Lecture Notes in Computer Science

Edited by G. Goos and J. Hartmanis

36

Sheila A. Greibach

Theory of Program Structures: Schemes, Semantics, Verification

Springer-Verlag
Berlin · Heidelberg · New York 1975

Author:
Prof. Sheila A. Greibach
Department of System Science
University of California
Los Angeles, CA 90024
USA

Library of Congress Cataloging in Publication Data

Greibach, Sheila, 1939-
  Theory of program structures.

  (Lecture notes in computer science ; 36)
  Bibliography: p.
  Includes indexes.
  1. Electronic digital computers--Programming.
2. Recursive programming. 3. Computer programs.
I. Title. II. Series.
QA76.6.G743 1975   001.6'42   75-31780

AMS Subject Classifications (1970): 68 XX
CR Subject Classifications (1974): 5.24

ISBN 3-540-07415-5 Springer-Verlag Berlin · Heidelberg · New York
ISBN 0-387-07415-5 Springer-Verlag New York · Heidelberg · Berlin

FOR MY PARENTS AND JACK

PREFACE

The material in these lecture notes offers an exposition - aimed at graduate students rather than researchers in the field - of a topic often called "program schemata" or "schematology". The subject matter represents one approach to formalizing the elusive notion of the "semantics of programming languages". The idea is to model an "abstract flowchart" and study the interrelation between the syntax of programs (what can be said about their behavior from their format) and the semantics (what they actually "do", depending on the interpretation, the programming language, and perhaps even the implementation) and examine the application of formal proof systems to verify properties of programs.

Among the goals of such studies are to determine which constructs of programming languages are "essential" and what is the relative power of various features, and to develop general methods for checking or verifying a given program against its specifications.

The approach taken here through program and recursion schemes follows naturally from the methods of the formal language theory and the theory of computation. The results are studied not just for their own sake but for their assistance in casting light on problems such as program verification. Topics treated in this book include: program schemes and their basic properties; structured programs including block structure and WHILE programs; correctness and program verification; decision problems; recursion schemes, augmented schemes and verification of programs with recursion; and monadic recursion schemes.

These represent the notes for the current version of Engineering 223F, Theory of Computation, given jointly by the Department of System Science and the Department of Computer Science at the University of California, Los Angeles. Not all of the material has been (or could be) given in any one quarter. Asterisks in the Table of Contents represent material which can be omitted without interfering with continuity.

The course is intended for first or second year graduate students who have had a basic one quarter course in formal language theory (covering finite state machines and graphs, context-free languages, and the idea of Turing machines, algorithms and procedures), and sufficient experience with programming languages to appreciate the motivation and understand the relevant jargon. The emphasis is on constructions and examples, although most proofs are given in full detail.

Los Angeles   S. A. Greibach
August 11, 1975

ACKNOWLEDGEMENTS

Grateful thanks are due my secretaries without whose assistance this volume could never have been produced. The dedication and professional competence of my former secretary, Mrs. Nancy Grey, is evident in the diagrams she drew and in the bulk of the manuscript. Ms. Susan Frank most ably completed the job.

Thanks are also owed to various colleagues and students with whom I discussed the material in these notes. Particular acknowledgement is due to Professor E. P. Friedman and to Mr. J. Gallier who offered numerous corrections to the previous version of this manuscript and provided many helpful suggestions for the present version. Needless to say, all remaining difficulties in the manuscript are solely due to the author's negligence.

I should also like to thank my Chairperson, Professor J. W. Carlyle, for advice and encouragement in all my work and for exhortation to get this volume finished and published.

Although this volume is not a research monograph, one's research, advanced graduate teaching and expository writing are often inextricably intertwined. During the period in which this manuscript was prepared, the author's research in automata and formal languages was supported in part by the National Science Foundation under Grants GJ-803 and DCR7415091 and this support is acknowledged with appreciation.

NOTES TO THE READER

This book is written to be read sequentially from first chapter to last. However, sections marked in the Table of Contents by an asterisk can be skipped without affecting continuity. To assist browsing, an Index of Notation and an Index of Terms appear at the end.

Each chapter is numbered separately and theorems, lemmas, propositions and corollaries are numbered consecutively within each chapter; thus Theorem 6.7 is the 7th numbered result, but not necessarily the 7th theorem, in Chapter VI. The end of a proof is indicated by the symbol: ■ .

References appear at the end organized by chapters. The set of exercises is also organized by chapters. The reader is warned that some of the exercises have not been consumer tested. Any one using any of the exercises does so at his/her own peril.

The book is self-contained as to knowledge of program schemes, but a few sections are more meaningful for readers with an elementary knowledge of formal language theory. The background material can be found (for example) in Chapters 1-7 of Hopcroft and Ullman, "Formal Languages and their Relation to Automata", Addison-Wesley, 1969. Most of the material can be read without this background. More specifically, the basic notions of a Turing Machine, of computable functions and of undecidable properties are needed for Chapter VI (Decision Problems); the definitions of recursive, primitive recursive and partial recursive functions are helpful for Section F of Chapter IV and two of the proofs in Chapter VI. The basic facts regarding regular sets, context-free languages and pushdown store automata are helpful in Chapter VIII (Monadic Recursion Schemes) and in the proof of Theorem 3.14. For Chapter V (Correctness and Program Verification) it is useful to know the basic notation and ideas of the first order predicate calculus; a highly abbreviated version of this material appears as Appendix A.

TABLE OF CONTENTS

I. INTRODUCTION

The subject of these notes might be described as "abstract flowcharts" - the study of mathematical models for programs and flowcharts, and of the interrelation between the syntax of programs (what can be said about their behavior from their very format) and the semantics (interpretations and the functions computed under varying interpretations) and the application of formal proof systems to verify properties of programs.

The basic thrust of studies in this area has been to devise theories that would, for example, permit proofs that programs are correct, that programs terminate, that programs are optimal, and so on. The ultimate goals (somewhat utopian) include error-free compilers, automatic subroutine validation, mechanical aids to debugging, and detection of infinite looping. Not too surprisingly, the theoretical study began in the late fifties by Russian mathematicians such as Ianov, brought to the attention of Western computer scientists by Rutledge, McCarthy and others and then reformulated and developed further by Manna, Paterson, Karp, Miller, and Floyd among others, has not yet made truly significant progress toward these eventual aims, although there have been many interesting and useful developments. The alert reader will object that we are dealing with problems that are unsolvable in full generality and this of course is true. We shall see how often we do indeed end in the "Turing swamp" of undecidable properties. However, the hope is that in applications of interest we can try to skirt the swamp and concentrate on what can be done - and in particular what can be achieved using heuristic methods or interactive systems.

One of the models we shall examine in detail is the Luckham-Park-Paterson definition of program schemes. The study of program schemes has several goals. One is to present a precise formal model of the notion of a computer program in a way that is entirely independent of features or workings of any (real or abstract) computing machinery. The schemes under consideration are to embody just those features or constructs of programming languages that appear "essential" - to determine whether or not they are in some real sense essential and what is the relative power of different features is one of the objects of the study. A second purpose is to develop a basic theory of program optimization again independently of any particular machine or programming language. A third objective is to develop general methods (e.g. systems of rules of inference or transformations on programs) for checking or verifying a given program against its specifications. This last statement is a little circular since one must provide a formal definition of the "specifications" of a program and if by a "reasonable" specification of a program you mean a "recursively definable" one or a "computable program" you find that you are indeed checking two programs (probably in different languages) for equivalence.

So a study of formal notions of program equivalence is an important part of the theory - both for its own sake and for its importance when considering optimization

and correctness problems. Another theme is the question of translating programs
having one set of features into programs having different properties. A
translatability theorem - one which says that any scheme in one class can be
translated into an equivalent scheme in another class - results in our knowing
how to replace certain features of programs by others. This may provide normal
forms, it may help optimization and it may reduce a correctness problem to one we
already know how to solve. A nontranslatability theorem - saying that certain
features cannot be replaced by others - provides us with some insight into the
elusive notion of the "power of expression" of a programming language.

EXAMPLES

    Let us examine a few sample flowcharts to illustrate further the sort of
questions we shall be studying. Later we shall give formal definitions of schemes
and of other concepts, but right now let us rely on an intuitive understanding of
"flowchart", "interpretation", "equivalence".

    First look at Flowcharts A and B in Example I-1. Each contains one START box
where the program starts with some initially defined value of x   - we may also
consider x to be the name of a register or location whose initial contents is the
input to the program. There is one STOP box which indicates when the program halts;
at that time the current contents of registers y and u are the outputs. The
arrows represent the flow of control. Now a statement such as

$$y \leftarrow f(x)$$

indicates that function f is to be applied to the contents of register x and the
result is placed in register y . Similarly

$$y \leftarrow f(y)$$

indicates that y is updated by applying function f to the current contents of
register y and the resulting value is stored as the new contents of register y .
Statement P(y) can be regarded as a predicate or test statement or a Boolean
function. If the result of this test is positive, i.e. if property P or expression
P or statement P is true of the current contents of register y , then control
flows along the arrow labeled TRUE and otherwise along the FALSE arrow; it is
implicit that one or the other must occur.

    Notice that A and B are "abstract" flowcharts because functions f and g
and predicate P are undefined and represented by abstract symbols. One may
consider these as places for insertion of subroutines specifying f and g and P .
We are interested in two aspects of this situation. The study of what can be said
about flowcharts A and B without inserting the subroutines or actual operation

EXAMPLE I-1   -   "STRONG EQUIVALENCE"

No matter what functions you substitute for "f" and "g", no matter what statement you use for "P", for each initial value of x, either both A and B loop or both A and B halt with the same values in registers y and u.

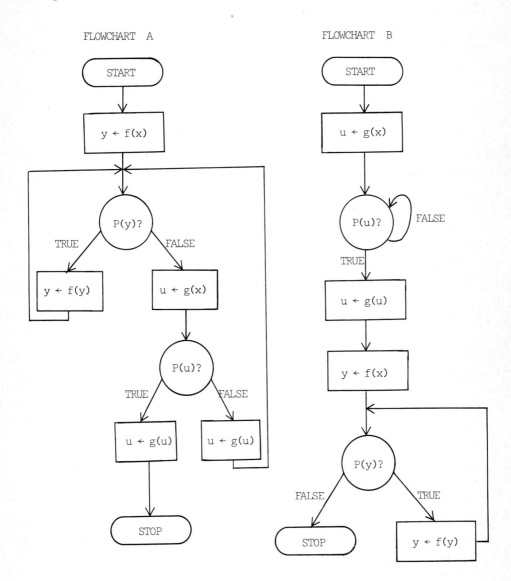

FLOWCHART A

FLOWCHART B

symbols for f , g and P - the examination of what holds for all possible choices for f and g and P over all possible input domains - might be considered the study of the syntax of abstract flowcharts or program schemes. If we consider varying the interpretation - varying subroutines for g , f and P and alternative input domains, e.g. integers, real numbers, complex numbers, arrays, lists, natural language data - and their effect on the flowcharts we are in a sense studying the semantics of flowcharts. So the study of program schemes is related to the study of both the syntax and the semantics of programming languages.

There are other things to observe in these sample flowcharts. Suppose flow-chart A is started with some value a in input register x . First $f(a)$ is placed in register y . If $P(f(a))$ is true, then y is updated to $f(f(a))$ (which we shall take the liberty of abbreviating $f^2(a)$) and test P is reapplied, now to $f^2(a)$. If P is true of each $f^n(a)$ for all n , then there is no way to leave this loop and the computation cannot reach the STOP box. On the other hand, if m is the least nonzero positive integer with P false for $f^m(a)$, then the computation finally proceeds along the FALSE arrow with the contents of y at $f^m(a)$ and places $g(a)$ in register u . If P is true of $g(a)$ then u is updated to $g^2(a)$ and the computation halts with $u = g^2(a)$ and $y = f^m(a)$. If P is not true of $g(a)$ then first u is updated to $g^2(a)$ and then the computation retests y . Since the value of y is unchanged, the FALSE arrow is again followed. Next u is changed to $g(a)$. But now when P is applied to $g(a)$ the same, FALSE, path must be followed and A is in an unbreakable loop. Thus if either P is not true for $g(a)$ or if there is no $m \geq 1$ such that P is false for $f^m(a)$, the computation never halts. Otherwise, it halts with $g^2(a)$ in register u and $f^m(a)$ in register y where m is the least nonzero positive integer with $P(f^m(a))$ false. This holds regardless of the actual functions and values involved.

Examining B we see that under input a the computation specifies u as $g(a)$ and then applies test P to $g(a)$. If $P(g(a))$ is false, then the computation loops. Otherwise, u is set to $g^2(a)$. Then y is set to $f(a)$. If P is false for $f(a)$, the computation halts. Otherwise y is reset to $f^2(a)$ and P is again applied and again a false answer causes a stop and a true answer resets y to $f^3(a)$ and reapplies P . If there is a m such that P is false for $f^m(a)$, $m \geq 1$, the computation halts, but otherwise it loops forever. Hence B halts if and only if P is true of $g(a)$ and false for some $f^m(a)$ and when it halts u is set to $g^2(a)$ and y to $f^m(a)$ where m is the least nonzero positive integer for which $P(f^m(a))$ is false.

So we observe that for any choice of interpretations for f , g and P and for any input a , either both A and B enter infinite loops (in which case there is no output and we are not interested in the succeeding register contents) or both A and B terminate with the same values for the u and y locations.

So we shall say that A and B are strongly equivalent - for all interpretations they either both diverge (loop infinitely) or else both converge (halt, terminate) with the same outputs.

We shall study the question of the strong equivalence of flowcharts at length, and in particular examine when the strong equivalence problem is decidable. We shall see that in the general case it is undecidable and not even partially decidable - one cannot even find an algorithm to list by exhaustion all pairs of strongly equivalent schemes.

Example I-2 illustrates another theme of our discussion. Here we assume that the input location or variable x is always set to some nonnegative integer. Initially u and y are set to the input value, say n . If $u = 0$ then $n = 0$ and the program halts with output $z = 2n$. Otherwise, y is reset to $n + 1$ and u to $n - 1$ and u is again tested for 0 . This process continues until u is set to 0 . This occurs after $u \leftarrow u - 1$ is applied n times and the loop is traversed n times. At this point y is set to $n + 1 + \ldots + 1 = n + n = 2n$. Then the program halts with output n . This is the only way the program can halt. Hence we can say that for any input n , if n is a nonnegative integer and the program halts on input n , then the value of the output register is $z = 2n$. Formally we shall say that the program is <u>partially correct</u> for input predicate " x is a nonnegative integer" and output predicate "$z = 2x$" in the sense that whenever the input criterion is true for the input x and the computation halts, then the output criterion is true for the output value of register z and the initial input value of register x . Further we can see that whenever the input statement is true, the computation must halt. We shall express both conditions together by saying that the program is <u>totally correct</u> for the particular input and output predicates cited. We shall investigate at length the concepts of partial and total correctness and examine systems for proving programs partially correct.

To illustrate the concept of interpretation, examine flowchart C in Example I-3. If we assume that our inputs are all nonnegative integers, and that f is the function $f(n) = n$, $g(n) = n - 1$ and $P(n)$ is true if and only if $n = 0$, we have the program in Example I-2 which computes $z = 2x$. On the other hand, with the same input domain and the same "meaning" for g and P , if we set $f(n) = 2n$, then each time around the loop we double the current value of y and so under this interpretation C computes $z = 2^x x$. If the domain is strings of a's - members of a^* - including the empty string, if $P(w)$ is true if and only if w is the empty string, and $f(w) = wb$ for any string w and $g(a^n) = a^{n-1}$ for any $n \geq 1$, then under this interpretation C is totally correct for input predicate " x is a string of a's " and output predicate "$z = xb^{|x|}$" . We shall frequently be dealing with statements that start "For all interpretations ... " or "There exists an interpretation such that ...". In some cases such as in the study of program correctness we shall be concerned with the behavior of a flowchart under specific interpretations.

EXAMPLE I-2 - CORRECTNESS

The program below is totally correct for z = 2x and input x a
nonnegative integer.

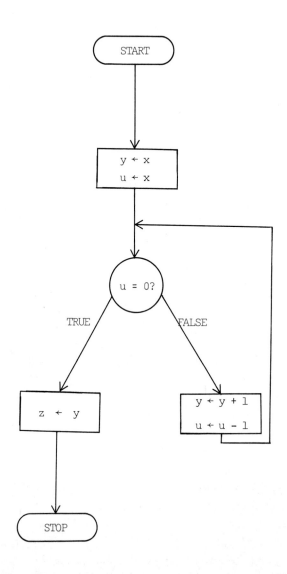

EXAMPLE I-3 - INTERPRETATIONS

FLOWCHART C

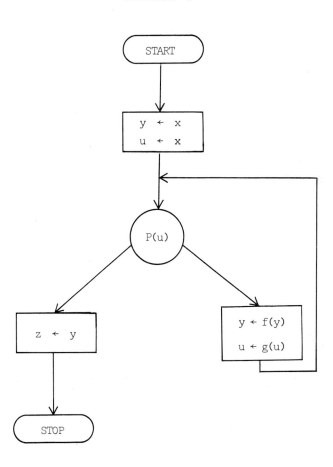

Let x be the input variable and z the output variable. If $f(n) \overset{\text{def}}{=} n + 1$
and $g(n) \overset{\text{def}}{=} n - 1$ and P(n) is true if and only if n = 0 , and the inputs are
nonnegative integers, then C computes z = 2x . If P and g are the same but
$f(n) \overset{\text{def}}{=} 2n$, then C computes $z = 2^x x$. If inputs are members of a^* , P(w)
is true if and only if w = e (the empty string), $f(w) \overset{\text{def}}{=} xb$ and $g(a^n) \overset{\text{def}}{=} a^{n-1}$
for $n \geq 1$, then C takes $x = a^n$ into $z = a^n b^n$.

Flowchart C illustrates another topic of study. It can be considered a graphical translation of the English program on the next page. This is a special kind of flowchart called a "WHILE scheme". One of its salient points is that it has no "GOTOs" - the only loops are subsumed by the WHILE statements. We shall examine special structural properties of schemes, such as block form, and conversions to such forms; these may really be considered syntactic properties of flowcharts since they depend primarily on the graph structure. However they are very useful in discussing semantic considerations.

EXAMPLE I-4 - EXPRESSION OF FLOWCHART C AS A "WHILE-SCHEME"

START

$y \leftarrow x$

$u \leftarrow x$

WHILE P(u) is FALSE DO

$\quad\quad\quad\quad\quad y \leftarrow f(y)$

$\quad\quad\quad\quad\quad u \leftarrow g(u)$

ENDWHILE

$z \leftarrow y$

STOP

II. PROGRAM SCHEMES - BASIC DEFINITIONS AND CONCEPTS

A. SYNTAX - THE MODEL

We give two closely related definitions of program schemes, one in the form of flow diagrams or abstract flowcharts and the other a linear representation of this form.

Program schemes are sequences of expressions in a particular formal meta-language and we define them in parts as follows.

ALPHABET

    a. <u>Function letters</u> - for each $n \geq 1$ there are an infinite number of n-placed or n-ary function letters (we use $f,g,h,\ldots$ with or without subscripts)

    b. <u>Predicate letters</u> - for each $n \geq 1$ there are an infinite number of n-placed or n-ary predicate letters (we use $T,P,Q,p,q,\ldots$ with or without subscripts)

    c. <u>Variables</u> - there are an infinite number of individual variables or locations or registers (we use $x,y,z,u,v,\ldots$ with or without subscripts)

    d. <u>auxiliary symbols</u> - numerals START STOP ( ) ← , TRUE FALSE (or 1 0 or T F)

    e. <u>augmented symbols</u> - constants (we use $a,b,c,\ldots$ with or without subscripts), = (equality)

TERMS

    a. A variable u or constant c is a <u>functional term</u>.

    b. If f is an n-ary function letter and $x_1,\ldots,x_n$ are variables, then $f(x_1,\ldots,x_n)$ is a <u>functional term</u>.

    c. If T is an n-placed predicate letter and $x_1,\ldots,x_n$ are variables, then $T(x_1,\ldots,x_n)$ is a <u>predicate term</u>.

    d. The auxiliary symbols START and STOP are <u>terms</u>.

STATEMENTS

    a. ASSIGNMENT STATEMENTS - if t is a functional term and u is a variable then

    is an assignment statement

b. TEST STATEMENTS - if t is a predicate term then

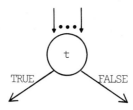

is a test statement (we can substitute 1 0 or T F
for TRUE FALSE)

c. START and STOP statements:

Thus assignment statements can have any number of entries but only one exit, test statements can have any number of entries but two exits, START statements have no entries and one exit and STOP statements have any number of entries but no exits.

DEFINITION An interconnection of statements such that each entry point leads from an exit point and each exit point leads to some entry point is a FLOW DIAGRAM.

DEFINITION A PROGRAM SCHEME is a finite flow diagram P such that
1. P contains well-formed assignment and test statements, exactly one START statement and at least one STOP statement.
2. Every statement is connected to (lies on a path from) the START statement.
3. The variables are divided into three not necessarily disjoint sets, $\bar{X}$ - input variables, $\bar{Y}$ - program variables, and $\bar{Z}$ - output variables, such that:
   a. A variable in $\bar{X}$ - $\bar{Y}$ never appears on the left hand side of an assignment statement,
   b. A variable in $\bar{Z}$ - $\bar{Y}$ appears on the left hand side of an assignment statement only if that statement is immediately connected to STOP; a variable in $\bar{Z}$ - $\bar{X}$ - $\bar{Y}$ never appears in a test statement or the right hand side of an assignment statement, and

c. on every path from START all variables not in $\overline{X}$ are assigned to
    before they are computed upon; i.e. for each variable u not in $\overline{X}$
    any path from START to any statement involving u must contain an
    assignment statement with u on the left hand side.

There are several points to notice. This definition is really a definition of
a particular kind of graph. Later we shall give a linear definition. Notice that
the sets of input, output and program variables need not be disjoint and that 3a.
and b. could just as well be taken as a definition of the concept of input,
program and output variables. If every variable is simultaneously an input, output
and program variable then we generally will not designate these sets. Quite often
we simply assume that every variable is a program variable and only observe whether
there are program variables that are not input variables and also what are the
output variables.

The definition of program scheme is "recursive" or "computable" in the sense
that we can decide whether a given flow diagram (finite of course) meets this
definition. Conditions 1 and 3a and b are clearly verifiable by inspection of the
diagram. Since accessibility is decidable for finite state graphs, we can determine
whether a given statement lies on a path from START and so verify condition 2.

Condition 3c says that every variable must either be an input variable or else
be specified before being used on every path from the START. Consider any variable
u not in $\overline{X}$. For our present purposes, regard the diagram as a finite state graph,
with START as the initial node, and as final nodes, each place in which u is a
program variable - every test statement involving u and every assignment statement with u on the right hand side. Label each arrow from an assignment statement
of the form $u \leftarrow t$ where t does not involve u by a and every other arrow by
b. Now we can construct a regular expression for the set of all and only label
sequences on paths from START to the final nodes and determine whether it designates
any member of b^{*}; if it does, this stands for a "bad" path - one from START to
a usage of u without passing through an assignment of u. Equivalently, one can
notice that if P has n statements then there is a bad path if and only if there
is a bad path of length n or less. Frequently we avoid the problem by assuming all
variables to be input variables.

Function letters are sometimes called computation or operator symbols. Test
statements are also referred to as conditional transfers (if the branches go to
different next statements) or unconditional transfers or GOTOs (if the branches go
to the same place).

There are various ways of augmenting the program schemes. For example, a test
may have more than two exits, an assignment statement might update several variables
simultaneously (e.g. $(u,v) \leftarrow (t_1,t_2)$) or a term might have functional terms as
variables (e.g. $u \leftarrow f(g(f(x_1),g(u_1,u_2)))$ or $T(g(x,f(y)))$. Questions such as

strong equivalence, termination, correctness and freeness can generally be answered for such augmented schemes by answering the same questions in our simpler language; these additions may provide notational convenience but do not affect the power of schemes.

There are other methods of augmenting schemes which may or may not increase the power of the language in certain cases. For example one can add constants or resets - zero-placed functions. One can also consider the effect of adding an equality test - a special two place predicate, say $E(x,y)$ - which is restricted to be interpreted as equality - $E(x,y)$ is true if and only if $x = y$. Yet another is to add a counter which as we shall see later means adding special unary functions and predicates which are always restricted to be interpreted as $+1$, -1 or test for zero - the counter operations. Similarly one might add pushdown stores or arrays. We shall postpone all such definitions and considerations for later.

A minor notational point is that, strictly speaking, one should fix once and for all what symbols are to be 1-place functions, 1-place predicates, 2-place functions, variables, etc. This would lead to an unpleasant degree of subscripting. So we shall try to play both games. That is, for the formalism and the proofs we shall assume that this has been done and everything is clearly marked and unambiguous and consistent. For example, if we have a subscheme:

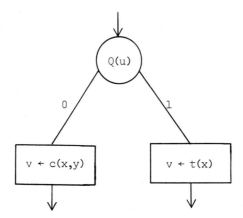

then we know that u,v,x,y are used as variables and nothing else, c is a 2-placed function letter, t a monadic function letter and Q a unary predicate letter and nothing else. So that particular scheme could also have a piece:

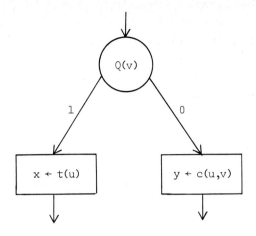

but must not have pieces such as:

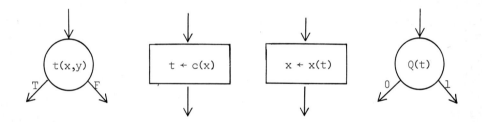

B. SEMANTICS - INTERPRETATIONS AND COMPUTATIONS

INTERPRETATIONS

Now that we have our formal language in hand, we must see how it is used.
First we must discuss the concept of interpretation.

DEFINITION   An interpretation I for a program scheme P consists of:

1. A nonempty set of elements D called the domain of the interpretation.
2. An assignment to each n-ary function symbol f of a total n-ary function
    $I(f)$ from D^n into D .
3. An assignment to each n-ary predicate symbol T of a total n-ary function
    $I(T)$ from D^n into $\{0,1\}$ (or equivalently, into $\{T,F\}$ or
    $\{TRUE,FALSE\}$ - $I(T)$ is a Boolean function).
4. For any constant c in P , a member $I(c)$ of D .

A pair (P,I) where I is an interpretation of a scheme P is called a program. Suppose the input vector for P is $\bar{X} = (x_1,\ldots,x_k)$, and to each input register x_i we assign a member a_i of the domain D of I . We often write $\bar{a}$ for input vector $\bar{a} = (a_1,\ldots,a_k)$. Then we use $(P,I,\bar{a})$ for the computation of (P,I) on input $\bar{a}$. Occasionally the interpretation also includes the input values; both approaches are useful and a matter of taste; the notation should make our definition clear.

If the domain D of interpretation I is finite, then I is a finite interpretation. If D is a recursive set and all functions and predicates assigned by I are total recursive functions, then I is recursive.

COMPUTATION

Now we must give a precise definition of the computation of program (P,I) on input $\bar{a}$. The intuitive meaning should be clear, although the formalism is a bit cumbersome. We consider a computation to be a sequence of vectors, each a computation state.

A computation state consists of a statement or instruction - the statement of P currently being executed - and a vector of values assigned to the variables of P at that stage in the computation. We can let the symbol Λ correspond to those variables (program or output variables which are not also input variables) which are undefined at this stage. The statement being executed could also be denoted by its address or position in the flow diagram. If s is the sequence of computation states, let $s(i)$ be the statement in the i-th state of s , that is, the statement executed in the i-th step of the computation, and let $val(u,i)$ denote the value assigned to variable u after $s(i)$ is executed. Thus the i-th state of s can be represented as

$$(s(i),val(u_1,i),\ldots,val(u_r,i))$$

if $u_1,\ldots,u_r$ is the list of all variables used in P .

We define the computation states inductively, letting D be the domain of I .

1) Initially we have $s(1) = START$, the start statement, and $val(x_j,1) = a_j$ if x_j is the j-th input variable and $val(u,1) = \Lambda$ (is undefined) if u is not an input variable. Then $s(2)$ is the statement entered by the arrow leaving the exit of the START statement.

2) If $s(i+1)$ is the assignment statement

$$y \leftarrow f(v_1,\ldots,v_n)$$

and $I(f)$ is the function from D^n into D assigned to f by interpretation I , then

$$val(y,i+1) = I(f)(val(v_1,i),\dots,val(v_n,i)) \,,$$
$$val(u,i+1) = val(u,i) \,, \quad \text{for} \quad u \neq y \,, \quad \text{and}$$
$s(i+2)$ is the statement entered by the arrow leaving
the exit point of $s(i+1)$.

2') If $s(i+1)$ is the assignment statement

$$y \leftarrow v$$

where y and v are variables, then

$$val(y,i+1) = val(v,i) \,,$$
$$val(u,i+1) = val(u,i) \,, \quad \text{for} \quad u \neq y \,, \quad \text{and}$$
$s(i+2)$ is the same as in 2) .

2") If $s(i+1)$ is the assignment statement

$$y \leftarrow c$$

for constant c and $I(c)$ is the member of D assigned to c by
interpretation I , then

$$val(y,i+1) = I(c) \,,$$
$$val(u,i+1) = val(u,i) \,, \quad \text{for} \quad u \neq y \,, \quad \text{and}$$
$s(i+2)$ is the same as in 2) .

3) If $s(i+1)$ is the test statement

$$T(v_1,\dots,v_n)$$

and $I(T)$ is the function from D^n into $\{0,1\}$ assigned to T by
interpretation I , then

$val(u,i+1) = val(u,i)$ for all variables u , and
if $I(T)(val(v_1,i),\dots,val(v_n,i)) = 0$ then $s(i+2)$ is the
statement entered by the arrow labeled 0 leaving $s(i+1)$
and otherwise $s(i+2)$ is the statement entered by the
arrow labeled 1 leaving $s(i+1)$.

4) If $s(i+1) = STOP$ then

$val(u,i+1) = val(u,i)$ for all variables u , $s(i+2)$ is undefined, and
computation sequence s has $i+1$ states and is a complete terminated
computation.

DEFINITION   Let s be the computation sequence for program (P,I) on input $\bar{a}$.
If there is an i such that s(i) = STOP , then we say that computation (P,I,$\bar{a}$)
halts or terminates or converges in i steps, written (P,I,$\bar{a}$)↓ , and the output
of P under I with input $\bar{a}$ is denoted by

$$val(P,I,\bar{a}) = (val(z_1,i),\ldots,val(z_m,i))$$

where $\bar{Z} = (z_1,\ldots,z_m)$ is the vector of output variables of P . If s is
infinite, then the computation (P,I,$\bar{a}$) diverges or loops, written (P,I,$\bar{a}$)↑ .
In this case val(P,I,$\bar{a}$) is undefined, indicated by val(P,I,$\bar{a}$)↑ .

EXAMPLE II-1
    Let us use the flowchart in Example II-1 to illustrate the concept of
interpretation and computation. Consider an interpretation I for which the domain
D is the nonnegative integers, I(T)(n) = 0 if and only if n = 0 ,
I(g)(n) = n $\pm$ 1 (where n $\pm$ m = n - m for n $\geq$ m and n $\pm$ m = 0 otherwise) and
I(f)(n,m) = n + m .
    We can write out explicitly the computation states for computation (P,I,(2,3))
where the initial value of x_1 is 2 and of x_2 is 3 . We have attached letters
to the right of the statement boxes except for the unique START and STOP statements
for convenience in naming the statements executed at each step.

STATE		
	1	(START,2,3,Λ)
	2	(A,2,3,Λ)
	3	(B,2,3,2)
	4	(C,2,3,2)
	5	(D,2,4,2)
	6	(E,2,4,1)
	7	(F,2,4,1)
	8	(G,2,6,1)
	9	(E,2,6,0)
	10	(F,2,6,0)
	11	(STOP,2,6,0)

EXAMPLE II-1

Input variables - x_1 , x_2 Output variable - x_2

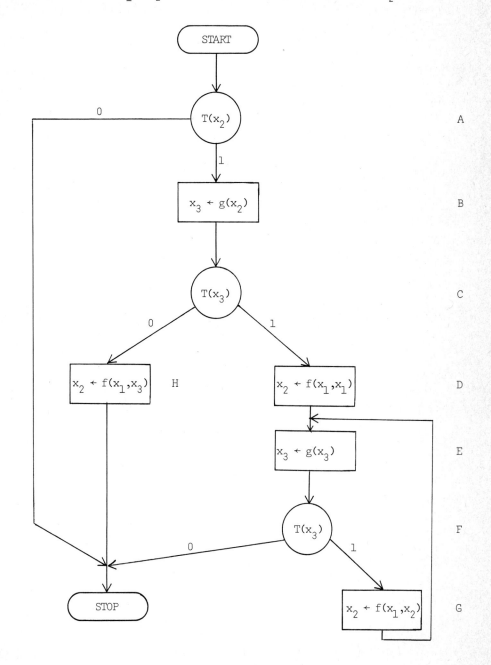

Thus, for example, $s(5) = D$, $val(x_3,7) = 1$, $val(x_2,5) = 4$, etc.
Finally, $val(P,I,(2,3)) = val(x_2,11) = val(x_2,10) = 6$.

In this case it is not difficult to see that $val(P,I,(n,0)) = 0$,
$val(P,I,(n,1)) = n$, $val(P,I,(0,m)) = 0$ for $n,m \geq 0$ and for $n,m \geq 1$,
$val(P,I,(n,m)) = nm$.

C. LINEAR DEFINITION OF PROGRAM SCHEMES

Instead of representing a program scheme in graph form as a flow diagram, we
can represent it in linear form by having each statement preceeded by a numeral
called the address of the statement and having each test statement followed by two
numerals, the transfer addresses.

Well-formed statements now are:

Assignments   k. $y \leftarrow f(v_1,\dots,v_n)$ where k is a numeral, the address
                    of the statement, $y,v_1,\dots,v_n$ are variables and f
                    is an n-placed function letter

               k. $y \leftarrow v$ for y,v variables

               k. $y \leftarrow c$ for y a variable and c a constant

Tests   k. $T(v_1,\dots,v_n)$ r,s where k is a numeral, the address
                    of the statement, r and s are numerals, the transfer
                    addresses, T is an n-placed predicate letter and
                    $v_1,\dots,v_n$ are variables

STOP   k.   STOP where k is a numeral, the address of the STOP
                    statement.

DEFINITION   A _program scheme_ P is a finite sequence of statements such that:
(1) the address of each statement is its position in the sequence,
(2) all transfer addresses are addresses in P ,
(3) there is at least one STOP statement, the last statement is either STOP or a test statement, and each statement lies on some path from 1, and
(4) the variables of P are divided into three not necessarily disjoint sets $\overline{X}$, $\overline{Y}$ and $\overline{Z}$ such that any variable not in $\overline{X}$ is assigned to in any path from 1 before it is computed on, any variable in $\overline{X} - \overline{Y}$ is never assigned to, any variable in $\overline{Z} - \overline{Y}$ is assigned to only just before a STOP statement, and no variable in $\overline{Z} - \overline{X} - \overline{Y}$ is computed upon.

Condition (4) is decidable in the same way and by the same reasoning as condition (3) in the other model. Some authors use the weaker condition that any variable not in $\overline{X}$ is assigned to in any computation before it is computed on. Since it is undecidable whether a particular statement can ever be reached in any computation under any interpretation for any input, this condition will be undecidable and thus in our view undesirable. We prefer definitions to be effective, particularly definitions of the basic object under discussion. So this problem is avoided either by using the condition we have given which obviously implies the alternative one, or by always assuming all variables to be input variables, which shortcuts the whole problem.

We assume that computations always start at statement 1 and so we did not need a START statement in this model.

We define interpretation in this model exactly as in the flow diagram model. However, the timing of computations is now off by ½ step. For this model, in a computation sequence s , s(i) is the address of the statement to be executed at stage i and val(u,i) is the value of variable u _before_ stage i but after instruction s(i-1) has been executed.

We now give an inductive definition of computation sequence s for scheme P , interpretation I and input $\overline{a}$.

1. Let s(1) = 1 , val(x,1) = a if x is an input variable with initial value a , and let val(y,1) be undefined if y is not an input variable.

2. If s(i) = k and we have

   k. $y \leftarrow f(v_1,\ldots,v_n)$

then s(i+1) = k+1 , val(u,i+1) = val(u,i) for u ≠ y , and val(y,i+1) = I(f)(val(v_1,i),...,val(v_n,i)) .

2'. If $s(i) = k$ and we have

      k. $y \leftarrow v$

for variable v then $s(i+1) = k+1$, $val(u,i+1) = val(u,i)$ for $u \neq y$,
and $val(y,i+1) = val(v,i)$.

2". If $s(i) = k$ and we have

      k. $y \leftarrow c$

for constant c , then $s(i+1) = k+1$, $val(u,i+1) = val(u,i)$ for $u \neq y$
and $val(y,i+1) = I(c)$.

3. If $s(i) = k$ and we have

      k. $T(v_1,\ldots,v_n)$ r , s

then $val(u,i+1) = val(u,i)$ for all variables i and

$$s(i+1) \quad = \quad \begin{cases} r & \text{if } I(T)(val(v_1,i),\ldots,val(v_n,i)) = 1 \\ \\ s & \text{if } I(T)(val(v_1,i),\ldots,val(v_n,i)) = 0 \end{cases}$$

4. If $s(i) = STOP$, then $s(i+1)$ is undefined, s has exactly i steps and
if $\bar{Z} = (z_1,\ldots,z_n)$, then $val(P,I,\bar{a}) = (val(z_1,i),\ldots,val(z_n,i))$.

Thus except for timing this definition is essentially the same as the previous
one. It is obvious that the two models are the same. Going from the linear to the
flow diagram model is obvious; in the reverse construction note that if we must make
a correspondence between nodes and addresses such that the statement in the flow
diagram given address k is an assignment that does not lead into the statement
given address $k+1$, then we add a forced transfer as $k+1$ and readdress the rest
of the statements.

For example, it is obvious that Example II-2 is a sequential form of
Example II-1. Notice the extra test added in line 8 to provide a forced transfer
back to line 6.

EXAMPLE II-2

LINEAR FORM OF SCHEME   II-1

1. $T(x_2)$ 10,2

2. $x_3 \leftarrow g(x_2)$

3. $T(x_3)$ 9,4

4. $x_2 \leftarrow f(x_1, x_1)$

5. $x_3 \leftarrow g(x_3)$

6. $T(x_3)$ 10,7

7. $x_2 \leftarrow f(x_1, x_2)$

8. $T(x_3)$ 6,6

9. $x_2 \leftarrow f(x_1, x_3)$

10. STOP

EXAMPLE

Let us consider Example II-3, a classic example of a scheme which halts for all finite interpretations but fails to halt for some infinite interpretations. Let us see why this is true.

Suppose the initial value of x_1 is a. After the first two assignments, registers x_1 and x_2 both contain $f(a)$. If $T(f(a)) = 1$, the program automatically halts. If we are trying to find an interpretation and input for which P diverges, we know that we must have $T(f(a)) = 0$. In the next step, x_1 is updated as $f^2(a)$. If $T(f^2(a)) = 0$, then P halts. In order to diverge we must have $T(f^2(a)) = 1$. Next x_1 is reassigned as $f^3(a)$. If $T(f^3(a)) = 1$, P halts so $T(f^3(a)) = 0$. Reassigning x_1 as $f^4(a)$ and x_2 as $f(x_2) = f^2(a)$, we see by the previous reasoning that we must have $T(f^4(a)) = 1$. The next choice point is determined because to be consistent with our previous assumptions regarding the interpretation of T, we must have $T(x_2) = T(f^2(a)) = 1$.

We summarize some stages of the interpretation and computation in Example II-3'.

EXAMPLE II-3

A SCHEME WHICH HALTS UNDER ALL FINITE INTERPRETATIONS
BUT NOT UNDER SOME INFINITE INTERPRETATIONS

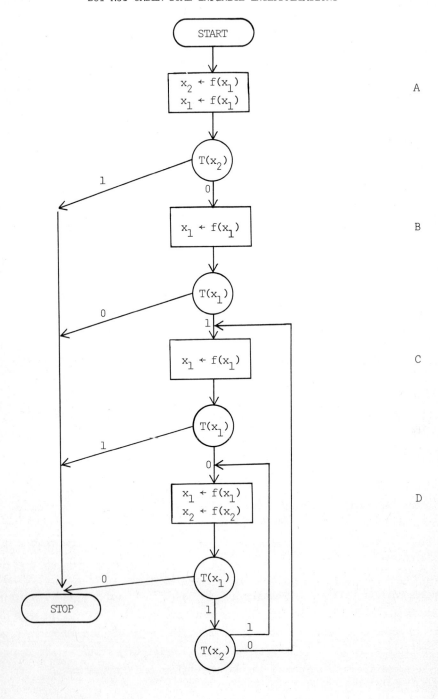

EXAMPLE II-3'

SOME STEPS IN A COMPUTATION OF EXAMPLE II-3 WHICH NEVER HALTS

ASSIGNMENT BOX	x_1	$T(x_1)$	x_2	$T(x_2)$
A	$f(a)$	0	$f(a)$	0
B	$f^2(a)$	1		
C	$f^3(a)$	0		
D	$f^4(a)$	1	$f^2(a)$	1
D	$f^5(a)$	1	$f^3(a)$	0
C	$f^6(a)$	0		
D	$f^7(a)$	1	$f^4(a)$	1
D	$f^8(a)$	1	$f^5(a)$	1
D	$f^9(a)$	1	$f^6(a)$	0
C	$f^{10}(a)$	0		
D	$f^{11}(a)$	1	$f^7(a)$	1
D	$f^{12}(a)$	1	$f^8(a)$	1
D	$f^{13}(a)$	1	$f^9(a)$	1
D	$f^{14}(a)$	1	$f^{10}(a)$	0
C	$f^{15}(a)$	0		

Examining the list in Example II-3', one can see that the n for which x_1 is assigned $f^n(a)$ in C (or in A) must have $T(f^n(a)) = 0$ in any nonhalting definition and those for which x_1 is first assigned $f^n(a)$ in D must have $T(f^n(a)) = 1$. The n for which $T(f^n(a))$ must be 0 form an arithmetic progression and in fact we have $T(f^n(a)) = 0$ if and only if there is an integer k for which $n = k(k+1)/2$. Clearly if the set of values

$$f(a), f^2(a), f^3(a), \ldots, f^r(a), \ldots$$

is infinite then no two are the same and so there is an interpretation of T which causes P to diverge. For example, if the domain of I is the nonnegative integers, $I(f)(n) = n+1$ and $T(n) = 0$ if and only if there is an integer k for which $n = k(k+1)/2$ and the input is $a = 0$, then $(P,I,0)$ will diverge.

On the other hand, suppose that domain D of interpretation I is finite. Let f_I stand for $I(f)$. Since D is finite, the sequence

$$f_I(a), f_I^2(a), f_I^3(a), \ldots, f_I^r(a), \ldots$$

contains only finitely many distinct values and hence there are $n, m \geq 1$ such that $f_I^n(a) = f_I^{n+m}(a)$. Thus after n , the sequence of values $f_I^n(a), f_I^{n+1}(a), \ldots, f_I^{n+m}(a)$ repeats forever. If $I(T)(f_I^{n+i}(a)) = 1$ for $0 \leq i \leq m$, then eventually we will specify x_1 as some $f_I^{n+i}(a)$ in C for which the value of $I(T)$ will be 1 and P will halt. On the other hand, if one of these m values of $I(T)$ is 0 then 0 will repeat "too often" in the sequence

$$I(T)(f_I^n(a)), \ldots, I(T)(f_I^{n+r}(a)), \ldots$$

and hence at some point after D we shall have $I(T)$ as 0 for the current value of x_1 and halt. So P will eventually halt.

Thus P halts on all finite interpretations but diverges for certain infinite interpretations.

D. EQUIVALENCE

It is clear that any interpretation I of a scheme P can be extended to a general interpretation I' of all schemes by using the same domain and assigning functions over the domain of I to the function and test symbols of the language that were not assigned meanings under I . The interpreted programs (P,I) and (P,I') are obviously identical. For convenience we shall for the most part in the following discussion restrict our attention to those interpretations that assign a meaning to every function and test symbol of the language. Such interpretations, which we might call universal interpretations, are interpretations of every scheme.

DEFINITION   Suppose a program scheme P has n input variables and D is the domain of an interpretation I . We say that (P,I) <u>halts everywhere</u> (or <u>converges everywhere</u>) if for all inputs $\bar{a}$ in D^n the computation $(P,I,\bar{a})$ halts.

DEFINITION   A program scheme P <u>halts for all interpretations</u> or P <u>always halts</u> if (P,I) halts everywhere for all interpretations I . The <u>termination problem</u> for P is the problem of determining whether P always halts.

Equivalently, if P has n input variables, then P always halts if for every interpretation I and every input $\bar{a}$ in D_I^n (where D_I is the domain of I), the computation $(P,I,\bar{a})$ halts.

Loosely speaking, two schemes are said to be equivalent if under all interpretations they compute the same values. There are several different possible notions of equivalence. Assume now that P has the same input variables as P' and the same output variables.

DEFINITION   Two interpreted schemes (programs) (P,I) and (P',I') with the same domain D are <u>strongly equivalent</u>, written $(P,I) \equiv (P',I')$, if for all input vectors $\bar{a}$ over the common domain either $(P,I,\bar{a})$ and $(P',I',\bar{a})$ both diverge or $(P,I,\bar{a})$ and $(P',I',\bar{a})$ both halt and $\text{val}(P,I,\bar{a}) = \text{val}(P',I',\bar{a})$.

DEFINITION   Two schemes P and P' are <u>strongly equivalent</u>, written $P \equiv P'$, if for all interpretations I , (P,I) and (P',I) are strongly equivalent.

Strong equivalence requires that for any interpretation and input either the values of the computations of P and P' are both undefined or they are both defined and are equal. Several notions of equivalence may be defined in a similar way by restricting the set of interpretations. Thus:

DEFINITION   Two schemes P and P' are <u>finitely equivalent</u>, written $P \underset{F}{\equiv} P'$ if and only if (P,I) is strongly equivalent to (P',I) for every finite interpretation I . Two schemes P and P' are <u>recursively</u> equivalent, written $P \underset{R}{\equiv} P'$ if and only if (P,I) is strongly equivalent to (P',I) for every recursive interpretation I .

These equivalence relations are not the same. Obviously strong equivalence implies recursive equivalence and recursive equivalence implies finite equivalence. None of the reverse inclusions hold. We are already in a position to show that finite equivalence does not imply recursive equivalence. Consider the scheme of P of Example II-3 which halts for all finite interpretations but diverges for some infinite but recursive interpretations (for the interpretation of P we saw that caused divergence is obviously recursive). We can diagram P as:

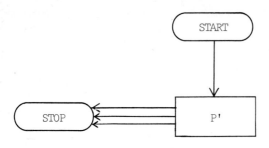

Now let us alter P to P_1 :

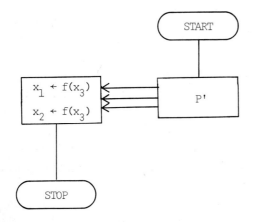

Now P_1 has a new input variable x_3 which is never computed on until the
very end. So P_1 just like P will halt for all finite interpretations and the
output will be $(f(x_3),f(x_3),x_3)$ regardless of input or f or what P did in the
meantime. But P_1 will diverge for some infinite interpretations. Thus if we
consider the trivial scheme P_2 :

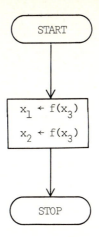

we see that P_1 and P_2 are equivalent for all finite interpretations (and indeed for all interpretations wherein P_1 halts) but there is a recursive interpretation for which P_2 halts and P_1 diverges.

Now of course these counterexample schemes are not of great interest in themselves. Their purpose is to exhibit a pathology which one must watch out for in any "real" scheme.

There are many other possible notions of equivalence, depending on the under-lying phenomena one wishes to model and study. In our later discussion of block structure and transformations to structured form we shall meet some definitions yet more rigorous than "strong equivalence" - notions of computational equivalence or structure preservation where one demands that not only the end result be the same but that the outputs be obtained in roughly similar ways. One stronger notion is total equivalence which only holds between always halting schemes.

DEFINITION   Scheme P is <u>totally equivalent</u> to scheme P' if P and P' always halt and P is strongly equivalent to P' .

Now we introduce some "weaker" definitions of equivalence, relaxing some of the demands of strong equivalence.

In some cases - notably in considerations of program verification - one is seeking something less than complete equivalence; one might be willing to settle for a "fail-safe" condition. That is, one might agree that the program might have bugs and fail to halt but when it halts it must do the right thing. This notion leads to the definition of weak equivalence.

DEFINITION   We say that interpreted programs (P,I) and (P',I') with the same domain D are weakly equivalent, written (P,I) ≈ (P',I') , if for all input vectors $\bar{a}$ over domain D , whenever both computation (P,I,$\bar{a}$) and computation (P',I',$\bar{a}$) halt, then val(P,I,$\bar{a}$) = val(P',I',$\bar{a}$) . We say that P and P' are weakly equivalent, written P ≈ P' , if for all interpretations I , (P,I) is weakly equivalent to (P',I) .

If P and P' are weakly equivalent, then whenever both halt, they do the same thing. We may be interested in knowing that, say, P does a little more - that P halts whenever P' does but perhaps halts in some other places.

DEFINITION   Suppose I and I' are interpretations with the same domain. We say that program (P,I) extends program (P',I') , written (P,I) > (P',I') , or (P',I') is included in (P,I) , written (P',I') < (P,I)) if they are weakly equivalent and whenever (P',I',$\bar{a}$) halts, (P,I,$\bar{a}$) halts, but not necessarily vice versa. We say that P is an extension of P' , P > P' (or P' is included in P , P' < P) if (P,I) is an extension of (P',I) for every interpretation I .

DEFINITION   A relationship ∿ between schemes is a reasonable equivalence relation if P ∿ Q always implies that P is weakly equivalent to Q and if whenever P and Q are strongly equivalent then P ∿ Q .

Weak equivalence requires that for any interpretation and input the computations of P and P' yield the same values whenever both computations halt. If one computation diverges it does not matter what the other one does.

The term "weak equivalence" is somewhat unfortunate since weak equivalence is not in fact an equivalence relationship in the usual meaning of the term. It is obviously symmetric but it is not transitive, since every scheme is weakly equivalent to any scheme that never halts. For example, consider P_1 , P_2 and P_3 below:

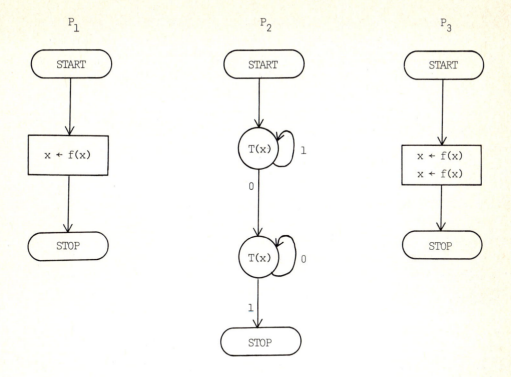

Obviously P_1 and P_3 are weakly equivalent to P_2 (i.e. $P_1 \simeq P_2$ and $P_2 \simeq P_3$) but are not weakly equivalent to each other (i.e. $P_1 \not\simeq P_3$) . We shall frequently denote situations such as P_2 where an infinite loop must occur in all inter-pretations by:

Now weak equivalence, finite equivalence, recursive equivalence and strong equivalence are all reasonable equivalences although the first is not a true equivalence relationship and the last three are. Reasonable equivalences stand between weak and strong - they must hold between schemes that behave identically for all interpretations and must fail between schemes which can be demonstrated to produce different results on the same interpretation. Total equivalence is not a reasonable equivalence because it does not hold for schemes which can diverge, and

although transitive and symmetric is not reflexive and so it is not an equivalence
relationship.

Notice that if P_1 and P_2 contain different function or test letters then
strong equivalence between P_1 and P_2 implies a kind of degeneracy, in that
certain functions and predicates are not really needed. We need a different type
definition of equivalence to handle the case in which different schemes compute the
same function under varying interpretations of the functions they do not have in
common.

DEFINITION   Call interpretations I and I' with domains D and D' respectively
compatible if for any n-place function f interpreted by both I and I' ,
$I(f)(\overline{a}) = I'(f)(\overline{a})$ and for any n-place predicate T interpreted by both I and
I' , $I(T)(\overline{a}) = I'(T)(\overline{a})$ for any $\overline{a}$ in D^n and $(D')^n$, and for any constant c
assigned in both I and I' , $I(c) = I'(c)$.

Suppose we call an interpretation of P minimal if it interprets only function
letters and predicate letters actually present in P . Then one might define a
relation

$$P_1 \sim P_2$$

if and only if for each minimal interpretation I_1 of P_1 there is a compatible
minimal interpretation I_2 of P_2 with the same domain such that (P_1,I_1) is
strongly equivalent to (P_2,I_2) and for each minimal interpretation I_2 of P_2
there is a compatible minimal interpretation I_1 of P_1 with the same domain such
that (P_1,I_1) is strongly equivalent to (P_2,I_2) .

LOCAL TRANSFORMATIONS
    We shall be particularly concerned with transformations on schemes which
preserve strong equivalence. Some of these will be global transformations acting
on the scheme as a unit and others will be local, replacing parts of a scheme with
other strongly equivalent subschemes.
    A few examples of local transformations appear in Example II-4. The reader can
verify for each pair of subschemes R and S , that if a scheme P is transformed
by replacing subscheme S by subscheme R in such a way that entry point 1_S of S
is replaced by entry point 1_R of R and exit point e_S of S by exit point e_R
of R (or e_{S0} by e_{R0} and e_{S1} by e_{R1} if there are two corresponding exit
points after a test) then the resulting scheme P' is strongly equivalent to P .
    These transformations can be used to trace equivalences and sometimes obtain
simplifications.

EXAMPLE II-4   SOME LOCAL EQUIVALENCE PRESERVING TRANSFORMATIONS

1. Interchanging assignment and test statements

Valid for u ≠ v

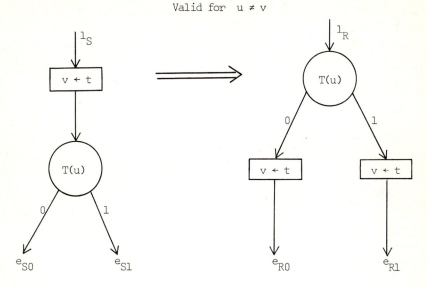

2. Interchanging assignment statements

Valid if u does not appear in t and v does not appear in t'

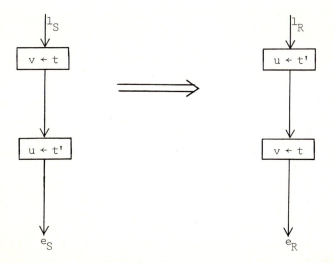

3. Elimination of "overprinted" assignments

      Valid if u does not appear in t' or in a test statement
of B or the right hand side of an assignment of B :

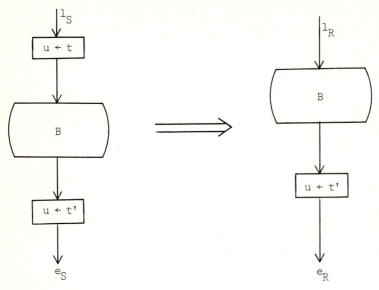

4. Detection and explicit display of tight loops

      Valid if u does not appear on the left hand side of
an assignment of B

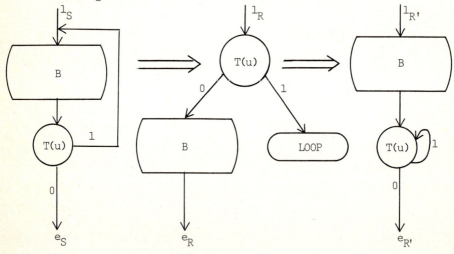

5. Loop unwinding

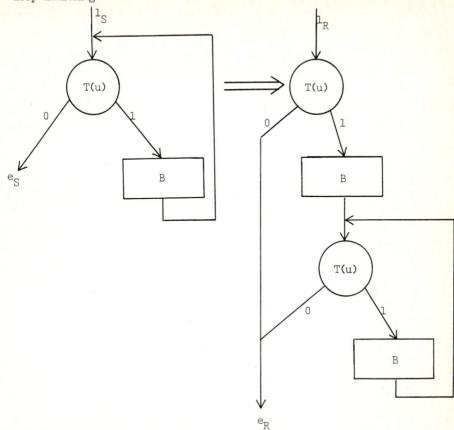

E. CORRECTNESS

When we say that some program we have just written is "correct", what do we really mean? We do not mean "correct" in some absolute sense - correctness is not in this case an ethical judgment. We simply mean that it does what we want it to do. In other words, it fits some pre-arranged condition or relationship between input and output values. If we later decide that we really wanted some other output, then the program may no longer be "correct" for our purposes.

Mathematically it would make no sense to define an absolute concept of correctness. We define only a relative concept. The definition of partial correctness is designed to capture the idea that a program when fed with a proper input or inputs - an input vector satisfying some input criterion - will give, if and when it halts, an output or outputs fulfilling some designated criterion.

In the next definitions, let us assume that P is a scheme with n input variables, denoted by $\overline{X}$, and m output variables, denoted by $\overline{Z}$ with $\overline{X}$ and $\overline{Z}$ disjoint and that I is an interpretation of P with domain D . Let $A(\overline{X})$ be a total function from D^n into {TRUE,FALSE} and $B(\overline{X},\overline{Z})$ a total function from $D^n \times D^m$ into {TRUE,FALSE} .

DEFINITION Program (P,I) is <u>partially correct</u> with respect to input criterion $A(\overline{X})$ and output criterion $B(\overline{X},\overline{Z})$ if for all $\overline{a}$ in D^n , whenever $A(\overline{a})$ = TRUE and $(P,I,\overline{a})$ halts, then $B(\overline{a},val(P,I,\overline{a}))$ = TRUE .

DEFINITION Program (P,I) is <u>totally correct</u> with respect to input criterion $A(\overline{X})$ and output criterion $B(\overline{X},\overline{Z})$ if for all $\overline{a}$ in D^n , whenever $A(\overline{a})$ = TRUE , then $(P,I,\overline{a})$ halts and $B(\overline{a},val(P,I,\overline{a}))$ = TRUE .

If we omit the input criterion in discussing partial or total correctness it is understood that we take as input criterion the function which is TRUE on all of D_n - i.e., all possible input vectors are regarded as legitimate input.

There are several points to notice. We have not said how functions A and B are to be described, although for all practical considerations this is extremely important. Next, notice that $\hat{B}(\overline{X})$ = {$\overline{Z}$ | $B(\overline{X},\overline{Z})$ = TRUE} need not correspond to a function, i.e., $\hat{B}(\overline{a})$ could have no members or more than one member for input $\overline{a}$. Thus there could be more than one function computed by programs totally correct for B if $B(a,b)$ = $B(a,b')$ = TRUE for $b \neq b'$. This situation might occur if, for example, one wants the program to retrieve certain data but does not care about the order in which they are presented, or the program is to find a person or object meeting certain specifications and if more than one "correct" object exists, no preference is expressed as to which should be selected.

Partial correctness is analogous to weak equivalence in that it is a sort of fail-safe condition. If $A(\overline{a})$ = FALSE the input criterion is invalid and $\overline{a}$ presumably never occurs as input and so we make no claims as to the behavior of program (P,I) with "bad" input. If $(P,I,\overline{a})$ does not halt there is no output and this is also regarded as a don't-care situation. There are fairly realistic situations where we would be perfectly satisfied with this sort of "correctness" - for example, in data security or protection systems. We presume - or have empirical evidence - that the system does not fail often or catastrophically and wish to know that when it is working and output is given (of whatever kind, for the output could be just internal transfer of data) then the result is "good" or, more likely, nothing "bad" happens.

In other situations we might wish - or hope - for total correctness - that our program halts for all valid inputs and gives the right answer. Total correctness is analogous to total equivalence and only applies to programs that always halt over the subdomain of valid inputs and to candidates for B which specify at least one "good" output $\overline{b}$ (with $B(\overline{a},\overline{b})$ = TRUE) for each "good" input $\overline{a}$ (with $A(\overline{a})$ = TRUE).

Statements of either partial or of total correctness can be rendered meaningless by choice of A or B . For example, any program that always loops is partially correct for any A and B while any program is partially correct for B if B is defined as TRUE everywhere, and any program is totally correct with respect to A and B if A is defined as FALSE everywhere.

EXAMPLE

Let P be the scheme in Example II-1. Suppose D is the nonnegative integers and interpretation I over D assigns $I(g)(n) = n \doteq 1$, $I(f)(n,m) = n+m$ and $I(T)(n) = 0$ if and only if $n = 0$. Then we have already seen that (P,I) is totally correct for A and B where $A(n,m)$ = TRUE if and only if n and m are nonzero positive integers, and $B((n,m),z)$ = TRUE if and only if $z = nm$.

Now let I' have the same domain as I and the same values for T and g but set $I'(f)(n,m) = nm$. Then (P,I') is totally correct for A' and B' where $A'(n,m)$ = TRUE if and only if n and m are integers with $n \geq 1$, $m \geq 2$ and $B'((n,m),z)$ = TRUE if and only if $z = n^m$.

Appendix A contains a brief summary of some relevant ideas of satisfiability and validity of well-formed formulas in the predicate calculus. Using these ideas it gives a definition of partial and total correctness of a scheme with respect to a well-formed formula as output criterion. The treatment is cursory and nonrigorous. Readers who have not seen these ideas before should examine this appendix before we return to the treatment of correctness and program verification in Chapter V, and finally conclude this treatment in Chapter VII.

III. PROGRAM SCHEMES - BASIC PROPERTIES

A. HERBRAND OR FREE INTERPRETATIONS

We have seen that there are schemes which halt on all finite interpretations but not on some infinite interpretations. Can we carry this any further? Are there any schemes which halt on all countable interpretations but diverge on some uncountable interpretations - say under interpretations with domain the real numbers?

The answer is no and the method of proof provides us with a powerful technique for dealing with questions on the power of various models of schemes, with questions on termination, equivalence and extension, and with the justification of program verification procedures.

The basic idea is that if we are concerned with a problem such as "Does (P,I) halt for all interpretations I ?" it is quite irrelevant whether the value of, say, $f(x,g(y,z))$ is 2 or 3 or 4.75 or John Jones or anything else; what matters is that there is some interpretation I under which its value is different from the value of some other term (although under other interpretations all values might coincide). If we know that under certain circumstances both P and P' halt with value $f(x,g(y,z))$, then we know that they have identical outputs, without considering the actual value of $f(x,g(y,z))$ under any particular interpretation. If a certain sequence of outcomes of tests leads P to halt with output $f(x,g(y,z))$ and P' with $g(f(x,x),y)$, then we know that some specification of f and g would lead to P and P' halting with different outcomes.

For these purposes one might as well consider just those interpretations in which a functional term denotes its own value. We are considering the domain of an interpretation to be a formal language. We view, for example, $f(x,g(y,z))$ as some string in this language. Notice that in effect we adopted this strategy when we studied Example II-3 to determine when that scheme diverged.

For a scheme P we can define a language U(P) (sometimes called a <u>Herbrand Universe</u>) over the alphabet of all variables, constants and function letters appearing in P plus parentheses and commas as special symbols. We define U(P) inductively as follows:

1) If v is a variable used in P , v is in U(P) .
2) If c is a constant used in P , c is in U(P) .
3) If f is an n-placed function letter used in P and $t_1,\ldots,t_n$ are in U(P) , then $f(t_1,\ldots,t_n)$ is in U(P) .
4) U(P) is the smallest language satisfying (1), (2) and (3).

The interested reader can easily check that U(P) is a context-free language.

We can always extend U(P) to add any finite number of variables, constants and function letters we choose subject to the rule of formation 3) above. If we are dealing with two schemes P and P' we shall always tacitly assume that U(P) = U(P') and that we have included all variables, constants, and function letters in P or P' .

A free interpretation, loosely speaking, is a minimal one - one in which we make as few decisions as possible in fulfilling the definition of an interpretation of P . In particular, we establish no relations whatsoever among members of the domain and establish no connections between objects, functions, and the values of functions on those objects, except those required by formal identity. Thus f(x,g(y,z)) must be equal to itself and must be the result of applying f to x and g(y,z) - but we assume that it is distinct from, say, g(f(x,x),y)) and that there is no relationship whatsoever between g(y,z) and f(x,x) or g(x,x) .

DEFINITION   An interpretation I of a scheme P is a _free interpretation_ (or _Herbrand interpretation_) of P if:

1) The domain of I is U(P) .
2) If c is a constant symbol, I(c) = c and if x is a variable, I(x) = x .
3) If f is an n-placed function symbol in P , $n \geq 1$, then I(f) is the
    function from $(U(P))^n$ into U(P) defined by

$$I(f)(t_1,\ldots,t_n) = f(t_1,\ldots,t_n) \text{ for all } t_1,\ldots,t_n \text{ in } U(P) .$$

4) If T is an n-placed test letter in P , then I(T) is any function
    from $(U(P))^n$ into {0,1} .

When we looked for an interpretation to make the scheme in Example II-3 diverge, we constructed a free interpretation of that scheme under which it diverged. In fact this was the correct procedure, as the next series of results we will show.

We distinguish between a _path_ through a scheme P (which is any sequence of boxes, or addresses of instructions which follows the arrows from the START box) and an _execution sequence_ (which is the series of addresses of instruction actually followed during some computation under some interpretation). We now show that every execution sequence is the execution sequence of some computation under a free interpretation.

Our first result yields a very useful technique for handling schemes. Its method of proof depends on ideas we shall need later when we provide justification for program verification procedures. For this reason, we shall give the proof in some detail.

LEMMA 3.1   Every execution sequence is the execution sequence of a computation under some free (Herbrand) interpretation. In particular, if P is a scheme, I an interpretation, and $\bar{a}$ an input vector, and if s is an execution sequence of computation $(P,I,\bar{a})$, there is a free interpretation I* such that s is an execution sequence for computation $(P,I*,\bar{X})$, and if $(P,I,\bar{a})$ halts with complete execution sequence s , then $(P,I*,\bar{X})$ halts with complete execution sequence s and $val(P,I,\bar{a}) = I(val(P,I*,\bar{X}))(a)$ - i.e., $val(P,I,\bar{a})$ can be obtained as the result of substituting $\bar{a}$ for $\bar{X}$ in the formal function $val(P,I*,\bar{X})$ and then evaluating the functions according to I .

PROOF

We shall regard execution sequence s as being defined by $s(1),s(2),\ldots,s(i),\ldots$ the sequence of statements or instructions executed by the part of computation $(P,I,\bar{a})$ denoted by s . We shall assume that scheme P is described in linear form.

We shall simultaneously construct the free interpretation I* and the computation $(P,I*,\bar{X})$. As we go along we construct for each n-placed predicate letter T two disjoint sets, $Q(s,T,0)$ and $Q(s,T,1)$, of n-tuples of members of $U(P)$ and define $I*(T)(\bar{t}) = j$ if $\bar{t}$ is in $Q(s,T,j)$.

The procedure for constructing the Q-sets can be roughly described thus.

1) Follow the execution sequence s , recording the values of the variables at each point but, instead of using an interpreted value of a function, use its name; thus $f(x)$ substitutes for $I(f)(a)$.

2) Whenever $s(i)$ is a test or conditional transfer instruction:

        k. $T(u_1,\ldots,u_n)$ r , ℓ $r \neq \ell$

and the current value of the list of variables, $(u_1,\ldots,u_n)$, recorded in functional form, is $\bar{t} = (t_1,\ldots,t_n)$, each t_j in $U(P)$, place $\bar{t}$ in $Q(s,T,1)$ if $s(i+1) = r$ and place $\bar{t}$ in $Q(s,T,0)$ if $s(i+1) = \ell$.

3) Except as directed in 2), do not change the value of any Q-set; start with all Q-sets empty.

4) At the "end", if $\bar{t}$ has been placed in neither $Q(s,T,0)$ nor $Q(s,T,1)$, place it in either one arbitrarily.

We shall give a somewhat more formal and detailed explication of the procedure and its justification. First, as a point of notation, we shall compose interpreted functions in the usual way. Thus $I(f(g(x)))(a) = I(f)(I(g)(a))$ and $I((f(x_1),g(x_2)))(a_1,a_2)) = (I(f)(a_1),I(g)(a_2))$.

Let s(i) be the statement plus address executed at step i of computation
$(P,I,\bar{a})$ and s*(i) be the statement plus address executed at step i of
$(P,I^*,\bar{X})$. For each variable u , let val(u,i) be the value of variable u
before executing s(i) in computation $(P,I,\bar{a})$ - i.e., after step i-1 and just
as step i starts - and let val*(u,i) be the corresponding value in computation
$(P,I^*,\bar{X})$. We show by induction on i that s(i) = s*(i) and for each variable
u , if u is defined at step i , then $val(u,i) = I(val^*(u,i))(\bar{a})$. Further,
if $\bar{t} = (t_1,\ldots,t_n)$ is placed in Q(s,T,j) at step i during execution of a test
statement $T(u_1,\ldots,u_n)$, then $j = I^*(T)(\bar{t}) = I(T)(I(\bar{t})(\bar{a})) =$
$I(T)(val(u_1,i),\ldots,val(u_n,i))$. Thus at each step we shall have the relation we
desire at the conclusion (if it halts) and the computation on the free interpretation
I* will exactly parallel the original computation on interpretation I .

These relations between s , and s* , val(u,i) and val*(u,i) and between
val(u,i) , val*(u,i) and the Q sets will hold for all i whether or not s is
finite and the computation halts. Further, the Q-sets and I* always exist and are
well-defined. However, the procedure we are about to define is an algorithm and
actually halts and constructs the Q-sets only if s is finite.

We proceed by induction as follows.
1) Initially, s(1) = s*(1) = 1 and for each input variable x_j ,
    $val^*(x_j,1) = x_j$. Clearly $I(val^*(x_j,1))(\bar{a}) = a_j$.
    All the sets Q(s,T,0) and Q(s,T,1) are empty initially.

Suppose that we have carried out our program successfully up to the execution
of statement s(i) in $(P,I,\bar{a})$ and s*(i) = s(i) in $(P,I^*,\bar{X})$. There are the
following possibilities for s(i) .

2) s(i) is the assignment statement

    k. $y \leftarrow f(u_1,\ldots,u_n)$

Then $val^*(u,i+1) = f(val^*(u_1,i),\ldots,val^*(u_n,i))$ and $val^*(v,i+1) = val^*(v,i)$
for $v \neq y$ by definition of a computation, and the various Q-sets are left
unchanged. Since
$$val(y,i+1) = I(f)(val(u_1,i),\ldots,val(u_n,i))$$
$$= I(f)(I(val^*(u_1,i))(\bar{a}),\ldots,I(val^*(u_n,i))(\bar{a}))$$
$$= I(f(val^*(u_1,i),\ldots,val^*(u_n,i))(\bar{a})$$
$$= I(val^*(y,i+1))(\bar{a})$$
we have the desired relation for y . Clearly the situation is unchanged for
$v \neq y$. Under any interpretation, if s(i) = s*(i) = k , we must have
s(i+1) = s*(i+1) = k+1 .

2') s(i) is the assignment statement

> k.   y ← u

for variable u . Then val*(y,i+1) = val*(u,i) and val*(v,i+1) = val*(v,i)
for v ≠ y and s*(i+1) = s(i+1) = k+1 , and we leave the Q-sets unchanged.
It should be obvious that we still maintain the desired relations.

2") s(i) is the assignment statement

> k.   y ← c

for a constant c . Then val*(y,i+1) = c and val*(v,i+1) = val*(v,i) for
v ≠ y and we leave the various Q-sets unchanged. Since val(y,i+1) = I(c) =
I(c)($\bar{a}$) = I(val*(y,i+1))($\bar{a}$) , we have the desired relation for y . Clearly
s*(i+1) = s(i+1) = k+1 and we maintain the desired relations for v ≠ y .

3) s(i) is the test statement

> k. $T(u_1,\ldots,u_n)$ r , ℓ   and   r ≠ ℓ

There are two subcases.

(a) If s(i+1) is the statement with address r , then we place in Q(s,T,1)
the n-tuple (val*(u_1,i),...,val*(u_n,i)) and define for interpretation
I* :
I*(T)(val*(u_1,i),...,val*(u_n,i)) = 1
In this case, obviously s*(i+1) = r = s(i+1) , by definition of a
computation under I* . The fact that s(i+1) = r implies, by the
definition of a computation:
1 = I(T)(val(u_1,i),...,val(u_n,i))
  = I(T)(I(val*(u_1,i))($\bar{a}$),...,I(val*(u_n,i))($\bar{a}$))
  = I(T)(I((val*(u_1,i),...,val*(u_n,i))($\bar{a}$)
as desired, taking $\bar{t}$ = (val*(u_1,i),...,val*(u_n,i)) .
For each variable u , val*(u,i+1) = val*(u,i) so the equation
connecting val*(u,i+1) and val(u,i+1) still holds.

(b) If s(i+1) is the statement with address ℓ , then we place in
Q(s,T,0) the n-tuple (val*(u_1,i),...,val*(u_n,i)) and define
for interpretation I* :
I*(T)(val*(u_1,i),...,val*(u_n,i)) = 0 .
In this case, obviously s*(i+1) = ℓ = s(i+1) .
The rest of the argument can be pursued as in (a).

4) s(i) is the forced transfer

> k. $T(u_1,\ldots,u_n)$ r , r

We make no changes in Q(s,T,0) or Q(s,T,1) and all values of the variables
are likewise unchanged. Under any interpretation we must have
s*(i+1) = s(i+1) = r .

5) $s(i)$ is the STOP statement.

Then s and s^* are completed execution sequences. Under any interpretation the computation must halt at this point and the values of the variables are unchanged. In particular, if the output variables are $z_1,\ldots,z_n$ then

$$\text{val}(P,I,\bar{a}) = (\text{val}(z_1,i),\ldots,\text{val}(z_n,i))$$
$$= (I(\text{val}^*(z_1,i))(\bar{a}),\ldots,I(\text{val}^*(z_n,i))(\bar{a}))$$
$$= I(\text{val}(P,I^*,\bar{X}))(\bar{a}) \ .$$

Now case 5) tells us that if s is a complete finite execution sequence and so $(P,I,\bar{a})$ converges, then $(P,I^*,\bar{X})$ also converges with complete terminated execution sequence $s^* = s$ and the outputs have the desired relations, i.e., $\text{val}(P,I,\bar{a}) = I(\text{val}(P,I^*,\bar{X}))(\bar{a})$.

Let T be an n-placed predicate letter, and let $\bar{t}$ be in $[U(P)]^n$. Then $\bar{t}$ is in $Q(s,T,0)$ or $Q(s,T,1)$ if and only if either it is placed there by 3) during some step i of s , or it is never placed in $Q(s,T,0) \cup Q(s,T,1)$ by any application of 3), in which case it is arbitrarily placed in $Q(s,T,0)$. Notice that under this convention the Q-sets are always well-defined but the placement of $\bar{t}$ in $Q(s,T,0)$ or $Q(s,T,1)$ is algorithmic - done effectively by our procedure - only if s is finite.

It remains only to verify that I^* is a legitimate interpretation - in particular that the definition of $I^*(T)$ is consistent for each test T . Thus we need only verify that if T is an n-placed predicate letter in P and $\bar{t} \in (U(P))^n$, then $I^*(T)(\bar{t})$ is uniquely defined as a value in $\{0,1\}$. So we must show that $Q(s,T,0) \cap Q(s,T,1) = \phi$.

Now we place $\bar{t}$ in, say, $Q(s,T,0)$ only in two circumstances. We can assign it arbitrarily at the "end" in which case we place it in just one of these sets. Or we place it in $Q(s,T,0)$ at step i of the computation. Suppose at i we placed $\bar{t}$ in $Q(s,T,0)$ because $s(i)$ was the test k . $T(u_1,\ldots,u_n)$ r,m , $m = s(i+1)$ and $\text{val}^*(u_k,i) = t_k$, $1 \le k \le n$, $\bar{t} = (t_1,\ldots,t_n)$. Then we had at this point: $0 = I^*(T)(\bar{t}) = I(T)(I(\bar{t})(\bar{a})) = I(T)(\text{val}(u_1,i),\ldots,\text{val}(u_n,i))$ and $\text{val}(u_k,i) = I(\text{val}^*(u_k,i))(\bar{a})$, $1 \le k \le n$. If we placed $\bar{t}$ in $Q(s,T,1)$ at step j , then $s(j)$ must have been some test k' . $T(v_1,\ldots,v_n)$ r',m' , $s(j+1) = r'$ and further we must have $\text{val}^*(v_k,j) = t_k$ for $1 \le k \le n$. Then by construction:

$$1 = I^*(T)(\bar{t}) = I(T)(I(\bar{t})(\bar{a})) = I(T)(\text{val}(v_1,j),\ldots,\text{val}(v_n,j))$$
$$= I(T)(I(\text{val}^*(v_1,j))(\bar{a}),\ldots,I(\text{val}^*(v_n,j))(\bar{a}))$$
$$= I(T)(I(t_1)(\bar{a}),\ldots,I(t_n)(\bar{a}))$$
$$= I(T)(I(\text{val}^*(u_1,i))(\bar{a}),\ldots,I(\text{val}^*(u_n,i))(\bar{a}))$$
$$= I(T)(\text{val}(u_1,i),\ldots,\text{val}(u_n,i))$$
$$= 0$$

which is a contradiction, since I is supposed to be a legitimate interpretation and hence $I(T)$ must be single valued.

Thus we must have $Q(s,T,0) \cap Q(s,T,1) = \phi$ for each test T and so I^* is a legitimate free interpretation with the desired properties. ∎

We can rephrase the previous lemma to provide in effect a syntactic definition of what it means for a path to be an execution sequence. If we are given any path s from START through a scheme P, we can build the sets $Q(s,T,0)$ and $Q(s,T,1)$ for each test T as before. We construct the various values $val^*(u,j)$ as before following s and place $\bar{t}$ in $Q(s,T,j)$ when demanded by the algorithm, step (3), but do not worry as to whether this is a consistent definition. As before, this is an actual construction only for s finite.

DEFINITION   A path sequence s from START is <u>consistent</u> if for each test T, $Q(\acute{s},T,0) \cap Q(s,T,1) = \phi$.

COROLLARY 3.2   A path in P from START is an execution sequence for P if and only if it is consistent.

We can carry on the algorithm simultaneously for paths s_1 in P_1, s_2 in P_2, ... , and s_n in P_n . Then we can extend our definition:

DEFINITION   A set of paths, s_1 in scheme P_1 , s_2 in scheme P_2 , ... , s_n in scheme P_n , each starting from START, is <u>consistent</u> if for any test T appearing in any P_i ,

$$(\bigcup_{i=1}^{m} Q(s_i,T,0)) \cap (\bigcup_{i=1}^{m} Q(s_i,T,1)) = \phi .$$

EXAMPLE
Let us return once again to Example II-3, and test two paths for consistency using our algorithm. As we did before, we only put down the names of the boxes with assignment statements; this uniquely determines each path.

Path s = A B C D D C STOP

We find that s forces us to make the following assignments:

BOX	Value of U(P) tested	Q-set placement
A	$f(x_1)$	$Q(s,T,0)$
B	$f^2(x_1)$	$Q(s,T,1)$
C	$f^3(x_1)$	$Q(s,T,0)$
D	$f^4(x_1)$	$Q(s,T,1)$
	$f^2(x_1)$	$Q(s,T,1)$
D	$f^5(x_1)$	$Q(s,T,1)$
	$f^3(x_1)$	$Q(s,T,0)$
C	$f^6(x_1)$	$Q(s,T,1)$

STOP

We made only assignments $Q(s,T,0) = \{f(x_1),f^3(x_1)\}$ and
$Q(s,T,1) = \{f^2(x_1),f^4(x_1),f^5(x_1),f^6(x_1)\}$. Since $Q(s,T,0) \cap Q(s,T,1) = \phi$, the
path is consistent. It corresponds, for example, to free interpretation I* with
$I^*(T)(f^n(x_1)) = 0$ for n = 1 or n = 3 and $I^*(T)(f^n(x_1)) = 1$ elsewhere. Notice
that since only values of $f^n(x_1)$ through n = 6 were computed, the value of
I*(T) elsewhere is irrelevant.

Path s' = A B C D D C D C STOP

We find that s' forces the following assignments:

BOX	Value of U(P) tested	Q-set placement	
A	$f(x_1)$	$Q(s',T,0)$	
B	$f^2(x_1)$	$Q(s',T,1)$	
C	$f^3(x_1)$	$Q(s',T,0)$	
D	$f^4(x_1)$	$Q(s',T,1)$	
	$f^2(x_1)$	$Q(s',T,1)$	
D	$f^5(x_1)$	$Q(s',T,1)$	
	$f^3(x_1)$	$Q(s',T,0)$	@%¢ε@@
C	$f^6(x_1)$	$Q(s',T,0)$	INCONSISTENT
D	$f^7(x_1)$	$Q(s',T,1)$	
	$f^4(x_1)$	$Q(s',T,0)$	
C	$f^8(x_1)$	$Q(s',T,1)$	

STOP

We notice that $f^4(x_1)$ was first assigned to $Q(s',T,1)$ in going from D to D and then to $Q(s',T,0)$ in going from D to C . This is inconsistent. No interpretation can make both decisions and so no computation can follow path s' . Hence s' is a path which is not an execution sequence.

Since any execution sequence must be an execution sequence under some free interpretation, any infinite execution sequence must be an infinite execution sequence under some free interpretation. So if P fails to halt for some interpretation and some input, there is a free interpretation under which it fails to halt. Thus we can characterize the condition of always halting in terms of consistent paths or in terms of halting under all free interpretations.

THEOREM 3.3 (1) A scheme P is always halting if and only if every consistent path through P from START is finite.

(2) A scheme P is always halting if and only if it halts everywhere under all free interpretations.

We can characterize strong equivalence in a similar fashion. If s is a consistent path (execution sequence) through P and s' is a consistent path (execution sequence) through P' (each beginning at START of course) we can apply our algorithm simultaneously to s and s' and if {s,s'} is a consistent set of paths - so for all tests T ,
$((Q(s,T,0) \cup Q(s',T,0)) \cap (Q(s,T,1) \cup Q(s',T,1)) = \phi$ - then we can construct a free interpretation $I_{s,s'}$ under which P follows execution sequence s and P' follows execution sequence s' . Namely we assume $U(P) = U(P')$ as discussed before. For n-place test T and $\bar{t}$ in $[U(P)]^n$, $I_{s,s'}(T)(\bar{t}) = 0$ if $\bar{t}$ is in $Q(s,T,0) \cup Q(s',T,0)$ and $I_{s,s'}(\bar{t}) = 1$ if $\bar{t}$ is in $Q(s,T,1) \cup Q(s',T,1)$.

THEOREM 3.4 For two schemes P and P' with the same list $\bar{X}$ of input variables the following statements are equivalent:
(1) P is strongly equivalent to P' .
(2) For every free interpretation I , (P,I) is strongly equivalent to (P',I) .
(3) For all consistent pairs of sequences s through P and s' through P' ,
val$(P,I_{s,s'},\bar{X}) = $ val$(P',I_{s,s'},\bar{X})$ whenever either is defined.

PROOF
By the definition of strong equivalence, (1) implies (2). Evidently (2) implies (3) since $I_{s,s'}$ is a particular free interpretation.

Suppose (3) holds. Consider computations $(P,I,\overline{a})$ and $(P',I,\overline{a})$. If the first corresponds to some path s through P and the other to some path s' through P' , clearly {s,s'} is a consistent pair. Suppose one path, say s , is finite. This is true if and only if $(P,I,\overline{a})$ converges. But then by (3) and lemma 3.1:

$$val(P,I,\overline{a}) = I(val(P,I_{s,s'},\overline{X}))(\overline{a}) = I(val(P',I_{s,s'},\overline{X}))(\overline{a}) = val(P',I,\overline{a})$$

Similarly, if $(P',I,\overline{a})$ converges, so does $(P,I,\overline{a})$ and the outputs are the same. Hence for every interpretation I , (P,I) is strongly equivalent to (P',I) and so P is strongly equivalent to P' . ■

Similar results can be shown for other definitions of equivalence.

THEOREM 3.5   For schemes P and P' :
(1) P and P' are weakly equivalent if and only if for every free interpretation I , (P,I) is weakly equivalent to (P',I) .
(2) P and P' are totally equivalent if and only if for every free interpretation I , (P,I) is totally equivalent to (P',I) .
(3) P and P' are recursively equivalent if and only if for every recursive free interpretation I , (P,I) and (P',I) are strongly equivalent.
(4) P is an extension of P' if and only if for every free interpretation I , (P,I) is an extension of (P',I) .

Thus free interpretations will be one of our primary tools for handling such questions. Notice that in a free interpretation the domain is recursive and the functions assigned to function letters are recursive but the interpretations of the predicate letters may not be recursive.

B.   TREE SCHEMES AND ALWAYS HALTING SCHEMES
The next result, on always halting schemes, requires use of what has been variously known as König's Lemma or the Fan Lemma or the Infinity Lemma.

KONIG'S LEMMA (INFINITY LEMMA, FAN LEMMA)
If T is a finitely branching tree (each node is directly connected to finitely many sons) and T is infinite, then there exists at least one infinite path through T starting at the root of T .

This lemma is nonconstructive. It only says that there is an infinite path, but gives no formula or algorithm for constructing the path. Whether the proof can be made constructive in an individual case depends on the infinite tree T and how T is specified. An infinite path in T can be described by an infinite sequence of nodes, $n_0, n_1, \ldots, n_i, \ldots$ such that (1) n_0 is the initial node and (2) n_{i+1} is a son (direct descendant) of n_i for each i. The proof of the existence of this path consists in showing that given n_i, there is an n_{i+1} lying in this path. The argument starts by saying that since T is infinite and n_0 has some finite set of sons, $\{m_{01}, \ldots, m_{0k_0}\}$, the subtree rooted at least one m_{0j} is infinite; let n_1 be this son, m_{0j}. At each step, the subtree rooted at n_i is infinite. Then n_i has finitely many sons, $\{m_{i1}, \ldots, m_{ik_i}\}$, and the subtree rooted at one son must be infinite; we let n_{i+1} be that son.

To make this proof constructive, the names of nodes should form a recursive set, there should be a total recursive function f such that $f(n)$ lists all the sons of node n, and the predicate "The subtree rooted at n is infinite" should be total recursive.

Let P be any program scheme. Using our algorithm for testing whether a path is an execution sequence, we construct a tree $T(P)$ of all possible execution sequences for P under free interpretations. The tree $T(P)$ may be finite or infinite; our main result on the subject will say that $T(P)$ is finite if and only if P is always halting. The nodes of $T(P)$ are labelled with execution sequences. At level n (declaring the root or initial node to be at level 1) $T(P)$ will have exactly one node for each execution sequence of length n (i.e. containing n statements) and each node will be labelled with the corresponding execution sequence.

The root or initial node will be labelled by the unique execution sequence of length 1, containing just the initial or start statement. If node q at level n is labelled with execution sequence s, it is directly connected to (has as sons) exactly those nodes q' labelled with execution sequences s' of length $n+1$ such that $\{s, s'\}$ is a consistent pair.

Notice that $T(P)$ is a proper tree. An execution sequence s of length $n \geq 2$ is consistent with exactly one execution sequence s' of length $n-1$; namely, if s consists of statements $(k_1, k_2, \ldots, k_n)$, then s' is $(k_1, k_2, \ldots, k_{n-1})$. The tree $T(P)$ is finite branching for if s is an execution sequence of length n and $s = (k_1, \ldots, k_n)$ we need only consider the possibilities for statement k_n. If it is a STOP statement, s is a complete execution sequence and has no consistent extensions so it labels a node with no sons. If k_n is an assignment statement, or a forced transfer, there is exactly one statement k_{n+1} such that $(k_1, k_2, \ldots, k_n, k_{n+1})$ is consistent, namely the unique statement following k_n. If k_n is a conditional transfer (test) then, since our tests are binary, there are at most two statements k_{n+1} and k_{n+1}' which can consistently extend s ; at least one must so extend s since either the 0 or the 1 branch must be valid. In this case the node labelled s has either 1 or 2 sons. So T(P) is certainly finite branching.

If T(P) is finite then there are only finitely many possible execution sequences for P and a uniform bound on the length of any execution sequence exists. Then P is always halting and there is a uniform bound N on the length of any computation in P .

If T(P) is infinite, then, since it is finite branching, there must be an infinite path through T(P) . Since node i in such a path is labelled with an execution sequence of length i and the sequence labelling node i has a consistent extension labelling node i+1 in this path, the path must represent an infinite execution sequence of P . Hence P has at least one infinite execution sequence and hence at least one computation that diverges. So if T(P) is infinite, P is not always halting. If the tree T(P) has infinitely many levels it is infinite and so P is not always halting. If there is no uniform bound N on the length of computations in P , T(P) has infinitely many levels and P is not always halting. Thus we have established:

THEOREM 3.6   If P is always halting, there is a uniform bound N such that for any interpretation I and any input $\bar{a}$, computation $(P, I, \bar{a})$ contains at most N steps.

This result is "partially constructible" in the sense that if P is known to be finite, then tree T(P) is known to be finite and we can actually construct T(P) from P since it is decidable whether a given finite path in P is an execution sequence. However, as we shall see later, there is no way of deciding whether P is always halting.

We can construct given T(P) a tree T*(P) - finite or infinite - which in some sense can be considered equivalent to scheme P . If node q on level n in T(P) is labelled with execution sequence $s = (k_1, \ldots, k_n)$, replace label s with a label containing the statement or instruction named by k_n . Thus our new tree T'(P) will have as labels the instructions of P ordered so that a path through T'(P) gives the proper sequence of statements executed by an appropriate computation in P . We can almost consider T'(P) to be a scheme strongly equivalent to P . If a node q is now labelled with a test $T(u_1, \ldots, u_n)$ and has two branches to nodes q_1 and q_2 labelled with statements r_1 and r_2 , one must correspond to the 0 branch from $T(u_1, \ldots, u_n)$ and one with t to the 1 branch; simply label the branches in T'(P) by 0 and 1 in appropriate fashion. If q has only one son q_1 there is only one consistent outcome to the test $T(u_1, \ldots, u_n)$ at this point. We can either treat this as a forced transfer and label the branch from q to q_1 by both 0 and 1, or else "pinch out" node q and let the subtree rooted at q_1 become the subtree rooted at q . The tree $T^*(P)$ formed from $T'(P)$ by this process can be regarded as a scheme strongly equivalent to P .

It is evident that if $T(P)$ is infinite we cannot really "construct" $T^*(P)$. But if $T(P)$ is finite, we can carry out this process and now $T^*(P)$ really is a program scheme strongly equivalent to P ; its graph is a tree.

DEFINITION   A scheme P is a <u>tree program scheme</u> if its graph is a tree.

COROLLARY 3.7   Any always halting scheme P is totally equivalent to some tree program scheme $T^*(P)$ and if P is known to be always halting, $T^*(P)$ can be constructed from P .

EXAMPLE
   Consider the program scheme P in Example III-1. Except for the START and STOP boxes, all statement boxes in P have been named by integers for convenience.
   On the second page of Example III-1, we display the execution sequence tree $T(P)$. Statements are named by the appropriate numbers. Thus the only execution sequence of length 1 consists of just the START statement, the only one of length 2 consists of START followed by statement 1, the only one of length 3 consists of (START,1,2) while there are two execution sequences of length 7: (START,1,2,3,4,5,6) and (START,1,2,3,4,5,STOP).. For convenience the diagram of $T(P)$ also shows the labels 0 and 1 on the appropriate branches from test statements and also exhibits the values of y_1 and y_2 when either is updated. This helps show that, for example, when we return to the test in box 6 in path (START,1,2,3,4,5,6,7,6) , we are applying test T to $y_1 = f(x)$ while earlier in this path we took branch 1 on applying test T to $y_2 = f(x)$ in box 3; hence we are now constrained to follow branch 1 again.
   Following $T(P)$ through in detail we see that it is finite and there are 4 possible complete execution sequences: (START,1,2,3,STOP) , (START,1,2,3,4,5,STOP), (START,1,2,3,4,5,6,8,3,STOP) , and (START,1,2,3,4,5,6,7,6,8,3,STOP) . Thus no computation in P can take more than 12 steps.
   On the next page of Example III-1, we construct $T'(P)$ from $T(P)$ by substituting for the full list of each execution sequence the statement named in the last step of the sequence.

   Finally we build $T^*(P)$ from $T'(P)$ by eliminating single exit test statements which obviously cannot affect the outcome of the computations.

EXAMPLE III-1   ALWAYS HALTING PROGRAM SCHEME   P .

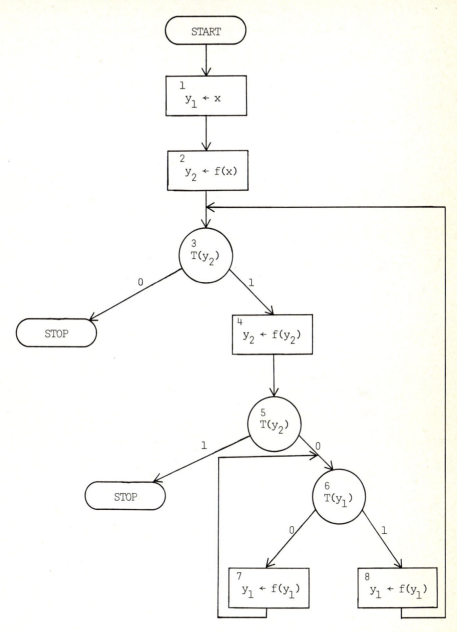

EXAMPLE III-1   CONTINUED

THE EXECUTION SEQUENCE TREE   T(P)

(with values added at assignments)

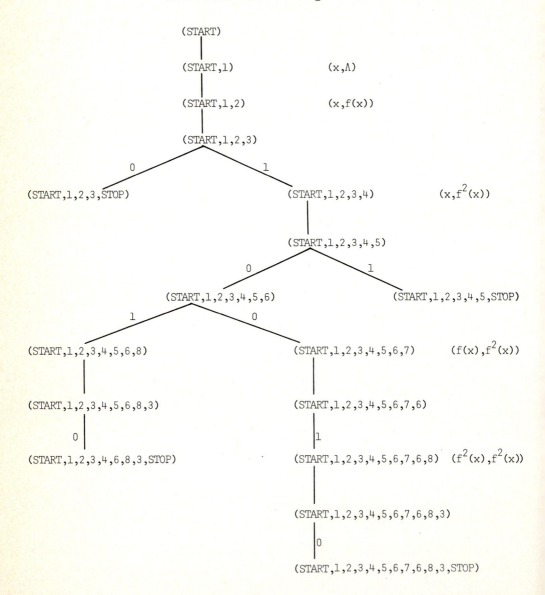

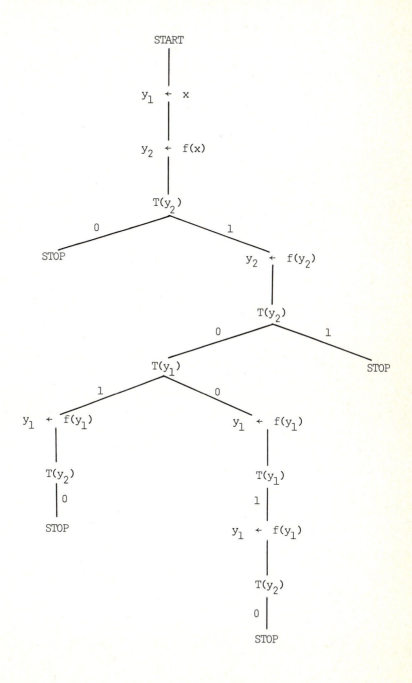

EXAMPLE III-1   CONTINUED
THE STATEMENT LABELLED EXECUTION SEQUENCE TREE   T'(P)

EXAMPLE III-1   CONCLUDED

TREE PROGRAM SCHEME T*(P) STRONGLY EQUIVALENT TO   P

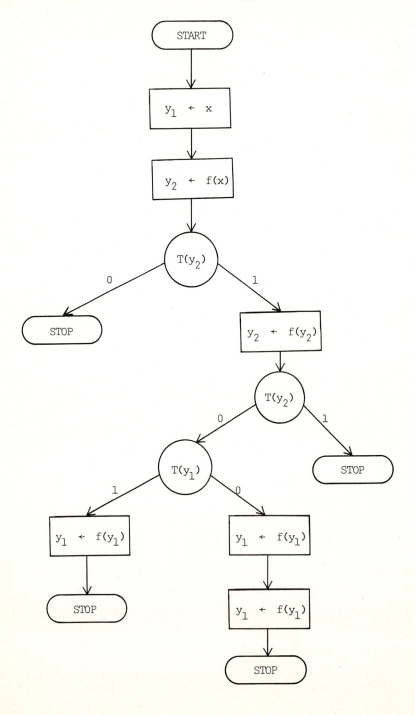

We can easily test tree program schemes for strong equivalence. For if P and P' are tree program schemes, there are at most finitely many paths through these two schemes and hence finitely many consistent pairs {s,s'} where s is a consistent path through P and hence an execution sequence in P and s' is a consistent path through P' and hence an execution sequence in P' . So, let us find all paths s through P and s' through P' . For each pair {s,s'} we can construct the Q-sets as in the algorithm and test {s,s'} for consistency. If {s,s'} is a consistent pair, we construct the corresponding free interpretation $I_{s,s'}$ and follow the paths s and s' (which of course are finite) and see whether $val(P,I_{s,s'},\bar{X}) = val(P',I_{s,s'},\bar{X})$. Schemes P and P' are strongly equivalent if and only if this equation holds for every consistent pair s,s' . So we have shown:

THEOREM 3.8   Strong equivalence is decidable for tree program schemes.

A scheme which is known to be always halting can be effectively transformed into a strongly equivalent tree program scheme. Hence:

COROLLARY 3.9   Strong equivalence is decidable for always halting program schemes.

C. rREE SCHEMES
    A useful property for schemes to have is "freeness".

DEFINITION   A program scheme P is <u>free</u> if every path from START is an execution sequence.

Using our results concerning consistent paths, we can given alternative definitions of free schemes.

THEOREM 3.10   The following statements regarding a program scheme P are equivalent:
(1) P is free.
(2) For each path s through P and each predicate T in P ,
     $Q(s,T,0) \cap Q(s,T,1) = \phi$.
(3) Under any free interpretation I , the computation $(P,I,\bar{X})$ never applies the same n-placed test T twice to the same n-tuple of members of U(P) .

EXAMPLES:

The flowcharts A and B in Example I-1 are not free. In flowchart A the path from P(y) = FALSE through P(u) = FALSE retests P(y) without updating y and so the same path must be followed afterwards. Flowchart B contains the tight loop around P(u) which is not free.

An always looping scheme is one with no consistent paths from START to STOP, i.e. a scheme all of whose computations diverge. A simple example is:

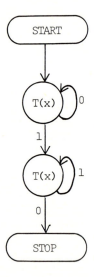

The scheme above is not free. If we remove the requirement that a scheme contain at least one STOP statement, there are free always looping schemes such as:

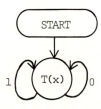

If we use:

We usually assume that this is to be replaced by a "free" subscheme such as:

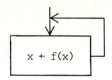

Flowchart C in Example I-3 is free. Every time P(u) is applied, the value of u in a free interpretation has been changed to a new one. The path which traces out the loop n times, n > 0 , corresponds to a free interpretation with $P(f^n(x))$ = TRUE but $P(f^k(x))$ = FALSE for $0 \le k \le n-1$. For similar reasons, the flowchart of Example II-1 is clearly free.

We have already seen that the flowchart of Example II-3 is not free - we saw that for example path START A B C D D C D C STOP was inconsistent.

The flowchart P in Example III-1 is obviously not free since it contains infinite paths but no infinite execution sequence. However the strongly equivalent tree program scheme T*(P) is clearly free since we have eliminated the useless tests. This situation is general as we now observe.

Following the usual arguments for finite state graphs, we can determine whether P contains any infinite path. If P has n statements, clearly P contains a loop if and only if it contains a path with n+1 or more statements. A free scheme always halts if and only if its graph contains no loops since in a free scheme a loop corresponds to an infinite path and hence to an infinite execution sequence.

THEOREM 3.11   For free program schemes (i.e. if a "birdie" tells you a scheme is free) it is decidable whether P is always halting.

Now our construction of tree scheme T*(P) from P and T(P) could, if T(P) happens to be finite, be organized so that T*(P) is free - we merely eliminate single exit tests. Hence we again show:

THEOREM 3.12   If P is an always halting scheme we can construct a strongly equivalent free tree program scheme.

THEOREM 3.13   If P is a tree scheme we can construct a strongly equivalent free tree program scheme.

We have seen examples of schemes which are not free. There are schemes which are not even strongly equivalent to any free scheme. Such a scheme appears in Example III-2. Intuitively speaking, Example III-2 cannot be "freed" because we must use the two tests as a clock, to see how long it takes to find $f^n(x)$ with $P(f^n(x)) = 0$ and then to run through this cycle again and update x to $g^n f^n(x)$. To justify this statement formally, we need some additional notation and results.

DEFINITION   A program scheme P is <u>monadic</u> if all functions and tests appearing in P are monadic (1-placed).

When dealing with monadic program schemes we often omit the parentheses in functional descriptions, so e.g. $f(g(f(f(x))))$ is written as $fgffx$. This is always done in defining value languages.

DEFINITION   For a monadic scheme P with a single output variable, the <u>value language of P</u> is the language

$$L(P) = \{val(P,I,\overline{X}) \mid I \text{ free interpretation, } (P,I,\overline{X}) \text{ halts}\}$$

where each $val(P,I,\overline{X})$ is written without parentheses.

We shall return to the concept of value languages later in our study of monadic recursion schemes; this concept is a powerful tool in studying the relative power of monadic program schemes and monadic recursion schemes. For the present we need only the following simple fact.

THEOREM 3.14   Let P be a monadic free scheme with one output variable z. Then the value language $L(P)$ is regular.

PROOF
We can assume that P is in linear form, that z is not an input or a program variable and that no input variable is a program variable. Also we can assume that all statements are of the forms:

    k. $u \leftarrow f(u)$
    k. $u \leftarrow v$
    k. $u \leftarrow c$
    k. $T(u)$ r,s

where c is a constant and u and v are variables.

Since there is only one output variable, z , and all functions are monadic, at any given time at most one variable in the computation under a free interpretation can contain a value which ultimately affects the final output value. Since P is free, all paths are execution sequences under some free interpretation. Thus if we concentrate on just the contents of that register which we believe will ultimately be transferred to z , and ignore other values, we cannot be trapped into following a "bad" path. If v is our "guessed" variable and we have stored the current value of v , that suffices. All continuations of the current path must be valid (consistent).

We shall construct a right linear context-free grammar G to generate L(P) . This suffices to show that L(P) is regular. The nonterminals of G are of the forms (k,0) and (k,v) where k is an address and v is a variable. The presence of nonterminal (k,0) indicates that we are simulating a computation currently in address k but have not yet started computing the ultimate output z . The presence of (k,v) indicates that we are simulating a computation currently in address k and have guessed that the contents of v will ultimately be transformed into the desired output.

Let 1 be the start address of P . Then the initial symbol of G is (1,0) and G contains a production

$$(1,0) \rightarrow (1,x)x$$

for each input variable x . For any statement

$$k. \quad T(u) \quad r,s$$

G contains productions

$$(k,0) \rightarrow (r,0)$$
$$(k,0) \rightarrow (s,0)$$
$$(k,u) \rightarrow (r,u)$$
$$(k,u) \rightarrow (s,u)$$

for every variable u . For any statement

$$k. \quad u \leftarrow f(u)$$

G contains

$$(k,0) \rightarrow (k+1,0)$$
$$(k,u) \rightarrow (k+1,u)f$$
$$(k,v) \rightarrow (k+1,v)$$

for every variable $v \neq u$. For any statement

k. $u \leftarrow y$

where y is a variable G contains

$$(k,0) \rightarrow (k+1,0)$$
$$(k,y) \rightarrow (k+1,u)$$
$$(k,v) \rightarrow (k+1,v)$$

for every variable $v \neq u$. For any statement

k. $u \leftarrow c$

where c is a constant, G contains

$$(k,0) \rightarrow (k+1,0)$$
$$(k,0) \rightarrow (k+1,u)c$$
$$(k,v) \rightarrow (k+1,v)$$

for every variable $v \neq u$. Finally, for any statement

k.   STOP

G contains

$$(k,z) \rightarrow e$$

where e is the empty string

     This construction works because G is free and we are dealing with free interpretations. When we come to a test we can nondeterministically select either path - some free interpretation will take either path. The final output under any free interpretation must be either $f_1 \ldots f_n x$ for some input variable x or else $f_1 \ldots f_n c$ for some constant c . In the first case, G guesses this will occur by the production $(1,0) \rightarrow (1,x)x$ and records the fact that the grammar is

generating values currently stored in x . In the second case, G uses
nonterminals (k,0) and if it ever encounters k.   u ← c can nondeterministically
decide that the ultimate output is started here and so use rule (k,0) → (k+1,u)c .

   When statement k. STOP is reached, a series of right guesses will have
produced $(k,z)f_1 \ldots f_n x$ or $(k,z)f_1 \ldots f_n c$ and the (k,z) is now erased, leaving
the proper output in place. Otherwise, the derivation blocks at this point if not
earlier.   ■

   This result allows us to conclude that the scheme P in Example III-2 is not
strongly equivalent to any free scheme since $L(P) = \{g^n f^n x \mid n \geq 1\}$ is not
regular.

   Unfortunately, "freeness" is not itself a decidable property. This is the
first undecidability result we encounter. The proof employs the Post
Correspondence Problem.

DEFINITION   Let $\sum$ be a vocabulary and let $A = (\alpha_1, \ldots, \alpha_n)$ and $B = (\beta_1, \ldots, \beta_n)$
be two ordered lists of n nonempty members of $\sum^+$, $n \geq 1$, each α_i , β_i in
$\sum^+$. The Post Correspondence Problem for (A,B) has a solution if there exists
$m \geq 1$, $i_1, \ldots, i_m$ in $\{1, \ldots, n\}$ such that

$$\alpha_{i_1} \ldots \alpha_{i_m} = \beta_{i_1} \ldots \beta_{i_m}$$

   An alternative formulation is that given two finite code sets, the Post
Correspondence Problem inquires whether any word is coded alike in both codes.

   We use the following well-known result due to Post:

THEOREM 3.15   For $\#\sum \geq 2$, it is undecidable whether the Post Correspondence
Problem has a solution.

   Now we want to show that given a pair (A,B) of lists over a two symbol
alphabet, say {a,b} , we can effectively construct a scheme P(A,B) such that
P(A,B) is free if and only if the Correspondence Problem for (A,B) has NO
solution. It will then follow that freeness is undecidable. For it if were
decidable whether a scheme is free, then we could decide the Correspondence Problem
as follows: Given (A,B) , construct P(A,B) , turn on the machine which decides
whether P(A,B) is free; if P(A,B) is free print the answer NO - (A,B) has no
solution - and otherwise print the answer YES - (A,B) has a solution.

EXAMPLE III-2

A SCHEME NOT STRONGLY EQUIVALENT TO ANY FREE PROGRAM SCHEME

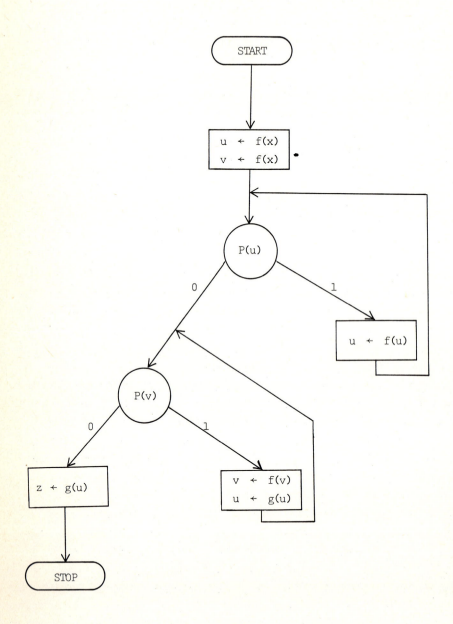

The main idea is as follows. For convenience let a and b be regarded as two distinct monadic function letters so $a(x)$ and $b(x)$ are formally distinct functions. We shall again omit parentheses in composing functions, and use, for example, $abaa(x)$ instead of $a(b(a(a(x))))$. We also let interpreted functions compose in the usual way so that, for example, $I(abaa)(x) = I(a)(I(b)(I(a)(I(a)(x))))$. Clearly $I(w_1)(x) = I(w_2)(x)$ for all interpretations I of a and b and all values of x if and only if $w_1 = w_2$.

For each sequence $s = (i_m, \ldots, i_1)$ of integers from $\{1, \ldots, n\}$, there will be a free interpretation I_s of $P(A,B)$ under which the value of variable u is built up as $\alpha_{i_1} \ldots \alpha_{i_m}(x)$ and the value of variable v is built up as $\beta_{i_1} \ldots \beta_{i_m}(x)$ and then a test T is applied to u and v in succession. If the Correspondence Problem for (A,B) has a solution

$$\alpha_{i_1} \ldots \alpha_{i_m} = \beta_{i_1} \ldots \beta_{i_m}$$

and $s = (i_m, \ldots, i_1)$ under the free interpretation I_s we shall at this point have $val(u) = \alpha_{i_1} \ldots \alpha_{i_m}(x) = \beta_{i_1} \ldots \beta_{i_m}(x) = val(v)$ and then apply test T twice to the same value of the variables u and v. If that occurs, $P(A,B)$ is not free. Hence if the correspondence problem for (A,B) has a solution, we can ensure that $P(A,B)$ is not free. The rest of the work consists of ensuring that this is the only way in which $P(A,B)$ can be "unfree" so that if the Correspondence Problem for (A,B) has no solution then $P(A,B)$ is free.

The construction appears in Example III-3. We allow composite functions in assignment statements for convenience. This can be simulated by simple functions, to meet our definition. That is, we now allow a statement such as $u \leftarrow abaa(u)$ which can be simulated by applying in order $u \leftarrow a(u)$, $u \leftarrow a(u)$, $u \leftarrow b(u)$, and finally $u \leftarrow a(u)$.

Since the scheme in Example III-3 could obviously not appear in one page or be conveniently represented as a whole, we describe it by subschemes, a useful abbreviation technique we shall frequently employ. The triangles such as:

represent addresses of subschemes. The full scheme $P(A,B)$ is obtained by pasting the triangles with the same name on top of each other and then substituting a straight line.

EXAMPLE III-3

For A = $(\alpha_1,...,\alpha_n)$ and B = $(\beta_1,...,\beta_n)$, each α_i,β_i in $\{a,b\}^+$, construction of scheme P(A,B) such that P(A,B) is free if and only if the Correspondence Problem for (A,B) has no solution.

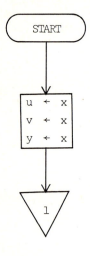

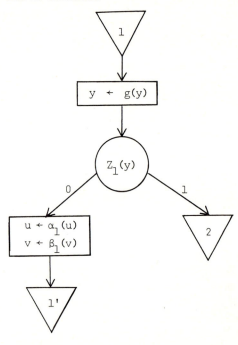

Subscheme for i , $2 \le i \le n$

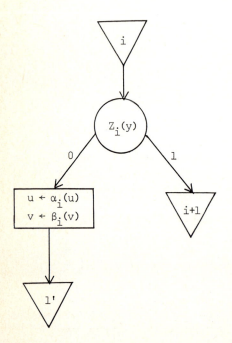

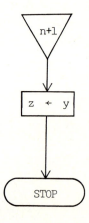

EXAMPLE III-3   CONTINUED

Subscheme for 1'

Subscheme for i' , 2 ≤ i ≤ n

Subscheme for (n+1)'

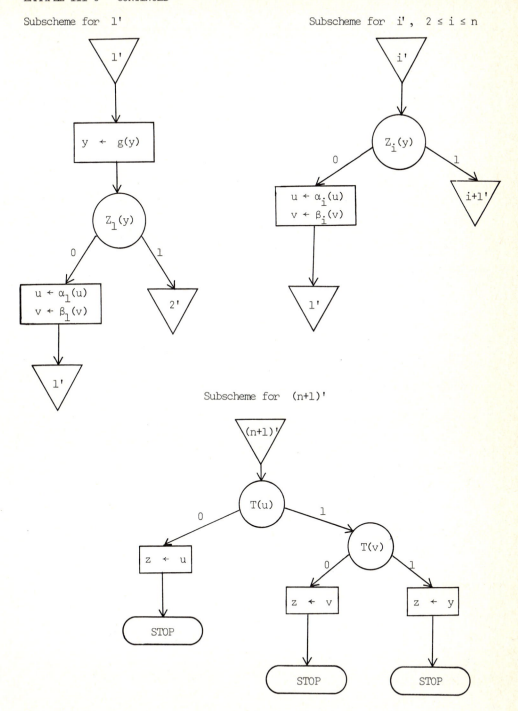

We assume that for each i , $1 \le i \le n$, Z_i is a different monadic predicate letter and that T is a monadic predicate letter distinct from all the Z_i . Further, g is a monadic function letter distinct from a and b .

Given a sequence $s = (i_1, \ldots, i_m)$ we can define a (not unique) free interpretation I_s by the correspondence:

$$I_s(Z_{i_r})(g^r(x)) = 0 \qquad\qquad 1 \le r \le m$$

$$I_s(Z_k)(g^r(x)) = 1 \qquad\qquad 1 \le k \le i_r - 1 , \quad 1 \le r \le m$$

$$I_s(Z_k)(g^{m+1}(x)) = 1 \qquad\qquad 1 \le k \le n$$

$$I_s(T)(\alpha_{i_m} \ldots \alpha_{i_1}(x)) = 1$$

The values of the $I_s(Z_k)$ and $I_s(T)$ are unimportant elsewhere and can be specified arbitrarily. It is clear that this correspondence works both ways – if I is a free interpretation such that for some $m+1 > 2$, $I(Z_k)(g^{m+1}(x)) = 1$ for all k , $1 \le k \le n$, and for each $r \le m$ there is an $i_r \in \{1, \ldots, n\}$ such that $I_s(Z_{i_r})(g^r(x)) = 0$ and $I_s(Z_k)(g^r(x)) = 1$ for $1 \le k \le i_r - 1$, then clearly I can be represented as I_s for $s = (i_1, \ldots, i_m)$.

Let $s = (i_1, \ldots, i_m)$. Under I_s , $P(A,B)$ will apply each Z_k to $y = g(x)$ in succession, returning answer 1, until finally for Z_{i_1} the answer is 0 whereupon u becomes $\alpha_{i_1}(x)$ and v becomes $\beta_{i_1}(x)$ and the computation proceeds to subscheme 1' and now applies these tests to $y = g^2(x)$. This continues until finally the computation returns to 1' with y as $g^m(x)$ and u as $\alpha_{i_m} \ldots \alpha_{i_1}(x)$ and $val(v) = \beta_{i_m} \ldots \beta_{i_1}(x)$. Then y is reassigned as $g^{m+1}(x)$. This time all the tests Z_k applied to y return answer 1 and finally the computation enters subscheme $(n+1)'$.

So in particular, if the Correspondence Problem for (A,B) has the solution

$$\alpha_{i_1} \ldots \alpha_{i_m} = \beta_{i_1} \ldots \beta_{i_m}$$

then if $s = (i_m, \ldots, i_1)$, the computation under I_s will ultimately enter subscheme $(n+1)'$ with $val(u) = val(v) = \alpha_{i_1} \ldots \alpha_{i_m}(x)$. Then the result of test T on u will be 1 and so the output of the next test is constrained to be 1 as T is applied twice to the same value. Hence $P(A,B)$ cannot be free.

On the other hand, until we reach $(n+1)'$ we only apply the tests Z_k which are all distinct and are applied only after y has been updated by assignment $y \leftarrow g(y)$. Thus until and unless the computation reaches subscheme $(n+1)'$, there is no way of violating the definition of a free scheme. But the computation on free interpretation I can enter $(n+1)'$ only after all the Z_k have tested out 1 on some $g^{m+1}(x)$, $m+1 \geq 2$, for the first time. As we mentioned above, this can be seen to correspond to a free interpretation I_s for some $s = (i_1,\ldots,i_m)$ and u will have as value $\alpha_{i_m} \ldots \alpha_{i_1}(x)$ and v as value $\beta_{i_m} \ldots \beta_{i_1}(x)$. If the Correspondence Problem for (A,B) has no solution, these values must be distinct and so we do not violate the definition of freeness. Hence if the Correspondence Problem for (A,B) has no solution, $P(A,B)$ is free. Thus, $P(A,B)$ is free if and only if the Correspondence Problem for (A,B) has no solution.

We have just shown that:

THEOREM 3.16   It is undecidable whether a program scheme is free.

We can extend this result a little. If we examine Example III-4, we see that we have altered $P(A,B)$ to form $\tilde{P}(A,B)$ by changing subscheme $(n+1)'$. Since f and g are assumed to be distinct from the function letters a and b and from each other, if we enter $(n+1)'$ with different values for u and v the subscheme will not violate the definition of freeness. But if we enter $(n+1)'$ with $\mathrm{val}(u) = \mathrm{val}(v)$, then the subscheme behaves like the scheme in Example III-2, which we have seen is not strongly equivalent to any free scheme. Hence, similar arguments will show that now $\hat{P}(A,B)$ is strongly equivalent to some free scheme if and only if the Correspondence Problem for (A,B) has no solution.

THEOREM 3.17   It is undecidable whether there is a free scheme which is strongly equivalent to a given scheme.

EXAMPLE III-4

If we replace subscheme $(n+1)'$ in Example III-3 by the
following subscheme, the resulting scheme $\hat{P}(A,B)$ is
strongly equivalent to a free scheme if and only if the Correspondence
Problem for (A,B) has no solution.

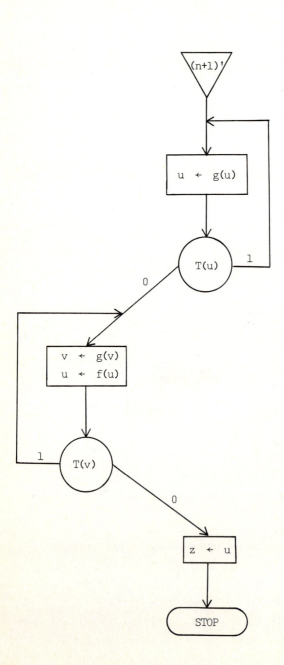

D. LIBERAL SCHEMES AND A GLOBAL TRANSFORMATION

We shall briefly examine a condition on schemes which implies freeness and which can be tested. We do this primarily because it gives us our first example of an equivalence preserving global transformation on schemes. This is a topic we study more closely in the next chapter.

In the next definition and for the rest of this chapter we assume that only assignments of the form

$$u \leftarrow f(v_1,\ldots,v_r)$$

are allowed where u and the v_i are variables. Some of the results are in fact not true if we allow, e.g., composite assignments such as

$$u \leftarrow f(g(x),g(y))$$

DEFINITION   A scheme P is <u>liberal</u> if for each free interpretation I , the computation $(P,I,\overline{X})$ never computes the same member of $U(P)$ twice, i.e., never assigns twice the same member of $U(P)$ to a variable.

We shall show that every liberal scheme is strongly equivalent to a free scheme. The converse is not true. Example III-5 contains a free scheme P which is not strongly equivalent to any liberal scheme. Under free interpretation I , if $2n+1 = \text{Min } \{k \geq 3 \mid k \text{ odd, } I(T)(f^k(x)) = 0\}$, then (P,I,x) halts with output $(f^n(x),f^{2n+1}(x))$. To compute $f^{2n+1}(x)$ and test it, we must first compute $f^n(x)$, and store it until $f^{2n+1}(x)$ is tested; the time lag $n+1$ becomes arbitrarily large so either we need arbitrarily many registers - violating the definition of a program scheme - or else we must recompute $f^n(x)$ - violating the definition of a liberal scheme.

We demonstrate the fact that every liberal scheme is strongly equivalent to a free scheme by describing a transformation t on schemes such that:

  (1) If P is liberal, $t(P)$ is liberal.
  (2) Scheme $t(P)$ is free if and only if it is liberal.
  (3) Scheme $t(P)$ is strongly equivalent to scheme P in all cases.

The transformation t does not necessarily preserve freeness if the original scheme is not liberal. The basic idea is that a test should occur only after one of its variables has been assigned to. This is accomplished by performing all possible

EXAMPLE III-5

A FREE SCHEME WHICH IS NOT STRONGLY EQUIVALENT TO ANY LIBERAL SCHEME

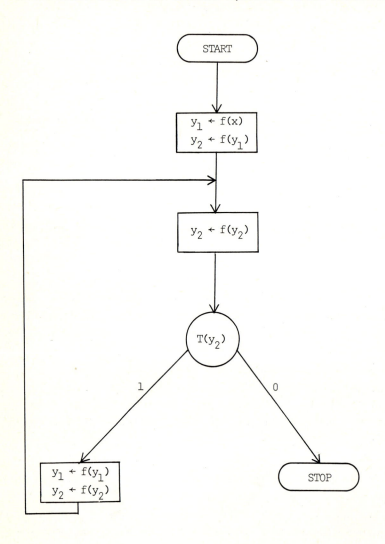

INPUT VARIABLE - x   OUTPUT VARIABLES - y_1, y_2

tests involving a variable u directly after assigning to variable u and storing
the results in the addresses of statements. Thus we are really using the addresses
as states in a finite state control. This is a very useful technique in
constructing schemes with preselected properties.

The construction appears in Example III-6 for a particular subclass. The
construction for the full class is similar but vastly more complicated.

The transformation t is not itself of great significance - although useful
in certain proofs - but it does illustrate reasonably well the concept of a
global equivalence preserving transformation on schemes.

In this transformation t we have changed the order of appearance of tests
but the application of assignment statements is unchanged. For each execution
sequence in P there is one in t(P) in which the order of applications of
assignment statements is the same. If P is liberal, obviously t(P) is liberal.
Now in t(P) we have a test Q(u) only after either another test Q'(u) ,
$Q \neq Q'$ or an assignment to u . Hence we cannot test u by Q twice in a row
without assigning to u . Thus if t(P) is liberal it must be free. On the
other hand, every assignment in t(P) is directly followed by all possible tests
involving the variable assigned to and so if P is not liberal it cannot be free.
Hence t(P) is free if and only if it is liberal.

If P is liberal, then t(P) is liberal and so free. Obviously P is
always strongly equivalent to t(P) .

THEOREM 3.18   If P is liberal we can effectively construct a free liberal scheme
t(P) strongly equivalent to P .

Suppose t(P) is not liberal and the smallest "illiberal" execution sequence
has length m . If we examine the tree scheme corresponding to paths in t(P) of
length less than m this must be free. Hence if this execution sequence has a
subpath passing twice through the same address we can "snip" out the subpath and
still have a legitimate execution sequence.

By our conditions on the form of assignment statements in P and so in t(P) ,
this first occurrence of "illiberality" must be due to an assignment at time i ,
$u \leftarrow f(v_1,\ldots,v_s)$ followed at time i+j by $y \leftarrow f(y_1,\ldots,y_s)$ with $val(v_k,i) =$
$val(y_k,i+j)$ all k , $1 \leq k \leq s$ under the particular free interpretation leading
to this execution sequence. But we must have computed previously each $val(v_k,i)$
and $val(y_k,i+j)$, so if this is the first violation of liberality, then formally
each $v_k = y_k$, i.e., they are the same variables. Further, between i and i+j
we cannot recompute any v_k or we shall have to reassign v_k and $val(v_k,i)$ again

EXAMPLE III-6

TO "FREE" A LIBERAL SCHEME

TRANSFORMATION t CARRIES SCHEME P INTO SCHEME t(P)

P IS STRONGLY EQUIVALENT TO t(P)

Here we construct t(P) by subschemes from P for the special case of one input variable x and two monadic predicates T_1 and T_2 and r variables altogether, $u_1,...,u_r$. The transformation can be extended to any number of predicates which need not be monadic; however, the subscripting becomes formidable.

We assume P to be in linear form. We let an address p in P correspond to all possible addresses $(p,i_1,...,i_r,j_1,...,j_r)$ in t(P) where each i_k and j_k is in $\{0,1,\Lambda\}$ with Λ standing for "unassigned".

For an address p in P , define function F by:

1) $F(p,i_1,...,i_r,j_1,...,j_r) = p$ if p is not the address of a test statement

2) $F(p,i_1,...,i_r,j_1,...,j_r) = \bar{p}$ if p is the address of a test statement and $\bar{p}$ is the address of the first nontest statement entered from p if $T_1(u_k) = i_k$ and $T_2(u_k) = j_k$ for each assigned u_k (i.e. for each k with $i_k \neq \Lambda \neq j_k$).

3) $F(p,i_1,...,i_r,j_1,...,j_r) = $ LOOP   if neither (1) nor (2) holds.

EXAMPLE III-6   CONTINUED

INITIAL SUBSCHEME

For $i,j \in \{0,1\}$, if $F(p,i,\Lambda,\ldots,\Lambda,j,\Lambda,\ldots,\Lambda) = \bar{p}$ then $S_{ij} = (\bar{p},i,\Lambda,\ldots,\Lambda,j,\Lambda,\ldots,\Lambda)$; if $F(p,i,\Lambda,\ldots,\Lambda,j,\Lambda,\ldots,\Lambda) = \text{LOOP}$ then $S_{ij} = \text{LOOP}$

In P we have: In t(P) we have:

EXAMPLE III-6

ASSIGNMENT SUBSCHEMES

For $m,n \in \{0,1\}$, if $\bar{i}_k = i_k$, $\bar{j}_k = j_k$ for $k \neq \ell$, $1 \leq k \leq r$, $\bar{i}_\ell = m$, $\bar{j}_\ell = n$ then if $F(q,i_1,\ldots,i_r,j_1,\ldots,j_r) = \bar{q}$ let $S_{mn} = (\bar{q},\bar{i}_1,\ldots,\bar{i}_r,\bar{j}_1,\ldots,\bar{j}_r)$ and if $F(q,i_1,\ldots,i_r,j_1,\ldots,j_r) = \text{LOOP}$ let $S_{mn} = \text{LOOP}$

If P contains a statement: Then t(P) contains for all possible
                                              $w = (p,i_1,\ldots,i_r,j_1,\ldots,j_r)$ subschemes:

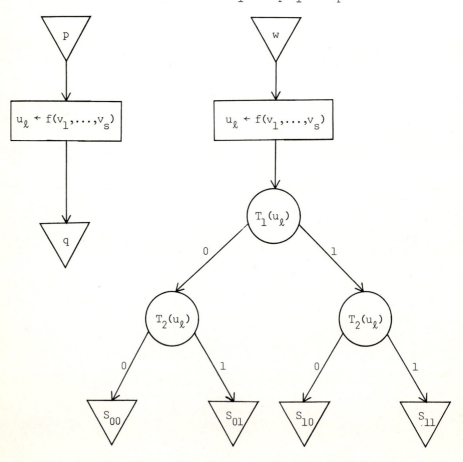

EXAMPLE III-6   CONCLUDED

In t(P) we also have a subscheme

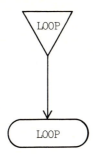

where LOOP stands for any free but always looping subscheme. An example is:

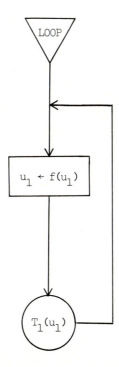

violating the definition of a liberal scheme. Hence no v_k is altered during the subpath from i to i+j . If this subpath passes twice through the same address we can snip out that section and obtain an execution sequence of length strictly less than m in which this same instance of "illiberality" occurs. This is impossible, so the subpath from i to i+j cannot pass twice through the same address. Also, the subpath from i through i+j is "illiberal" regardless of the value of the $v_k = y_k$ at i . Hence, if the subpath from START to i passes twice through the same address, then eliminating this cycle results in an execution sequence from START to i to i+j of length less than m , which is an instance of "illiberality" contradicting the minimality of m.. Thus no cycle can occur between START and i or between i and i+j . If t(P) contains N statements, then we must have $m \leq 2N+2$. Hence we can decide whether t(P) is liberal by trying all paths and hence all execution sequences of length less than or equal to 2N+2 .

So we can decide liberality and so freeness for t(P) . But P is liberal if and only if t(P) is liberal and free.

THEOREM 3.19   It is decidable whether a scheme is liberal.

IV. STRUCTURED PROGRAMS

A. CANONICAL FORMS

We define a <u>canonical form</u> for schemes as a class $\mathscr{S}$ of schemes such that there is an algorithm which transforms any scheme into a strongly equivalent member of $\mathscr{S}$. Thus one has:

$$\mathscr{C} \xrightarrow{\quad t \quad} \mathscr{S}$$

where $\mathscr{C}$ is the whole class of schemes, $\mathscr{S}$ is the canonical subclass and t is a total recursive function taking any scheme P into a strongly equivalent scheme t(P) in $\mathscr{S}$. We call t a <u>canonical transformation</u>; it is strong equivalence preserving since if P and P' are strongly equivalent, obviously t(P) and t(P') are strongly equivalent.

The transformation t we saw at the end of the last section, which changes liberal schemes into free schemes, is such a canonical transformation. The corresponding canonical class of schemes is the class of schemes such that tests are applied initially on the input variables and are applied after assignment statements on the program variables involved, and at no other time. This transformation t is clearly recursive and equivalence preserving. The class of free schemes is not a canonical form class, since, as we saw, there are schemes not strongly equivalent to any free scheme.

In this chapter we study two canonical forms for schemes and programs associated with structured programming - block structure and WHILE-schemes or GOTO-less schemes. Our approach is analytic rather than synthetic. We do not study directly the question of how to write a program in structured form, but rather explore the conditions on the syntax of a program implied by such a form and the techniques of transforming a pre-existing program into this form. In a later chapter we see the utility of such forms in simplifying program verification techniques.

Just transforming a program or scheme into a given canonical form may not be enough if the transformation preserves strong equivalence but nothing else. We may also require canonical transformations to preserve "structure" in some sense of this rather vague notion. For example, we may wish blocks or modules already existing in the original program to remain blocks or subschemes in the new program. We may wish parts of the program already in canonical form to remain so in the new program. Or we may wish to preserve "loop structure" - map cycles into cycles and not produce any new cycles. We might also be interested not just in preservation of final outcome, but also in the intermediate values of program variables. For example, the transformation t in the last chapter changed only the application of test statements; the sequence of nontest instructions performed in any computation was unchanged and all program variables ran through the same sequence of values during a computation.

We can consider the preservation of structure in either semantic or syntactic terms - either in terms of the sequence of values of registers or in terms of the sequence of instructions performed.

One basic idea is that structurally akin schemes P and P' should not only do the same thing when output is given, but also should compute the same output in roughly the "same way". One fairly strong way of expressing this concept is that under the same interpretation and input they should have the same "computation record".

DEFINITION   Let P be a program scheme, I an interpretation and $\bar{a}$ an input to program (P,I). Let P have r variables, $u_1,\ldots,u_r$. The computation record of the computation $(P,I,\bar{a})$ is the sequence

$$\rho(P,I,\bar{a}) \;=\; (\rho_1,\ldots,\rho_i,\ldots)$$

finite if $(P,I,\bar{a})$ converges and otherwise infinite, such that for each i,

$$\rho_i \;=\; (val(u_1,i),\ldots,val(u_r,i)) \;.$$

The test added computation record for $(P,I,\bar{a})$ is the sequence

$$\bar{\rho}(P,I,\bar{a}) \;=\; (\bar{\rho}_1,\ldots,\bar{\rho}_i,\ldots)$$

where $\bar{\rho}_i = \rho_i$ if i is not the execution of a test statement, and

$$\bar{\rho}_i \;=\; ((val(u_1,i),\ldots,val(u_r,i),T(val(v_1,i),\ldots,val(v_s,i)))$$

if i is the execution of test statement $T(v_1,\ldots,v_s)$. If $\{u_{j_1},\ldots,u_{j_k}\}$ is any subset of $\{u_1,\ldots,u_r\}$ including all input and output variables, the computation record of the computation $(P,I,\bar{a})$ relative to $\{u_{j_1},\ldots,u_{j_k}\}$ is the sequence $(\rho'_1,\ldots,\rho'_i,\ldots)$ where $\rho'_i = (val(u_{j_1},i),\ldots,val(u_{j_k},i))$ for each i, and the test added computation record relative to $\{u_{j_1},\ldots,u_{j_k}\}$ is

$$(\bar{\rho}'_1,\ldots,\bar{\rho}'_i,\ldots) \;,$$

where $\bar{\rho}'_i = \rho'_i$ if i is not a test statement involving only members of $\{u_{j_1},\ldots,u_{j_k}\}$, and

$$\bar{\rho}'_i = (val(u_{j_1},i),\ldots,val(u_{j_k},i),T(val(v_1,i),\ldots,val(v_s,i)))$$

if i is a test statement $T(v_1,\ldots,v_s)$ and $\{v_1,\ldots,v_s\} \subseteq \{u_{j_1},\ldots,u_{j_k}\}$.

Thus the computation record of a computation contains the successive listings of the values of the variables - it is the listing of computation states minus the name of the instruction executed at time i . The test added computation record contains this list of values plus the formal record of tests applied. If test T is applied at step i to, say, values 1 and 5, the test added computation record contains for step i the formal statement "T(1,5)" , identifying the particular test applied and the values to which it is applied. The computation record or test added computation record relative to some subset of variables considers only values of those variables and tests applied to those variables. It is useful when comparing programs with different program variables but the same input and output variables.

DEFINITION   Two computation records are equivalent if they are identical when consecutive duplications have been removed from each record - i.e. ρ_{i+1} is removed if $\rho_i = \rho_{i+1}$.

There are several ways in which we can try to capture the idea that " P and P' have the same structure". We now assume that P and P' have the same set of variables.

SEMANTIC
1) P and P' are computationally equivalent if for every interpretation I and input $\bar{a}$ the computation records $\rho(P,I,\bar{a})$ and $\rho(P',I,\bar{a})$ are equivalent.

2) P and P' are strongly computationally equivalent if for every interpretation I and input $\bar{a}$ the test added computation records $\bar{\rho}(P,I,\bar{a})$ and $\bar{\rho}(P',I,\bar{a})$ are equivalent.

3) P and P' are computationally isomorphic if for every interpretation I and input $\bar{a}$ the computation records are identical, i.e. $\rho(P,I,\bar{a}) = \rho(P',I,\bar{a})$.

4) P and P' are strongly computationally isomorphic if for every interpretation I and input $\bar{a}$ the test added computation records are identical, i.e. $\bar{\rho}(P,I,\bar{a}) = \bar{\rho}(P',I,\bar{a})$.

If any one of relations (1) through (4) hold for P and P' , then P and P' are strongly equivalent. However none of these relationships need necessarily hold for P and P' strongly equivalent. Clearly (4) implies (2) and (3) and either (2) or (3) imply (1). No other implications hold. One can construct schemes computationally equivalent but not strongly computationally equivalent (because, say, the order of some tests are interchanged) or computationally isomorphic (because, say, some value is computed twice in a row); schemes strongly computationally equivalent but not computationally isomorphic; schemes both computationally isomorphic and strongly computationally equivalent but not strongly computationally isomorphic.

The transformation t studied in the last chapter preserves computational isomorphism but not strong computational equivalence - P and t(P) are not only strongly equivalent but also computationally isomorphic. They may not be strongly computationally equivalent since the transformation t can rearrange the order of application of tests or introduce new tests or - in the case of a cycle involving only tests - eliminate tests. (Strictly speaking, whether t(P) and P are or are not computationally equivalent can depend on the subscheme substituted for tight LOOPs; if we are not concerned with making this subscheme free we can use one which will not affect computational isomorphism.)

We now consider some similar concepts which can be regarded as more syntactic than semantic in nature.

SYNTACTIC

5) P and P' are <u>structurally similar</u> if for each interpretation I and input $\overline{a}$, the sequence of nontest instructions executed during $(P,I,\overline{a})$, listed in order of execution, is identical to the same list for computation $(P',I,\overline{a})$.

6) P and P' are <u>strongly structurally similar</u> if for each interpretation I and input $\overline{a}$, the sequence of instructions executed during computation $(P,I,\overline{a})$, listed in order of execution, is identical to the same list for computation $(P',I,\overline{a})$.

7) P is a <u>homomorphic image</u> of P' if there is a function h from the addresses of P' into the addresses of P , such that (1) for each address i in P' , i and h(i) name identical instructions and (2) for each interpretation I and input $\overline{a}$, if $(k_1,...,k_i,...)$ lists in order of execution the addresses of nontest instructions executed during computation $(P',I,\overline{a})$, then $(h(k_1),...,h(k_i),...)$ lists in order of execution the addresses of nontest instructions executed during computation $(P,I,\overline{a})$.

8) P is a <u>strong homomorphic image</u> of P' if there is a function h from the addresses of P' into the addresses of P , such that (1) for each address i in P' , i and h(i) name identical instructions and (2) for each interpretation I and input $\bar{a}$, if $(k_1,...,k_i,...)$ lists in order of execution the addresses of all instructions executed during computation $(P',I,\bar{a})$, then $(h(k_1),...,h(k_i),...)$ lists in order of execution the addresses of all instructions executed during computation $(P,I,\bar{a})$.

The lattice of implications among (1) - (8) and strong equivalence appears below. No implications shown can be reversed and no implications not in the diagram hold. Conditions (7) and (8) represent an attempt to formalize the idea of preserving loop structure, since cycles in P' correspond to cycles in P and cycles in P , if repeated often enough, correspond to cycles in P' .

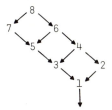

strong equivalence

The strongest definition of structural similarity is the concept of <u>graph isomorphism</u> which is, of course, tantamount to complete identity. This concept can be defined for subschemes as well as for schemes.

DEFINITION A flow diagram P is a <u>graph homomorphic image</u> of flow diagram P' under graph homomorphism h , if h is a function from the address set of P' into the address set of P such that (1) for each address i in P' , i and h(i) name identical instructions and (2) if there is an arrow from statement i to statement j in P' , there is an arrow from h(i) to h(j) in P and if the arrow from i to j is labelled, then the arrow from h(i) to h(j) has the same label. If the function h is one-one and onto, then h is a <u>graph isomorphism</u> and P and P' are <u>graph isomorphic</u>.

Graph isomorphism is a completely syntactic concept and is clearly testable. The methods used later in Chapter VI can be adapted to show that none of (1) - (8) are decidable - it is not decidable whether any of these relations hold between two schemes P and P' and if (i) does not always imply (j) , then even if (i) is known to hold, it is undecidable whether (j) holds. It can also be noted

that even if P is a strong homomorphic image of P' and P' is a strong
homomorphic image of P , it is not necessarily true that P and P' are graph
isomorphic. Essentially the reason is that in condition (8) we place restrictions
only on the parts of the schemes that are reachable - on those instructions
actually executed during some computation.

We can also consider restricted or relativized versions of these relations
among schemes. For example, a restricted version of (1) to (8) can be obtained by
eliminating all mention of variables that do not appear in both P and P' .
Instead of assuming that P and P' have identical variable sets, we only assume
that they have the same sets of input variables and of output variables. Thus, for
example, we could define:

1') P and P' are <u>computationally equivalent in the restricted sense</u> if for
    every interpretation I and input $\bar{a}$ the computation record of (P,I,$\bar{a}$)
    relative to the common variable set of P and P' is equivalent to the
    computation record of (P',I,$\bar{a}$) relative to the common variable set of
    P and P' .

Alternatively, one can consider strong equivalence relative to some fixed
subinterpretation. Suppose I is an interpretation over some fixed domain D
which interprets all function letters, predicate letters and constants appearing
in either P or P' but not in both P and P' ; it can also interpret symbols
not in either P or P' . Suppose I' is an interpretation of all letters in P
and P' with domain D' . If D is a subset of D' and whenever I(f)($\bar{a}$) or
I(T)($\bar{a}$) or I(c) is defined - for a function letter f , predicate letter T
or constant c and $\bar{a}$ a vector over D - then I'(f)($\bar{a}$) = I(f)($\bar{a}$) or
I'(T)($\bar{a}$) = I(T)($\bar{a}$) or I'(c) = I(c) respectively, then we call I' <u>an extension</u>
<u>of I to all of P and P'</u> .

DEFINITION   Scheme P is <u>strongly equivalent to P' relative to I</u> if for any
interpretation I' extending I to all of P and P' , program (P,I') is
strongly equivalent to program (P',I') .

We now examine two very useful structure preserving transformations. To assist
in the discussion, we introduce the concept of a single entry subgraph.

DEFINITION   Let G be a directed labelled graph and G' a subgraph of G . We
call G' <u>a single entry subgraph of G</u> if there is a node n in G' , called the
<u>entry node of G'</u> such that
(1) Every node in G' lies on some path from n .
(2) There is no direct connection (single step path) from any node in G - G'
    to any node in G' - {n} .

The <u>exit node</u> set of G', $E(G')$ can be described as the set of all

(1) pairs (k,r) where k is a node in G', r is a node in $G - G'$ and k has exactly one branch and that branch is unlabelled and leads to r, and

(2) triples (k,r,i) where k is a branch node in G', r is a node in $G - G'$ and k is directly connected to r by an arrow labelled i.

We are interested in the case where G is a flow diagram. If a pair (k,r) is in $E(G')$, k is the address of an assignment statement which is followed by the instruction in node r, while if (k,r,i) is in $E(G')$, then k is the node of a test statement and the outcome i leads to node (or address) r in $G - G'$.

The first transformation illustrated in Example IV-1 is the Duplicate Operation. It is a local operation, applied to a subgraph of a scheme. To apply it, we assume that A and B are single entry subgraphs in a scheme P, with entry nodes n_A and n_B respectively. The exit node set $E(A)$ contains either a pair (k,n_B) or a triple (k,n_B,i). We construct B', a graph isomorphic copy of B; let h be the one-one function from the nodes of B onto the nodes of B' which establishes this isomorphism. We form P' by adding B' to P, replacing the exit node from A to B by one from A to B' - so that (k,n_B) is replaced by $(k,h(n_B))$ or (k,n_B,i) by $(k,h(n_B),i)$ - leaving the other nodes of A untouched. The exit node set of B' is the set

$$E(B') = \{(h(k),r) \mid (k,r) \in E(B)\} \cup \{(h(k),r,i) \mid (k,r,i) \in E(B)\} \ .$$

It is clear that P' is strongly equivalent to P. In fact, all the other relations (1) - (8) hold between P and P'. Moreover, P is a graph homomorphic image of P'; the homomorphism f is defined by letting $f(h(n)) = n$ for n in B (which means $h(n)$ is in B') and $f(m) = m$ for any node in $P' - B'$. So this transformation - the duplicate operation - preserves structure in a very strong fashion.

Notice that the duplicate operation is valid in many cases where B is not a single entry subgraph; however, in such cases it is often harder to state precisely and justify. The second illustration in Example IV-1 gives one such case. Here we have a single node n which is connected to a node m and possibly to other nodes $\alpha_1,\ldots,\alpha_r$. Subgraph B contains all and only nodes reachable from m. It may not be single entry and there may be connections from B back to m. The new scheme P' is formed by adding a node m' with the same label $(\lambda(m))$ as m, and a graph isomorphic copy B' of B. The connection from n to m is replaced by one from n to m' with the same label, if any; the connections between m'

EXAMPLE IV-1   SOME TRANSFORMATIONS PRESERVING COMPUTATIONAL ISOMORPHISM

DUPLICATE   OPERATION

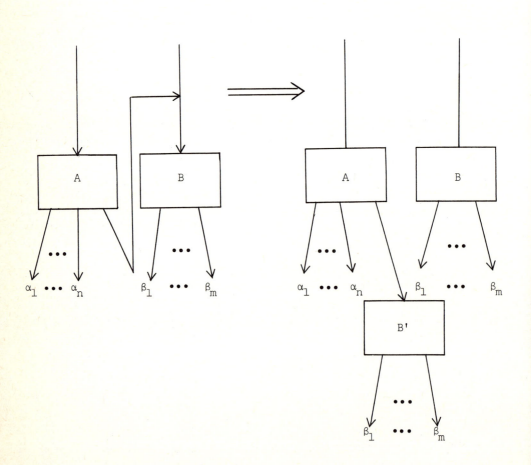

A and B are single entry subgraphs

B' is graph isomorphic to B

EXAMPLE IV-1   CONTINUED

SPECIAL CASE OF DUPLICATE OPERATION

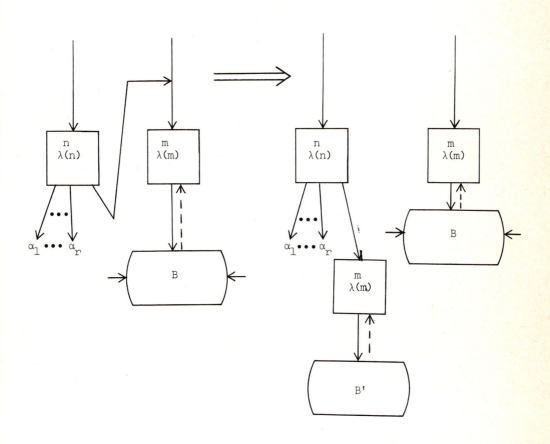

Node n is connected to $\alpha_1,\ldots,\alpha_r$ and m

B contains all nodes reachable from node m

B' is graph isomorphic to B

EXAMPLE IV-1   CONCLUDED

UNWIND   LOOP   OPERATION

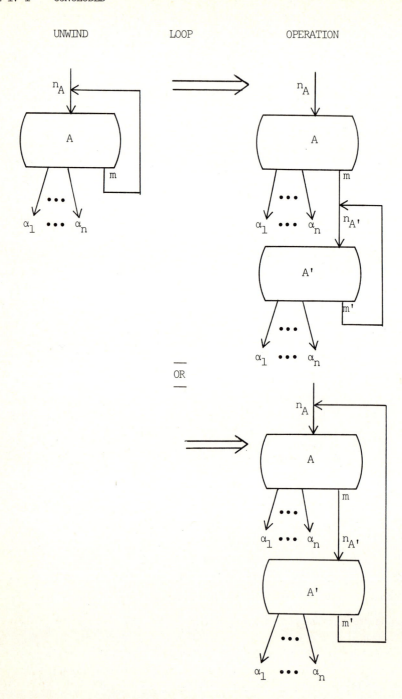

and B' are isomorphic to the connections between m and B (so that m' plus
B' forms a graph isomorphic copy of m plus B). There are no connections into
B' except from m' . All other connections in the scheme are unchanged. Again,
P is a strong homomorphic image of P' and so a fortiori P and P' are
strongly equivalent.

The last operation depicted in Example IV-1 is the Unwind Loop Operation.
Here A is a single entry subgraph with entry node n_A and a self-loop back to
n_A . We now add a single entry subgraph A' graph isomorphic to A and connect
A to $n_{A'}$, , the entry of A' . There are two possibilities. If node m in A
was connected to n_A , then the corresponding node m' in A' can be connected
either back to the entry node of A or A' or to the entry node n_A of A .
Both possibilities are shown. Scheme P is a strong homomorphic image of each of
the two resulting schemes; all three schemes are strongly equivalent.

In the rest of this chapter we shall generally describe transformations and
operations on schemes and subgraphs pictorially, rather than giving the formal
description as we just did for the Duplicate Operation.

B. BLOCK STRUCTURE

We shall give two equivalent definitions of a block structured scheme and
demonstrate their equivalence. Then we shall describe and illustrate a procedure
for converting a scheme (or program) into block structure. The first definition
is really a restriction on graphs. We shall need some purely graph oriented
definitions.

DEFINITION   Let G be a directed labelled graph and G' a single entry subgraph
of G with entry node e . A node n in G' is a G'-ancestor of a node m in
G' if every path from e to m passes through n ; if G = G' , then n is an
ancestor of m or n dominates m .

DEFINITION   A graph G is tree-like if whenever a node n in G is directly
connected to a node m , either n is an ancestor of m or m is an ancestor
of n or n = m .

Let us illustrate the concept of "tree-like" with a few simple examples.
Suppose G is tree-like with entry node e and there is a direct connection from
n to m . Situations (1), (2) and (3) below are permissible:

(1) n is an ancestor of m   (2) m is an ancestor of n   (3) n = m

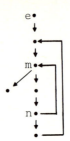
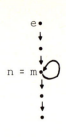

The situations which violate the definition of "tree-like" involve a "diamond" as in (4) or a triangle as in (5):

(4) "Diamond"   (5) "Triangle"

Of course, there can be many nodes between e and n in (4) and (5) or between e and p and p and m in (4).

A program scheme whose graph is tree-like - taking the START node as the entry node - is sometimes said to be in normal form.

We can list some obvious consequences of the definitions of "ancestor" and "tree-like".

LEMMA 4.1   In any graph G , the ancestor relationship is transitive.

PROOF

If m is an ancestor of n and n is an ancestor of p , then m must be an ancestor of p since any path from the entry node to p must pass through n and hence through m .   ∎

Obviously the ancestor relationship cannot be symmetric; we cannot have n an ancestor of m and m an ancestor of n unless no path through the entry ever reaches either n or m .

LEMMA 4.2   In any graph G , if m is an ancestor of p , m is an ancestor of
any node on any path from m to p that does not pass through m en route.

PROOF

     Suppose m is an ancestor of p and n ≠ m lies on some path from m to p
which does not pass through m except at the start or finish. If m is not an
ancestor of n , then there is a path from the entry node to n which does not
pass through m ; if we add on the path from n to p we have a path from the
entry node to p which does not pass through m , contradicting the hypothesis
that m is an ancestor of p . ■

LEMMA 4.3   If a graph G is tree-like and m is any node in G , then the
subgraph S_m consisting of m and all its descendants (all nodes of which m is
an ancestor) is a tree-like single entry subgraph with entry node m .

PROOF

     First note that any single entry subgraph of a tree-like graph must itself
be tree-like for if the ancestor relationship fails to hold in a subgraph it cannot
hold in the whole graph. Next, every node in S_m lies on some path from m by
definition of S_m .
     Now we must show that S_m is single entry with entry node m . Suppose p
is a node in S_m , p ≠ m and s is a node in G - S_m directly connected to p .
Since G is tree-like, either p is an ancestor of s or s is an ancestor of
p . If p is an ancestor of s , then by the transitivity of the ancestor
relationship, m is an ancestor of s and so s is in S_m . If s is an
ancestor of p then every path from the entry node e of G to p must pass
through both s and m ; if it passes through m only once it must go either
e - m - s - p or e - s - m - p . If the first case ever occurs, then by
Lemma 4.2 m is an ancestor of s and so s is in S_m . In the second case the
path from e to s and then directly to p is a path from e to p not passing
through m and so contradicts the fact that m is an ancestor of p . ■

     We define blocks inductively. A **block** is a particular kind of flow diagram.

DEFINITION

1) The following are blocks:

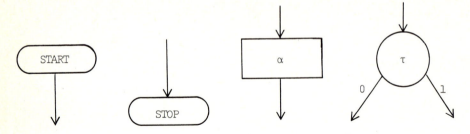

where   α   is any assignment statement and   τ   is any predicate statement.

2) If B_1 and B_2 are blocks, so is their block composition B_3 :

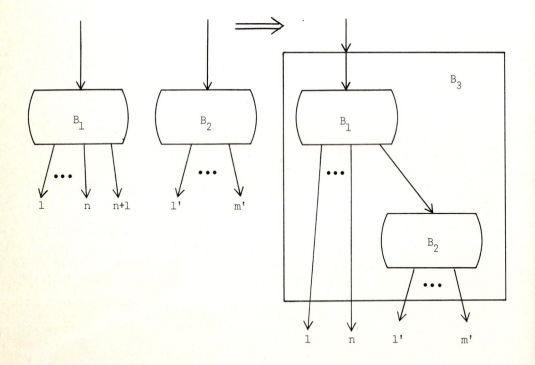

3) If B is a block so is its <u>block iterate</u> B'

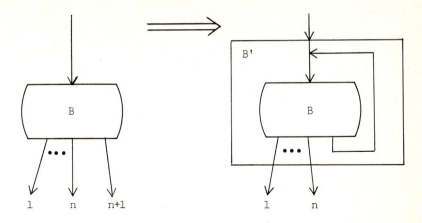

DEFINITION   A single entry flow diagram is a <u>block</u> if and only if it can be built up from the basic blocks in (1) by a finite number of applications of block composition and block iteration.

DEFINITION   A program (P,I) is a <u>block structured program</u> if P is a block — i.e., if its graph is a block.

DEFINITION   If B is a block, then a <u>subblock</u> of B is any subgraph of B which is itself a block.

The definition of a block given here is really a bottom-up definition, building large blocks from smaller subblocks. When one actually constructs a block structured program, one proceeds top-down — first defining the role of the outer-most block (what process it is to realize), then that of its immediate subblocks, and so forth. A single node (labelled by a process for which one intends to build a submodule) can be considered a block. The equivalence of the top-down and bottom-up definitions can be justified by the block replacement lemma, stated without proof.

BLOCK REPLACEMENT LEMMA 4.4
    If G is a block with a subblock B_1 , the result of replacing B_1 by any other block B_2 with the same exit connections is a block, G' . Pictorially:

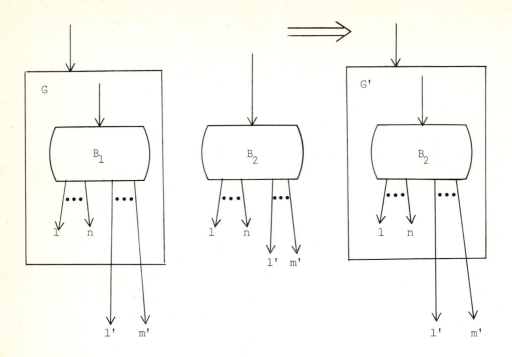

Now we show that the concepts of a block and of a tree-like flow diagram are the same.

THEOREM 4.5   Every block is a single entry tree-like flow diagram and every single entry tree-like flow diagram is a block.

PROOF

Obviously a block is a single entry flow diagram and the basic blocks are tree-like. We need only see that the operations of block composition and block iteration preserve the property of being tree-like. If B is formed by directly connecting node n of block B_1 by block composition to entry node e_2 of block B_2 , clearly n is an ancestor of e_2 , so that if both B_1 and B_2 are tree-like, clearly B is tree-like. If B is formed by block iteration by directly connecting exit node n of Block B_1 to entry node e_1 of B_1 , then n remains a descendant of e_1 in B , so if B_1 is tree-like then B is also tree-like.

Now suppose that G is a single entry tree-like flow diagram; let e be the entry node of G . Let d_G be the number of direct connections in G from a node to either itself or an ancestor. If $d_G = 0$, G is a tree and a tree is obviously a block. We proceed by induction on d_G . Suppose $d_G = d \geq 1$ and we have proven that G' is a block for every single entry tree-like flow diagram G' with

$d_{G'} \leq d-1$. For a node n , let $a(n)$ be the length of the shortest path from e to n .

Let A contain each node k in G such that either k is directly connected to itself or there is a direct connection from a descendant of k to k . Since $d_G \geq 1$, $A \neq \phi$. Let n be a member of A for which $a(n)$ is minimal. Let m be a descendant of n (or n itself) directly connected to n and let S_n be the set containing n plus its descendants. By our previous observation, Lemma 4.3, S_n is a single entry tree-like subgraph of G . Let e be the entry node of G . There are two cases. If $e = n$, then $S_n = G$. If we form G' by changing the connection from m to n to an exit from G' , then G' is a single entry tree-like flow diagram with $d_{G'} = d-1 < d$, so G' is a block by the induction hypothesis. Since G is formed from G' by block iteration (connecting exit node m to the entry node e), G is a block.

Suppose $n \neq e$. If e were in S_n , then there would be a direct connection from some descendant of e in S_n back to e and e would be in A with $a(e) = 0 < a(n)$, a contradiction. So $G \neq S_n$. We claim that S_n is a closed subgraph in that there are no exits from S_n to $G - S_n$. For suppose node k in S_n is directly connected to node p in $G - S_n$ (k may or may not be n). If k is an ancestor of p , then n is an ancestor of p and so p is in S_n , a contradiction. Hence p is an ancestor of k . The direct connection from k to p shows that p is in A , and so $a(n) \leq a(p)$ by the minimality of $a(n)$. The shortest path from e to n can be extended to a path from e to k containing n exactly once; this extended path must contain p , an ancestor of k . Since $a(n) \leq a(p)$, the path must go $e - n - p - k$. By Lemma 4.2 n is an ancestor of p and p is in S_n , a contradiction. Hence there are no exits from S_n . There is at least one node s in $G - S_n$ directly connected to n ; s must be an ancestor of n . If any other node in $G - S_n$ were directly connected to n , then two ancestors of n would be directly connected to n , a contradiction of the fact that G is tree-like. Essentially G is formed by block composition from $G - S_n$ and S_n . Form G' by removing all of S_n from G and replacing the connection from s to n by an exit out of G' . Then G' is clearly a single entry tree-like subgraph with $d_{G'} \leq d_G - 1$ and hence by the induction hypothesis G' is a block. Similarly, S_n is a single entry tree-like flow diagram. Form S_n' from S_n by changing the direct connection from m to n to an exit from m . Then S_n' is a single entry tree-like flow diagram with $d_{S_n'} = d_{S_n} - 1 \leq d_G - 1$ and by the induction hypothesis S_n' is a block. Then S_n is formed from S_n' by block iteration (reconnect m to n , the entry node of S_n) and is a block. Finally, G is formed from G' and S_n by block composition (reconnect s to n) and thus is a block. ∎

Notice that our proof that a tree-like single entry flow diagram is a block actually gives an algorithm for dividing such a graph G into subblocks. Namely, one finds A , selects n to minimize a(n) and separates out S_n . If S_n is equal to G , then G is formed by block iteration from S_n' which is S_n minus one connection; the algorithm is now applied to S_n' . If $G \neq S_n$, then G is formed by block composition from $G - S_n$ and S_n and we can apply the algorithm to these smaller blocks. We could instead replace S_n by a single node labelled by S_n and treat that version of $G - S_n$ separately and S_n separately. If we follow such a procedure we get a division into major blocks, a concept we shall return to later.

Now that we have shown that tree-like single entry flow diagrams are blocks and vice versa and in the process given a construction for expressing any tree-like single entry flow diagram as a block construction of tree subschemes, we are in a position to show how to convert a program to block structured form.

THEOREM 4.6   BLOCK STRUCTURE THEOREM

Every program scheme P can be converted into a strongly equivalent block program scheme P' with the same set of variables, such that P is a graph homomorphic image of P' .

PROOF

We shall convert a program scheme P into a strongly equivalent tree-like program scheme P' and use Theorem 4.5 above to assert that P' is a block.

There are two possible approaches. In one approach we in effect build the execution sequence tree for P . We start with node (1,0) labelled START. A node (k,r) will be at level r of the new tree-like structure and be labelled with the instruction named by k . Suppose statement k in P is connected by an arrow (with or without a label) to statement p in P and that we have constructed node (k,r) in P' to date. If (k,r) has no ancestor of the form (p,r') , r' < r , place node (p,r+1) labelled by statement p on the tree, with an arrow from (k,r) to (p,r+1) which contains any label on the arrow from k to p . If there is already an ancestor (p,r') , r' < r , of (k,r) on the tree, then do not create (p,r+1) but instead add an arrow from (k,r) back to (p,r') containing any label also on the arrow from k to p . If P has N statements, this process must terminate in a scheme P' with at most N levels. Clearly P' is tree-like and is strongly equivalent to P . This transformation is global and structure preserving. In fact P is a strong homomorphic image of P' under the homomorphism h taking each (k,r) back into k .

An alternative method of proof uses repeated applications of a local transformation, the duplicate operation, which also preserves graph homomorphic images. Call a direct connection in P from n to m anomalous if n ≠ m and n is not an ancestor of m and m is not an ancestor of n. Let e be the entry node of P. For any node n, let S_n be the subgraph containing n and all nodes reachable from n. For any subgraph G, let $a(G,P)$ be the number of anomalous connections in G - i.e., the number of direct connections between nodes of G which are anomalous with respect to the whole scheme P; if $G = P$, we can write $a(P) = a(P,P)$.

We can show by induction on $a(P)$ that:

CLAIM Given a flow diagram P we can construct a flow diagram P' such that P is a graph homomorphic image of P' and $a(P') = 0$.

If $a(P) = 0$, there is nothing to prove. Assume that we have shown the result for any flow diagram G with $a(G) \le d-1$ and that $a(P) = d \ge 1$. Let n and m be any two nodes in P such that the direct connection from n to m is anomalous. Let G_1 be a graph isomorphic copy of S_m with entry node m_1 of G_1 mapped by the graph isomorphism f onto m. Now the direct connection from n to m is either not present in G_1 because n is not in S_m or has become a direct connection from $f^{-1}(n)$ to $f^{-1}(m) = m_1$ which is not anomalous in G_1 because m_1 is the entry node of G_1 and so the ancestor of $f^{-1}(n)$; any other direct connection anomalous in G_1 is the image of a direct connection anomalous in P. Hence $a(G_1) \le a(P) - 1$, and we can apply the induction hypothesis to G_1. Thus G_1 is a graph homomorphic image of a flow diagram G_2 with $a(G_2) = 0$; let h_1 be the graph homomorphism. Now we can form P_1 from P by adding G_2 with entry node m_2 and replacing the direct connection from n to m by one from n to m_2. Since the connection between n and m is anomalous, no nodes are disconnected by this process. If $h_2(k) = h_1(f(k))$ for k in G_2 and $h_2(k) = k$ otherwise, clearly h_2 is a graph homomorphism from P_1 onto P. Since G_2 is tree-like, certainly $a(G_2,P_1) = 0$. The direct connection from n to m is replaced by one from n to m_2 which is not anomalous since n is an ancestor of m_2; other anomalous connections in P_1 are in P already. Hence $a(P_1) = a(P,P_1) + a(G_2,P_1) = a(P,P_1) \le a(P) - 1$. We can now apply the induction hypothesis and obtain a flow diagram P' such that P_1 is a graph homomorphic image of P' and $a(P') = 0$. Hence P is a graph homomorphic image of P' since P is an image of P_1 and P_1 of P'. This completes the proof. ∎

Although we did not give the details which are tedious, P' can be obtained from P by a finite number of applications of the duplicate operation.

EXAMPLE

The scheme in P in Example IV-2 is not tree-like. (Here we let A,B,C,D,E
stand for arbitrary assignment statements or sets of assignment statements, in
order to exhibit the structure of the example uncluttered by extraneous formulae.)
The direct connection from the node labelled $T(x_1)$ following the node labelled D
up to the node labelled B is anomalous since the path START A $T(x_1)$ D $T(x_1)$
does not contain B and the path START A $T(x_1)$ B does not contain the node
labelled $T(x_1)$ following D . Similarly the two direct connections at the bottom
of the diagram, from test $T(x_2)$ to test $T(x_1)$ and from test $T(x_1)$ to E are
anomalous. The other direct connections in the graph are not anomalous. For
example, the direct connection from test $T(x_2)$ up to the node labelled A is not
anomalous since A is an ancestor of every node in the graph except START.

Scheme P is a graph homomorphic image of the scheme P' in Example IV-3,
which is tree-like. Scheme P' is formed from P by duplicating nodes when
anomalous connections occur. Thus the direct connection from the node labelled
$T(x_1)$ which follows D , to B is anomalous in P . In P' , this connection
is removed and a direct connection to a copy of B is substituted. The copy of B
leads into a copy of the subscheme reachable from B until A occurs. We do not
need to duplicate A since any connection to A must be acceptable; hence the
diagram loops back to A . Similarly, the anomalous direct connection from the node
$T(x_1)$ which follows C to E is anomalous and is replaced by a connection to a
copy of E and the node following E , $T(x_2)$; the connections from this instance
of $T(x_2)$ are now legal and so no duplicates are needed.

MAJOR BLOCKS

The division of a tree-like scheme into major blocks will be important in the
sequel, so it is worth stressing at this point. Let P be a tree-like program
scheme. Notice that the fact that P is tree-like means that the relationship of
ancestry or dominance among nodes of P extends to subblocks - a subblock with
entry node n is an ancestor of a subblock with entry node m if n is an
ancestor of m .

A division of P into major blocks will correspond roughly speaking to a
bottom-up parsing of P into blocks which are themselves almost trees - trees
with reinitializations. Let us define:

DEFINITION Let G be a graph and G' a single entry subgraph of G with entry
node e . We call G' a <u>tree with reinitializations</u> if whenever there is a
direct connection from a node n in G' to a node m in G' either n is an
ancestor of m or m = e .

4-21

EXAMPLE IV-2   A PROGRAM SCHEME THAT IS NOT TREE-LIKE

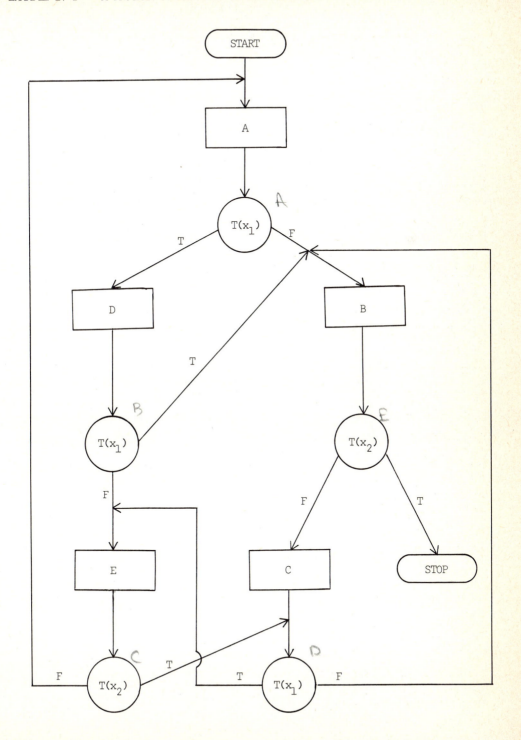

EXAMPLE IV-3   A TREE-LIKE PROGRAM SCHEME

The scheme in Example IV-2 is a graph homomorphic image of this scheme.

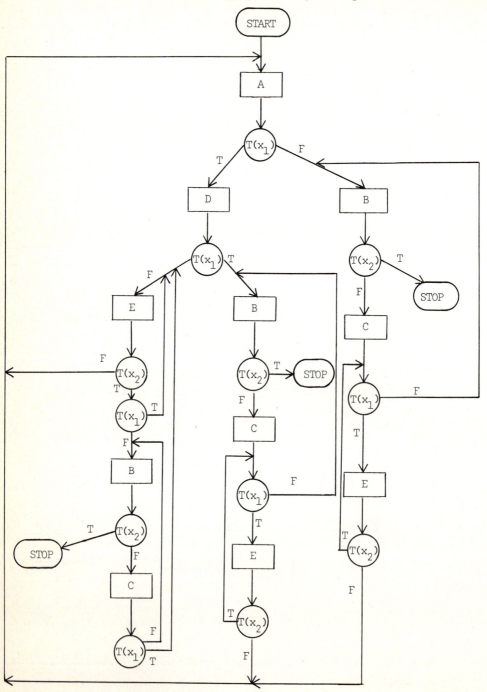

Thus a tree with reinitializations is a tree-like subgraph in which we have strengthened the conditions on a direct connection from n to m to eliminate the case   n = m   for n ≠ e and substitute "m = e" for " m is an ancestor of n ". For example, (1) below is a tree with reinitializations while (2) and (3) are not although they are tree-like.

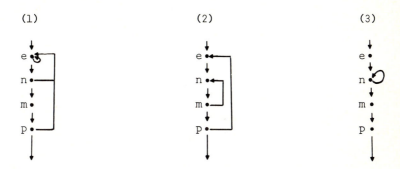

      (1)   (2)   (3)

A division of P into major blocks $(B_0,\ldots,B_n)$ is obtained by first isolating disjoint subgraphs which are trees with reinitializations (making these pieces as large as possible) and giving them names and placing isomorphic copies last (rightmost) in the list (among B_n, B_{n-1} etc.). Then these subgraphs are replaced with nodes labelled by their names and having the same entry and exit conditions. This gives a new tree-like graph P_1' and the same procedure is applied to P_1' . This continues until we wind up with some P_i which is itself a tree with reinitializations and then P_i is B_0 and the list is complete. For convenience in later constructions, we impose other conditions on our division ((4) and (5) below).

Somewhat more formally:

DEFINITION   Let P be a block. A <u>division of P into major blocks</u> is a list $(B_0,\ldots,B_n)$ of graphs such that:

(1) each graph B_i is a tree with reinitializations, i.e. a single entry tree-like graph with each arrow leading either out of the block B_i or from a node to a descendant of that node or from a node back to the entry node of B_i

(2) each node in a block B_i is labelled either with a statement of P or with the name of a block B_j with $i + 1 \leq j \leq n$, and if the name of B_j appears in B_i with $j > i$ it appears exactly once and does not appear in B_k for $k \neq i$

(3) blocks B_i can be substituted for their names in other blocks until each B_i becomes (graph isomorphic to) a subblock of P and B_0 becomes (graph isomorphic to) P .

(4) in each block B_i every branch from a node labelled with a subblock name B_j leads either out of the block B_i or back to the entry node of the block B_i, and

(5) any exit arrow from a block B_i is labelled either with some block B_j, with $1 \le j \le i-1$, such that B_i is a subblock of B_j (i.e. B_i is either the name of a node in B_j or the name of a node in a subblock of B_j), or else to STOP.

The conversion of a tree-like scheme into block form given by our algorithm will result into a division into major blocks. At each stage, if we are considering B_i (and we take $B_0 = B_e$ where e is the entry node to the original flow diagram) we consider a node p such that there is a connection from some node m, a descendant of p, back to p; we take as B_p the node p plus all descendants of p; we can leave in B_i in place of p a node labelled B_p. Since we always select p to be as close to the entry node of B_i as possible, condition (4) of the definition of major block will be automatically satisfied.

We always try in a division into major blocks to make the individual subblocks as large as possible, and the number of subblocks as small as possible, consistent with conditions (1) - (5). Our algorithm will also make our subblocks as large as possible.

COROLLARY 4.7   Every tree-like scheme can be divided into major blocks.

Example IV-4 gives a division of the scheme of Examples IV-2 and IV-3 into major blocks. Exit nodes in these diagrams are those with arrows leading to figures ⬡ which indicate the connections in the larger diagram. Thus in B_{11} there is a node labelled B_{111} which has both an exit back to the entry of B_{11} and an exit to graph B_0; the former appears directly on the diagram of B_{11} while the latter corresponds to an arrow directed to ⬡B_0. On the diagram of B_{111}, both connections are indicated by arrows, one to ⬡B_0 and one to ⬡B_{11}.

The zigzags labelled α or β will be explained and used in section H of this chapter and should be ignored at present

EXAMPLE IV-4   BLOCK STRUCTURE
THE SCHEME OF EXAMPLE IV-3 DIVIDED INTO MAJOR BLOCKS

BLOCK B_0

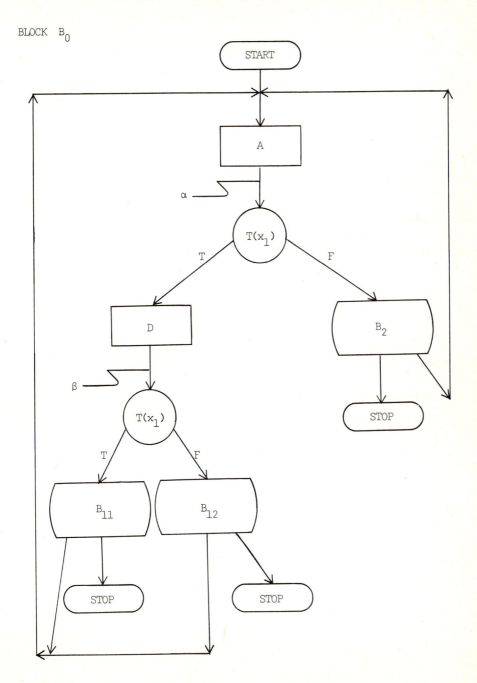

EXAMPLE IV-4   CONTINUED

THE BLOCK STRUCTURE OF EXAMPLE IV-3

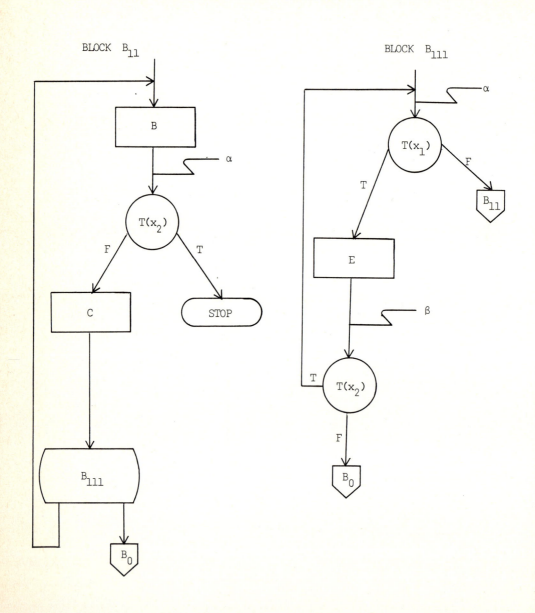

EXAMPLE IV-4   CONTINUED

THE BLOCK STRUCTURE OF EXAMPLE IV-3

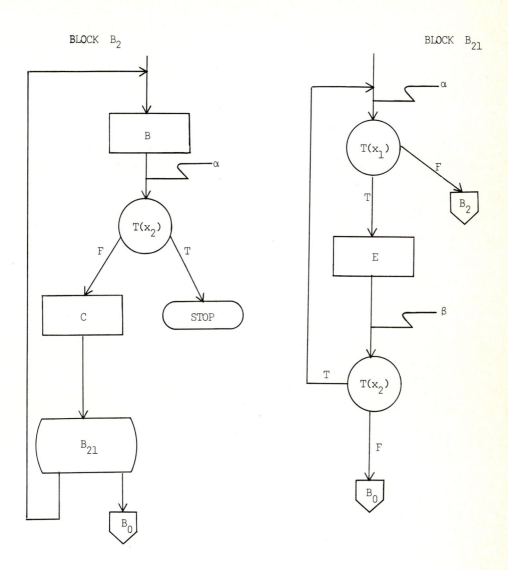

EXAMPLE IV-4   CONCLUDED

THE BLOCK STRUCTURE OF EXAMPLE IV-3

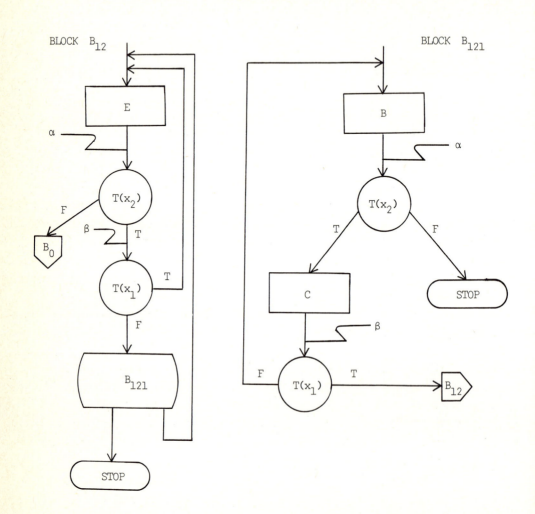

C. WHILE SCHEMES AND GOTO-LESS PROGRAMS

In the previous section we examined a particular canonical form for schemes, namely block structured schemes, in which the program is built in modules connected in a tree-like fashion. In this section we carry this idea one step forward and examine schemes written in a "line-like" form - the so-called "WHILE schemes" or "GOTO-less schemes".

The role of the "GOTO" statement has caused considerable controversy among programming language experts. Essentially such a statement is a transfer (conditional or unconditional) which allows an exit from any part of a block to any other block or even into the middle of a block. This feature can be extremely convenient in constructing the program or algorithm, but equally inconvenient when it comes to documentation of program behavior or analysis of program structure.

We shall not discuss here whether programming languages should or should not allow unrestricted "GOTOs". We only make a few comments on the formal, mathematical side. There is no doubt that "WHILE schemes" are more elegant, easier to describe and possibly easier to document. As we shall see in the next chapter, they possess certain formal advantages for program verification methods. However, since - as we shall see shortly - they do provide a canonical form for schemes, restricting programs to this format does not affect the decidability or undecidability of various problems. Any property undecidable for general program schemes remains undecidable for WHILE-schemes.

There is no way to change undecidable properties to decidable properties without a loss of power of expression. So that sort of consideration cannot be an argument for or against the use of any particular canonical form. However, when the property happens to be decidable in general or for a particular subclass, use of a particular format may make life easier. Further, although WHILE schemes form a canonical form for the whole class of schemes, they do not do so for many subclasses. That is, if we have a canonical transformation

$$\mathscr{C} \quad \xrightarrow{\quad t \quad} \quad \mathscr{S}$$

for a canonical form $\mathscr{S}$, and $\mathscr{C}_1$ is a proper subset of $\mathscr{C}$ that is NOT a canonical form, then t may not map members of $\mathscr{C}_1$ into $\mathscr{S} \cap \mathscr{C}_1$ and there may indeed be members of $\mathscr{C}_1$ which are not strongly equivalent to any member of $\mathscr{S} \cap \mathscr{C}_1$. As we shall see, this is certainly true if $\mathscr{S}$ is the class of WHILE schemes, and $\mathscr{C}_1$ the class of single variable schemes.

Finally, any format that does indeed assist program documentation should be given serious consideration. Sometimes it is harder to determine how to use an existing program or subroutine than to construct a new one!

We shall give a definition of a "simple" WHILE scheme and then see that it must be enlarged somewhat to provide a canonical form. Our definition is an inductive one, like the definition of a block.

A WHILE scheme is a particular kind of single entry single exit subgraph.

DEFINITION   A single entry single exit subgraph of a graph G is a single entry subgraph G' with a single exit node d such that:

(1) For every node n in G' there is at least one path from n to d .
(2) There is no direct connection from any node in G' - {d} to any node in G - G' .

DEFINITION   A subgraph G' of G is zero exit or closed if no arrow leaves G' ; it is zero entry if no arrows enter G' .

As we give our definition of a WHILE scheme in graphical form, we shall simultaneously give a definition in a simple programming language which has as basic instructions:

   assignment statements
   START and STOP statements
   both positive and negative test statements - $T(u_1,\ldots,u_n)$ and
     NOT $T(u_1,\ldots,u_n)$
and has three rules of composition:

   block or linear composition
   IF ... THEN ... ELSE ... ENDIF   or   IF ... THEN ... ENDIF
   WHILE ... DO ... ENDWHILE .

In this and the next chapter we let our tests have as outcomes T and F or TRUE and FALSE .

DEFINITION OF WELL-STRUCTURED SUBSCHEME

(1) The following are well-structured subschemes:

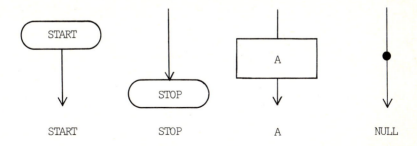

where A is any assignment statement and NULL - the straight arrow -
stands for any identity instruction such as u ← u . All are single entry
single exit blocks; the STOP statement is, of course, a zero exit block,
and START is zero entry. (A NULL node by convention disappears when
followed by any other node.)

(2) If B_1 and B_2 are well-structured subschemes, B_1 is not zero exit and B_2 is not zero entry, then B_3 , the block or chain composition of B_1 and B_2 is a well-structureed subscheme, zero entry if B_1 is so and zero exit if B_2 is so.

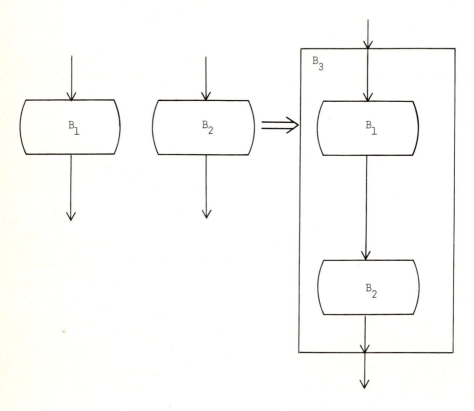

In our "programming language" B_3 is written as:

$$B_1 \atop B_2 \qquad \text{or} \qquad B_1 \; ; \; B_2$$

(3) If Q is any m-placed predicate letter, $\bar{u} = (u_1,\ldots,u_m)$ is any vector of m
    variables, B_1 and B_2 are single entry single exit well-structured sub-
    schemes and neither B_1 nor B_2 is zero entry (begins with START) nor zero
    exit (ends with STOP), then the following IF-THEN compositions, B_3 , B_4 and
    B_5 are well-structured single entry single exit subschemes:

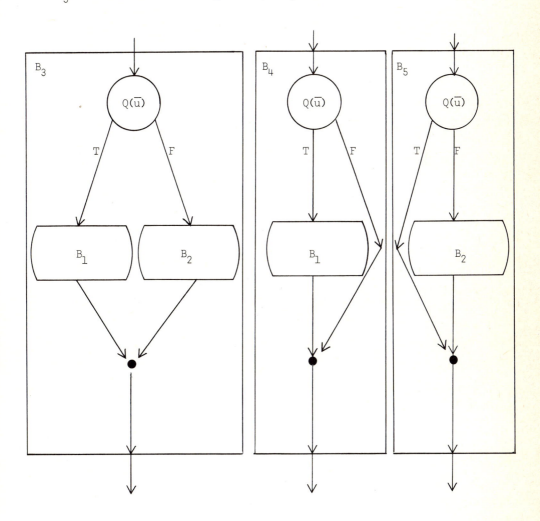

B_3: IF $Q(\bar{u})$ THEN B_1 ELSE B_2 ENDIF B_4: IF $Q(\bar{u})$ THEN B_1 ENDIF
         or
     IF NOT $Q(\bar{u})$ THEN B_2 ELSE B_1 ENDIF B_5: IF NOT $Q(\bar{u})$ THEN B_2 ENDIF

(4) If Q is any m-placed predicate letter, $\bar{u} = (u_1,\ldots,u_m)$ is any vector of m
variables, and B is a single entry single exit well-structured subscheme
which is not zero entry or zero exit, nor null then the following WHILE-
compositions B_1 and B_2 are single entry single exit well structured
subschemes:

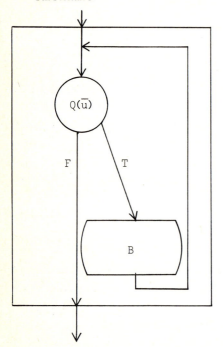 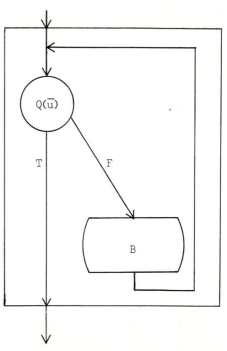

B_1: WHILE $Q(\bar{u})$ DO B ENDWHILE B_2: WHILE NOT $Q(\bar{u})$ DO B ENDWHILE

Finally we can define:

DEFINITION   A finite graph or subscheme is <u>well-structured</u> if it can be built out of the basic blocks in (1) by a finite number of applications of chain (block) composition, IF-THEN composition and WHILE composition.

DEFINTION   A <u>simple WHILE program scheme</u> is a program scheme whose graph is well-structured.

We shall usually describe WHILE schemes in terms of our little "programming language". Notice that there is no need to provide semantics for our programming language. That is already done by the correspondence with the graphical form whose semantics have been given in detail. If we are given an interpretation I for a WHILE program scheme P then we can substitute the interpreted functions -   I(f) and I(Q) - into our language as well as into the graph representation.

DEFINITION   If P is a simple WHILE program scheme and I is an interpretation of P , then (P,I) is a <u>simple WHILE program.</u>

Our next main task is to consider extensions to our language. Most of these extensions are a matter of convenience but one of them does add expressive power. First, however, we shall digress a little to provide an equivalent graph oriented definition of a simple WHILE scheme. Just as we saw that a block could be defined as a single entry tree-like flow diagram, so we shall notice that a well-structured subscheme can be defined as a single entry single exit <u>line-like</u> flow diagram. Readers uninterested in graph considerations can skip this section.

D.   LINE-LIKE SUBGRAPHS
First we add to the previous concept of ancestry or domination the concept of back domination and combine the two in the concepts of chain domination and of cycle domination. These ideas also play an important role in graph oriented discussions of program optimization.

DEFINITION   Let G be a single entry single exit subgraph with entry node e and exit node d . For any nodes n and m in G , we say that:
(1) n <u>dominates</u> m (n is an <u>ancestor</u> of m) if n lies on every path from e to m , (abbreviated n d m) ,
(2) n <u>back dominates</u> m if n lies on every path from m to d (abbreviated n bd m) ,

(3) n <u>chain dominates</u> m if n dominates m and m back dominates n
(abbreviated n ch m) , and

(4) n <u>cycle dominates</u> m if n both dominates and back dominates m
(abbreviated n cy m) .

The concept of "back dominates" is really the reverse or "dual" of the concept of "dominates" or "is an ancestor of" in the sense that in graph G with single entry e and single exit d , n back dominates m if and only if m dominates n (m is an ancestor of n) in the graph G' obtained by reversing the arrows of G , making d the entry and e the exit.

Chain domination and cycle domination are illustrated below.

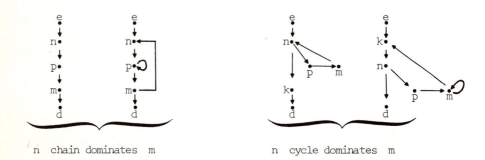

 n chain dominates m   n cycle dominates m

Using Lemma 4.1 and the "duality principle" (i.e. that domination and back domination can be exchanged by reversing the directions of all the arrows on a single entry single exit graph) we have the following lemma.

LEMMA 4.8   The relationships of domination, back domination, chain domination and cycle domination are transitive.

Again using the duality principle, Lemma 4.2 becomes the following lemma.

LEMMA 4.2'   (a) If n dominates m , n also dominates every node on every path from n to m not passing through n .
(b) If n back dominates m , n also back dominates every node on every path from m to n not passing through n .

Lemmas 4.8 and 4.2' can be used to show the next results; the proof is left to the reader as an exercise.

LEMMA 4.9   Let G be a graph with single entry e and single exit d . For nodes n,m and p the following hold.

(1) If n and m dominate p , either n dominates m or m dominates n .

(2) If n and m back dominate p , either n back dominates m or m back dominates n .

(3) If m and p are directly connected to n , m and p cannot both dominate n .

(4) If n is directly connected to both m and p , m and p cannot both back dominate n .

Now we are ready for a formal definition of "line-like".

DEFINITION   Let G be a single entry single exit subgraph with entry node e and exit node d . Then G is <u>line-like</u> if:

(A) for every pair of nodes n and m such that n is directly connected to m , then n ≠ m and either

   (1) n chain dominates m , or

   (2) n cycle dominates m , or

   (3) m cycle dominates n , or

   (4) n dominates m but does not chain dominate or cycle dominate m and there is a node p such that n chain dominates p and p back dominates m , or

   (5) m back dominates n but does not cycle dominate n nor does n chain dominate m and there is a node q such that q chain dominates m and q dominates n .

(B) for any nodes n , m , and p , if n and m both cycle dominate p , then n cycle dominates m or m cycle dominates n .

We can illustrate these concepts with some simple examples. Each of the graphs (1) - (5) below are "line-like" and in graph (i) the direct connection (arrow) from n to m satisfies condition (i) of part (A) of the definition of line-like.

(1) n chain dominates m   (2) n cycle dominates m   (3) m cycle dominates n

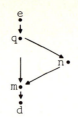

(4) n dominates m

    n chain dominates p

    p back dominates m

    n does not back dominate m

    m does not back dominate n

(5) m back dominates n

    q chain dominates m

    q dominates n

    n does not dominate m

    m does not dominate n

It is clear from inspection that graphs (1) - (3) above are blocks but (4) and
(5) are not. We shall see in the proof of the next lemma that condition (1) of part
(A) of the definition of line-like corresponds to block composition, the WHILE
construction necessitates conditions (2) and (3), and the IF-THEN construction
requires (4) and (5); eliminating the IF-THEN construction would yield a much neater
definition of line-like. By way of contrast, here are three blocks (tree-like
graphs) which are not line-like:

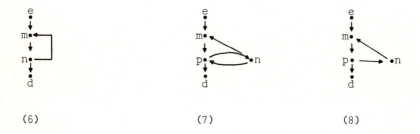

(6)   (7)   (8)

In all three, the trouble lies in the connection from n to m ; m is an ancestor
of (dominates) n so the definition of tree-like is satisfied. However, while in
(6), m chain dominates n , n cannot dominate m nor can m back dominate n ,
so the arrow from n to m violates part (A) of the definition of line-like. In
(7), m chain dominates p and p cycle dominates n , but again the arrow from
n to m cannot satisfy any of (1) - (5) of part (A) of the definition of line-like.
On the other hand, (8) satisfies part (A) of the definition of line-like - m chain
dominates p and both m and p cycle dominate n . But (8) violates part (B) of
the definition of line-like since neither of m and p can cycle dominate the
other. The situation illustrated in (8) is the reason for part (B) of the definition
of line-like; graph (8) cannot be the graph of a WHILE scheme.

The proof of the first half of our characterization theorem is not difficult. The demonstration that a well-structured subscheme is line-like clearly motivates the definitions of chain domination and cycle domination.

LEMMA 4.10 A well-structured subscheme is line-like.

PROOF

It is obvious that the basic blocks in part (1) of the definition of well-structured subscheme are line-like, if we allow the NULL node graph to be so described. We need only examine the three forms of composition of blocks in (2) - (4) of the definition of well-structured, to see that they take line-like graphs into line-like graphs.

In (2) B_3 is the block or chain composition of B_1 and B_2 . The only direct connection added is from the exit node d_1 of B_1 to the entry node e_2 of B_2 . The only entry to e_2 in B_3 is from d_1 so d_1 dominates e_2 ; similarly the only exit from B_1 is via the connection from d_1 to e_2 , so e_2 back dominates d_1 and in fact all of B_1 . Hence d_1 chain dominates e_2 . Thus B_3 is line-like if B_1 and B_2 are so.

There are 3 subcases in (3); we only examine the first. In the first subcase B_3 is formed by connecting a query node q to the entry node e_1 of B_1 and the entry node e_2 of B_2 , while the exit nodes d_1 of B_1 and d_2 of B_2 are connected to a NULL node p which is now the exit for B_3 . Then q dominates e_1 and e_2 but neither (of e_1 and e_2) back dominates q nor does q back dominate e_1 or e_2 . However, the common exit node p back dominates d_1 and d_2 by definition and hence e_1 and e_2 and finally q . Thus q chain dominates p and the connections from q to e_1 and e_2 satisfy (4) of part (A) of the definition of line-like while the connections from d_1 and d_2 to p satisfy (5) of part (A) of the definition of line-like.

Finally the two compositions in (4) are graphically similar, and so we discuss only the first. Graph B_1 is formed by connecting a query node q a branch node - to two nodes, the entry node e of B and the NULL node p which is the exit for B_1 ; the exit node d of B is directly connected back to q . We can only enter B_1 from q and B can only be entered by the connection from q to e , so q dominates e and d . We can only leave B via the connection from d to q ; thus q back dominates e and d . Hence q cycle dominates e and d ; the connection from q to e satisfies (2) of the definition of line-like while the connection from d to q satisfies (3). Notice that q chain dominates the exit node p ; alternatively one might omit p and regard q as both entry and exit node to B_1 .

Block composition, (2), and IF-THEN composition, (3), do not affect cycle domination so we need consider part (B) of the definition of line-like only for WHILE composition, (4). But the query node q cycle dominates all of B and these are the only cycle dominations added in B_1 so if (B) is line-like then B_1 is line-like. ∎

To reverse Lemma 4.10, we need a few additional implications of our definitions. First, we have a result true for any single entry single exit graph G .

LEMMA 4.11   Let G be a single entry single exit graph with entry e and exit d . Let n,m and p be three different nodes in G .
(1) If n cy m and m ch p , then n cy p .
(2) If n and m ch p , then n ch m or m ch p .
(3) If n ch m and p , then m ch p or p ch m .
(4) If n and m cy p , then n ch m or m ch n or n cy m or
    m cy n .

PROOF
    Part (1) is an obvious consequence of Lemma 4.8 and the definitions of chain and cycle domination. In (2), if n ch p and m ch p , by Lemma 4.9(1) either n d m or m d n . The cases are symmetric, so suppose n d m . Thus there is a path from e to n not passing through m (the shortest path from e to n must have this property). If m did not back dominate n , then there would be a path from n to d not passing through m ; since p bd n this path would pass through p . Putting the two paths together we would get a path from e to p not passing through m , contradicting the fact that m d p . Hence m bd n and so n chain dominates m . Then (3) is obtained by the dual of the arguments in (2); details are left to the reader.
    Finally, for (4), notice that if n and m both cycle dominate p then both n and m dominate and back dominate p . Thus by Lemma 4.9(1) and (2), n dominates m or m dominates n and n back dominates m or m back dominates n . This yields exactly the four possibilities mentioned in (4). ∎

Notice that part (B) of the definition of line-like is needed to eliminate two of the four possibilities mentioned in Lemma 4.11(4). If G is line-like and both n and m cycle dominate p , then n cycle dominates m or m cycle dominates n .
    We wish to show that if P is a flow diagram with a line-like graph, then P is well-structured. The plan of attack is to divide P into smaller line-like pieces and proceed by induction on the number of nodes in the graph of P . To facilitate this division of P , we introduce another definition and another lemma.

DEFINITION   For nodes n and m in a single entry single exit graph, let

$$S(n,m) = \{n,m\} \cup \{k \mid n \text{ dominates } k \text{ and } m \text{ back dominates } k\}$$

LEMMA 4.12   Let G be a single entry single exit line-like graph with entry e
and exit d . Let n and m be distinct nodes such that either n = m or n
chain dominates m . Then:
(1) S(n,m) is line-like with single entry n and single exit m .
(2) If n ≠ m and e ≠ d , S(e,n) ∩ S(m,d) = φ .

PROOF
     Whether n = m or n ch m , every member of S(n,m) - {n} is dominated
by n and every member of S(n,m) - {m} is back dominated by m . Thus
S(n,m) has single entry n and single exit m . All relations of dominance and
back dominance true in G are certainly true in S(n,m) . Clearly S(n,m)
satisfies (B) of the definition of line-like if G does.
     Let r and s be in S(n,m) with a direct connection from r to s . If
this arrow satisfies (1), (2) or (3) of part (A) of the definition of line-like in
G it does so in S(n,m) . So it remains to consider (4) and (5); by the duality
principle we need only consider (4). There is a node p in G such that r
dominates s , r chain dominates p and p back dominates s . We consider two
cases. If n = m we cannot have r = n or else r cy s which already satisfies
(A3) of the definition of line-like. So r ≠ n , n cycle dominates r and r
chain dominates p . By Lemma 4.11, n cycle dominates p and thus p is in
S(n,m) = S(n,n) and so the definition of line-like is satisfied in S(n,m) as in
G . On the other hand, if n ≠ m then by hypothesis, n chain dominates m .
Now both m and p back dominate r . If m back dominates p , p is in
S(n,m) and again we are done. Otherwise, by Lemma 4.9, p back dominates m .
Hence the shortest path from r to d in G must go r - m - p - d and thus
since r dominates p , by Lemma 4.2', r dominates m . Thus r chain
dominates m . Hence the arrow from r to s in S(n,m) still satisfies (4) of
part (A) of the definition of line-like, now using m instead of p .
     Hence we can conclude that in all cases S(n,m) is line-like. Now assume that
n ≠ m , e ≠ d , and n chain dominates m . Suppose k is in both S(e,n) and
S(m,d) . Then k is not e , n , m or d . Thus n back dominates k and
since n dominates m and m dominates k , n cycle dominates k by Lemma 4.8.
Similarly, m dominates k and since m back dominates n and n back dominates
k , m also cycle dominates k by Lemma 4.8. But n chain dominates m which
violates (B) of the definition of line-like. Thus S(e,n) ∩ S(m,d) = φ . ∎

Now we are ready for the main lemma.

LEMMA 4.13   Let P be a flow diagram whose graph G is a line-like single entry single exit graph with entry node e and exit node d , such that either d is labeled with a STOP statement or d has exactly one arc leading out of G . Then P is a well-structured graph.

PROOF

We proceed by induction on #G , the number of nodes in G . If G has only one node, this node cannot be labeled with a test statement or else it would either have two arcs leading out of G or else there would be a self-loop which is forbidden by the definition of line-like. Hence, the lemma is true for #G = 1 .

Now suppose we have established the lemma for graphs with fewer than #G nodes and that #G ≥ 2 . We consider two main cases, e ≠ d and e = d . First let us assume that e ≠ d .

There are three subcases to consider. First suppose that e is not a branch node. Then e is directly connected to exactly one node n . Clearly e chain dominates n and G = {e} ∪ S(n,d) . The subscheme corresponding to {e} is well-structured and e is not in S(n,d) which is line-like by Lemma 4.12. Thus P is the block composition of the subschemes corresponding to {e} and to S(n,d) . By the induction hypothesis S(n,d) corresponds to a well-structured subgraph, and so P is well-structured.

Now assume that e is a branch node directly connected to nodes n and m and that e cycle dominates one of the two nodes. The arguments are symmetric, so suppose e cycle dominates m . If there is any path from e to d not containing n consider the shortest such path; it must go e - m - d . Since e back dominates m , those path must go e - m - e - d and thus there is a shorter such path, a contradiction. Thus every path from e to d contains n and e chain dominates n and n chain dominates d . By Lemma 4.12, S(e,e) ∩ S(n,d) = φ . For any node k , either k lies on a path from n to d and so either n = k or n dominates k and k is in S(n,d) or else k lies on a path from m to e and so is in S(e,e) . Thus G = S(e,e) ∪ S(n,d) and so G is a chain connection of S(e,e) and S(n,d) . Thus, applying the induction hypothesis to S(e,e) and S(n,d) which are line-like by Lemma 4.12, P is well-structured.

Finally assume that e is directly connected to nodes n and m and that e cycle dominates neither n nor m . By Lemma 4.9, e cannot chain dominate both n and m so suppose e does not chain dominate m . By the definition of line-like, there is a node p such that e chain dominates p and p back dominates m and hence n . Suppose there is more than one such node p . The set of nodes chain dominated by e must be itself a chain by Lemma 4.11(3) and so let p be the least upper bound of this set - i.e., if e chain dominates p' then p' = p or p chain dominates p' . We establish the following simple observations.

(i) S(n,p) ∩ S(m,p) = {p}

Suppose k is in S(n,p) ∩ S(m,p) and k ≠ p . Thus n and m both dominate k . Either n dominates m or m dominates m by Lemma 4.9. The arguments are similar; suppose n dominates m . Then the shortest path foom e to k goes e - n - m - k . But using the direct connection from e to m we can get a shorter such path, a contradiction. Hence k cannot exist and we have shown (i).

(ii) S(e,e) = {e}

Suppose k is in S(e,e) and k ≠ e . The shortest path from e to d containing k must go either e - n - k - d or e - m - k - d ; the arguments are similar so suppose it goes e - n - k - d . Since e back dominates k this path must go e - n - k - e - d and so e cy n contrary to hypothesis. Thus S(e,e) = {e} .

(iii) Either n = p or S(n,p) ∩ S(p,d) = {p} ; either m = p or
       S(m,p) ∩ S(p,d) = {p} .

Suppose n ≠ p and k is in S(n,p) ∩ S(p,d) for k ≠ p . Thus both n and p dominate k . Now p cannot dominate n , so by Lemma 4.9, n dominates p . By hypothesis p back dominates e so every path from e to d contains p and thus also n . Hence e chain dominates n . But p is the least upper bound of nodes chain dominated by e so n = p , a contradiction. The other half of (iii) is established similarly.

By similar reasoning to the arguments for (i) - (iii) we can show (iv) and (v); the proof is left to the reader as an exercise.

(iv) If k can be reached from both n and m , either k = p or p dominates
      k .

(v) G = {e} ∪ S(n,p) ∪ S(m,p) ∪ S(p,d) .

Let S'(n,p) be obtained by substituting the NULL node for p and similarly for S'(m,p) . Similar to Lemma 4.12, it can be shown that S'(n,p) and S'(m,p) are line-like, and so correspond to well-structured subschemes, as does S(p,d) . If n ≠ p ≠ m , G is by (i) - (v) the chain connection of the IF-THEN connection of {e} , S'(n,p) and S'(m,p) to S(p,d) ; for n = p , G is the chain connection of the IF-THEN connection of {e} and S'(m,p) to S(p,d) , and similarly if p = m . Hence P is well-structured in this case too.

Finally if e = d there is an arc from e leading out of G and one from e to some node n . Then e cy n and G is the WHILE connection of {e} and S(n,e) so we are done. ∎

THEOREM 4.14   A program scheme P is a simple WHILE scheme if and only if its graph is line-like.

E. EXTENSIONS OF THE DEFINITION OF A WHILE SCHEME

We now consider some extensions of our definition, which depend on enlarging the definitions of functional terms and predicate terms.

Extended Functional Term - defined inductively:
(1) If x is a variable, x is an extended functional term.
(2) If c is a constant symbol, c is an extended functional term.
(3) If f is an n-placed function letter and $t_1,\ldots,t_n$ are extended functional terms, then $f(t_1,\ldots,t_n)$ is an extended functional term.

Extended Predicate Term:

If Q is an m-placed predicate letter and $t_1,\ldots,t_n$ are extended functional terms, then $Q(t_1,\ldots,t_n)$ and (NOT $Q(t_1,\ldots,t_n)$) are extended predicate terms.

Boolean Expression

Any connection of extended predicate terms using AND and OR (∧ and ∨) is a Boolean expression.

First let us consider some partial extensions which do not increase the expressive power of WHILE schemes.

PROPOSITION 4.15 Adding the following constructions to the definition of a well-structured subscheme does not increase expressive power.

(1) Extended Assignment Statements:

If t is an extended functional term and u is a variable, the following can be considered to be a well-structured subscheme:

(Proof is obvious)

(2) Simply Extended IF-THEN and WHILE Constructions:

If $t_1,\ldots,t_m$ are extended functional terms, Q is an m-placed test letter and B_1 and B_2 are well-structured subschemes, the following can be considered to be well-structured:

C_1:   IF $Q(t_1,\ldots,t_m)$ THEN B_1 ELSE B_2 ENDIF

C_2:   IF $Q(t_1,\ldots,t_m)$ THEN B_1 ENDIF

C_3:   IF NOT $Q(t_1,\ldots,t_m)$ THEN B_1 ENDIF

W_1:   WHILE $Q(t_1,\ldots,t_m)$ DO B_1 ENDWHILE

W_2:   WHILE NOT $Q(t_1,\ldots,t_m)$ DO B_1 ENDWHILE

(Proof is obvious)

(3) Extended IF - THEN Constructions

     If Q is any Boolean expression and B_1 and B_2 are well-structured subschemes the following can be considered well-structured:

        IF Q THEN B_1 ELSE B_2 ENDIF

        IF Q THEN B_1 ENDIF

This can be shown by induction on the number of connectives by noting that:

        IF Q_1 OR Q_2 THEN B_1 ELSE B_2 ENDIF

is strongly equivalent to:

        IF Q_1 THEN B_1 ELSE IF Q_2 THEN B_1 ELSE B_2 ENDIF ENDIF

and

        IF Q_1 AND Q_2 THEN B_1 ELSE B_2 ENDIF

is strongly equivalent to:

        IF Q_1 THEN IF Q_2 THEN B_1 ELSE B_2 ENDIF ELSE B_2 ENDIF

(4) Partially Extended WHILE Construction:

     If $Q_1,\ldots,Q_n$ are extended predicate terms and B is a well-structured subscheme, the following can be considered a well-structured subscheme:

        WHILE (Q_1 OR Q_2 OR $\ldots$ OR Q_n) DO B ENDWHILE

This is easily shown. For example, we note that for $n = 2$, this statement is strongly equivalent to:

WHILE Q_1 DO B ENDWHILE;

WHILE Q_2 DO B ;

WHILE Q_1 DO B ENDWHILE

ENDWHILE

We should like to allow the use of arbitrary Boolean expressions in WHILE constructions. This does represent an extension of the power of our programming language. Consider the program scheme P whose graph appears in Example IV-5; in our language P becomes:

START ; WHILE Q(x) and T(x) DO x ← f(x) ENDWHILE ; STOP

We claim that P is not strongly equivalent to any simple WHILE progaam scheme. Suppose P is strongly equivalent to a simple WHILE scheme P' with N assignment statements. In a simple WHILE scheme we do not allow extended functional terms or extended predicate terms. Any step of a computation under a free interpretation in such a scheme can increase the length of the value of a variable by at most one letter. First consider the free interpretation I such that $I(Q)(x) = I(T)(x) = I(Q)(f^n(x)) = I(T)(f^n(x)) = $ TRUE for $1 \le n \le N+1$ and $I(Q)(f^{N+2}(x)) = I(T)(f^{N+2}(x)) = $ FALSE . Under this interpretation computation (P',I,x) must halt with output $f^{N+2}(x)$. In order to do so, the computation must certainly construct $f^{N+2}(x)$ but this will take at least N+1 assignment statements. Thus there must be a time, before any value $f^{N+1}(x)$ has yet been constructed, when the computation passes twice through the same assignment statement. Since P' is a WHILE scheme this can only occur by means of a WHILE construction. That is, at some time when all the value of the variables to date are of the form $val(y) = x$ or $val(y) = f^n(x)$ for $1 \le n \le N$, the computation enters some WHILE construction, passes the test, goes around the loop, re-enters, passes the test and repeats the loop. Since P' is a simple WHILE scheme, this construction must be of one of the forms:

(1) WHILE Q(u) DO B ENDWHILE
(2) WHILE NOT Q(u) DO B ENDWHILE
(3) WHILE T(u) DO B ENDWHILE
(4) WHILE NOT T(u) DO B ENDWHILE

Since the treatment of Q and T in P is symmetric, we need only look at the first two cases. In the first case, let I_1 be the free interpretation defined by $I_1(T)(E) = I(T)(E)$ and $I_1(Q)(E) = $ TRUE for all members E of the domain. When

EXAMPLE IV-5   A SCHEME NOT STRONGLY EQUIVALENT TO ANY SIMPLE WHILE SCHEME

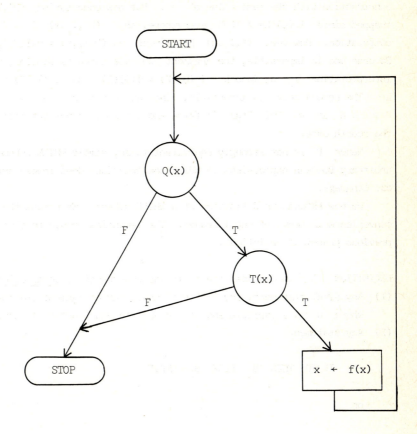

START

WHILE Q(x) AND T(x) DO x ← f(x) ENDWHILE

STOP

computation (P',I,x) entered this WHILE construction, all values computed to date
were of the form $\text{val}(y) = x$ or $\text{val}(y) = f^n(x)$ for $n \leq N$, and so up to this
point computation (P',I_1,x) follows the same path and enters the WHILE
construction with the same value of u. But now computation (P',I_1,x) is
trapped since $I_1(Q)(E) = \text{TRUE}$ everywhere; thus (P',I_1,x) is a divergent
computation. However, (P,I_1,x) halts with $\text{val}(P,I_1,x) = \text{val}(P,I,x) = f^{N+2}(x)$.
So case one is impossible; the argument for case three is similar, using free
interpretation I_2 defined by $I_2(Q)(E) = I(Q)(E)$ and $I_2(T)(E) = \text{TRUE}$ for all
E. The second case is impossible, since at this point $\text{val}(u) = f^n(x)$,
$0 \leq n \leq N$ and so NOT $Q(u)$ is false and the loop is not entered; similarly for
the fourth case.

Hence P is not strongly equivalent to any simple WHILE scheme. Thus allowing
arbitrary Boolean expressions in WHILE constructions does indeed extend the power of
our language.

We now extend our definition of a WHILE scheme. We phrase the definition for
convenience in terms of our language. The semantics should be obvious from the
previous graphical defintions.

DEFINITION   Let us consider the following constructions acceptable:
(1) Any START statement; any STOP statement; any assignment statement $u \leftarrow t$
    where u is a variable and t is an extended functional term.
(2) Any statement

           IF Q THEN B_1 ELSE B_2 ENDIF

    or

           IF Q THEN B_1 ENDIF

    where Q is an Boolean expression and B_1 and B_2 are acceptable
    constructions.
(3) Any statement

           WHILE Q DO B ENDWHILE

    where Q is any Boolean expression and B is any acceptable construction.
(4) Any construction

        B_1 ; B_2

    where B_1 and B_2 are acceptable constructions.

DEFINITION   A finite sequence of acceptable constructions starting with START and ending with STOP and containing no other START or STOP statements is a WHILE scheme. If P is a WHILE scheme and I an interpretation of P , then (P,I) is a WHILE program or structured program or GOTO-less PROGRAM.

F.   WHILE PROGRAMS, STEP PROGRAMS, AND PRIMITIVE RECURSIVE FUNCTIONS
    We shall see that there are several senses in which WHILE programs and WHILE schemes are universal. We first examine the "weakest" sense - the fact that WHILE programs can do everything that Turing machines can do.
    We can use some elementary facts from recursive function theory to show that every partially computable or partial recursive function from nonnegative integers to nonnegative integers can be computed by a WHILE program of a particularly simple form.   This result can be extended to functions computable over other domains by standard encoding techniques.
    A particular subset of the total recursive functions, the primitive recursive functions, can be computed by a special type of WHILE program, a STEP program or LOOP program.   We define a STEP construction:

        STEP   u   DO   B   ENDSTEP

as the particular WHILE construction:

        $v \leftarrow u$;   WHILE $v \neq 0$ DO   B ; $v \leftarrow v \doteq 1$ ENDWHILE

where v is a new variable and a loop results if the value of v is not a nonnegative integer. A STEP program or LOOP program can be defined by restricting interpretations to the nonnegative integers and replacing the WHILE construction (3) in the definition of acceptable construction by (3) STEP u DO B ENDSTEP where B is an acceptable construction.

DEFINITION   The operation of primitive recursion defines from functions h and g the function f by the formula:

$$f(0,x_2,\ldots,x_n) = h(x_2,\ldots,x_n)$$
$$f(x+1,x_2,\ldots,x_n) = g(x,f(x,x_2,\ldots,x_n),x_2,\ldots,x_n)$$

Notice that f can be defined from h and g by primitive recursion as the output of the following program:

$$u \leftarrow h(x_2,\dots,x_n)$$

$$v \leftarrow 0$$

STEP x DO

$$u \leftarrow g(v,u,x_2,\dots,x_n)$$

$$v \leftarrow v+1$$

ENDSTEP

$$z \leftarrow u$$

DEFINITION   The family of primitive recursive functions is the least family of functions closed under functional composition and primitive recursion and containing the base functions:

$$S(x) \;=\; x+1$$

$$Z(x) \;=\; 0$$

$$P_{i,n}(x_1,\dots,x_n) \;=\; x_i$$

Block composition certainly corresponds to functional composition. Thus we have shown:

THEOREM 4.16   Every primitive recursive function can be computed by a program (P,I) where P is a STEP scheme not employing any IF-THEN construction and I is an interpretation over the nonnegative integers assigning to function letters only functions S , Z , $P_{i,n}$ and $x \doteq 1$ and to predicate letters only the interpretation "Is x = 0 ?" .

Meyers and Ritchie have shown that the converse is true - that STEP programs compute precisely the primitive recursive functions. We get from primitive recursive functions to partial recursive functions by the minimization operation.

DEFINITION   The operation of minimization defines from a function f the function:

$$\mu_y(f(y,x_2,\dots,x_n)) \;=\; \begin{cases} m & \text{if } m = \text{Min } \{y \mid f(y,x_2,\dots,x_n) = 0\} \\[2mm] \text{undefined if } \{y \mid f(y,x_2,\dots,x_n) = 0\} = \phi \end{cases}$$

Observe that $\mu_y f$ can be obtained from f by the following WHILE program:

$$u \leftarrow f(0,x_2,\ldots,x_n)$$

$$z \leftarrow 0$$

WHILE $u \neq 0$ DO

$$z \leftarrow z + 1$$

$$u \leftarrow f(z,x_2,\ldots,x_n)$$

ENDWHILE

It can be shown that every partial recursive (partially computable) function on the nonnegative integers can be obtained by applying minimization once to a primitive recursive function. Thus it is a trivial consequence of elementary recursive function theory that

THEOREM 4.17 Every partially computable function can be computed using the set of program schemes obtained by applying one WHILE construction to a STEP scheme and using interpretations of function letters limited to $S(x)$, $Z(x)$, $P_{i,n}(x_1,\ldots,x_n)$ and $x \stackrel{.}{-} 1$ and interpretations of predicate letters limited to "Is $x = 0$?" .

This theorem is not really adequate for our purposes. It does indeed say that any program could be written in a very simplified structured form. But the program this theorem gives you may be exceedingly inefficient as regards time or space. It may be very difficult to construct or analyze. It may have no obvious relationship to the approach you really want to use. When you convert an existing program to this form - and the theorem is effective, there is an algorithm for the conversion - the resulting program will in general have no relationship to the original program except the very input-output relation.

We want to know something more. We want to know not just that WHILE programs can compute every partial recursive function somehow or other but that the class of WHILE schemes is a canonical form. Notice that this does not follow from the previous theorem since we want to know about behavior under all interpretations.

G. UNIVERSALITY OF WHILE SCHEMES   -   SWITCH VARIABLES

It is not difficult to see that every scheme is strongly equivalent to a WHILE scheme relative to some fixed subinterpretation. Just add switch variables to indicate which statement is now being executed and let the interpretation to which you are relativized include constants and tests for constants. This is essentially the Böhm-Jacoppini result.

THEOREM 4.18   Let I be the interpretation with domain $D = \{0,1\}$ and $I(0) = 0$, $I(1) = 1$ and for predicate letter Z , $I(Z)(0) = \text{TRUE}$ and $I(Z)(1) = \text{FALSE}$. Given any program scheme P (not employing $0,1$ or Z) we can construct a WHILE scheme P' strongly equivalent to P relative to I .

PROOF

There are many alternative lines of proof. Suppose that P is expressed in linear form. For each address k in P we add a new variable u_k and construct a block B_k of program as indicated. We let u_{STOP} be a new variable and let 0 and 1 be constants.

If k is the address of a test statement $T(y_1,\ldots,y_n)$ r,s (where r is the transfer on TRUE and s on FALSE) block B_k is:

$u_k \leftarrow 1$

IF $T(y_1,\ldots,y_n)$ THEN $u_r \leftarrow 0$ ELSE $u_s \leftarrow 0$ ENDIF

If k is the address of a STOP statement, then B_k is

$u_k \leftarrow 1$; $u_{STOP} \leftarrow 0$

If k is an assignment statement A , then B_k is:

$u_k \leftarrow 1$; A ; $u_{k+1} \leftarrow 0$

In each case the block $\overline{B}_k$ is defined from B_k by:

IF $Z(u_k)$ THEN B_k ENDIF

The desired WHILE scheme P' is simply:

START

$u_1 \leftarrow 0$; $u_2 \leftarrow 1$; $u_3 \leftarrow 1$; $\ldots$; $u_m \leftarrow 1$; $u_{STOP} \leftarrow 1$

WHILE NOT $Z(u_{STOP})$ DO $\overline{B}_1, \ldots, \overline{B}_m$ ENDWHILE

STOP

where m is the number of statements in P .   ■

This construction is scarcely optimal. It is easy to see that instead of $m+1$ new variables, $\log m$ will suffice and indeed even fewer switch variables are usually needed since one needs u_k only if $k = 1$ or k is a statement addressed by a GOTO (is a transfer address in a test statement). By taking advantage of other features of particular schemes, still fewer switch variables may suffice in particular cases.

The transformation is global. The schemes P and P' are strongly computationally equivalent in the restricted sense - if we omit from the test added computational histories of $(P,I',\bar{a})$ and $(P',I',\bar{a})$ all values of the new variables and all tests involving these variables (i.e. test Z) for an interpretation I' extending I to all of P and P' , then the resulting lists are equal. However the loop structure of P has been drastically changed and there is no simple relationship between the graphs of P and P' .

This construction cannot be fixed up to admit strong equivalence since the WHILE scheme P' constructed is actually a simple WHILE scheme and we saw that simple WHILE schemes did not form a canonical class. We can obtain strong equivalence by using our new variables not to mark the next statement to be executed but rather to store the values of the registers at certain critical points. Adding new variables is crucial as we shall mention later.

H. THE STRONG EQUIVALENCE CONSTRUCTION

We now give a construction for transforming any program scheme P into a strongly equivalent WHILE scheme. We assume that P is tree-like and has a division $B_0,\ldots,B_n$ into major blocks as described at the end of section B. We proceed by blocks from the inside out, starting with innermost blocks without any subblocks - i.e. without any nodes labeled with a block name.

To each block B_i we shall associate a WHILE subscheme $p(B_i)$. If B_i has an exit to a block B_j (which might be B_i itself) we construct a Boolean expression $E(B_i,B_j)$ such that the computation leaves B_i for B_j if and only if $E(B_i,B_j)$ is true. We build $p(B_i)$ from the $E(B_i,B_j)$, the $p(B_j)$ associated with subblocks of B_i and a special tree scheme $p'(B_i)$.

If node c in block B_i contains a test $T(x_1,\ldots,x_k)$, we call c a critical point and associate new variables $u(i,c,x_1),\ldots,u(i,c,x_k)$ indexed by the block, the critical point, and the variable tested at the critical point.

First form block B_i' from B_i by replacing arrows to the entry node by exits labeled B_i . Let e be the entry node of B_i . Since B_i' is a tree, there is a unique path from the node e to each node including the exit nodes. For each node N we can define a conditional expression $E(B_i,N)$ by induction on the length of the shortest path from e to N . Notice that either $N = e$ or there is a unique node m directly connected to N . We proceed by cases.

(1) For N = e , $E(B_i,e) =$ TRUE

(2) If $E(B_i,m)$ has been defined and m is labeled with an assignment statement
     and the arrow from m leads to node N (which may be an exit)
     $E(B_i,N) = E(B_i,m)$.

(3) If $E(B_i,m)$ has been defined and m is labeled by subblock B_j and an arrow
     leads from m to exit node N for block B_k (and any arrow from m must
     lead out of B_i by definition of a division into major blocks), then
     $E(B_i,N) = E(B_i,m) \land E(B_j,B_k)$.

(4) If $E(B_i,m)$ has been defined and m is labeled by test $T(x_1,\ldots,x_k)$ at
     critical point c , and a branch labeled b leads to node N (which may be
     an exit node), then $E(B_i,N)$ is either

$$E(B_i,m) \land T(u(i,c,x_1),\ldots,u(i,c,x_k))$$

     if b = TRUE or else, if b = FALSE:

$$E(B_i,m) \land \text{NOT } T(u(i,c,x_1),\ldots,u(i,c,x_k))$$

     Finally, if $N_1,\ldots,N_r$ is the set of notes which are labeled as exits to
B_j , $E(B_i,B_j)$ is defined as:

$$E(B_i,N_1) \lor \ldots \lor E(B_i,N_r)$$

EXAMPLE

     Let us give the construction for block B_{21} from Example IV-4 which gave a
division of the scheme of Example IV-3 into major blocks. The critical points are
α and β and the new variables are $u(21,\alpha,x_1)$ and $u(21,\beta,x_2)$. The Boolean
expression which gives the conditions under which a computation goes from the entry
node of B_{21} to the exit for block B_2 is:

$E(B_{21},B_2)$:   NOT $T(u(21,\alpha,x_1))$

Similarly:

$E(B_{21},B_0)$: $T(u(21,\alpha,x_1)) \land$ NOT $T(u(21,\beta,x_2))$

and

$E(B_{21},B_{21})$: $T(u(21,\alpha,x_1)) \land T(u(21,\beta,x_2))$

     Notice that no two of the conditions (i.e. no two of $E(B_{21},B_0)$, $E(B_{21},B_2)$
and $E(B_{21},B_{21})$) can hold at the same time but, assuming the variables in question
have been properly defined, one of the three conditions must always hold.

Next we must construct a subscheme $p'(B_i)$. We assume that either B_i is an innermost block or we have already constructed $p(B_j)$ for any subblocks B_j of B_i . For each node N in B_i' we define a subscheme S_N inductively, this time by distance from exit nodes of B_i' .

(1) If N is labeled by assignment statement A :

    (a) and the arrow from N goes to an exit node, S_N is:

        A

    (b) and the arrow from N goes to a node m which is not an exit, S_N is:

        A ; S_m

(2) If N is labeled by subblock B_j all arrows must lead to exit nodes and S_N is $p(B_j)$.

(3) If N is labeled with test $T(x_1,\ldots,x_k)$ at critical point c
    (a) and all branches lead out of B_i' , S_N is:

$$u(i,c,x_1) \leftarrow x_1 ; \ldots ; u(i,c,x_k) \leftarrow x_k$$

    (b) and a branch labeled b_1 leads to node m which is not an exit and
    the branch labeled b_2 leads to an exit node, S_N is either

$$u(i,c,x_1) \leftarrow x_1 ; \ldots ; u(i,c,x_k) \leftarrow x_k$$

        IF $T(x_1,\ldots,x_k)$ THEN S_m ENDIF

    if b_1 = TRUE or else, if b_1 = FALSE :

$$u(i,c,x_1) \leftarrow x_1 ; \ldots ; u(i,c,x_k) \leftarrow x_k$$

        IF NOT $T(x_1,\ldots,x_k)$ THEN S_m ENDIF

    (c) and the branch labeled TRUE leads to node m_1 and the branch labeled
    FALSE leads to node m_2 and neither m_1 nor m_2 are exit nodes, then
    S_N is:

$$u(i,c,x_1) \leftarrow x_1 ; \ldots ; u(i,c,x_k) \leftarrow x_k$$

        IF $T(x_1,\ldots,x_k)$ THEN S_{m_1} ELSE S_{m_2} ENDIF

Finally, $p'(B_i)$ is S_e where e is the entry node to B_i .

EXAMPLE

We continue the construction of $p(B_{21})$ from Example IV-4. Clearly we can take as $p'(B_{21})$:

$$u(21,\alpha,x_1) \leftarrow x_1$$

        IF $T(x_1)$ THEN E ; $u(21,\beta,x_2) \leftarrow x_2$ ENDIF

Finally we can define $p(B_i)$. If B_i is itself a tree, $B_i = B_i'$ and we let $p(B_i) = p'(B_i)$. Otherwise $p(B_i)$ is defined to be:

$$p'(B_i)$$

$$\text{WHILE} \quad E(B_i, B_i) \quad \text{DO} \quad p'(B_i) \quad \text{ENDWHILE}$$

Notice that $E(B_i, B_i)$ must be defined since if there were no exit to B_i , B_i would be a tree. The expression $E(B_i, B_i)$ contains and tests variables $u(i,c,x_r)$ which have already been specified in $p'(B_i)$ or else the exit to B_i would not have been reached; it also tests variables $u(j,c,x_r)$ for subblocks B_j and the computation must pass through $p(B_j)$ and define these variables before reaching an exit that tests them. Each variable $u(i,c,x_r)$ stores the value of x_r when critical point c was last encountered and is not affected by any subsequent respecifications of x_r . Thus if we have taken a path leading to the exit to B_i , $E(B_i, B_i)$ will be TRUE for appropriate values of the variables and the computation will re-enter the loop; otherwise it will leave the loop.

EXAMPLE

We conclude the construction of $p(B_{21})$. Using our formula and the previously defined expression for $p'(B_{21})$ we have for $p(B_{21})$:

$$u(21,\alpha,x_1) \leftarrow x_1$$

$$\text{IF} \quad T(x_1) \quad \text{THEN} \quad E ; \quad u(21,\beta,x_2) \leftarrow x_2 \quad \text{ENDIF}$$

$$\text{WHILE} \quad T(u(21,\alpha,x_1)) \quad \wedge \quad T(u(21,\beta,x_2))$$

$$\text{DO} \quad u(21,\alpha,x_1) \leftarrow x_1 ;$$

$$\text{IF} \quad T(x_1) \quad \text{THEN} \quad E ; \quad u(21,\beta,x_2) \leftarrow x_2 \quad \text{ENDIF}$$

$$\text{ENDWHLLE}$$

Finally we can define the WHILE scheme P' which is strongly equivalent to the original tree-like scheme P by:

$$\text{START}$$
$$p(B_0)$$
$$\text{STOP}$$

Example IV-6 gives the complete construction of a WHILE scheme strongly equivalent to the flowchart in Examples IV-2, IV-3 and IV-4.

We have just shown:

THEOREM 4.19 Given a program scheme P we can construct a strongly equivalent WHILE scheme P' using new variables; P and P' are computationally equivalent in the restricted sense.

EXAMPLE IV-6   CONSTRUCTION OF A WHILE SCHEME P' STRONGLY EQUIVALENT
                TO THE PROGRAM SCHEME P IN EXAMPLE IV-4

CONSTRUCTION OF $p(B_{21})$:

$E(B_{21},B_2)$:   NOT $T(u(21,\alpha,x_1))$

$E(B_{21},B_0)$: $T(u(21,\alpha,x_1))$ $\wedge$ NOT $T(u(21,\beta,x_2))$

$E(B_{21},B_{21})$: $T(u(21,\alpha,x_1))$ $\wedge$ $T(u(21,\beta,x_2))$

$p(B_{21})$ is :

$\qquad$ $u(21,\alpha,x_1)$ $\leftarrow$ x_1 ;

$\qquad$ IF $T(x_1)$ THEN E ; $u(21,\beta,x_2)$ $\leftarrow$ x_2 ENDIF

$\qquad$ WHILE $T(u(21,\alpha,x_1))$ $\wedge$ $T(u(21,\beta,x_2))$

$\qquad\qquad$ DO $u(21,\alpha,x_1)$ $\leftarrow$ x_1 ;

$\qquad\qquad\qquad$ IF $T(x_1)$ THEN E ; $u(21,\beta,x_2)$ $\leftarrow$ x_2 ENDIF

$\qquad$ ENDWHILE

EXAMPLE IV-6   CONTINUED

BLOCKS B_2 , B_{11} and B_{111}

BLOCK B_2

$E(B_2,B_2)$:   NOT $T(u(2,\alpha,x_2))$ $\wedge$ $E(B_{21},B_2)$

$E(B_2,B_0)$:   NOT $T(u(2,\alpha,x_2))$ $\wedge$ $E(B_{21},B_0)$

$E(B_2,STOP)$: $T(u(2,\alpha,x_2))$

$p(B_2)$:

$\qquad$ B ; $u(2,\alpha,x_2)$ $\leftarrow$ x_2

$\qquad$ IF NOT $((x_2)$ THEN C ; $p(B_{21})$ ENDIF

$\qquad$ WHILE NOT $T(u(2,\alpha,x_2))$ $\wedge$ $E(B_{21},B_2)$

$\qquad\qquad$ DO B ; $u(2,\alpha,x_2)$ $\leftarrow$ x_2 ;

$\qquad\qquad\qquad$ IF NOT $T(x_2)$ THEN C ; $p(B_{21})$ ENDIF

$\qquad$ ENDWHILE

CLEARLY B_{111} and B_{21} are isomorphic except for block names and we can take:

$\qquad$ $p(B_{111}) = p(B_{21})$; $E(B_{111},B_{11}) = E(B_{21},B_2)$; $E(B_{111},B_0) = E(B_{21},B_0)$

$\qquad$ and $E(B_{111},B_{111}) = E(B_{21},B_{21})$

THEN we can also identify $p(B_{11}) = p(B_2)$

$\qquad$ $E(B_{11},B_{11}) = E(B_2,B_2)$; $E(B_{11},B_0) = E(B_2,B_0)$; $E(B_{11},STOP) = E(B_2,STOP)$

EXAMPLE IV-6   CONTINUED

BLOCK B_{121}

BLOCK B_{121}

$E(B_{121},B_{121})$:   NOT $T(u(121,\alpha,x_2))$ $\wedge$ NOT $T(u(121,\beta,x_1))$

$E(B_{121},B_{12})$:   NOT $T(u(121,\alpha,x_2))$ $\wedge$ $T(u(121,\beta,x_1))$

$E(B_{121},STOP)$: $T(u(121,\alpha,x_2))$

$p(B_{121})$:

        B ; $u(121,\alpha,x_2) \leftarrow x_2$;

        IF NOT $T(x_2)$ THEN C ; $u(121,\beta,x_1) \leftarrow x_1$ ENDIF

        WHILE NOT $T(u(121,\alpha,x_2))$ $\wedge$ NOT $T(u(121,\beta,x_1))$

                DO B ; $u(121,\alpha,x_2) \leftarrow x_2$;

                        IF NOT $T(x_2)$ THEN C ; $u(121,\beta,x_1) \leftarrow x_1$ ENDIF

        ENDWHILE

EXAMPLE IV-6   CONTINUED

BLOCK B_{12}

$E(B_{12},B_{12})$: $(T(u(12,\alpha,x_2)) \wedge T(u(12,\beta,x_1)))$

$\vee (T(u(12,\alpha,x_2)) \wedge \text{NOT } T(u(12,\beta,x_1)) \wedge E(B_{121},B_{12}))$

$E(B_{12},B_0)$: $\text{NOT } T(u(12,\alpha,x_2))$

$E(B_{12},\text{STOP})$: $T(u(12,\alpha,x_2)) \wedge \text{NOT } T(u(12,\beta,x_1)) \wedge E(B_{121},\text{STOP})$

$p(B_{12})$:

E ; $u(12,\alpha,x_2) \leftarrow x_2$; $u(12,\beta,x_1) \leftarrow x_1$

IF $T(x_2) \wedge T(x_1)$ THEN $p(B_{121})$ ENDIF

WHILE $[(T(u(12,\alpha,x_2)) \wedge T(u(12,\beta,x_1)))$

$\vee (T(u(12,\alpha,x_2)) \wedge \text{NOT } T(u(12,\beta,x_1)) \wedge E(B_{121},B_{12}))]$

DO E ; $u(12,\alpha,x_2) \leftarrow x_2$; $u(12,\beta,x_1) \leftarrow x_1$;

IF $T(x_2) \wedge \text{NOT } T(x_1)$ THEN $p(B_{121})$ ENDIF

ENDWHILE

EXAMPLE IV-6   CONCLUDED

BLOCK B_0

$E(B_0,B_0)$:   (NOT $T(u(0,\alpha,x_1))$ $\wedge$ $E(B_2,B_0))$

                        $\vee$ $(T(u(0,\alpha,x_1))$ $\wedge$ $T(u(0,\beta,x_1))$ $\wedge$ $E(B_{11},B_0))$

                        $\vee$ $(T(u(0,\alpha,x_1))$ $\wedge$ NOT $T(u(0,\beta,x_1))$ $\wedge$ $E(B_{12},B_0))$

The final WHILE scheme P' :

START

A ; $u(0,\alpha,x_1)$ $\leftarrow$ x_1 ;

IF $T(x_1)$ THEN D ; $u(0,\beta,x_1)$ $\leftarrow$ x_1 ;

                    IF $T(x_1)$ THEN $p(B_{11})$ ELSE $p(B_{12})$ ENDIF

            ELSE $p(B_2)$

ENDIF

WHILE $E(B_0,B_0)$ DO

                A ; $u(0,\alpha,x_1)$ $\leftarrow$ x_1 ;

                IF $T(x_1)$ THEN D ; $u(0,\beta,x_1)$ $\leftarrow$ x_1 ;

                                IF $T(x_1)$ THEN $p(B_{11})$ ELSE $p(B_{12})$ ENDIF

                        ELSE $p(B_2)$

                ENDIF

ENDWHILE

STOP

I. NEW VARIABLES ARE NEEDED

We now show that adding variables in the previous constructions is essential. We exhibit a program scheme P with one variable such that any strongly equivalent WHILE scheme must have more variables. Our proof actually shows that there is a program which is not strongly equivalent to any WHILE program with the same number of variables. Both the counterexample and its justification are due to Ashcroft and Manna (1971).

Consider the program scheme P in Example IV-7; it has one variable x . We shall demonstrate that for a particular interpretation I , (P,I) is not strongly equivalent to any single variable WHILE scheme. We now allow WHILE schemes in the extended sense, with arbitrary Boolean expressions.

Let the domain D of interpretation I be the set of all pairs (u,v) with u in $\{a,b\}^*$ and v in $\{a,b,\$\}^*$ such that v contains at most one occurrence of $\$$. We shall actually only consider input from the subdomain $D' = \{(e,y\$v) \mid y,v \in \{a,b\}^+ \}$.

For the tests, let $I(A)((u,av)) = \text{TRUE}$ for any $(u,av) \in D$, and let $I(A)$ be uniformly FALSE elsewhere. Let $I(B)((u,bv)) = \text{TRUE}$ for any $(u,bv) \in D$, and let $I(B)$ be uniformly FALSE elsewhere. For any c in $\{a,b,\$\}$, and (u,cv) in D , let $I(a)((u,cv)) = (ua,v)$ and $I(b)((u,cv)) = (ub,v)$ and let $I(a)$ and $I(b)$ be the identity elsewhere.

From now on we are only discussing programs under interpretation I and so if we discuss the computation of a scheme S with input z we mean computation (S,I,z) . For (u,v) in domain D , call u the <u>head</u> and v the <u>tail</u>.

It can be shown by induction on $|y|$, that for input $(e,y\$v)$ in D' the computation must halt with output (ay,v) . Thus during the computation in P or in any strongly equivalent single variable scheme the value of the single register x must at all times be of the form $(u',y'v)$ where u' is an initial substring of ay and y' is a terminal substring of $y\$$. If the tail of $val(x)$ at some point in the computation starts with a , then the second symbol added to the head afterwards must be a ; similarly if the tail starts with b , the next symbol but one added to the head must be b .

Now suppose that (P,I) is strongly equivalent to (P',I) for some WHILE scheme P' with a single register x . Let k be the length of the longest Boolean expression in P' . At any given place in P' the next step can depend on at most the first (i.e. leftmost) k symbols in the tail of the value of register x . We shall consider only inputs in D' . It will suffice to show that P' gives the wrong output for some input from D' .

EXAMPLE IV-7   A PROGRAM SCHEME NOT STRONGLY EQUIVALENT TO
                ANY WHILE SCHEME WITHOUT MORE VARIABLES

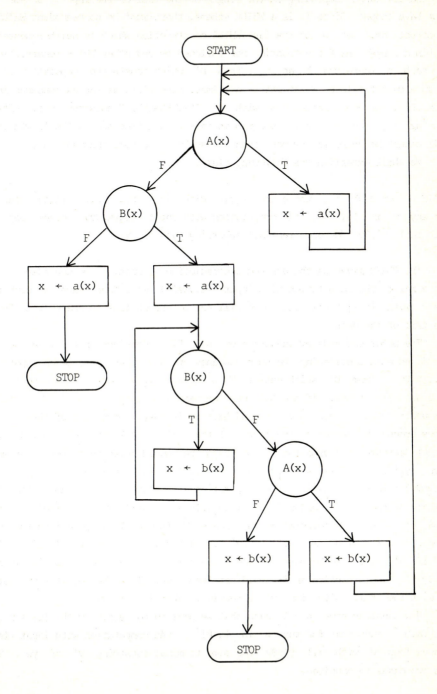

Since the length of the head of the output for an input from D' can grow arbitrarily large (depending on the length of the tail of the input), scheme P' must have loops. Since it is a WHILE scheme, there must be nonredundant WHILE constructions. Let W be the last WHILE construction which is neither nested within a larger WHILE construction nor followed by any other WHILE construction. For each n there must be an input from D' which causes the computation in P' to go around the loop W at least n times; otherwise, as far as concerns input from D', we could replace W with n "IF-THEN-ENDIF" constructions. After leaving W, the rest of the program is in effect a tree and so the length of the tail cannot be decreased by more than N symbols for some constant N.

We shall extablish the following claim:

CLAIM: For each n, there are y,z,v with $|z| = n$, $yz,v \in \{a,b\}^{+}$ such that for any w in $\{a,b\}^{+}$, the computation with input $(e,ywz\$v)$ leaves loop W with tail $y'z\$v$ for some terminal substring y' of yw.

The CLAIM gives us the desired contradiction at once, if we consider $|z| \geq N+1$; the computation with input $(e,ywz\$v)$ will then leave W with tail $y'z\$v$ with $|y'z| \geq N+1$ and there will not be enough time to erase $y'z$ from the tail of the output.

The proof proceeds by induction on n. First consider $n = 0$. As we mentioned when considering the nonredundancy of W, there must be an input $(e,y_1y_2\$v')$ from D' which enters W with tail $y_2\$v'$ and goes around the loop at least $k+1$ times. If the tail were unchanged by a cycle around W, then the computation could never leave W and halt as it must; hence each of these $k+1$ times around W decreases the length of the tail by at least one symbol and yet cannot decrease it beyond the $\$$ or the output would never be correct. So we must have $|y_2| \geq k$. Take $y = y_1y_2$ and $v = y_2v'$. For any input $(e,yw\$v) = (e,y_1y_2w\$y_2v')$, the computation will always see the same leftmost k symbols of the tail as under input $(e,y_1y_2\$y_2v')$ until W is entered with tail $y_2w\$y_2v'$. This new computation must leave W (since all computations for input from D' halt) with some tail $y'y_2v'$ for a terminal substring y' of $y_2w\$$. But if $y' = e$, the computation would see tail y_2v' and behave as it did on tail $y_2w\$y_2v'$ — in particular it would not leave W. Thus the computation must leave W with some tail $y'\$v$ for y' a terminal substring of yw.

Now consider some $n \geq 0$ such that we have found y,z,v with $|z| = n$, yz, $v \in \{a,b\}^{+}$ such that for any w in $\{a,b\}^{+}$, the computation with input $(e,ywz\$v)$ leaves loop W with tail $y'z\$v$ for some terminal substring y' of yw. There are two cases to consider.

First, assume that for each w the computation actually left W with tail $y'z\$v$ for y' a nonempty substring of yw . Now take our new $z' = az$. For any w' in $\{a,b\}^+$, the computation with input $(e,yw'z'\$v)$ leaves loop W by hypothesis with tail $y'z\$v$ for y' some nonempty terminal substring of $yw'a$; since y' is nonempty, $y' = y''a$ and so the tail is $y''z\$v$ for y'' some terminal substring of yw' . This settles this case.

Otherwise there must be some string wc , $c \in \{a,b\}$ such that the computation on input $(e,ywcz\$v)$ left W with tail $z\$v$. The cases are symmetric, so let us consider only $c = a$. Then the computation on input $(e,ywaz\$v)$ left W with tail $z\$v$. The last tail before that was $az\$v$ so by our remark at the start, the next symbol added to the head after leaving W must be a . Now let $z' = bz$. The computation on any input $(e,y\overline{w}z'\$v)$ leaves W with some tail $y'z\$v$ for y' a terminal substring of $y\overline{w}b$. If y' is empty, the previous tail started with b and so the next symbol added to the head after leaving W will be b . But all computations leaving W with the same tail - in this case, $z\$v$ - must afterwards behave alike since control depends only on the tail. This is a contradiction. Hence the computation on input $(e,y\overline{w}z'\$v)$ must leave W with some tail $y''z'\$v$ for y'' a terminal substring of $y\overline{w}$. This settles the other case and establishes the CLAIM. ■

COROLLARY 4.20   There is a flowchart program which is not strongly equivalent to any WHILE program with the same number of registers.

COROLLARY 4.21   Any canonical transformation mapping program schemes into WHILE schemes cannot preserve computational equivalence.

V. CORRECTNESS AND PROGRAM VERIFICATION

In this chapter we discuss techniques for program verification and their mathematical justification. The basic idea behind these methods was originally presented by Floyd; mathematical formulations and logical justifications were developed by Cooper and Manna, and others, and continued in King's Ph.D. thesis in which he presented the development of a partial implementation for these techniques. A somewhat different axiomatic approach has been pursued by Hoare et al. The reader who has never made acquaintance with the formalism of the first order predicate calculus should at this point turn to Appendix A for a brief and unrigorous exposition of the material relevant to this chapter.

The procedure we shall develop is part algorithm and part heuristics, and interactive in nature. There are many possible approaches and we shall examine in detail only one. The general idea is to devise for an input criterion A , output criterion B , and program (P,I) a well-formed formula $W(P,A,B)$ which is satisfiable in the logical sense if and only if (P,I) is partially correct with respect to A and B . To pursue this subject with full rigor, one must actually appeal to the second order logic in which one is allowed to quantify over predicates (or sets). Instead of going into this aspect we devise the well-formed formula $W(P,A,B)$ as a sort of logical scheme which uses as functions and predicates not only those in P but also A and B themselves plus certain special inductive assertions which we shall examine later. We shall see that for an interpretation I interpreting A and B as well as P , (P,I) is partially correct with respect to $I(A)$ and $I(B)$ if and only if there is an interpretation I' , extending I by providing interpretations for the inductive assertions, under which $W(P,A,B)$ holds over the domain of I .

A. PATH VERIFICATION

For simplicity we shall assume that in the flowcharts we consider, the input variables $\overline{X}$ are totally disjoint from the program variables $\overline{Y}$, and the output variables $\overline{Z}$ are a subset of the program variables $\overline{Y}$.

We assume that we are given a flowchart scheme P and a path σ in P . This path may be from START to STOP or it may be from any statement in P to any other statement in P . We assume that we are given an initial predicate A and final predicate B . We wish to construct mechanically - i.e. by an algorithm which can be implemented on a computer - a VERIFICATION CONDITION $V(P,\sigma,A,B)$ with the following property. We assume now that input variables $\overline{X}$ and program variables $\overline{Y}$ are disjoint.

DEFINITION   A logical formula $V(P,\sigma,A,B)$ is a <u>verification condition</u> for path σ
in scheme P if for every interpretation I of P , A , and B , and every
input $\bar{a}$, whenever:
(1) Program (P,I) starts path σ with $\bar{X} = \bar{a}$ and $\bar{Y} = \bar{b}$ and follows the
     path σ with $\bar{Y} = \bar{b}'$ at the end of the path σ ,
and
(2) $I(A)(\bar{a},\bar{b})$ is true,
     then $I(B)(\bar{a},\bar{b}')$ holds if and only if $I(V(P,\sigma,A,B))(\bar{a},\bar{b})$ is true.

    Thus the path verification condition is required to be true whenever the
initial condition A holds and the path is followed and condition B holds at
the end of the path; it is required to be false whenever the initial condition A
holds and the path is followed but condition B is false at the end of the path.
The verification condition we shall construct will be vacuously true if σ is not
in fact a consistent path or if A does not hold at the start of the path.
    There are several ways of constructing path verification conditions. Our
approach will be to use the algorithm for testing whether a path is consistent which
we have already explored at length, but it will be relativized to starting the
computation at the start of σ rather than at START and ending the computation at
the end of σ rather than at STOP (of course, in some cases σ may begin at START
and end at STOP).
    Let us assume that $\sigma = (\sigma_1,...,\sigma_t)$ with σ_i the address of the statement
executed in step i of path σ . We use the linear representation of P , and
the convention that in a statement k . $T(v_1,...,v_n)$ r,s , r is the address of
the next statement if $T(v_1,...,v_n)$ holds, and s is the address entered if the
test is false. We build up the sets $Q(\sigma,T,\text{TRUE})$ and $Q(\sigma,T,\text{FALSE})$ much as before,
along with the values $val(y,i)$ of each variable at step i in this path. At step
0 we set $val(y,0) = y$ and $val(x,0) = x$ for each program variable y or input
variable x , and all Q sets are empty. We proceed by steps, for i running
from 1 to t . At step 1, σ_1 is executed.
1) If σ_i is assignment statement k . $u \leftarrow f(v_1,...,v_q)$, then set
   $val(u,i) = f(val(v_1,i-1),...,val(v_q,i-1))$, and $val(v,i) = val(v,i-1)$
   for each variable $v \neq u$, and leave the Q sets unchanged.
1') If σ_i is assignment statement k . $u \leftarrow y$ with u and y variables, then
    set $val(u,i) = val(y,i-1)$, and $val(v,i) = val(v,i-1)$ for each variable
    $v \neq u$, and leave the Q sets unchanged.
1") If σ_i is assignment statement k . $u \leftarrow c$ with c a constant, then set
    $val(u,i) = c$ and $val(v,i) = val(v,i-1)$ for each variable $v \neq u$, and
    leave the Q sets unchanged.

2) If σ_i is a conditional transfer $k \cdot T(v_1,\ldots,v_q)$ r,s and $r \neq s$ and
   $i \neq t$, place $(val(v_1,i-1),\ldots,val(v_q,i-1))$ in $Q(\sigma,T,\text{TRUE})$ if $\sigma_{i+1} = r$
   and in $Q(\sigma,T,\text{FALSE})$ if $\sigma_{i+1} = s$; let $val(u,i) = val(u,i-1)$ everywhere.
3) If σ_i is a forced transfer $k \cdot T(v_1,\ldots,v_q)$ r,r or is a conditional
   transfer but $i = t$, make no changes; i.e. leave the Q sets unchanged and
   let $val(u,i) = val(u,i-1)$ everywhere.
4) If σ_i is $k \cdot \text{STOP}$ then of course $t = i$. Then leave the Q sets alone
   and let $val(u,i) = val(u,t) = val(u,i-1)$ everywhere.

Now suppose $\overline{Y} = (y_1,\ldots,y_r)$ and the list of all predicates in P is
$T_1,\ldots,T_s$; we assume that A and B are predicate symbols distinct from all the
T_i . Then we define $V(P,\sigma,A,B)$ as:

$$\left[A(\overline{X},\overline{Y}) \wedge \left(\bigwedge_{i=1}^{s} \left(\bigwedge_{\overline{t}\in Q(\sigma,T_i,\text{TRUE})} T_i(\overline{t}) \right) \wedge \left(\bigwedge_{\overline{t}\in Q(\sigma,T_i,\text{FALSE})} \text{NOT } T_i(\overline{t}) \right) \right) \right]$$

$$\supset B(\overline{X},val(y_1,t),\ldots,val(y_r,t))$$

Observe that if σ is not a consistent path, then the hypothesis in formula
$V(P,\sigma,A,B)$ is always false, i.e., inconsistent, and so $V(P,\sigma,A,B)$ is always true.
Hence in this case, $V(P,\sigma,A,B)$ trivially satisfies the definition of a verification
condition.

For convenience we designate by $V(P,\sigma,A,B,I)$ the formula resulting after
assigning the correct "meanings" to A and B and the function and predicate
symbols of P according to interpretation I - that is, $V(P,\sigma,A,B,I) =$
$I(V(P,\sigma,A,B))$ which can be regarded as the corresponding verification condition
for path σ in program (P,I) with initial condition $I(A)$ and terminal condition
$I(B)$.

Suppose program (P,I) is started at the start of path σ with $\overline{X} = \overline{a}$ and
$\overline{Y} = \overline{b}$, and then follows path σ with $\overline{X} = \overline{a}$ and $\overline{Y} = \overline{b}' = (b_1',\ldots,b_r')$ at the
end of the path. Moreover, suppose that $I(A)(\overline{a},\overline{b})$ is true. By the very definition
of a computation in a scheme under an interpretation, $b_i' = I(val(y_i,t))(\overline{a},\overline{b})$ for
$1 \leq i \leq r$. Notice that if σ is indeed the path followed in these circumstances,
then for $\overline{t}$ in $Q(\sigma,T,\text{TRUE})$, $I(T(\overline{t}))(\overline{a},\overline{b}) = \text{TRUE}$ and for $\overline{t}$ in $Q(\sigma,T,\text{FALSE})$,
$I(T(\overline{t}))(\overline{a},\overline{b}) = \text{FALSE}$ and so $I(\text{NOT } T(\overline{t}))(\overline{a},\overline{b}) = \text{TRUE}$. Hence if $I(A)(\overline{a},\overline{b})$ holds
and σ is the appropriate path, then the hypothesis in the implication in
$V(P,\sigma,A,B,I)$ must be true when evaluated at $\overline{X} = \overline{a}$ and $\overline{Y} = \overline{b}$. Thus
$V(P,\sigma,A,B,I)(\overline{a},\overline{b})$ holds if and only if $I(B)(\overline{a},\overline{b}')$ holds.

LEMMA 5.1 The quantifier-free formula $V(P,\sigma,A,B)$ as defined above satisfies the
definition of a verification condition for path σ in program P .

We might define correctness for a subpath by:

DEFINITION   Program (P,I) and path σ are <u>correct with respect to A and B</u> if whenever A holds at the start of subpath σ in program (P,I) and the program follows σ , then B holds at the end of path σ .

Then we can rephrase the previous lemma by:

LEMMA 5.2   Program (P,I) and path σ are correct with respect to A and B if and only if $\forall \overline{X} \, \forall \, \overline{Y} \, V(P,σ,A,B,I)$ holds over the domain of I (equivalently, if and only if $\forall \overline{X} \, \forall \, \overline{Y} \, V(P,σ,A,B)$ has model I).

EXAMPLE
   Example V-1 gives a simple WHILE scheme P and the program (P,I) under a particular interpretation I . Ultimately we shall verify that program (P,I) does indeed compute z = x! .
   We consider α , β , and γ as names of locations in P and in (P,I) as illustrated. Instead of A and B we shall use as predicate letters $A_α$, $A_β$, $A_γ$.
   For our program (P,I) we shall assign to these extra predicate letters the following meanings.

$$A_α(x,y_1,y_2,z) \text{ under } I : (x \geq 0)$$

$$A_β(x,y_1,y_2,z) \text{ under } I : (x \geq 0) \land (y_2 \geq 0) \land (z = y_1!) \land (x = y_1 + y_2)$$

$$A_γ(x,y_1,y_2,z) \text{ under } I : (z = x!)$$

We consider three paths. Path $σ_1$ is the path from α to β which reaches β only at the end and otherwise does not pass through β . Path $σ_2$ is the path from β back to β once while $σ_3$ is the direct one step path from β to γ .
   Path $σ_1$ encounters no tests so the Q sets are empty and the verification condition $V(P,σ_1,A_α,A_β)$ is constructed as:

$$A_α(x,y_1,y_2,z) \supset A_β(x,c,x,f(c)) .$$

Under interpretation I this becomes $V(P,σ_1,A_α,A_β,I)$:

$$(x \geq 0) \supset [(x \geq 0) \land (x \geq 0) \land ((0 + 1) = 0!) \land (x = (0 + x))]$$

EXAMPLE V-1   A SCHEME P

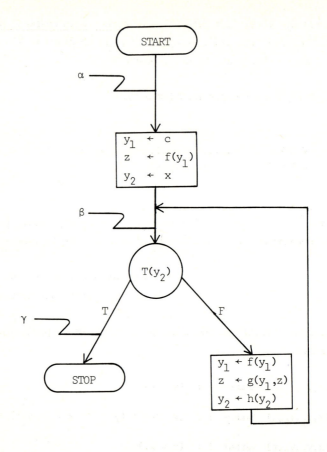

EXAMPLE V-1 (Continued)   PROGRAM (P,I)

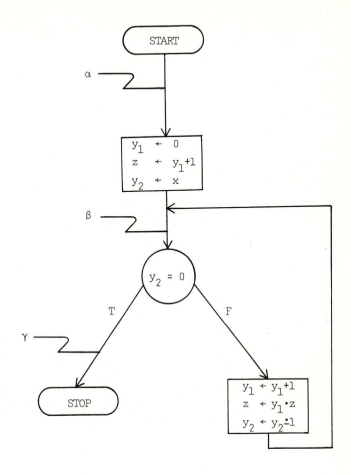

Interpretation I - domain is nonnegative integers, I(c) = 0 ,

I(f)(n) = n+1 ,   I(h)(n) = n ± 1 ,   I(g)(n,m) = n•m ,

I(T)(n) = TRUE if and only if n = 0

This formula is "clearly" true for any integer x. Notice that the truth of the statement is "obvious" because we consider "obvious" the fact that 0 is an identity for addition so $0 + 1 = 1$ and $0 + x = x$ for any x and because "0!" is defined to be 1. These "obvious" facts must be built into any procedure for mechanically verifying such a formula.

Path σ_2 encounters test $T(y_2)$ and is followed only when the outcome of the test is FALSE, so y_2 is in $Q(\sigma_2,T,\text{FALSE})$. Thus the verification condition $V(P,\sigma_2,A_\beta,A_\beta)$ for path σ_2 is:

$$[A_\beta(x,y_1,y_2,z) \wedge \text{NOT } T(y_2)] \supset A_\beta(x,f(y_1),h(y_2,g(f(y_1),z)))$$

Under interpretation I this becomes:

$$[(x \geq 0) \wedge (y_2 \geq 0) \wedge (z = y_1!) \wedge (x = y_1 + y_2) \wedge (y_2 \neq 0)]$$

$$\supset [(x \geq 0) \wedge ((y_2 \overset{.}{-} 1) \geq 0) \wedge ((y_1 + 1) \cdot z = (y_1 + 1)!)$$

$$\wedge (x = y_1 + 1) + (y_2 \overset{.}{-} 1))]$$

To see that this formula is true for all nonnegative integers x, y_1, y_2 and z one must know various "obvious" facts about addition, monus and minus, and manipulation of identities (the meaning of " = " in such a formula) - for example, that if $y_2 \neq 0$ and y_2 is a nonnegative integer, then $(y_1 + 1) + (y_2 \overset{.}{-} 1)$ $= (y_1 + 1) + (y_2 - 1) = y_1 + (1 + (y_2 + (-1))) = y_1 + ((y_2 + (-1)) + 1) = y_1 + (y_2 + (-1 + 1))$ $= y_1 + (y_2 + 0) = y_1 + y_2$ - for another example, somewhat more subtle, that the formula $z = y_1!$ in the hypothesis means that in the conclusion, $y_1!$ can be substituted for z anywhere. It is fairly clear that such abilities must be built into any useful mechanical theorem prover and indeed that sort of thing has been successfully implemented several times. However, verification of this formula also requires "knowing" that $(n+1)! = (n+1) \cdot n!$ Building this into the verification procedure is, intuitively, tantamount to knowing already that (P,I) is correct with respect to A_α and A_γ - that it does compute $z = x!$.

For σ_3, the final verification condition is:

$$[A_\beta(x,y_1,y_2,z) \wedge T(y_2)] \supset A_\gamma(x,y_1,y_2,z)$$

Under I this is interpreted:

$$[(x \geq 0) \wedge (y_2 = 0) \wedge (z = y_1!) \wedge (x = y_1 + y_2) \wedge (y_2 = 0)] \supset (z = x!)$$

which we can verify using simple facts about addition, 0, and identity.

If the flowchart P has a loop-free graph - if P is a tree - then the construction of $W(P,A,B)$ is now quite simple. If P is loop-free there are only a finite number of paths $\sigma_1,\ldots,\sigma_n$ from START to STOP which are consistent and hence execution sequences. The input condition $A(\overline{X})$ is a function only of the inputs, of course, while the output condition $B(\overline{X},\overline{Y})$ can be regarded as a function of the input and of the final values of all the program variables (some of these values, of course, may play no role in the statement of the condition). Notice that under these conditions, when σ_i is a complete execution sequence from START to STOP, the path verification condition $V(P,\sigma_i,A,B,I)$ for any interpretation I is a function of the input $\overline{X}$ alone.

DEFINITION   If P has a loop-free graph, let

$$W(P,A,B) = V(P,\sigma_1,A,B) \ \wedge \ \ldots \ \wedge \ V(P,\sigma_n,A,B)$$

where $\sigma_1,\ldots,\sigma_n$ is the list of all execution sequences of P.

For convenience we shall let $W(P,A,B,I)$ stand for $I(W(P,A,B))$; notice that it, too, is a function of $\overline{X}$.

First suppose that (P,I) is totally correct with respect to A and B . Consider any input vector $\overline{a}$. Notice that by our previous results each conjunct $V(P,\sigma_i,A,B,I)(\overline{a})$ in the formula $W(P,A,B,I)(\overline{a})$ is of the form $Z_i \supset B(\overline{a},\overline{b})$ where formula Z_i is true if and only if $A(\overline{a})$ holds under interpretation I(i.e., $I(A)(\overline{a})$ is true) and σ_i is the path actually followed by computation $(P,I,\overline{a})$. Further, if σ_i is the correct path of the computation, then $\overline{b}$ is the value of the vector $\overline{Y}$ at the end of the computation. Thus if $A(\overline{a})$ is false under I , each Z_i is false and so the conditional is vacuously true and $W(P,A,B,I)(\overline{a})$ is true. If $A(\overline{a})$ is true and the computation followed path σ_i , then Z_j is false for $j \neq 1$ and so $V(P,\sigma_j,A,B,I)(\overline{a})$ true, while Z_i is true. Since (P,I) is totally correct with respect to A and B , $B(\overline{a},\overline{b})$ must also hold and $V(P,\sigma_i,A,B,I)(\overline{a})$ be true. So in this case, $W(P,A,B,I)(\overline{a})$ is true. Hence if (P,I) is totally correct with respect to A and B , I is a model under which $\forall \overline{X} \ W(P,A,B)$ is satisfied.

On the other hand, suppose I is a model under which $\forall \overline{X} \ W(P,A,B)$ is satisfied - that is, $W(P,A,B,I)(\overline{a})$ holds for every input $\overline{a}$ in the domain of I . Consider any input $\overline{a}$ for which $A(\overline{a})$ is true. Now P is loop-free and so always halting; there is a path σ_i which computation $(P,I,\overline{a})$ follows from START to STOP. Thus Z_i is true here, and for $W(P,A,B,I)(\overline{a})$ to hold, in particular $V(P,\sigma_i,A,B,I)(\overline{a})$ must hold and thus $B(\overline{a},\overline{b})$ must be true under I , where $\overline{b}$ is the vector of values of $\overline{Y}$ at the end of the computation.

We have shown that:

THEOREM 5.3   Let P be a program scheme with a loop-free graph, and let I be
any interpretation of P . Program (P,I) is totally correct with respect to A
and B if and only if $\forall \overline{X} W(P,A,B,I)$ is valid (equivalently, if and only if
$\forall \overline{X} W(P,A,B)$ is satisfied by model I).

Thus verification of programs with loop-free flowcharts is simple (in theory)
- try verifying all possible paths. Of course, this exhaustive search procedure
is seldom practicable.

We can restate Theorem 5.3 for the special case of always halting schemes.
Suppose a program scheme P with a loop-free graph has input variables $\overline{X}$ which
are not program variables and output variable set $Z = (z_1,...,z_r)$ disjoint from
$\overline{X}$. Assume that at the end of every completed path (whenever STOP is reached)
each z_i is specified. For any execution sequence σ , let val(u,σ) denote the
value of variable u after the computation of P on a free interpretation I_σ
following path σ . Let $B_\sigma(\overline{X},\overline{Z}) = (z_1 = \mathrm{val}(z_1,\sigma)) \wedge ... \wedge (z_r = \mathrm{val}(z_r,\sigma))$ and
$\rho(P,\sigma) = V(P,\sigma,\mathrm{TRUE},B_\sigma)$. Finally, if $\sigma_1,...,\sigma_n$ is a list of all the execution
sequences in P , let

$$\rho(P) = \rho(P,\sigma_1) \wedge ... \wedge \rho(P,\sigma_n) .$$

Now the arguments for Theorem 5.3 can be used to show that (P,I) is totally
correct with respect to TRUE and $I(\rho(P))$. Thus we can show (cf Theorem A.1 in the
appendix).

COROLLARY 5.4   If P is an always halting program scheme we can construct a
quantifier-free well-formed formula $\rho(P)$ such that P is totally correct with
respect to TRUE and $\rho(P)$.

B.   PROGRAM VERIFICATION
   Now we are ready to tackle the more general case in which the flowchart does
have loops. We first examine the mathematical justification for the verification
procedure and then outline the procedure and discuss various problems connected
with it.
   We are going to introduce new predicates and new predicate letters to fill
certain special roles. To avoid too much notational complication, let us introduce
some conventions. The formula we shall develop for P containing A and B as
dummy symbols we shall call W(P) . When the predicates A   - the input condition

- and B - the output condition - have been specified we use the notation W(P,A,B) to indicate that the actual interpreted predicates have been substituted for A and B . Finally when the function and predicate letters of P have been replaced by their "meanings" in an interpretation I , we denote this by W(P,A,B,I) . We may regard W(P,A,B,I) as a partial interpretation of W(P) . We shall soon see why it is in general only a "partial" interpretation of W(P) . It is W(P,A,B,I) with which we shall be most concerned, for this will express set of verification conditions for the whole program (P,I) .

The new predicates we add are called <u>inductive assertions</u> and are assigned to certain preselected points in the program. These points can be selected quite freely, subject to certain conditions, so this set S of <u>induction points</u> will not be unique; this will mean that W(P) is not itself unique but is really "subscripted" by S . The choice of S is not significant as to the theory but may be very important as to the applications.

DEFINITION   For a flowchart scheme P , a set S of addresses in P is a set of <u>induction points</u> if:
(1) S contains the address of the initial statement and the addresses of all STOP statements, and
(2) S cuts all loops in P .

If S is a set of induction points, there is a finite set $\Pi(S)$ of all path segments which start with a member of S , end with a member of S and otherwise do not pass through any point of S . Every path from START to STOP can be divided into path segments from $\Pi(S)$. Sets with these properties do exist; for example, the set of all addresses in P is certainly a candidate for S . For a WHILE scheme, it suffices to include in S the initial statement, all STOP statements, and the start of each WHILE statement.

To each point t in S we assign an arbitrary predicate letter A_t which corresponds to a predicate $A_t(\overline{X},\overline{Y})$, except that the input condition predicate $A(\overline{X})$ is always assigned to the initial point in the scheme and the ouput condition predicate $B(\overline{X},\overline{Y})$ is always assigned to all STOPs in the scheme. Thus every node or address in S is tagged with a predicate which we call an <u>inductive assertion</u>.

From the paths in $\Pi(S)$ we can select the set $\{\sigma_1,\ldots,\sigma_m\}$ containing all and only consistent paths which start at a tagged point, end at a tagged point and otherwise do not pass through any tagged point. Suppose each σ_i starts at t_i and ends at r_i (in some cases we have $t_i = r_i$) . Then we define W(P) as the well-formed formula:

$$V(P,\sigma_1,A_{t_1},A_{r_1}) \land \ldots \land V(P,\sigma_m,A_{t_m},A_{r_m})$$

Now suppose that I is an interpretation of P and meanings have been assigned to A and B; we shall use A instead of $I(A)$ and B instead of $I(B)$. Further assume that we have somehow extended I to an interpretation I' which assigns inductive assertions to the letters A_t and so to the tagged points t. We shall likewise use A_t for $I'(A_t)$. Finally, suppose that under these circumstances I' is now a model for $\forall \bar{X} \forall \bar{Y} W(P,A,B)$, i.e. $\forall \bar{X} \forall \bar{Y} W(P,A,B,I)$ holds over the domain of I under these inductive assertions. Let us see what this implies.

Let $\bar{a}$ be an input vector such that $A(\bar{a})$ holds and computation $(P,I,\bar{a})$ halts with output $\bar{b}$. This computation follows some path σ which can be divided into segments $\tau_1, \ldots, \tau_q$ such that each τ_i starts at tagged point t_i in S and ends with tagged point t_{i+1} in S and does not pass through any member of S otherwise, and furthermore t_1 is the START or initial statement and t_{q+1} is a STOP statement. Let $\bar{b}_i$ be the vector of values of $\bar{Y}$ at the end of path segment τ_i of this computation. We can set $\bar{b}_0$ arbitrarily just for convenience in the inductive argument, since the registers in $\bar{Y}$ are initially unspecified and must be assigned during the computation. Note that $\bar{b}_q = \bar{b}$, the vector of values at the end of the computation.

We now establish by induction on i that $A_{t_i}(\bar{a}, \bar{b}_{i-1})$ holds for $1 \leq i \leq q+1$. Clearly $A_{t_1}(\bar{a}, \bar{b}_0) = A(\bar{a})$ by definition and $A(\bar{a})$ holds by hypothesis. Suppose we have established the desired result for all $i < k$ and let us consider A_{t_k}. Since I' is a model for $\forall \bar{X} \forall \bar{Y} W(P,A,B)$ each of the conjuncts must be true for $\bar{X} = \bar{a}$ and $\bar{Y} = \bar{b}_{k-2}$. In particular, $V(P, \tau_{k-1}, A_{t_{k-1}}, A_{t_k}, I')(\bar{a}, \bar{b}_{k-2})$ must hold, since τ_{k-1} is one of the consistent path segments σ_i in $\Pi(S)$. By the induction hypothesis, $A_{t_{k-1}}(\bar{a}, \bar{b}_{k-2})$ must hold; by assumption τ_{k-1} is the legitimate path segment in this situation ending with $\bar{Y} = \bar{b}_{k-1}$. Thus the hypotheses in the path verification condition $V(P, \tau_{k-1}, A_{t_{k-1}}, A_{t_k}, I')$ must hold by the same arguments we saw before and thus the conclusion must also be true; that is, $A_{t_k}(\bar{a}, \bar{b}_{k-1})$ must hold.

If we consider the special case $k = q+1$, then $A_{t_{q+1}}(\bar{a}, \bar{b}_q) = B(\bar{a}, \bar{b})$ also holds. So we have shown that for any input for which condition A is satisfied, and for which program (P,I) halts, condition B holds for the output. In other words, (P,I) is partially correct with respect to A and B.

We we have established first:

LEMMA 5.5 Let (P,I) be a program with input criterion A and output criterion B. Suppose that $A(\bar{a})$ holds, $(P,I,\bar{a})$ converges with output $\bar{b}$ and we have an assignment of inductive assertions under which $\forall \bar{Y} W(P,A,B,I)(\bar{a})$ holds, i.e. $\forall \bar{Y} W(P,A,B,I)(\bar{a})$ is satisfiable. Then $B(\bar{a}, \bar{b})$ is true.

More generally, we have:

THEOREM 5.6   For a flowchart scheme P and interpretation I of P with input condition A and output condition B , if I can be extended to an interpretation I' by assigning meanings to the inductive assertions such that I' is a model for $\forall \overline{X} \forall \overline{Y} W(P,A,B)$, then (P,I) is partially correct with respect to A and B .

We can also establish a converse of sorts. We have shown that if one is clever enough to find inductive assertions - Boolean functions to assign to the various A_t - such that the compound verification condition W(P,A,B) holds everywhere in the domain of I , then in fact (P,I) is partially correct with respect to A and B . If one guessed wrong and the verification condition does not hold, however, this says nothing as to the correctness of (P,I) . It may be that (P,I) is partially correct with respect to A and B and one or more of the inductive assertions is "wrong" and will not give us the desired answer. Or (P,I) may indeed not be partially correct with respect to A and B . We will never find out which, in this fashion, although the way in which the particular inductive assertions fail us and the verification conditions are violated may give us clues as to the location and nature of the possible bugs in our program.
     However, what we can say is that if (P,I) is partially correct with respect to A and B , then some choice of inductive assertions will work - there are inductive assertions (but we may of course not be able to find them) which assigned to the A_t make $\forall \overline{X} \forall \overline{Y} W(P,A,B,I)$ true.
     The assertions which will always work are the obvious ones and of no use in any practical situation. Namely, let $A_t(\overline{a},\overline{b})$ be true if and only if $A(\overline{a})$ holds and the computation $(P,I,\overline{a})$ at some point enters tagged point t with $\overline{Y} = \overline{b}$. (Under this definition, A_t is partial computable, if A is, but not necessarily computable and of course if we had a handy way of expressing and computing this sort of A_t we could easily verify our program ad hoc.) So let us assume that (P,I) is partially correct with respect to A and B and see what this means.
     We wish to see that for any choice of $\overline{X} = \overline{a}$ and $\overline{Y} = \overline{b}$ each path verification condition in W(P,A,B,I) holds. That is, we must examine each $V(P,\sigma,A_t,A_r,I)(\overline{a},\overline{b})$ where σ is a consistent path from tagged point t to tagged point r not passing through any other tagged point en route from t to r . If the hypothesis of the conditional expression $V(P,\sigma,A_t,A_r,I)(\overline{a},\overline{b})$ is false, then the verification condition is vacuously true. If it is true, then $A_t(\overline{a},\overline{b})$ is true and by definition of A_t , $A(\overline{a})$ is true and computation $(P,I,\overline{a})$ at some point enters tagged point t with $\overline{Y} = \overline{b}$. Further σ is the continuation of this computation and reaches r with $\overline{Y} = \overline{b}'$. So there is certainly a time when computation $(P,I,\overline{a})$ reaches r with this specification of $\overline{Y}$. Now if r is not a STOP statement, inductive assertion A_r was assigned by our definition and thus $A_r(\overline{a},\overline{b}')$ holds by definition.

But this is the conclusion in conditional expression $V(P,\sigma,A_t,A_r,I)(\bar{a},\bar{b})$ and so the whole expression is true. On the other hand, if r is the STOP statement, we can now conclude that computation $(P,I,\bar{a})$ halts at point r with output $\bar{b}'$. Since (P,I) is partially correct for A and B , $B(\bar{a},\bar{b}')$ holds. As this is the conclusion of $V(P,\sigma,A_t,B,I)(\bar{a},\bar{b})$, the verification condition $V(P,\sigma,A_t,B,I)$ is also true for $\bar{X} = \bar{a}$ and $\bar{Y} = \bar{b}$. Since this holds for all conjuncts, we can conclude that $W(P,A,B,I)(\bar{a},\bar{b})$ is true. This applies to any choice of $\bar{a}$ and $\bar{b}$, so we see that $\forall X \forall Y W(P,A,B,I)$ is satisfiable.

Thus we have:

LEMMA 5.7   Let (P,I) be a program with input predicate A and output predicate B . If $A(\bar{a})$ and $B(\bar{a},\bar{b})$ are true and $(P,I,\bar{a})$ halts with output $\bar{b}$, then there is a choice of inductive assertions under which

$$\forall \bar{Y} W(P,A,B,I)(\bar{a})$$

holds.

Putting everything together:

THEOREM 5.8   For any program (P,I) and any input predicate A and output predicate B , (P,I) is partially correct with respect to A and B if and only if I can be extended to a model for $\forall \bar{X} \forall \bar{Y} W(P,A,B,I)$.

EXAMPLE

Let us return briefly to Example V-1. Our choice of tagged points α , β , and γ was not accidental, nor was our selection of A_α , A_β , and A_γ . Let the input condition be $A(x) : (x \geq 0)$ and the output condition $B(x,z) : (z = x!)$ Thus $A = A_\alpha$ and $B = A_\gamma$. We can regard our selection of A_β , namely:

$$(x \geq 0) \wedge (y_2 \geq 0) \wedge (z = y_1!) \wedge (x = y_1 + y_2)$$

as the inductive assertion for point β . Then the three paths in $\Pi(S)$ for $S = \{\alpha,\beta,\gamma\}$ are the paths we have previously called σ_1 , σ_2 and σ_3 and the condition $W(P,A,B,I)$ is

$$V(P,\sigma_1,A,A_\beta,I) \wedge V(P,\sigma_2,A_\beta,A_\beta,I) \wedge V(P,\sigma_3,A,B,I)$$

We have already seen that each of these path verification conditions holds for all choices of x,y_1,y_2 and z . Since $\forall x(U \wedge V)$ is always logically equivalent to $(\forall x U) \wedge (\forall x V)$, we have shown that $W(P,A,B,I)$ holds for all x,y_1,y_2 and z

in the domain of I . Thus $\forall x \forall y_1 \forall y_2 \forall z \ W(P,A,B,I)$ is true for this assignment of A_β and hence (P,I) is partially correct for A and B , as claimed.

Of course we are usually interested in verifying not just partial correctness but also total correctness. We can do so using a variant of the previous methods, using now a formula $\exists \overline{X} \forall \overline{Y} \ [A(\overline{X}) \wedge W(P,A,\text{NOT } B,I)]$.

First suppose that we are dealing with input criterion A and program (P,I) . If t is not a STOP statement, let inductive assertion $A_t(\overline{a},\overline{b})$ hold if and only $A(\overline{a})$ holds and computation $(P,I,\overline{a})$ ever enters tagged point t with $\overline{Y} = \overline{b}$. The previous arguments (in the proof of Lemma 5.7) show that $V(P,\sigma,A_{t_1},A_r,I)(\overline{a},\overline{b})$ must hold for any $\overline{a}$ and $\overline{b}$ and any consistent path segment σ from tagged point t to tagged point r not passing through any other tagged point for which r is not the STOP statement. What about $V(P,\sigma,A_t,B,I)(\overline{a},\overline{b})$ if σ ends in tagged point r which is a STOP? Suppose $A(\overline{a})$ holds. Then if the hypothesis of $V(P,\sigma,A_t,B,I)(\overline{a},\overline{b})$ holds, computation $(P,I,\overline{a})$ enters t with $\overline{Y} = \overline{b}$ and then follows σ to r and halts, so $(P,I,\overline{a})$ converges. Thus if $A(\overline{a})$ holds but $(P,I,\overline{a})$ diverges, the hypothesis of $V(P,\sigma,A_t,B,I)(\overline{a},\overline{b})$ must be false for all B and $\overline{b}$ and so $V(P,\sigma,A_t,B,I)(\overline{a},\overline{b})$ must be vacuously true. Putting this together we see that:

LEMMA 5.9   If program (P,I) fails to halt for any input $\overline{a}$ for which $A(\overline{a})$ holds, then for any output criterion B , $\exists \overline{X} \forall \overline{Y} \ [A(\overline{X}) \wedge W(P,A,B,I)]$ is satisfiable. Alternatively, if for any input criterion A and output criterion B , $\exists \overline{X} \forall \overline{Y} \ [A(\overline{X}) \wedge W(P,A,B,I)]$ is not satisfiable, then (P,I) halts for any input satisfying input criterion A .

Now consider output criterion $B = \text{FALSE}$ - i.e. B never holds and suppose $\exists \overline{X} \forall \overline{Y} \ [A(\overline{X}) \wedge W(P,A,\text{FALSE},I)]$ is satisfiable. Thus we have input $\overline{X} = \overline{a}$ and a choice of inductive assertions A_t such that $\forall \overline{Y} \ [A(\overline{a}) \wedge W(P,A,\text{FALSE},I)(\overline{a})]$ holds. In particular, $A(\overline{a})$ holds. Suppose $(P,I,\overline{a})$ converges with output $\overline{b}$. By Lemma 5.5, $B(\overline{a},\overline{b}) = \text{TRUE}$, which is nonsense. Hence $(P,I,\overline{a})$ does not halt.

Thus:

LEMMA 5.10   Let (P,I) be a program with input criterion A . If $\exists \overline{X} \forall \overline{Y} \ [A(\overline{X}) \wedge W(P,A,\text{FALSE},I)]$ is satisfiable, then there is some input $\overline{a}$ for which $(P,I,\overline{a})$ fails to halt but $A(\overline{a})$ is true.

Finally:

THEOREM 5.11   Program (P,I) fails to halt for some input satisfying input
condition A if and only if $\exists \overline{X} \; \forall \; \overline{Y} \; [A(\overline{X}) \wedge W(P,A,FALSE,I)]$ is satisfiable.
Alternatively, program (P,I) halts for all input satisfying input condition A
if and only if $\exists \; \overline{X} \; \forall \; \overline{Y} \; [A(\overline{X}) \wedge W(P,A,FALSE,I)]$ is not satisfiable.

We can now give the corresponding result for total correctness. First,
suppose (P,I) is <u>not</u> totally correct for A and B . Either
(1) for some $\overline{a}$, $A(\overline{a})$ holds but $(P,I,\overline{a})$ diverges
or
(2) for some $\overline{a}$, $A(\overline{a})$ holds and $(P,I,\overline{a})$ converges with output $\overline{b}$ but
   $B(\overline{a},\overline{b})$ is false.
In case (1), Lemma 5.9 tells us that $\exists \; \overline{X} \; \forall \; \overline{Y} \; [A(\overline{X}) \wedge W(P,A,B,NOT\ B,I)]$ is
satisfiable (since it is satisfiable for any choice of output criterion). In case
(2), NOT $B(\overline{a},\overline{b})$ is true so by Lemma 5.7 (taking $\overline{X} = \overline{a}$)
$\exists \; \overline{X} \; \forall \; \overline{Y} \; [A(\overline{X}) \wedge W(P,A,NOT\ B,I)]$ is satisfiable (because $A(\overline{a})$ is true and
$\forall \; Y \; W(P,A,NOT\ B,I)(\overline{a})$ is satisfiable).
   Now conversely suppose $\exists \; \overline{X} \; \forall \; \overline{Y} \; [A(\overline{X}) \wedge W(P,A,NOT\ B,I)]$ is satisfiable. In
particular, suppose we have input $\overline{a}$ and a choice of inductive assertions for
which $\forall \; \overline{Y} \; [A(\overline{a}) \wedge W(P,A,NOT\ B,I)(\overline{a})]$ holds. If $(P,I,\overline{a})$ fails to converge,
(P,I) cannot be totally correct for input criterion A and any output criterion.
If $(P,I,\overline{a})$ converges with output $\overline{b}$, by Lemma 5.5, NOT $B(\overline{a},\overline{b})$ is true and
$B(\overline{a},\overline{b})$ is false and so (P,I) is not totally correct for A and B .
   Concluding:

THEOREM 5.12   Program (P,I) is not totally correct with respect to A and B
if and only if $\exists \; \overline{X} \; \forall \; \overline{Y} \; [A(\overline{X}) \wedge W(P,A,NOT\ B,I)]$ is satisfiable. Alternatively
(P,I) is totally correct with respect to A and B if and only if
$\exists \; \overline{X} \; \forall \; \overline{Y} \; [A(\overline{X}) \wedge W(P,A,NOT\ B,I)]$ is not satisfiable.

EXAMPLE
   Returning to Example V-1 we see that the "falsification" condition,
$\exists \; x \; \forall \; y_1 \; \forall \; y_2 \; \forall \; z \; [A(x) \wedge W(P,A,FALSE,I)]$ becomes:

$$\exists \; x \; \forall \; y_1 \; \forall \; y_2 \; \forall \; z \; [(x \geq 0) \wedge [((x \geq 0) \supset A_\beta(x,0,x,1))$$

$$\wedge \; ((A_\beta(x,y_1,y_2,z) \wedge (y_2 \neq 0)) \supset A_\beta(x,y_1+1,y_2 \doteq 1,(y_1+1)\cdot z))$$

$$\wedge \; ((A_\beta(x,y_1,y_2,z) \wedge (y_2 = 0)) \supset FALSE)]]$$

One can show that this formula is inconsistent over the domain of I . The argument would run roughly like this: let $n \geq 0$ be such that the formula holds for all y_1 , y_2 and z and $x = n$; let m be the smallest nonnegative integer such that $A_\beta(n,i,m,j)$ holds for some i and j . Since $n \geq 0$, $A_\beta(n,0,n,1)$ holds so there is some such m ; if $m = 0$, "FALSE" holds, a contradiction. But if $m \geq 1$, then $A_\beta(n,i+1,m-1,(i+1)\cdot j)$ also holds, contradicting the minimality of m . Hence there is no such integer n and the condition is unsatisfiable. However, it is obviously simpler to observe that over the given domain the WHLLE construction is in fact a STEP x construction and hence the program loop ends after x steps.

Examining what we have done so far, we see that $W(P)$ and so $W(P,A,B,I)$ consists of a conjunction of formulae $V(P,\sigma,A_t,A_r)$ for all paths σ starting at a tagged position and ending at a tagged position but not passing through any tagged position otherwise. Thus to verify partial correctness it suffices to find inductive assertions under which the verification conditions will hold for these individual paths.

So the verification procedure can be divided into steps:

1) Input the program (P,I) .

2) Input a choice of tagged points S .

3) Input a choice of inductive assertions A_t for each tagged point t in S .

4) Mechanically generate all verification conditions $V(P,\sigma,A_t,A_r,I)$ from the formal specification of program, set S of tagged points, and inductive assertions assigned to the tagged points.

5) Send verification conditions into a THEOREM PROVER. If all conditions are proven correct, print "PARTIALLY CORRECT WITH RESPECT TO A AND B " . If any verification condition is either proven incorrect by the THEOREM PROVER or else is rejected or not handled by the THEOREM PROVER, return to either 2) or 3), calling for new input.

There are pitfalls at all steps in the procedure. First the format for representing the program must be carefully thought out. The generation of verification conditions in 4) certainly can be done automatically, but again their format and presentation is of some importance. All this can affect the performance of the THEOREM PROVER.

The most obvious difficulty lies in the choice of inductive assertions. A wrong choice says nothing about the correctness of the program. One might say that the programmer should be able to provide inductive assertions - should have some idea what is going on at a particular point in the program. This is unfortunately often wishful thinking for various reasons. Using structured programming methods may help but is not a complete cure. This emphasizes the generally accepted need for better documentation methods, but is not the whole answer. The programmer may know what is supposed to occur at a given tagged point and may document this well enough to satisfy a human user, but may nevertheless not specify the inductive assertion in enough detail to satisfy the THEOREM PROVER. This is a very serious problem since the conditions left out may seem so obvious or irrelevant to the programmer as not to be worth specifying or so subtle that only an attempt to verify incomplete conditions will bring it out, and the final inductive assertions may prove very unwieldy. There are different heuristics to apply, of varying degrees of obviousness, and we shall point out a few in our examples.

What about mechanical generation of inductive assertions? This cannot be done in toto. There is no procedure which by exhaustive search - even unlimited exhaustive search - will eventually come up with "good" inductive assertions and establish partial correctness whenever partial correctness holds (or even when total correctness holds) even for very simple interpretations. In the next chapter we shall examine the reasons behind this phenomenon. The best one can hope for is some sort of interactive heuristic procedure in which the machine and programmer produce the assertions, the machine possibly providing some of the little details the programmer might forget or be unaware of; even in this more modest goal one must realize that success is not certain and sometimes programmer and machine together will not be able to verify partial correctness.

Even if the "right" inductive assertions are fed into the machine (and there is of course no unique right set of tagged points or inductive assertions), neither the practical nor the theoretical problems end there. There are still problems with the mechanical THEOREM PROVER. It is verifying conditions and checking expressions for tautologies in a fairly rich theory including identity, constants, arithmetic of the natural numbers, and probably much more complicated constructs. The predicates A and B have to be described properly for the THEOREM PROVER to deal with them. In the little example we saw - how do you describe " n! " ? Do you feed it in as a primitive together with a series of axioms to go with it? Or do you define it recursively from more basic operations? In the latter case you might realize in our example that you have really fed into THEOREM PROVER the fact that our program for n! is correct - in short you have built in what the machine is supposed to prove! This is a simplistic example of course, but the basic problem is real - getting the THEOREM PROVER to deal with some of the rather sophisticated primitives available in many programming languages and getting the programmer to describe the possibly yet more sophisticated notions behind the definition of "correct behavior" for a particular program.

The reader should NOT be deluded into thinking that the rather smooth and neat way in which Example V-1 was handled represents the "real life" situation, even for relatively small programs.

We shall conclude this chapter with further examples and a slightly different approach to verification. At the end of Chapter VII (on recursion augmented schemes) we discuss one method of extending verification to programs with procedures and calls.

C. FURTHER EXAMPLES

We shall illustrate and extend the ideas in the last section by looking at some further examples, one in our invented WHILE programming language, and others in "real" programming languages.

Example V-2 gives a program to compute a binomial coefficient, $z = \begin{pmatrix} x_1 \\ x_2 \end{pmatrix}$ subject to x_1 and x_2 being integers and $0 \le x_2 \le x_1$. The tagged points are the START and STOP points and α and β which are the start of the two WHILE loops in the program. The second page of the example gives the verification terms in terms of A, B, A_α, and A_β. Notice that we have already taken tacit liberties with our procedure - for example we have observed that at point α, y_4 and y_5 are "dummy" variables whose values are of no importance and hence A_α is not a function of y_4 and y_5.

What shall our inductive assertions be? For simplicity we shall assume that we are only dealing with the domain of nonnegative integers and thus statements such as "$x_1, x_2, y_1, y_2, y_3, y_4$ and y_5 are nonnegative integers" shall be omitted from the inductive assertions; strictly speaking, they should be included. We notice that node α dominates node β and there is no way of entering the second WHILE statement except through having the test "$y_1 \ne 0$" be positive; since we are dealing with nonnegative numbers, y_1 is always greater than or equal to 1 when we reach point β. Thus it is certainly safe to place "$y_1 \ge 1$" in the inductive assertion for A_β. Likewise we notice that in passing from α to β, y_4 and y_5 are respecified and z is multiplied by y_3 but the other variables are unchanged; thus it is safe to add $A_\alpha(x_1, x_2, y_1, y_2, y_3, z/y_3)$ to the conditions for A_β. Similarly, since input variables x_1 and x_2 are never changed during the program, we can add the input condition $A(x_1, x_2)$ to both A_α and A_β. These are heuristics which one can readily understand and implement without undue difficulty. The general idea is to search for "fail-safe conditions" which must by the flow of control be true whenever a tagged point is reached and routinely add these conditions to the inductive assertions for that point. These extra conditions may or may not be useful but they cannot "hurt". A scan of the verification conditions with abstract assertions (dummy symbols for the inductive assertions) is often useful in this respect.

EXAMPLE V-2   VERIFICATION OF A WHILE PROGRAM TO COMPUTE A BINOMIAL COEFFICIENT

START

$y_1 \leftarrow x_1 \dot{-} x_2$

$y_2 \leftarrow 1$

$z \leftarrow 1$

IF $y_1 \dot{-} x_2 = 0$ THEN $y_3 \leftarrow x_2 + 1$

             ELSE $y_3 \leftarrow y_1 + 1$

                    $y_1 \leftarrow x_2$

α ENDIF

WHILE $y_1 \neq 0$ DO

        $z \leftarrow z \cdot y_3$

        $y_4 \leftarrow 1$

        $y_5 \leftarrow y_2$

β WHILE $z \dot{-} y_5 \neq 0$ DO

                $y_4 \leftarrow y_4 + 1$

                $y_5 \leftarrow y_5 + y_2$

        ENDWHILE

        $z \leftarrow y_4$

        $y_1 \leftarrow y_1 \dot{-} 1$

        $y_2 \leftarrow y_2 + 1$

        $y_3 \leftarrow y_3 + 1$

ENDWHILE

STOP

EXAMPLE V-2 (Continued)   VERIFICATION CONDITIONS WITH ABSTRACT ASSERTIONS

(1) $[A(x_1,x_2) \land ((x_1 \dotminus x_2) \dotminus x_2 = 0)] \supset A_\alpha(x_1,x_2,x_1 \dotminus x_2,1,x_2+1,1)$

(2) $[A(x_1,x_2) \land ((x_1 \dotminus x_2) \dotminus x_2 \neq 0)] \supset A_\alpha(x_1,x_2,x_2,1,(x_1 \dotminus x_2)+1,1)$

(3) $[A_\alpha(x_1,x_2,y_1,y_2,y_3,z) \land (y_1 \neq 0)] \supset A_\beta(x_1,x_2,y_1,y_2,y_3,1,y_2,z \cdot y_3)$.

(4) $[A_\alpha(x_1,x_2,y_1,y_2,y_3,z) \land (y_1 = 0)] \supset B(x_1,x_2,z)$

(5) $[A_\beta(x_1,x_2,y_1,y_2,y_3,y_4,y_5,z) \land (z \dotminus y_5 \neq 0)] \supset A_\beta(x_1,x_2,y_1,y_2,y_3,y_4+1,y_5+y_2,z)$

(6) $[A_\beta(x_1,x_2,y_1,y_2,y_3,y_4,y_5,z) \land (z \dotminus y_5 = 0)] \supset A_\alpha(x_1,x_2,y_1 \dotminus 1,y_2+1,y_3+1,y_4)$

INDUCTIVE ASSERTIONS

Input Assertion $A(x_1,x_2)$: $x_2 \leq x_1$

Output Assertion $B(x_1,x_2,z)$: $z = \binom{x_1}{x_2}$

$A_\alpha(x_1,x_2,y_1,y_2,y_3,z)$: $(x_2 \leq x_1) \land (y_1 + y_2 = 1 + \mathrm{Min}(x_2,x_1-x_2)) \land (y_1+y_3 = x_1 + 1)$

$$\land \; (1 \leq y_2 \leq y_3) \land (y_1 < y_3)$$

$$\land \; (z = \binom{y_3 - 1}{y_3 - y_2})$$

$A_\beta(x_1,x_2,y_1,y_2,y_3,y_4,y_5,z)$: $A_\alpha(x_1,x_2,y_1,y_2,y_3,z/y_3)$

$$\land \; (1 \leq y_5 = y_4 \cdot y_2 \leq z) \land (y_1 \geq 1)$$

A slightly more subtle heuristic lies behind the conditions "$y_1 + y_2 = 1 + Min(x_2, x_1 - x_2)$" and "$y_1 + y_3 = x_1 + 1$" in A_α. A quick scan of verification conditions (5) and (6) shows that within the main loop whenever y_1 is decreased by 1 (and we have already agreed that at β, $y_1 \geq 1$ and so $y \doteq 1 = y - 1$) then y_2 and y_3 are increased by 1 and otherwise y_1, y_2 and y_3 are unchanged. Thus the strategy is to describe $y_1 + y_2$ and $y_1 + y_3$ as constants (with respect to x_1 and x_2 which do not change). Examining verification conditions (1) and (2) indicates that the first test really decides which is the minimum of $x_1 \doteq x_2$ and x_2 and that y_1 is then specified as $Min(x_2, x_1 - x_2)$ and y_3 as $Max(x_2, x_1 - x_2) + 1$ and y_2 as 1 in all cases, so $y_1 + y_3 = (x_1 \doteq x_2) + x_2 + 1 = x_1 + 1$, whence the desired relations. The same considerations tell us we must have "$1 \leq y_2 \leq y_3$" at α and hence at β since that condition obtains when y_2 and y_3 are first specified and y_2 and y_2 are incremented together; the reason for "$y_1 < y_3$" is similar.

The other conditions depend on knowledge of the algorithm involved. The condition "$1 \leq y_5 = y_4 \cdot y_2 \leq z$" in A_β reflects the fact that the inner loop is used to divide z by y_2 and the condition on z in A_α reflects the method for computing $\binom{n}{k}$ used – namely, instead of computing $\binom{n}{k}$ by first computing $n!$ and then dividing by $k!$ and $(n-k)!$ (a method which is undesirable for large n since $n!$ will cause overflow long before $\binom{n}{k}$ itself gets out of hand) one computes successively $\binom{k}{k}$, $\binom{k+1}{k}$, $\binom{k+2}{k}$, ... using the recurrence relation $\binom{n}{k} = \frac{n}{n-k} \binom{n-1}{k}$.

The interested reader can construct the complete verification conditions and notice what "obvious facts" are needed to check them. For example, to verify (1) one must know that $\binom{n}{n} = 1$, to verify (4) that $k \leq n$ implies $\binom{n}{k} = \binom{n}{n-k}$, to verify (5) that $k \leq n$ implies $n\binom{n-1}{n-k}$ is divisible by k, and to verify (6) the recurrence relation above.

Example V-3 is taken from "The Elements of Programming Style" by Kernighan and Plauger. It is a Fortran subroutine for sorting an array of N numbers into increasing order. As it is, it does not appear amenable to our methods. However, we can translate it into the WHILE program shown, with input variables X_o and n and output and program variable X. This is an "array augmented" flowchart, because we have allowed as variables not only "simple" variables (e.g. SAVE), but variables containing arrays (e.g. X and X_o) and subscripted variables such as $X(1)$ or $X(I)$. These are to be interpreted in the obvious fashion – X is an array of N variables, $X(1), X(2), ..., X(N)$. We have special subscript registers, in this example I and J, which contain integers for subscripts and to which instructions such as $I \leftarrow 1$ or $I \leftarrow I + 1$ can be applied. An expression $X(I)$ refers to the value of that variable $X(i)$ such that i is the contents of I. The special predicate DIMENSION $U(V)$ is true if and only if V contains an integer

EXAMPLE V-3   VERIFICATION OF A FORTRAN SUBROUTINE FOR AN INTERCHANGE SORT

```
      SUBROUTINE SORT  (X,N)

      DIMENSION  X(N)

C              SORT INCREASING, BY INTERCHANGE

      IF  (N.LT.2)  RETURN

      DO  20  I = 2,N

         DO  10  J = 1,I

            IF  (X(I) . GE. X(J))  GOTO  10

               SAVE = X(I)

               X(I) = X(J)

               X(J) = SAVE

10       CONTINUE

20    CONTINUE

      RETURN

      END
```

EXAMPLE V-3 (Continued)

AN ARRAY AUGMENTED FLOWCHART VERSION OF THE PREVIOUS SUBROUTINE

START

$X \leftarrow X_o$

$N \leftarrow n$

IF NOT DIMENSION X(N) LOOP ENDIF

IF NOT (N < 2) THEN $I \leftarrow 2$;

α ~~~~~~~~~~~~~~~~~~~ WHILE $I \leq N$ DO

$J \leftarrow 1$

β ~~~~~~~~~~~ WHILE $J \leq I$ DO

IF NOT $(X(I) \geq X(J))$ THEN

$SAVE \leftarrow X(I)$;

$X(I) \leftarrow X(J)$;

$X(J) \leftarrow SAVE$;

ENDIF

$J \leftarrow J + 1$

ENDWHILE

$I \leftarrow I + 1$

ENDWHILE

ENDIF

STOP

m and U is an array of dimension m . Any incorrect usage of these variables causes the whole instruction to be ignored - e.g. an instruction u ← V(L) is ignored if L does not contain a proper subscript, or if V is not an array variable or if L contains i , and V is an array variable but V(i) is undefined so far. This augmentation of flowcharts does not precisely correspond to the definition which we discuss in Chapter VII, but is close enough for our present purposes.

The translation of the original Fortran subroutine to this augmented WHILE program can be done mechanically. Now we can apply our techniques, keeping in mind the semantics involved. Then input condition A is:

$A(X_0,n)$: X_0 is an array of n numbers

and output condition B can be described as:

$B(X_0,n,X)$: (X_0 is an array of n numbers) ∧ (X is a permutation of X_0)
   ∧ (the numbers of X are sorted in increasing order,
       $X(1) \leq X(2) \leq ... \leq X(n)$)

We select the start of the two WHILE statements as tagged points. Using the "fail-safe" strategy mentioned before, we can place "$2 \leq I \leq N+1$" into A_α and "$2 \leq I \leq N$" and "$1 \leq J \leq I+1$" into A_β , as well as the input condition A . Finishing the definition of inductive assertions depends on observing how the subroutine behaves.

So we can have as inductive assertions:

$A_\alpha(X_0,X,N,I)$:   (X_0 is an array of N numbers)
           ∧ (X is a permutation of X_0)
           ∧ ($2 \leq I \leq N+1$)
           ∧ (For $1 \leq i \leq I-2$, $X(i) \leq X(i+1)$)

$A_\beta(X_0,X,N,I,J)$:   (X_0 is an array of N numbers)
           ∧ (X is a permutation of X_0)
           ∧ ($2 \leq I \leq N$) ∧ ($1 \leq J \leq I+1$)
           ∧ (For $1 \leq i \leq J-2$, $X(i) \leq X(i+1)$)
           ∧ (For $J \leq i \leq I-2$, $X(i) \leq X(i+1)$)
           ∧ (If $J \neq 1$, then $X(J-1) \leq X(I)$)

There are 7 paths to verify: one from START to STOP not passing through α , one from START to α , one from α to β , one from α to STOP and two from β back to β and one from β up to α . (Why is there no need to verify the path for which DIMENSION X(N) is false?) We leave it to the reader to check out these path verification conditions.

Perhaps the most important thing to notice is that there is really no need to convert to flowchart form as we did; once one gets the "hang" of it, the verification can be done directly for the Fortran subroutine.

Example V-4 is also from "The Elements of Programming Style". It is a piece of PL/I code which runs through a list of numbers determining whether or not they are prime; it tacitly assumes that the input is integer (which might have been checked elsewhere).

We could have transferred this program into flowchart format fairly simply. Instead we have marked it up for our purposes. The first thing we did in editing is to omit the comments, which are, however, useful in composing inductive assertions. Since we are only interested in checking that one sweep through the program correctly determines whether INPUT is prime, we have treated every return to the initial statement, labelled by ST1 , as a STOP statement. Thus there are 3 stops in the program. We have tagged the initial line by START and the input predicate

$A(X)$: X is an integer

and each of the stops by STOPi and the output condition $B(X,Z)$:

If X is a positive prime integer, Z = "X IS A PRIME NUMBER"

If X is an integer greater than or equal to 4 which is not
         prime, Z = "X IS NOT A PRIME NUMBER"

Otherwise, Z = "ILLEGAL INPUT N = X"

We also tag the DO loop with Tag1 and the inductive assertion $A_1(X,N,R)$. One candidate for A_1 in which the first 5 conjuncts come from our "fail-safe" heuristic and the last two from examination of the code is:

$(N > 3)$ $\wedge$ $(N = X)$ $\wedge$ (X is an integer) $\wedge$ $(2 \leq R \leq SQRT(N) + 2)$

$\wedge$ (R is an integer)

$\wedge$ (if R = 3 , 2 does not divide N)

$\wedge$ (if R > 3 , i does not divide R for $2 \leq i \leq R - 2$)

Since we are only checking correctness of algorithm, we ignore the format of the output (PUT EDIT) statement and translate it into a straight output specification. In some cases one might want to use inductive assertions to check output presentation, once correctness has otherwise been verified (subject only to these output instructions being themselves correct).

EXAMPLE V-4   VERIFICATION OF A PIECE OF PL/I CODE FOR DECIDING IF N IS PRIME

```
ST1: GET LIST  (N) ;
     IF  N < = 1  THEN
         DO;
             PUT EDIT ('ILLEGAL INPUT  N=' ,  N ,  ' < = 1' )
                 (SKIP ,  X(10) ,  A ,  F(5) ,  A) ;
             GOTO  ST1 ;
         END;
     IF  N > 3  THEN
         DO  R = 2,3  TO  SQRT(N)  BY  2 ;  /* R = 2,3,5,7,...*/
         IF  MOD(N,R) = 0  THEN
             DO;
                 PUT EDIT (N ,  'IS NOT A PRIME NUMBER')
                     (SKIP,  F(15) ,  A) ;
                 GOTO  ST1 ;
             END;
         END;


/* GET HERE FOR  N = 2  OR  3  OR IF FALL OUT OF LOOP*/
   PUT EDIT (N ,  'IS A PRIME NUMBER')(SKIP, F(15), A);
   GOTO  ST1 ;
```

EXAMPLE V-4 (Continued)   THE CODE EDITED FOR VERIFICATION


```
        START ∿∿∿  N ← X
   A(X)
                IF  N < = 1  THEN

                            OUTPUT ← " 'ILLEGAL INPUT N = ' N " < = 1'"
        STOP1 ∿∿∿∿∿∿∿∿∿∿∿∿∿∿∿
   B(X)
                END;

                IF  N > 3  THEN

        Tag1 ∿∿∿∿∿∿∿∿∿∿∿∿ DO  R = 2,3  TO  SQRT(N)  BY  2 ;
A₁(X,N,R)
                        IF  MOD(N,R) = 0  THEN

        STOP2 ∿∿∿∿∿∿∿∿∿∿∿∿∿∿∿∿ Z ← " N 'IS NOT A PRIME NUMBER' "
   B(X,Z)
                        END;

                END;

                Z ← " N  ' IS A PRIME NUMBER' "

        STOP3 ∿∿∿∿∿∿∿
   B(X,Z)
```

To illustrate what is happening, we write out the paths and verification conditions in terms of A , B and A_1 ; it is left to the reader to check out the actual conditions. The set of tagged points is
$S = \{START, STOP1, STOP2, STOP3, Tag1\}$.

(1)   START to STOP1:

   $[A(X) \wedge (X < = 1)] \supset B(X , \text{"ILLEGAL INPUT } N = X < = 1")$

(2)   START to Tag1

   $[A(X) \wedge (NOT (X < = 1)) \wedge (X > 3)] \supset A_1(X,X,2)$

(3)   START to STOP3

   $[A(X) \wedge (NOT (X < = 1)) \wedge (NOT (X > 3))] \supset B(X , \text{"X IS A PRIME NUMBER")}$

(4)   Tag1 to Tag1   -   there are really two paths for $R = 2$ and $R \neq 2$ and two conditions:

   $[A_1(X,N,2) \wedge (2 \leq SQRT(N)) \wedge (MOD(N,R) \neq 0)] \supset A_1(X,N,3)$

   and

   $[A_1(X,N,R) \wedge (R \geq 3) \wedge (R \leq SQRT(N)) \wedge (MOD(N,R) \neq 0)] \supset A_1(X,N,R+2)$

(5)   Tag1 to STOP2   -   there are really two paths as in (4), but one condition will do:

   $[A_1(X,NR) \wedge (R \leq SQRT(N)) \wedge (MOD(N,R) = 0)] \supset B(X, \text{"X IS NOT A PRIME NUMBER")}$

(6)   Tag1 to STOP3

   $[A_1(X,N,R) \wedge (R = SQRT(N) + 2)] \supset B(X , \text{"X IS A PRIME NUMBER")}$

D.   AXIOMATIC APPROACH

A variant of the method discussed in this chapter has been proposed by C. A. R. Hoare using a set of axioms and rules of inference to establish partial correctness of programs. The method of Hoare appears more flexible in that axioms and rules can be introduced to cover various constructs of particular programming languages and their implementations, but also appears, at least to this author, even more cumbersome and unwieldy than the Floyd-Manna-King approach when applied to simple flowchart-like programs. The formal mathematical justification for both approaches is the same. Basically, the approach used to date employs "forward substitution" from hypothesis assertion to conclusion assertion while the Hoare method uses "backwards substitution". Which method is preferable depends partly on one's taste and partly on the individual program under discussion. At times a combination or alternation of forward and backward substitutions might be more efficient.

We need to introduce more notation. First, the usual logical notation

$$\vdash W$$

implies that W is a theorem in our system - based on our set of axioms and rules of inference we have shown that W holds for all values of its variables over the domain of interest. The special notation introduced by Hoare is $A \{P\} B$.

DEFINITION   Let P be a program or piece of program and let A and B be assertions. If whenever A is true before the execution of P and P terminates then B is true of the values after the termination of P , we write $A \{P\} B$. If this can be formally proven in the axiom system, write $\vdash A \{P\} B$.

Hoare also uses the notation S_E^x when S and E are expressions and x is a variable to stand for the result of substituting E for x everywhere in S ; similarly, $S_{a,b,c}^{x,y,z}$ or $S_{\bar{a}}^{\bar{x}}$ would be the result of substituting a for x , b for y and c for z , if $\bar{x} = (x,y,z)$ and $\bar{a} = (a,b,c)$, etc.

If $x \leftarrow E$ is an assignment statement, x is an identifier for a simple variable and E is an expression of a programming language without side effects but possibly containing x , then the Axiom of Assignment is:

DO $\vdash A_E^x \{x \leftarrow E\} A$

Notice that this reverses the way we have been treating assignment statements in path verification conditions. Essentially we have been saying that to prove that B holds of the values after assignment $x \leftarrow E$ if A holds previously, one must establish $\vdash A \supset B_E^x$. Actually that is merely a difference in viewpoint, not in methodology, and the mathematical justification is the same.

One can provide rules for the three methods of composing WHILE programs, for example. If P_1 and P_2 are pieces of a program, we can state the Rule of Composition:

D1   If $\vdash A \{P_1\} A_1$ and $\vdash A_1 \{P_2\} B$, then $\vdash A \{P_1;P_2\} B$

Informally it can be phrased: suppose whenever A holds before P_1 , A_1 holds afterwards and whenever A_1 holds before P_2 , B holds afterwards; then if A holds and $\{P_1;P_2\}$ follows, B holds afterwards.

For a conditional IF-THEN or IF-THEN-ELSE construction we can state the Rules of Conditional Statements:

D2   If $\vdash (A \wedge Q) \{P_1\} B$, then $\vdash A \{IF \ Q \ THEN \ P_1 \ ENDIF\} B$

       IF $\vdash (A \wedge Q) \{P_1\} B$ and $\vdash (A \wedge NOT \ Q) \{P_2\} B$, then

       $\vdash A \{IF \ Q \ THEN \ P_1 \ ELSE \ P_2 \ ENDIF\} B$

In a WHILE construction, WHILE Q DO P_1 ENDWHILE , notice that Q can be assumed true when P_1 is initiated and false when the WHILE loop is ended (if it ever is). Thus if it is true that whenever A and Q hold at the start of P_1 , then A holds at the end of P_1 , then it is also true that whenever A holds at the start of the WHILE loop, then at the end A holds and NOT Q is true. Formally we can state the Rule of Iteration

D3   If $\vdash (A \wedge Q) \{P_1\} A$, then $\vdash A \{WHILE \ Q \ DO \ P_1 \ ENDWHILE\} (A \wedge NOT \ Q)$

We need some rules of inference, to allow us to deduce new "theorems" from the theorems and axioms already established. The simplest choice of inference rules for our system is perhaps the Rules of Consequence:

D4   If $\vdash A \{P\} B$ and $\vdash B \supset B_1$ then $\vdash A \{P\} B_1$

       If $\vdash A_1 \{P\} B$ and $\vdash A \supset A_1$ then $\vdash A \{P\} B$

Using D0 and D4 we can show that our treatment of assignments and Hoare's are basically the same. The Manna approach essentially has one verify $\vdash A \supset B_E^x$ in order to assert what is in Hoare's notation $\vdash A \{x \leftarrow E\} B$. But D0 gives us $\vdash B_E^x \{x \leftarrow E\} B$ and so if we also have $\vdash A \supset B_E^x$, then D4 gives us $\vdash A \{x \leftarrow E\} B$ as claimed. Thus one is only discussing whether the selection of assertions is done "bottom-up" from desired conclusion (B) to sufficient (but perhaps not necessary) hypothesis (A) or "top-down" from A to B . In actual practice, inductive assertions may be assigned by both strategies.

For an example of this approach, we return to the simple program in Example V-1; this is already complicated enough to prevent a completely detailed and rigorous proof. We can write this program as:

1		$y_1 \leftarrow 0$
2		$z \leftarrow y_1 + 1$
3		$y_2 \leftarrow x$
4		WHILE $y_2 \neq 0$ DO
41		$y_1 \leftarrow y_1 + 1$
42		$z \leftarrow y_1 \cdot z$
43		$y_2 \leftarrow y_2 \doteq 1$
		ENDWHILE
5		STOP

We shall refer to statements by the labels to their left, for convenience. Recall that the inductive assertion $A_\beta(x, y_1, y_2, z)$ was:

$$(x \geq 0) \wedge (y_2 \geq 0) \wedge (z = y_1!) \wedge (x = y_1 + y_2)$$

Instead of verifying the path from 1 to 4 , we now want to prove

$$\vdash \quad A \{1,2,3\} A_\beta$$

Applying rule DO three times from 3 back to 1 we get:

$$\vdash (x \geq 0) \wedge (x \geq 0) \wedge (z = y_1!) \wedge (x = y_1 + x) \{3\} (x \geq 0) \wedge (y_2 \geq 0) \\ \wedge (z = y_1!) \wedge (x = y_1 + y_2)$$

$$\vdash (x \geq 0) \wedge (x \geq 0) \wedge (y_1 + 1 = y_1!) \wedge (x = y_1 + x) \{2\} (x \geq 0) \wedge (x \geq 0) \\ \wedge (z = y_1!) \wedge (x = y_1 + x)$$

$$\vdash (x \geq 0) \wedge (x \geq 0) \wedge (0 + 1 = 0!) \wedge (x = 0 + x) \{1\} (x \geq 0) \wedge (x \geq 0) \\ \wedge (y_1 + 1 = y_1!) \wedge (x = y_1 + x)$$

Putting these together by two uses of the Rule of Composition D1 we get:

$$\vdash (x \geq 0) \wedge (x \geq 0) \wedge (0 + 1 = 0!) \wedge (x = 0 + x) \{1,2,3\} (x \geq 0) \wedge (y_2 \geq 0) \\ \wedge (z = y_1!) \wedge (x = y_1 + y_2)$$

In order to deduce $A \{1,2,3\} A_\beta$, we need to apply an axiom of arithmetic:

A1 $\vdash\ x + 0 = 0 + x$

an axiom concerning the factorial:

F1 $\vdash\ 1 = 0!$

a rule of inference regarding identity:

I1   If $\vdash\ u = v$ then $\vdash\ A \supset A_v^u$ and $\vdash\ A \supset A_u^v$

and three other rules of inference:

R1   If $\vdash\ A$ then $\vdash\ B \supset (A \wedge B)$
R2   If $\vdash\ A$ and $\vdash\ A \supset B$ then $\vdash\ B$
R3 $\vdash\ (A \wedge B) \supset (A \wedge A \wedge B)$

From A1 and F1 we have

$\vdash\ 0 + 1 = 1$ and $\vdash\ 1 = 0!$

Applying I1 we have

$\vdash\ (0 + 1 = 1) \supset (0 + 1 = 0!)$

and from R2

$\vdash\ 0 + 1 = 0!$

Two applications of R1 will give

$\vdash\ [(x \geq 0) \wedge (x \geq 0)] \supset [(x \geq 0) \wedge (x \geq 0) \wedge (0 + 1 = 0!) \wedge (x = 0 + x)]$

whence by R3 and R2

$\vdash\ (x \geq 0) \supset [(x \geq 0) \wedge (x \geq 0) \wedge (0 + 1 = 0!) \wedge (x = 0 + x)]$

and finally the Rule of Consequence D4 yields

$\vdash\ (x \geq 0) \{1,2,3\} (x \geq 0) \wedge (y_2 \geq 0) \wedge (z = y_1!) \wedge (x = y_1 + y_2)$

The proof that $\vdash A_\beta \wedge (y_2 \neq 0) \{41,42,43\} A_\beta$ is even longer so we shall skip several formal steps which are purely applications of rules of inference of the propositional calculus with identity. We start working back by:

$$\vdash (x \geq 0) \wedge ((y_2 \doteq 1) \geq 0) \wedge (z = y_1!) \wedge (x = y_1 + (y_2 \doteq 1)) \{43\} (x \geq 0)$$
$$\wedge (y_2 \geq 0) \wedge (z = y_1!) \wedge (x = y_1 + y_2)$$

$$\vdash (x \geq 0) \wedge ((y_2 \doteq 1) \geq 0) \wedge (y_1 \cdot z = y_1!) \wedge (x = y_1 + (y_2 \doteq 1)) \{42\} (x \geq 0)$$
$$\wedge ((y_2 \doteq 1) \geq 0) \wedge (z = y_1!)$$
$$\wedge (x = y_1 + (y_2 \doteq 1))$$

$$\vdash (x \geq 0) \wedge ((y_2 \doteq 1) \geq 0) \wedge ((y_1 + 1) \cdot z = (y_1 + 1)!) \wedge (x = (y_1 + 1) + (y_2 \doteq 1))$$
$$\{41\} (x \geq 0) \wedge ((y_2 \doteq 1) \geq 0)$$
$$\wedge (y_1 \cdot z = y_1!) \wedge (x = y_1 + (y_2 \doteq 1))$$

and finally from D1

$$(x \geq 0) \wedge ((y_2 \doteq 1) \geq 0) \wedge ((y_1 + 1) \cdot z = (y_1 + 1)!) \wedge (x = (y_1 + 1) + (y_2 \doteq 1))$$
$$\{41,42,43\} (x \geq 0) \wedge (y_2 \geq 0) \wedge (z = y_1!)$$
$$\wedge (x = y_1 + y_2)$$

Now we must add another factorial axiom

F2 $\quad \vdash (y + 1) \cdot y! = (y + 1)!$

and various arithmetic axioms regarding $+$ and $\doteq$ in order to be able to deduce using the usual rules of inference:

$$\vdash [A_\beta(x,y_1,y_2,z) \wedge (y_2 \neq 0)] \supset [(x \geq 0) \wedge ((y_2 \doteq 1) \geq 0)$$
$$\wedge ((y_1 + 1) \cdot z = (y_1 + 1)!) \wedge (x = (y_1 + 1) + y_2 \doteq 1))]$$

This will finally by D4 produce

$$\vdash A_\beta \wedge (y_2 \neq 0) \{41,42,43\} A_\beta$$

Now the Rule of Iteration yields:

$$\vdash A_\beta \{4\} A_\beta \wedge (y_2 = 0)$$

More formal manipulation will show

$$\vdash \quad A_\beta \ \land \ (y_2 = 0) \ \supset \ B$$

whence by D4

$$\vdash \quad A_\beta \ \{4\} \ B$$

and finally by D1

$$A \ \{1,2,3,4,5\} \ B$$

which verifies the program.

Observe that we have in this procedure worked out some of the steps previously left to the THEOREM PROVER. The previous procedure involves having the programmer select a set of inductive assertions and critical points, and then feed this into the computer parts: a VERIFICATION CONDITION GENERATOR and a THEOREM PROVER. In this alternative construction we still need inductive assertions as the nature of the Rule of Iteration for WHILE statements shows. Now the inductive assertions are fed directly into the THEOREM PROVER which has been augmented by the special axioms and rules D0,D1,D2,D3 and D4 in addition to all of the usual arithmetic axioms, rules of inference, rules for handling identities and special axioms for the primitives in question (such as the factorial axioms in our example). In effect the THEOREM PROVER works backwards from the output condition and the various inductive assertions using D0 - D3 to find what amounts to path verification conditions - implications $\vdash R \supset S$ it must establish. It turns its heavy machinery to work on these implications and if it succeeds everywhere will eventually use D1 - D4 and these implications to finally prove the verification theorem.

It does not seem clear which procedure is easier to implement or more efficient (if and when it works!). Both can be augmented to handle other constructions in any particular programming language. The first procedure is augmented by changing the PATH VERIFICATION CONDITION GENERATOR and the second by adding additional axioms or rules to the THEOREM PROVER.

VI. DECISION PROBLEMS

In this chapter we shall be concerned with some of the more formal aspects of
the subject, primarily with establishing the decidability or undecidability of some
of the properties we have been discussing such as equivalence and partial
correctness. We shall assume that the reader is familiar with the basic concepts
and results regarding computability and Turing machines although no knowledge of
proofs or precise formalisms is needed. We shall give our proofs in more detail
and somewhat more formally than in most of the previous sections. The reader
uninterested in the mathematical properties of schemes can skip most of this
chapter, but should at least peek at the theorems which state that almost everything
interesting about schemes or programs is undecidable. This is not meant as a
discouraging word, but rather to establish the limits of the theory and how far we
can go with ad hoc methods, special cases and interactive procedures before running
aground.

Let us review some definitions and facts. A function f from a set A to a
set B is total if it is defined on all of A ; it is partial if it is defined on
some subset of A (which might be A itself, a proper subset of A , or even the
empty set). The domain of f is that subset of A on which f is defined while
the range of f is $\{f(a) \mid f$ is defined on $a \in A\}$, the set of values of f .
The partial characteristic function of a set L is the function which has value 1
(or YES or TRUE) for members of L and which is undefined outside of L ; the
characteristic or total characteristic function of L is the function whose value
is 1 (or YES or TRUE) for members of L and is 0 (or NO or FALSE) outside of L .

There are several equivalent ways of defining a recursively enumerable set or
predicate.

DEFINITION   A set is recursively enumerable (r.e.) if and only if there is a Turing
machine which when given as input a member of the set will eventually halt and give
a YES answer but when given an input not in the set will either give a NO answer or
fail to halt.
A set is r.e. if and only if it is the range of a total recursive (total computable)
function.
A set is r.e. if and only if it is the domain of a partial recursive (partial
computable) function.
A set is r.e. if and only if its partial characteristic function is partial
recursive (partial computable).

There are various ways of defining a recursive set.

DEFINITION   A set is <u>recursive</u> if and only if there is a Turing machine which
always halts and tells whether or not the input belongs to the set (answer YES if
it does and NO if it does not).
A set is recursive if and only if its total characteristic function is total
recursive (total computable).
A set is recursive if and only if both it and its complement are recursively
enumerable.

The fact that a set is recursive if (and only if) both it and its complement
are recursively enumerable is very important. If we have two procedures, one which
always halts and gives a YES when the input is in set R , set but otherwise may
not halt and one which always halts and gives a NO answer when the input is not in
R but otherwise may not halt, we can put them together and get an algorithm which
does one step of the first procedure and then one step of the second procedure in
alternation and halts and gives the answer provided by whichever procedure halts
first.

Suppose we have a class C of objects for which a property P may or may not
be true and recursive set A of names of C such that $C = \{c_a \mid a \in A\}$. Each
member of C has at least one name; some members may have several or even
infinitely many names. However, each name in A refers to exactly one member of
C . Then we say that P is <u>decidable</u> for C   - really for the set of names A
for C   - if the set

$$\{a \in A \mid P \text{ holds for } c_a\}$$

is recursive. In other words, P is decidable for C as described by A if and
only if there is a Turing machine which on input a halts and gives the answer YES
if P holds for c_a and gives the answer NO if c_a does not have property P .

A property P is <u>partially decidable</u> if the set $\{a \in A \mid P \text{ holds for } c_a\}$
is recursively enumerable. That is, P is <u>partially decidable</u> if there is a Turing
machine which halts and gives answer YES on input a if c_a has property P and
which will either halt and give answer NO or else loop forever if c_a does not have
property P .

We shall use without proof the following basic fact of computability theory.

THEOREM 6.1   It is not partially decidable whether a Turing machine diverges on the
blank initial tape.

A. TWO TAPE FINITE STATE ACCEPTORS

We shall find it more convenient to use a result on two-tape finite state machines rather than directly employ the result for Turing machines. We shall consider a finite state machine with two tapes, each with its own read-only head moving from left to right, and observe its behavior when each tape has the same input.

DEFINITION   A <u>two-tape one-way deterministic finite state acceptor</u> $M = (K_1, K_2, \Sigma, \delta, q_o, q_a, q_r)$ consists of:

(1)   Two finite disjoint sets of <u>states</u>, K_1 and K_2 , a designated <u>initial state</u> q_o in $K_1 \cup K_2$, an <u>accepting state</u> q_a and a <u>rejecting state</u> q_r with neither q_a nor q_r in $K_1 \cup K_2$,

(2)   A finite set Σ of <u>input symbols,</u>

and

(3)   A <u>transition function</u> δ from $(K_1 \cup K_2) \times \Sigma$ into $(K_1 \cup K_2 \cup \{q_a, q_r\}) - \{q_o\}$.

An <u>instantaneous description</u> of M is a triple (q, w_1, w_2) containing the current state q of M , the input w_1 on Tape 1 which remains to be scanned and the input w_2 on Tape 2 which remains to be scanned. If $q \in K_1$ and $p = \delta(q,a)$ for a in Σ , we write $(q, aw_1, w_2) \vdash (p, w_1, w_2)$; if $q \in K_2$ and $p = \delta(q,a)$ for a in Σ , we write $(q, w_1, aw_2) \vdash (p, w_1, w_2)$. Then $\overset{*}{\vdash}$ is defined as the reflexive transitive closure of $\vdash$ in the usual way. That is $A \overset{*}{\vdash} A$, and $A \overset{*}{\vdash} B$ and $B \overset{*}{\vdash} C$ imply $A \overset{*}{\vdash} C$. We say that M <u>accepts</u> a pair of tapes (w_1, w_2) , finite or infinite, if $(q_o, w_1, w_2) \overset{*}{\vdash} (q_a, w_1', w_2')$ for any terminal subtapes w_1' of w_1 and w_2' of w_2 , while M <u>rejects</u> (w_1, w_2) if $(q_o, w_1, w_2) \overset{*}{\vdash} (q_r, w_1', w_2')$. If (w_1, w_2) is a pair of infinite tapes and M neither accepts nor rejects any pair (w_1', w_2') such that w_1' is a finite initial substring of w_1 and w_2' is a finite initial substring of w_2 , then M <u>diverges</u> on (w_1, w_2) . Let $L_a(M)$ be the set of all pairs of tapes <u>accepted</u> by M , $L_r(M)$ the set of all pairs of tapes <u>rejected</u> by M and $L_d(M)$ set of all the pairs of infinite tapes on which M <u>diverges</u>. Two machines M_1 and M_2 are <u>equivalent</u> if $L_a(M_1) = L_a(M_2)$ and $L_r(M_1) = L_r(M_2)$.

Observe that M accepts or rejects a tape if and only if it accepts or rejects some pair of finite initial subtapes. The sets $L_a(M)$ and $L_r(M)$ are always disjoint. If M_1 is equivalent to M_2 we necessarily have $L_d(M_1) = L_d(M_2)$.

An infinite tape w is <u>ultimately periodic</u> if $w = uvvv \ldots$ for finite tapes u,v with $v \neq e$, i.e. if w can be written as a finite (possibly empty) initial string u followed by arbitrarily many repetitions of a nonempty finite string v . We need the next result which relates Turing machines and two-tape acceptors with special attention to behavior on ultimately periodic input tapes.

THEOREM 6.2 For each Turing machine T , one can construct a two-tape one-way deterministic finite state acceptor M_T such that if $D = \{(w,w) \mid w$ input tape, finite or infinite$\}$:

(1) M_T never diverges on (w,w) if w is ultimately periodic, and

(2) $L_a(M_T) \cap D = \phi$ if and only if $L_d(M_T) \cap D \neq \phi$ if and only if T diverges when its initial input is the completely blank tape.

PROOF

We only sketch the construction, since this is not a treatise on computability theory. Suppose T has vocabulary V with blank symbol $B \in V$ and state set K , $K \cap V = \phi$ and initial state q_o . Let $\mathop{\mbox{\textcent}}$ be a new symbol. An instantaneous description (ID) of T can be written as xqy for $x,y \in V^*$, y nonempty, and q in K if the current tape contents is xy , T is in state q and T is scanning the symbol to the right of q - the rightmost symbol of y . We assume that T always sees a new blank symbol B when it is about to fall off its right or left edge. The computation of T on an initially blank tape can be described as C ; $q_oB \vdash w_1 \vdash w_2 \vdash \ldots$ and can be encoded as $E(C) = \mathop{\mbox{\textcent}}q_oB\mathop{\mbox{\textcent}}\mathop{\mbox{\textcent}}w_1\mathop{\mbox{\textcent}}\mathop{\mbox{\textcent}}\mathop{\mbox{\textcent}}w_2\mathop{\mbox{\textcent}}\mathop{\mbox{\textcent}}\mathop{\mbox{\textcent}}w_3\ldots$, assuming that new blanks B are added to the instantaneous description only as needed - i.e. when T goes left or right of its current tape.

Now M_T searches for input pair $(E(C),E(C))$. It acts as follows on input (w,w) :

(1) First M_T checks on Tape 2 that w starts with $\mathop{\mbox{\textcent}}q_oB$. If it does not M_T goes to q_r and if it does, M_T moves just right of B .

(2) If M_T has just scanned $\mathop{\mbox{\textcent}}^{n+1}w_n$ on Tape 2 and is positioned on Tape 1 at the start of this substring $(\mathop{\mbox{\textcent}}^{n+1}w_n)$, then M_T simultaneously scans $\mathop{\mbox{\textcent}}^{n+1}w_n$ on Tape 1 and scans to see whether the next substring on Tape 2 is $\mathop{\mbox{\textcent}}^{n+2}w_{n+1}$. Notice that ID w_{n+1} can differ in at most three positions from ID w_n (i.e., state, symbol scanned and symbol left of scanned symbol if the move is left). So this check requires M_T to remember at most the last 3 symbols at one time, which a finite state device can do. If M_T does not find this substring next on Tape 2 it goes to q_r and halts; otherwise it has just scanned $\mathop{\mbox{\textcent}}^{n+2}w_{n+1}$ on Tape 2 and is positioned to scan this same substring on Tape 1.

(3) If M_T during its scan of Tape 2 recognizes that it has just seen $\mathop{\mbox{\textcent}}^{n+1}w_n$ where w_n is a terminating or halting ID, then M_T halts in state q_a . Since this condition of w_n depends solely on the state and current symbol scanned, a finite state machine can easily recognize it.

Observe that this procedure stops only if either M_T in (2) recognizes that it is not scanning a pair starting $(E(C),E(C))$ and goes to q_r and rejects or if M_T in (3) recognizes that C is finite and that the input starts with $(E(C),E(C))$ and so M_T goes to q_a and accepts. Notice that since we have forced successive blocks of ¢'s to become larger and larger, if w is ultimately periodic it cannot be $E(C)$ for C infinite, and so M_T will never diverge on (w,w) if w is ultimately periodic.

Thus M_T accepts (w,w) if and only if $E(C)$ is an initial substring of w and C is finite. Thus $L_a(M_T) \cap D = \phi$ if and only if T diverges on the initial blank tape. Similarly, M_T diverges on (w,w) if and only if $w = E(C)$ and C is infinite. Hence $L_d(M_T) \cap D \neq \phi$ if and only if T diverges on the initial blank tape. ∎

Suppose it were partially decidable for two-tape one-way deterministic finite state acceptors M whether $L_a(M) \cap D = \phi$. Then we would have a partially computable decision procedure $\mathscr{P}$ (implementable by a Turing machine) which given the name of a two-tape one-way deterministic finite state acceptor M will halt and give answer YES if $L_a(M) \cap D = \phi$ while it either halts and answers NO or else never halts if $L_a(M) \cap D \neq \phi$. Now we can take the algorithm $\mathscr{A}$ of the previous theorem (total recursive function, implementable by an always halting Turing machine) which transforms the name of a Turing machine T into the name of a two-tape one-way deterministic finite state acceptor M_T such that $L_a(M_T) \cap D = \phi$ if and only if T diverges on the initially blank tape. We hook $\mathscr{A}$ to $\mathscr{P}$ to form $\mathscr{P}'$:

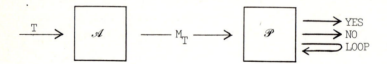

Clearly $\mathscr{P}'$ is itself a partially computable decision procedure.

If Turing machine T diverges on the initially blank tape, and $\mathscr{P}'$ is given the name of T as input, $\mathscr{P}'$ will transform T into M_T and discover via $\mathscr{P}$ that $L_a(M_T) \cap D = \phi$ and then halt with the answer YES. If T halts on the initially blank tape, when $\mathscr{P}'$ receives the name of T as input it changes T to M_T and, since $L_a(M_T) \cap D \neq \phi$, either halts with answer NO or else loops forever. Thus it would be partially decidable (by $\mathscr{P}'$) whether T diverges on the initially blank tape. But this is known to be false. Hence it is not partially decidable whether $L_a(M) \cap D = \phi$ for two-tape one-way deterministic finite state machines M . Since the algorithm $\mathscr{A}$ produced a machine M_T which was guaranteed to halt on (w,w) for w ultimately periodic, there cannot be such a partial decision procedure $\mathscr{P}$ even for machines guaranteed to halt on (w,w) for w ultimately periodic. The same argument applies to the problem $L_d(M) \cap D \neq \phi$.

Hence we have shown that:

THEOREM 6.3   The following problems are not partially decidable for two-tape one-way deterministic finite state acceptors M even if M is guaranteed not to diverge on (w,w) for w ultimately periodic:

$$L_a(M) \cap D = \phi$$
$$L_d(M) \cap D \neq \phi$$

We could use standard coding tricks to show that M_T could be taken to have a two symbol input alphabet. Hence:

COROLLARY 6.4   The following problems are not partially decidable for two-tape one-way deterministic finite state acceptors M with input alphabet {0,1} which are guaranteed to halt for (w,w) whenever w is ultimately periodic:

$$L_a(M) \cap D = \phi$$
$$L_d(M) \cap D \neq \phi$$

This corollary is the starting point for most of our proofs of undecidability. The general strategy will be to show that a property P of schemes is not partially decidable by finding an algorithm to transform each scheme S into a two-tape one-way deterministic finite state acceptor M(S) such that $L_a(M(S)) \cap D = \phi$ if and only if S possesses property P . Then the previous reasoning will show that the existence of a partial decision procedure for property P would imply the existence of one for $L_a(M) \cap D = \phi$ which we know to be impossible. So we can conclude that it is not even partially decidable whether a scheme possesses property P . The technical term for such a strategy is "many-one reducibility" (actually, one-one reducibility in our examples). We have shown that the problem of whether " S has P " is at least as hard as an "impossible" problem - " $L_a(M) \cap D = \phi$ " .

B.   UNDECIDABLE PROPERTIES OF SCHEMES

We shall show our undecidability results for monadic schemes with one function letter, one predicate letter and two program variables. Let S_n be the family of all schemes with:

1) n program variables $y_1,\ldots,y_n$
2) one monadic function letter f
3) one monadic predicate letter T
4) one input variable x

The general approach will be to set up a 1-1 correspondence between free interpretations of schemes in S_2 and infinite binary tapes. Obviously in a free interpretation of such a scheme (notice that S_n does <u>not</u> allow constants) only the values of T on $f^m(x)$ could affect the flow of computation and the ultimate output and so we can consider everything else to be fixed. Given an expression E of the form $f^m(x)$ and a free interpretation I , let

$$t_1(E) = a_0 a_1 a_2 \cdots a_i \cdots$$

where $a_0 = I(T)(E)$ and $a_i = I(T)(f^i(E))$ for $i \geq 1$.

Now it is clear that given an infinite binary tape t there is a free interpretation on S_n for which $t = t_I(x)$. The schemes in S_n that we shall use to establish our undecidability results will actually test only expressions of the form $f^m(x)$ for $m \geq 2$ and so for all purposes a tape t can be considered to correspond to a "unique" (unique as far as concerns operation of the schemes in question) free interpretation I such that

$$t = t_I(f^2(x)) \quad .$$

Consider the five schemes $P_i(M)$ diagrammed in Examples IV-1 through VI-5. In each case the idea is to establish a correspondence between a binary tape t , the input (t,t) to two-tape one-way deterministic finite state machine M , and a free interpretation I on $P_i(M)$ for which $t = t_I(f^2(x))$. We also use special schemes Z_1 and Z_2 in Example VI-6; Z_1 never halts and Z_2 always halts.

We can show by careful examination of the schemes in Examples VI-1 to VI-5 that the following statement holds in each case.

LEMMA 6.5   The computation of $P_i(M)$ under free interpretation I on input x :
(1) Enters address q_a if and only if $(t_I(f^2(x)),t_I(f^2(x)))$ is in $L_a(M) \cap D$.
(2) Enters address q_r if and only if $(t_I(f^2(x)),t_I(f^2(x)))$ is in $L_r(M) \cap D$.
(3) Never enters q_a or q_r if and only if $(t_I(f^2(x)),t_I(f^2(x)))$ is in $L_d(M) \cap D$.

EXAMPLES VI-1 - 5.   CONSTRUCTION OF SCHEMES $P_i(M)$ in S_2 from
a two-tape one-way deterministic finite state
acceptor $M = (K_1,K_2,\{0,1\},\delta,q_o,q_a,q_r)$

VI-1   Construction of $P_1(M)$ which always diverges if and only if $L_a(M) \cap D = \phi$

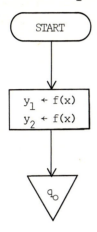

For each q in K_1 , subscheme:

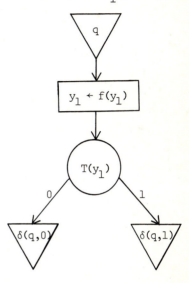

For q_a and q_r subschemes:

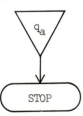

For each q in K_2 , subscheme:

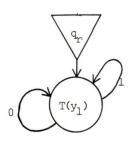

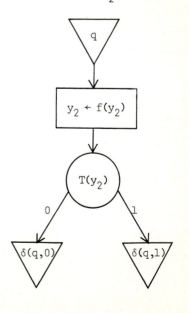

is the address of a subscheme

EXAMPLE VI-2   Construction of $P_2(M)$ which is NOT always halting (diverges
under some interpretation) if and only if $L_d(M) \cap D \neq \phi$

Initial subscheme

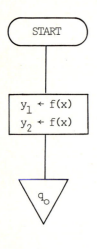

Subschemes associated with states:

For q in K_1

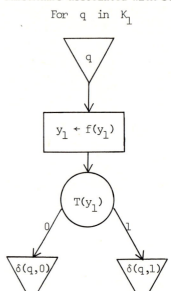

Terminal subscheme

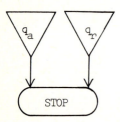

For q in K_2

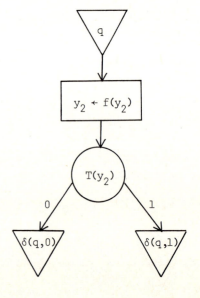

EXAMPLE VI-3   Construction of $P_3(M)$. If M halts on (w,w) whenever
w is ultimately periodic, then $P_3(M)$ halts for all
finite interpretations if and only if $L_a(M) \cap D = \phi$

Initial subscheme:

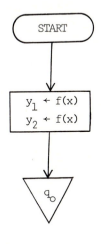

Subschemes associated with states:

For q in K_1

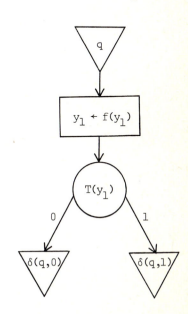

Subschemes for q_a and q_r

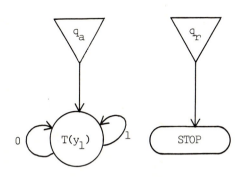

For q in K_2

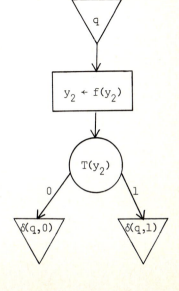

EXAMPLE VI-4   Construction of $P_4(M)$ such that $P_4(M)$ is NOT strongly
equivalent to Z_2 if and only if $L_d(M) \cap D \neq \phi$

Initial subscheme

Subschemes associated with states:

For q in K_1

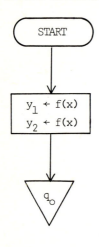

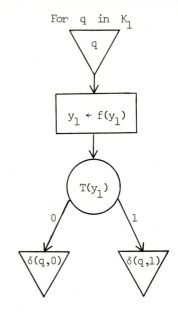

Subscheme for q_a , q_r

For q in K_2

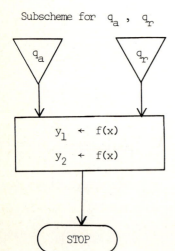

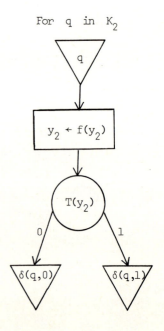

EXAMPLE VI-5   Construction of $P_5(M)$ which is weakly equivalent to Z_2 if and only if $L_a(M) \cap D = \phi$. If M converges on (w,w) for w ultimately periodic, then $P_5(M)$ is finitely equivalent to Z_2 if and only if $L_a(M) \cap D = \phi$.

Initial subscheme

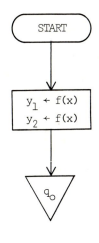

Subschemes associated with states:

For q in K_1

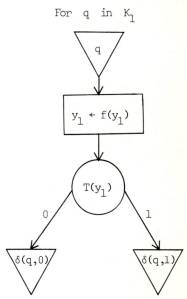

Subschemes for q_a , q_r

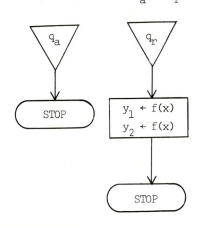

For q in K_2

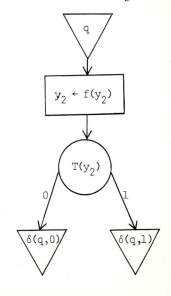

EXAMPLE VI-6   Special Schemes Z_1 and Z_2

Scheme Z_1 always diverges.   Scheme Z_2 always halts

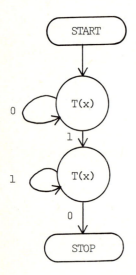

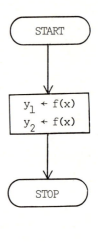

PROOF of Lemma 6.5

   The lemma follows directly from the definitions of $L_a(M)$, $L_r(M)$ and $L_d(M)$ and the following claim which can be proven by induction on $r+s$:

CLAIM   The computation $(P_i(M),I,x)$ for free interpretation I goes from address q with $val(y_1) = E_1$ and $val(y_2) = E_2$ to address p with $val(y_1) = f^r(E_1)$ and $val(y_2) = f^s(E_2)$ if and only if M on input $(t_I(f(E_1)),t_I(f(E_2)))$ goes from q to p reading r symbols on its first tape and s symbols on its second tape. ∎

THEOREM 6.6   The following properties of a scheme P are not partially decidable for schemes in S_2 , and special schemes Z_1 and Z_2 :

(1) P diverges under all interpretations
(2) P diverges under all finite interpretations
(3) P is strongly equivalent to Z_1
(4) P is finitely equivalent to Z_1
(5) P diverges under some interpretation
(6) P halts under all finite interpretations
(7) P is not strongly equivalent to Z_2
(8) P is not totally equivalent to Z_2
(9) P is weakly equivalent to Z_2
(10) P is finitely equivalent to Z_2

PROOF

(1) It is not partially decidable for two-tape one-way deterministic finite state machines M whether or not $L_a(M) \cap D = \phi$. Given such a machine M we can construct $P_1(M)$. Examining $P_1(M)$ we see that it diverges for a free interpretation I if and only if it never reaches address q_a ; from the previous lemma we see that $(P_1(M),I,x)$ fails to reach q_a if and only if $(t_I(f^2(x)),t_I(f^2(x)))$ is not in $L_a(M) \cap D$. On the other hand, if (t,t) is in $L_a(M) \cap D$, there is a free interpretation I for which $t = t_I(f^2(x))$ and hence in this case $(P_1(M),I,x)$ reaches q_a and halts. Since a scheme always diverges if and only if it diverges for all free interpretations, we see that $P_1(M)$ always diverges if and only if $L_a(M) \cap D = \phi$. Thus if we had a partial decision procedure which halts and gives the answer YES for every P which never converges we could have a procedure to partially decide whether $L_a(M) \cap D = \phi$. Hence it is not partially decidable whether P always diverges.

(2) Notice that if a scheme P does not diverge everywhere for some interpretation I, that is, if $(P,I,\bar{a})\downarrow$ for some input $\bar{a}$ in the domain of I,
then $(P,I',\bar{a})\downarrow$ for some finite subinterpretation I' of I. For a halting
computation is by definition finite and so the range of values of $val(u,i)$ for
every variable u and point i in the computation is finite. If we let D' be
this finite subset of the domain of I, let the interpretation of each predicate
letter be the restriction of its interpretation under I to subdomain D', and
for each function letter f let $I'(f)(\bar{b}) = I(f)(\bar{b})$ whenever $I(f)(\bar{b})$ is in D'
and elsewhere $I'(f)(\bar{b}) = \bar{a}$, it is evident that computation $(P,I',\bar{a})$ is
indistinguishable from computation $(P,I,\bar{a})$ and in particular halts. Hence P
diverges everywhere if and only if it diverges everywhere on all finite interpretations. Thus property (2) is equivalent to property (1) restated.

(3) Since Z_1 diverges everywhere, evidently P is strongly equivalent to Z_1 if
and only if P diverges everywhere. Hence property (3) is also a restatement of
(1).

(4) Again, P diverges everywhere under all finite inte pretations if and only if
P is finitely equivalent to Z_1 so we again have a restatement of (1).

(5) Now examine $P_2(M)$. A computation $(P_2(M),I,x)$ diverges under free interpretation I if and only if it never reaches q_a or q_r; thus by the lemma, the
computation diverges if and only if $(t_I(f^2(x)),t_I(f^2(x)))$ is in $L_d(M) \cap D$. If
(t,t) is in $L_d(M)$, then $(P_2(M),I,x)$ will diverge for any free interpretation
I such that $t = t_I(f^2(x))$. A scheme is not always halting if and only if it
diverges for some free interpretation. Hence $P_2(M)$ is not always halting
(diverges for some interpretation) if and only if $L_d(M) \cap D \neq \phi$, which is not
partially decidable.

(6) First recall that we actually showed that $L_a(M) \cap D \neq \phi$? is not partially
decidable even for two-tape one-way deterministic finite state machines with a two
symbol alphabet which always halt on (t,t) whenever t is ultimately periodic.
This was because in our construction of M_T from Turing machine T, we forced M_T
to halt on (t,t) unless t encoded an infinite computation of T on the blank
initial tape and by placing extra $\not c$'s in the encodement we made sure that such a
tape t could never be ultimately periodic. Hence we can assume that M halts on
(t,t) for t ultimately periodic.

Suppose $(P_3(M),I,a)$ diverges for some finite interpretation, I and input a in the domain of I . Since I has a finite domain, letting f_I stand for $I(f)$, we see that there are n and k such that $f_I^n(a) = f_I^{n+k}(a)$ and hence $f_I^n(a) = f_I^{n+mk}$ for all $m \geq 0$. Letting T_I stand for interpreted predicate $I(T)$, we see that in particular, the tape

$$t = T_I(f_I^2(a))T_I(f_I^3(a)) \ldots T_I(f_I^j(a)) \ldots.$$

is ultimately periodic. If we let I^* be the free interpretation with $t = t_{I^*}(f^2(x))$ we see that M halts on (t,t) since t is ultimately periodic and thus reaches q_a or q_r ; as $(P_3(M),I^*,x)$ follows the same infinite execution sequence as $(P_3(M),I,a)$ and in particular diverges, it must enter address q_a . This means that M accepts (t,t) and so $L_a(M) \cap D \neq \phi$. Thus if $P_3(M)$ diverges for any finite interpretation $L_a(M) \cap D \neq \phi$ and conversely, if $L_a(M) \cap D = \phi$, then $P_3(M)$ halts for all finite interpretations.

On the other hand, suppose that (t,t) is in $L_a(M) \cap D$. Then there is a free interpretation I with $t = t_I(f^2(x))$ for which computation $(P_3(M),I,x)$ will eventually enter address q_a in some finite number of steps, say n . After entering q_a , the computation loops forever without computing any new values of any of its variables. Thus this computation depends solely on the specification of T on $A = \{f^j(x) \mid 0 \leq j \leq n\}$. Let I' be the interpretation with domain A , $I'(f)(f^j(x)) = f^{j+1}(x) = I(f)(f^j(x))$ for $0 \leq j \leq n-1$, $I'(f)(f^n(x)) = f^n(x)$ and $I'(T)(E) = I(T)(E)$ for all E in A . Thus $(P_3(M),I',x)$ clearly follows the execution sequence of $(P_3(M),I,x)$ until entering q_a and then is trapped forever. Hence $P_3(M)$ diverges for finite interpretation I' . Thus if $L_a(M) \cap D \neq \phi$, $P_3(M)$ diverges for some finite interpretation.

Putting our conclusions together, we see that $P_3(M)$ halts for all finite interpretations if and only if $L_a(M) \cap D = \phi$. Hence there is no partial decision procedure to determine whether a scheme halts for all finite interpretations.

(7) Examining $P_4(M)$ we see that this scheme halts if and only if it ever enters q_a or q_r and when it halts the output is always $(f(x),f(x))$, since x is not a program variable, and this is the output of Z_2 under all circumstances. If (t,t) is in $L_d(M) \cap D$ then $(P_4(M),I,x)$ diverges for free interpretation I with $t = t_I(f^2(x))$ and so $P_4(M)$ certainly cannot be strongly equivalent to the always halting scheme Z_2 . On the other hand, $P_4(M)$ can fail to be strongly equivalent to Z_2 only if it ever diverges, that is only if $(P_4(M),I,x)$ diverges for some free interpretation I . Such a computation never reaches q_a or q_r so if tape t is chosen with $t = t_I(f^2(x))$, M diverges on (t,t) . Hence $P_4(M)$ is not strongly equivalent to Z_2 if and only if $L_d(M) \cap D \neq \phi$, which is not a partially decidable property.

(8) Since Z_2 is always halting, P is strongly equivalent to Z_2 if and only if P is totally equivalent to Z_2. Hence (8) is a restatement of (7).

(9) Examining $P_5(M)$ we see that if any computation $(P_5(M),I,a)$ enters address q_r it gives output $(f(a),f(a))$, the same output as (Z_2,I,a). If it ever enters address q_a it halts with an output $val(P_5(M),I,a) = (f^r(a),f^s(a))$ for some $r,s \geq 2$ whereas $val(Z_2,I,a) = (f(a),f(a))$. Hence $P_5(M)$ is weakly equivalent to Z_2 if and only if no computation $(P_5(M),I,a)$ ever enters q_a. This holds if and only if no computation of M ever enters state q_a. So $P_5(M)$ is weakly equivalent to Z_2 if and only if $L_a(M) \cap D = \phi$.

(10) Again we examine $P_5(M)$. As we did in (6) we notice that we can assume that M halts on (t,t) whenever t is ultimately periodic and this implies that $P_5(M)$ enters q_a or q_r for all finite interpretations. Hence $P_5(M)$ halts under all finite interpretations as does Z_2. So $P_5(M)$ is finitely equivalent to Z_2 if and only if no computation ever reaches q_a if and only if. $L_a(M) \cap D = \phi$. ∎

Now let us see some of the implications of these undecidability results. Perhaps the most important is that neither " P strongly equivalent to Q " nor " P is not strongly equivalent to Q " is partially decidable. This is why we could claim as we did that there is no point in giving a large list of elementary equivalence preserving transformations - either global or local - since no such list could be complete and result in ultimately establishing all possible equivalences.

Somewhat more formally, we claim that there can be no list of transformations on schemes:

$$t_1, t_2, \ldots, t_i, \ldots$$

such that:

(1) The function $F(i,P) = t_i(P)$ is total recursive.
(2) $F(i,P) = t_i(P)$ is strongly equivalent to P for each i.
(3) If P is strongly equivalent to Q there is a finite set $i_1, \ldots, i_r$ such that $Q = t_{i_1}(t_{i_2}(\ldots (t_{i_r}(P)) \ldots))$.

The existence of such a sequence would imply the existence of a partial decision procedure for " P is strongly equivalent to Q " as follows. We keep a counter with a number N and a pseudostack with up to N entries of the form (P',i) for a scheme P' (or, more accurately, the description or name of a scheme) and a number

i less than N . Let the function TOP(X) give the top of pseudostack X ,
POP(X) , remove the top of stack X , and PUSH(X,Y) , add Y to the top of X ;
let Height(X) give the number of entries in stack X and let L((P',i)) = P'
and R((P',i)) = i . Then we can express the procedure using the WHILE program in
Example VI-7.

The procedure exemplifies an idea called "dovetailing" - a way of
exhaustively searching an infinite tree. In this case the choice tree is infinite
branching (corresponding to a possibly infinite set of transformations) as well as
having potentially infinitely many levels, corresponding to the fact that any finite
number of transformations might be applied to take P into Q . A compound
transformation $t_{i_1} (t_{i_2} (... (t_{i_r} (P) ...))$ is regarded as a vector $(i_1, i_2, ..., i_r)$
and the procedure first tries the null vector (i.e. is P already equal to Q)
and then searches the set of all such vectors with $r \leq N+1$ and each $i_j \leq N$ for
N = 1,2,... . For each value of N a standard backtrack procedure over a finite
tree is employed. The stack keeps track of the effect of successive transformations
on P and the transformations performed at each step. Whenever N is updated,
everything is reinitialized. This is inefficient since the finite initial portions
of the infinite tree are constantly rescanned. By using another stack we could
avoid this problem. Each possible vector is tried in turn and the procedure halts
if and only if one of the corresponding compound transformations takes P into Q .
If such a complete list of transformations exists, then the procedure will halt and
give the answer YES if and only if P is strongly equivalent to Q . Thus it would
partially decide " P strongly equivalent to Q " . Since we know this is
impossible we must conclude that no such list of transformations exists.

THEOREM 6.7   If $t_1, t_2, ..., t_i, ...$ is a list of transformations on schemes such
that $F(i,P) = t_i(P)$ is total recursive, then either there is at least one t_i
which is not equivalence preserving (i.e. $t_i(P)$ is not strongly equivalent to P
for some scheme P) or there are schemes P and Q such that P and Q are
strongly equivalent and no application of the transformations takes P into Q
(i.e. the list is not complete with respect to strong equivalence).

EXAMPLE VI-7   A SPECIAL WHILE PROGRAM

    N ← 1

    S ← ϕ

    V ← P

    n ← 1

    WHILE V ≠ Q DO

              IF (0 ≤ HEIGHT(S) < N) AND (n ≤ N) THEN

                            S ← PUSH(S,(V,n+1))

                            V ← $t_n(V)$

                            n ← 1

              ENDIF

              IF (0 < HEIGHT(S) ≤ N) AND (n = N+1) THEN

                            U ← TOP(S)

                            V ← L(U)

                            n ← R(U)

                            POP(S)

              ENDIF

              IF (HEIGHT(S) = 0) AND (n = N+1) THEN

                            V ← P

                            n ← 1

                            N ← N+1

              ENDIF

              IF (HEIGHT(S) = N) AND (n ≤ N) THEN

                            V ← $t_n(V)$

                            n ← n+1

              ENDIF

ENDWHILE

ANSWER ← YES

STOP

An exhaustive simplification procedure with respect to strong equivalence would be an infinite set of transformations t_i such that $F(i,P) = t_i(P)$ is totally recursive in i and P , $t_i(P)$ is always strongly equivalent to P and whenever P is strongly equivalent to Q then there are $i_1,\ldots,i_r$ and $j_1,\ldots,j_s$ such that $t_{i_1}\ldots t_{i_r}(P) = t_{j_1}\ldots t_{j_s}(Q)$. The same sort of dovetailing argument used above shows that the existence of such a procedure would imply the partial decidability of strong equivalence. Hence:

THEOREM 6.8   There is no exhaustive simplification method for strong equivalence.

Similarly, there can be no minimal canonical forms for schemes in the following sense:

THEOREM 6.9   There is no subclass C of schemes such that there is a total recursive function mapping all schemes into C with strongly equivalent schemes mapped into the same scheme.

These results hold not only for strong equivalence but also for weak equivalence and for any "reasonable equivalence".

DEFINITION   A relation $\sim$ among schemes is called a "reasonable equivalence" if whenever $P \sim Q$, then P is weakly equivalent to Q and whenever P is strongly equivalent to Q , then $P \sim Q$.

THEOREM 6.10   For any reasonable equivalence relation $\sim$ and schemes P and Q in S_2 , " $P \sim Q$ " is not partially decidable.

PROOF
    We examine the schemes $P_6(M)$ and Z_3 in Example VI-8. Scheme Z_3 searches $f(x), f^3(x), f^5(x),\ldots$ for the first $f^{2n+1}(x)$ which is tested to be 1. For interpretation I , let T_I stand for $I(T)$ and f_I for $I(f)$. If for all $n \geq 1$, $T_I(f_I^{2n+1}(a)) = 0$ for some input a , then computation (Z_3,I,a) diverges. Otherwise, if $N = \text{Min}\{n \mid T_I(f_I^{2n+1}(a)) = 1\}$, computation (Z_3,I,a) halts and $\text{val}(Z_3,I,a) = (f_I^{2N+3}(a), f_I^{2N+3}(a))$.
    Now $P_6(M)$ is constructed from two-tape one-way deterministic finite state automaton $M = (K_1, K_2, \{0,1\}, \delta, q_0, q_a, q_r)$ as in Examples VI-1 – 5 except that it tests $f^{2n+1}(x)$ for 1 and uses $f^{2n}(x)$ as the previous schemes used $f^n(x)$. If computation $(P_I(M),I,a)$ at step i has $\text{val}(y_j,i) = f_I^{2n+1}(a)$ and tests $T_I(\text{val}(y_j,i)) = 1$, it goes to either subscheme I for $j = 1$ or II for $j = 2$ and these are halting subschemes which stop with $\text{val}(P_6(M),I,a) = (f_I^{2n+3}(a), f_I^{2n+3}(a))$ which is necessarily $\text{val}(Z_3,I,a)$ for this interpretation.

EXAMPLE VI-8   CONSTRUCTION of $P_6(M)$ from deterministic two-tape
one-way finite state acceptor $M = (K_1, K_2, \{0,1\}, \delta, q_o, q_a, q_r$

Initial subscheme:

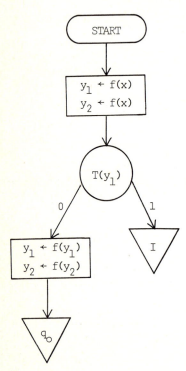

Subscheme for q_a :

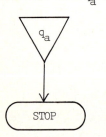

Special Subscheme I

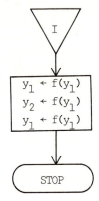

Special Subscheme II

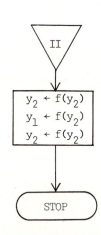

EXAMPLE VI-8   CONTINUED - Subschemes for states in $K_1 \cup K_2$

For q in K_1 For q in K_2

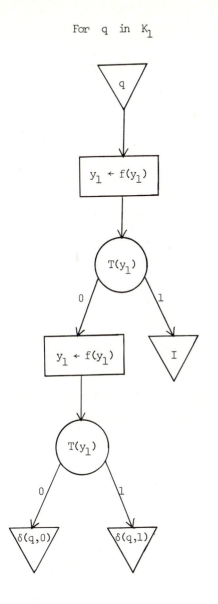
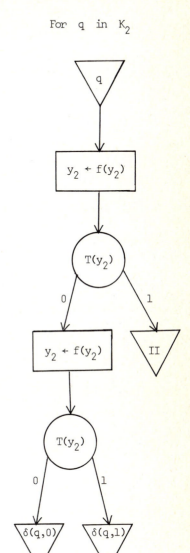

EXAMPLE VI-8   CONCLUDED - Subscheme for q_r and Scheme Z_3

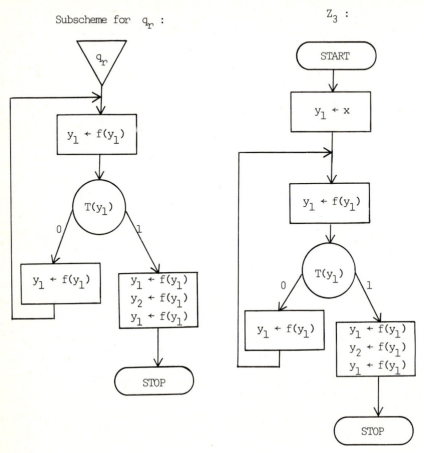

Subscheme for q_r : Z_3 :

If $L_a(M) \cap D = \phi$ then $P_6(M)$ is strongly equivalent to Z_3

If $L_a(M) \cap D \neq \phi$ then $P_6(M)$ is not weakly equivalent to Z_3

DEFINITION: A relation $\sim$ on schemes is a "reasonable equivalence" if whenever P

is strongly equivalent to Q , then $P \sim Q$ and whenever $P \sim Q$, then P is

weakly equivalent to Q .

For any reasonable equivalence relation $\sim$, $P_6(M) \sim Z_3$ if and only if

$L_a(M) \cap D = \phi$. Hence, for any reasonable equivalence relation $\sim$ and schemes

in S_2 , " $P \sim Q$ " is not partially decidable.

Similarly, if the computation reaches q_r with $val(y_1) = f_I^{2n}(a)$, we must have $T_I(f_I^{2n-j}(a)) = 0$ for $1 \leq 2n-j \leq 2n-1$ and since subscheme q_r is identical to scheme Z_3 after Z_3 is initialized, $(P_6(M),I,a)$ diverges if (Z_3,I,a) diverges and if (Z_3,I,a) halts then $val(P_6(M),I,a) = val(Z_3,I,a)$. If computation $(P_6(M),I,a)$ diverges, it must eventually compute $f_I^n(a)$ for all n and since it will halt if any of these values tests to 1 for n odd, $T_I(f_I^{2n+1}(a)) = 0$ for all $n \geq 1$ and so (Z_3,I,a) also diverges.

Thus we see that the only way computations $(P_6(M),I,a)$ and (Z_3,I,a) can have different outcomes - i.e. have one converge and the other diverge or both converge with different outputs - is if $(P_6(M),I,a)$ reaches state q_a . As we saw before, if $L_a(M) \cap D = \phi$ this can never happen. Hence if $L_a(M) \cap D = \phi$, $P_6(M)$ is strongly equivalent to Z_3 and a fortiori $P_6(M) \sim Z_3$.

On the other hand, suppose (t,t) is in $L_a(M) \cap D$. Let $t = a_0 a_1 a_2 \ldots$; we can assume t to be infinite since if M accepts (t,t) for t finite, it accepts (tt',tt') for any infinite tape t' . There is some N such that M halts after reading exactly N_1 symbols on Tape 1 and N_2 on Tape 2 with $N = Max(N_1,N_2)$. Let I be the free interpretation with $T_I(f^n(x)) = 0$, $0 \leq n \leq 3$, $T_I(f^{2n+4}(x)) = a_n$ for $n \geq 0$, $T_I(f^{2n+1}(x)) = 0$, $0 \leq n \leq N+1$ and $T_I(f^{2n+5}(x)) = 1$ for $n \geq N$. Thus $2N+5 = Min\{n \mid T_I(f^n(x)) = 1$ and n is odd$\}$ and so (Z_3,I,x) halts with output $(f^{2N+7}(x),f^{2N+7}(x))$. On the other hand computation $(P_6(M),I,x)$ will be able to complete the simulation of M on (t,t) and reach q_a with $val(y_1) = f^{2N_1+4}(x)$ and $val(y_2) = f^{2N_2+4}(x)$ since it will never compute $f^n(x)$ for $n > 2N+4$ and hence never apply T to $f^{2n+1}(x)$ with $n \geq N+2$. Hence $val(P_6(M),I,x) = (f^{2N_1+4}(x),f^{2N_2+4}(x)) \neq (f^{2N+7}(x),f^{2N+7}(x)) = val(Z_3,I,x)$. Thus $P_6(M)$ is not weakly equivalent to Z_3 which means that $P_6(M) \sim Z_3$ cannot hold. So if $P_6(M) \sim Z_3$, then $L_a(M) \cap D = \phi$.

Having established that $P_6(M) \sim Z_3$ if and only if $L_a(M) \cap D = \phi$ which is not partially decidable, we can conclude as usual that " $P \sim Q$ " is not partially decidable for schemes in S_2 . ∎

COROLLARY 6.11   There is no exhaustive simplification procedure for any reasonable equivalence relation.

We can contrast these negative results with the following "partially negative" or partially decidable results.

THEOREM 6.12   Let   Q   be any scheme which halts under all interpretations.   The following properties of schemes   P   and   R   are partially decidable although not decidable:

(1)   P   halts under some interpretation for some input
(2)   P   halts under some finite interpretation for some input
(3)   P   is not strongly equivalent to Z_1
(4)   P   is not finitely equivalent to Z_1
(5)   P   diverges somewhere under some finite interpretation
(6)   P   diverges everywhere under some finite interpretation
(7)   P   always halts
(8)   P   is strongly equivalent to   Q
(9)   P   is totally equivalent to   Q
(10)   P   is totally equivalent to   R
(11)   P   is not finitely equivalent to   R
(12)   P   is not weakly equivalent to   R

PROOF

Theorem 6.6 tells us that the negative of each of these statements is not partially decidable and so none of them are decidable.

Statements (1)-(4) are equivalent since we saw before that if a scheme halts for any interpretation, it halts for some finite interpretation.   Further, if   P   halts for any input under any interpretation, (P,I,x) converges for some free interpretation   I   and we can discover this by building the (possibly infinite) execution sequence tree and seeing whether STOP ever appears.   Hence (1)-(4) are partially decidable.

Any finite interpretation is necessarily recursive.   There are only a finite number of function letters and predicate letters in   P   and so for each finite domain   D   only a finite number of possible assignments of functions from D^m to   D   or D^m to   {0,1} .   We can recursively enumerate all finite interpretations.   A program must loop if it ever enters the same statement twice with all values specified alike.   If finite domain   D   of interpretation   I   has   d   objects and   P   has   n   statements and   m   variables of any kind, then any execution sequence under   I   with more than nd^m steps must twice enter the same statement with the same specification of all variables and hence must represent an infinite loop.   Hence for each input vector $\bar{a}$ computation $(P,I,\bar{a})$ diverges if and only if it fails to halt within nd^m steps.   So for each finite interpretation we can decide whether   P   halts for some inputs or all inputs.   Thus (5) and (6) are partially decidable.

We have already seen (in section B of Chapter III) that (7) is partially decidable and that whenever (7) holds for   P   we can convert   P   into an always halting tree scheme and decide strong equivalence and total equivalence (Theorems 3.6 and 3.8 and Corollaries 3.7 and 3.9).   Hence (7) - (11) are partially decidable.

As we saw, we can enumerate all finite interpretations, For each such interpretation I and each input vector $\bar{a}$ we can determine whether $(P,I,\bar{a})$ halts
and if so what is the output and thus decide strong equivalence for (P,I) and
(R,I) . If P and R are not finitely equivalent, we will eventually discover
this by trying all finite interpretations. This covers (11).

A scheme P is not weakly equivalent to a scheme R if and only if there is
an interpretation I and input $\bar{a}$ for which $(P,I,\bar{a})$ and $(R,I,\bar{a})$ both halt but
give different answers. In this case there is a finite interpretation I' for
which $val(P,I,\bar{a}) = val(P,I',\bar{a})$ $val(R,I',\bar{a}) = val(R,I,\bar{a})$. Thus it suffices to
test over all finite interpretations and so we get partial decidability for (12) as
for (11).   ■

C. UNDECIDABLE PROPERTIES OF PROGRAMS

We have already seen that every partial recursive function can be defined by a
program (P,I) where the interpretation I is restricted to include only the
functions $x + 1$ and $x \dot{-} 1$, the predicate $x = 0$ and the constant function 0
(where we take functions over the natural numbers). It can also be shown that we
can assume that the flowchart P contains only three program variables and one
input variable (this is a consequence of Minsky's theorem that every partial
recursive function can be computed using three registers or counters which one can
only increase by 1, decrease by 1 or test for 0; if the input is coded as 2^x and
output as 2^z then two registers suffice). So we can obtain the corresponding
undecidability results for programs over even a very limited interpretation using
the well-known results for partial recursive functions.

THEOREM 6.13   The following problems are undecidable for programs (P,I) where P
is a monadic flowchart with three program variables and I is any interpretation
over the natural numbers allowing $x + 1$, $x \dot{-} 1$, $x = 0$ and the constant 0.
(1) (P,I) diverges for all inputs.
(2) (P,I) is strongly equivalent to (Z_1,I) .
(3) (P,I) is partially correct for FALSE.
(4) (P,I) diverges for some inputs.
(5) (P,I) halts for all inputs.
(6) (P,I) is totally correct for TRUE.
(7) (P,I) is not strongly equivalent to (Z_4,I) .
(8) (P,I) is weakly equivalent to (Z_4,I) .
(9) (P,I) is not totally equivalent to (Z_4,I) .

(10) (P,I) is totally correct for z = x (even if (P,I) converges everywhere).

(11) (P,I) is totally correct for z = x (even if (P,I) is partially correct
      for z = x).

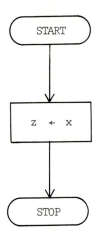

TRIVIAL SCHEME Z_4 is totally correct for z = x

PROOF

    Statements (1), (2) and (3) declare that partial recursive function val(P,I,n)
is nowhere defined; it is known that it is not partially decidable whether a partial
recursive function is everywhere undefined. Statement (4) says that partial
recursive function val(P,I,n) is not total recursive while statements (5) and (6)
say that it is total recursive; neither property is partially decidable for partial
recursive functions as defined by, e.g., Turing machines.

    Scheme Z_4 always halts and computes z = x - the identity. Thus state-
ments (7) and (9) say that a partial recursive function val(P,I,n) does not
compute z = x . If x is input but not program variable in P and we replace the
STOP statement in P by z ← x STOP to get P' we see that (P',I) is not
strongly equivalent to (Z_4,I) if and only if val(P,I,n) is not total recursive;
hence (7) and (9) are not partially decidable. Further, (P',I) is partially
correct for z = y and is totally correct for z = x if and only if val(P,I,n)
is total recursive; hence (11) is not partially decidable - i.e., total correctness
is not decidable even if partial correctness is given by an oracle. We can similarly
form P" from P by replacing STOP by z ← f(x) STOP where f is a function
interpreted by I as x + 1 . Thus whenever (P",I) halts it gives an answer
different from (Z_4,I) ; we see that (P",I) is weakly equivalent to (Z_4,I) if

and only if (P,I) diverges everywhere and hence (8) is not partially decidable.
For every Turing machine T one can construct a total recursive function g such
that g(n) = n if T started on the initially balnk tape does not stop within n
steps and g(n) = n + 1 if T started on the initially blank tape stops within n
steps. This function is the identity if and only if T diverges on the initially
blank tape. Hence it is not partially decidable whether a total recursive function
computes the identity; this settles (10).   ■

  In particular, we see that partial correctness is not decidable even for very
trivial output conditions and for programs whose flowchart structure is very simple.
This means that the program verification procedure must remain a procedure and not
an algorithm - success is NOT guaranteed. No algorithm can decide whether or not
a program is partially correct with respect to given input and output conditions.
Further the verification procedure cannot be completely mechanized. There is no
procedure implementable on a computer which given a program and an input condition
A and an output condition B will always halt and say YES whenever the program is
partially correct with respect to A and B but when the program is not partially
correct may say NO or may just give up or may even grind on forever. That is simply
another way of saying that partial correctness is not partially decidable. If we
could mechanize the production of inductive assertions in such a way that when
partial correctness held the assertion generator would finally find the "right"
assertions and the THEOREM PROVER finally establish the corresponding path
verification conditions, then we would in effect have a partial decision procedure.

  What does all this mean in a practical way? Certainly we have no intention of
writing programs for all partially computable functions; indeed time and space
considerations do not allow execution of all partially computable functions. The
functions actually computed form a very small subset of the primitive recursive
functions. We do not know, however, whether they fall into a class for which
partial correctness is partially decidable; one suspects not. In any case, since we
obtain our undecidability results for programs with very simple structure, there can
be nothing in the structure of "real" programs which will allow us by and of itself
to conclude that the properties of interest are at least partially decidable.

  The undecidability results do not say that a task is always impossible - just
that no program can be written to perform the task properly in all cases. But
programs could be written to handle special cases. Thus we cannot completely
mechanize the verification procedure so it will succeed eventually whenever it
should succeed. We can of course verify particular programs and we can improve the
verification procedure and increase the set of cases where it will work. As a
practical matter, complexity questions will probably swamp one first - classes of
programs for which verification is possible but it simply takes too long.

D. A DECIDABLE SUBCLASSES - IANOV SCHEMES

A Ianov scheme is essentially a one variable scheme. In the original model as interpreted by Rutledge such a scheme basically contained:

- a finite state control (finite set K of states)
- a finite set of monadic operators or function letters, $f_1, \ldots, f_n$
- a finite set of Boolean predicates or test letters, $T_1, \ldots, T_m$
- a single register for input, computations, and output
- a designated output function O

The program started with input x in the register. To start the computation off, at first all possible tests are applied to x , resulting in $(T_1(x), \ldots, T_m(x))$ an m-tuple of 0's and 1's. Depending on the outcome of these tests, control is passed to a state q which is now the first state. While in a state q , with register contents y , the program first calls in a function f_q associated with state q and replaces y by $f_q(y)$ - i.e., executes $y \leftarrow f_q(y)$. Then all the tests are applied to this new value of y and depending on q and the vector $(T_1(y), \ldots, T_m(y))$ control is passed either to the next state q' or to the output function resulting in a halt with output O(y) .

Thus we can see that a Ianov scheme is essentially a special form of one variable scheme. On the other hand, a one variable scheme is obviously liberal if we do not allow constants or reinitializing the register, and so applying the transformation t used to "free" a liberal scheme results in a free one variable scheme in the Rutledge format.

So we feel free to use the following definition for Ianov schemes.

DEFINITION   A Ianov scheme is a scheme with one input variable, x , one program variable, y , and one output variable z , which is composed entirely of the following kinds of subschemes for monadic function letters f and monadic predicate letters T :

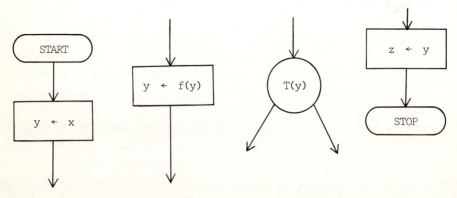

By courtesy we also allow the following subscheme since there are Ianov schemes with the unbreakable loop property:

The following results are immediate from the definition and previous constructions.

THEOREM 6.14   Given a Ianov scheme one can effectively construct a strongly equivalent free Ianov scheme.

THEOREM 6.15   It is decidable whether a Ianov scheme is free.
It is decidable whether a Ianov scheme is always halting.

There are several ways to demonstrate the decidability of strong equivalence (and of almost everything else) for Ianov schemes. One method is to use a variant of the Moore minimization algorithm for deterministic finite state machines to show that there is a minimal canonical form for Ianov schemes - every Ianov scheme can be converted into a minimal standard form scheme which is unique up to a graph isomorphism such that two schemes are strongly equivalent if and only if the corresponding canonical forms are graph isomorphic.

Another proof is based on the idea that in a free interpretation I of two Ianov schemes P and P' , if we write down in succession the values of y in sequence for P and P' , then:

(1) if val(P,I,x) = val(P',I,x) and both are defined we must have the two sequences of y-assignments identical,

(2) if at any point the two sequences of y-assignments differ - e.g. P has y ← f(y) and P' has y ← g(y) - then either P and P' are not strongly equivalent or else both computations must diverge; further if we assume as we may that both P and P' are free schemes then at this point to be strongly equivalent they must both be in a "dead end" with no path completion to STOP.

Call a node in a free scheme "live" if there is a path from it to a STOP statement; since the scheme is free this path is an execution sequence. Call a node "dead" if it is not live - if there is no path from it to STOP. We have mentioned previously that it is decidable whether there is a path between two nodes in a finite state graph (although it is not decidable whether there is an execution sequence between two nodes in a scheme that is not free). Hence it is decidable whether a node in a free scheme is live or dead. As a first step in proving the decidability of strong equivalence, we establish the decidability of weak equivalence.

LEMMA 6.16 Let P and P' be two free Ianov schemes such that P contains n distinct assignment statements and P' contains m distinct assignment statements. Schemes P and P' are not weakly equivalent if and only if there are paths σ in P and σ' in P' beginning at START such that
(a) the pair $\{\sigma,\sigma'\}$ is consistent
(b) both σ and σ' contain exactly k assignment statements for some k ,
(c) both σ and σ' terminate at live nodes, and
(d) the last node in σ contains an assignment $y \leftarrow f(y)$ and the last node in
 σ' contains an assignment $y \leftarrow g(y)$ such that $f \neq g$, and
(e) $1 \leq k \leq nm + 1$.

PROOF
    First suppose that there are paths σ in P and σ' in P' starting at START and satisfying (a) - (d); in particular, $\{\sigma,\sigma'\}$ is a consistent pair. At the end of σ , in any free interpretation following this path, $val(y) = fw(x)$ and at the end of σ' , $val(y) = gw'(x)$ for some strings w and w' of function symbols, with $|w| = |w'| = k-1$ (we are again omitting parentheses in composing monadic functions). Both paths end at live nodes and so can be extended to a path τ in P containing σ as initial subpath and continuing on to STOP and τ' in P' containing σ' as initial subpath and continuing on to STOP. At the end of σ and σ' the values of y in P and P' are different under any free interpretation and cannot become the same in any path continuation under a free interpretation and so afterwards τ cannot test the same expressions as τ' and vice versa. Hence $\{\tau,\tau'\}$ is also a consistent pair and so there is a free interpretation I under which computation (P,I,x) follows τ and (P',I,x) follows τ' . Both computations halt but must give different outputs. Hence P and P' are not weakly equivalent.
    On the other hand, suppose P and P' are not weakly equivalent. There is a free interpretation I under which (P,I,x) and (P',I,x) both halt but give different outputs. There is a first point at which they make different assignments. That is, there is a subpath σ of the execution sequence followed by (P,I,x) and a subpath σ' of that followed by (P',I,x) such that σ ends in an assignment $y \leftarrow f(y)$ and σ' ends in an assignment $y \leftarrow g(y)$, $f \neq g$, and this is the first such point; at the end of σ , $val(y) = fw(x)$ and at the end of σ' , $val(y) = gw(x)$ for some string w of function symbols. Clearly both paths end at live nodes, and $\{\sigma,\sigma'\}$ is consistent pair. Hence σ and σ' satisfy all of (a) - (d). Thus we know that we can find subpaths σ and σ' satisfying all of

(a) - (d) and furthermore they will satisfy:

(f) At the end of σ in a free interpretation, val(y) = fw(x) and
at the end of σ' , val(y) = gw(x) .

So now let σ and σ' be the smallest paths satsifying (a) - (d) plus (f).
We claim that (e), the length condition, must also be satisfied, so
$|w|$ = k-1 $\leq$ nm . Suppose it is not, so $|w|$ = k-1 $\geq$ nm + 1 . We can divide σ
into segments $\sigma_1,\ldots,\sigma_k$ and similarly σ' into $\sigma_1',\ldots,\sigma_k'$ such that each
segment contains exactly one assignment statement which occurs at the end of the
segment. There are only n assignment statements in P and m in P' and so
there are r and s , $1 \leq r \not\leq s \leq$ k-1 such that σ_r and σ_s end in the same
node p and σ_r' and σ_s' end in the same node q . If we "pinch out" segments
σ_{r+1} through σ_s from path σ and segments σ_{r+1}' through σ_s' from σ' , the
resulting paths are $\tau = \sigma_1,\ldots,\sigma_r,\sigma_{s+1},\ldots,\sigma_{k-1},\sigma_k$ and
$\tau' = \sigma_1',\ldots,\sigma_r',\sigma_{s+1}',\ldots,\sigma_{k-1}',\sigma_k'$. Since σ_r and σ_s ended at the same node
p and σ_r' and σ_s' ended at the same node q , τ and τ' are indeed legitimate
paths. Through σ_r , path σ has computed val(y) = w_1(x) and path σ' has
computed the same value for some w_1 of length r ; at the end of σ_s and σ_s' ,
val(y) = $w_2 w_1$(x) for $|w_2|$ = s-r and at the end of σ_{k-1} and σ_{k-1}' we have
val(y) = $w_3 w_2 w_1$(x) where w = $w_3 w_2 w_1$. Hence at the end of τ we have
val(y) = $fw_3 w_1$(x) and at the end of τ' we have val(y) = $gw_3 w_1$(x) . So τ and
τ' meet the same conditions as σ and σ' but contain fewer
$(|w_3 w_1| + 1 \not\leq |w_3 w_2 w_1| + 1)$ assignment statements. This contradicts the minimality
of σ and σ' . Thus σ and σ' meet all of (a) - (e) and we are done. ∎

If P and P' are free and contain at most r tests, a path with at most
nm + 1 assignment statements is altogether of length at most r(nm + 2) . Thus we
need only test paths of length up to r(nm + 2) and they are finite in number.
Hence:

THEOREM 6.17   Weak equivalence is decidable for Ianov schemes.

So we can decide weak equivalence for Ianov schemes; we can decide whether they
ever halt with different answers. If they are weakly equivalent, the only way they
can fail to be strongly equivalent is for one to halt and the other loop for the
same interpretation and input. We now show that this situation is detectable. We
use a somewhat more complex version of the previous argument. Call a node n
"loop-alive" if there is any path from n to STOP passing twice through the same
node.

LEMMA 6.18   Let P and P' be free Ianov schemes such that P contains n
assignment statements and P' contains m assignment statements. There is a free
interpretation I such that (P,I,x) halts but (P',I,x) diverges if and only if
there are finite paths σ in P and σ' in P' starting from START such that:

(a) {σ,σ'} is a consistent pair,

(b) σ ends in STOP and σ' ends at an assignment statement labeling a node that
     is either dead or else loop-alive,

(c) σ contains exactly k assignment statements and σ' contains exactly
     k + 1 assignment statements, and

(d) 0 ≤ k ≤ 2mn + 1

PROOF

First suppose we have paths σ and σ' satisfying (a) - (c). Since σ' ends
at a node that is either dead or loop-alive, σ' can be extended to an infinite
path τ (with σ' as finite initial subpath) which is an execution sequence
because P' is free. Now σ' contained one more assignment than σ so the values
of y under a free interpretation at the end of σ and of σ' must differ. Thus,
as the schemes are Ianov, any extension of σ' must be consistent with σ . So
{σ,τ} is a consistent pair. Thus there is a free interpretation I under which
computation (P,I,x) follows σ and so halts and computation (P',I,x) follows
τ and so diverges.

On the other hand, suppose there is a free interpretation I such that
(P,I,x) halts but (P',I,x) diverges. Let σ be the complete execution sequence
of (P,I,x) , containing k assignment statements for some k . If P and P'
have at most r predicate letters, then since they are free no path in either P
or P' can contain more than r test statements in a row. Hence we can find a
finite initial segment σ' of the execution sequence of (P',I,x) containing
exactly k + 1 assignments; {σ,σ'} is obviously a consistent pair. Clearly the
pair {σ,σ'} satisfies all of (a) - (c).

So we can again let {σ,σ'} be that pair satisfying (a) - (c) with k minimal.
If k ≤ 2mn + 1 we are done. Suppose k ≥ 2mn + 2 . We divide σ into $\sigma_1,\ldots,\sigma_k$
and σ' into $\sigma_1',\ldots,\sigma_k',\sigma_{k+1}'$ such that each path segment contains exactly one
assignment statement and all end in this assignment statement except that σ_k ends
at STOP. This time, since k ≥ 2mn + 2 , we can find r , s and t such that
$0 \le r \ne s \ne t \le k-1$ and σ_r, σ_s and σ_t end in the same node p while σ_r' ,
σ_s' and σ_t' end in the same node q . We now have two middle segments that could
be "pinched out". This is necessary to ensure that the shortened paths will still
form a consistent pair.

Let $w_1(x)$ be the value of y after σ_r , $w_2w_1(x)$ after σ_s , and
$w_3w_2w_1(x)$ after σ_t ; let z_1 , z_2 , and z_3 be similar values for path σ' .
There are two cases. First suppose that $w_2w_1 = z_2z_1$; since $|w_1| = |z_1| = r$,

$w_1 = z_1$ and $w_2 = z_2$. Let τ be path $\sigma_1, \ldots, \sigma_r, \sigma_{s+1}, \ldots, \sigma_t, \ldots, \sigma_k$ and τ' be path $\sigma_1', \ldots, \sigma_r', \sigma_{s+1}', \ldots, \sigma_t', \ldots, \sigma_k', \sigma_{k+1}'$. Notice that when the values of y are the same in corresponding parts of τ and τ' they must have been the same in σ and σ' because the excised pieces started with the same value of y in P and P' and ended with y still at the same value in P as in P'. Hence , $\{\tau, \tau'\}$ must still be a consistent pair which clearly satisfies (a) - (c), and this contradicts the minimality of k. The other case to consider is that $w_2 w_1 \neq z_2 z_1$. Now we let τ be $\sigma_1, \ldots, \sigma_r, \ldots, \sigma_s, \sigma_{t+1}, \ldots, \sigma_k$ and let τ' be path $\sigma_1', \ldots, \sigma_r', \ldots, \sigma_s', \sigma_{t+1}', \ldots, \sigma_k', \sigma_{k+1}'$. Now we can argue that the truncated paths τ and τ' are still consistent because they were consistent through s assignment statements and afterwards y contained different values in the two schemes so there is no way for inconsistency to arise. Thus $\{\tau, \tau'\}$ is again a consistent pair satsifying (a) - (c) and violating the minimality of k. So we can conclude that (d) is also true for $\{\sigma, \sigma'\}$. ■

COROLLARY 6.19   It is decidable for Ianov schemes P and P' whether there is any interpretation and input for which P halts but P' diverges.

Putting these things together we see that:

THEOREM 6.20   It is decidable whether two Ianov schemes are strongly equivalent.

All the properties of schemes shown to be undecidable in general in section B of this chapter can be shown by similar arguments to be decidable in the special case of Ianov schemes. This does not apply to the properties of programs discussed in section C if the flowchart is Ianov (single register, no resets or constants). Every partially computable function can be implemented by a single register machine, even under relatively simple interpretations. The result of Minsky on two counter machines also shows that:

THEOREM 6.21   Every partial recursive function from non-negative integers to non-negative integers can be expressed as $f(n) = \text{val}(P, I, n)$ for P a Ianov scheme and I an interpretation permitting only functions px and x/p and predicate " p divides x " for every prime p, constant 1, and special input function 2^x and output function $\log_2 x$.

Using similar but much longer arguments, it can be shown that:

THEOREM 6.22   Strong equivalence is decidable for Ianov schemes with constants and resets (instructions $y \leftarrow x$ in the body of the scheme).

VII. RECURSION SCHEMES

In this chapter we start the discussion of an alternative model for programs, designed to reflect recursive properties of programming languages. We shall see that this model does indeed represent an augmentation of the flowchart model we have been studying up to now. One topic of concern will be when recursion equations can be translated into flowchart form - when recursion schemes are flowchartable.

We examine these models not only as mathematical entities but also as a means of determining what the mathematical properties of schemes tell us regarding programming problems and languages. In studying alternative models an important point to consider is their relative power.

While we have an intuitive notion of what we mean by saying that one programming language or class of programming languages has more power than another, serious difficulties arise when we try to formalize this notion. Even quite rudimentary languages are nevertheless universal in the sense that we can write programs in them for any partial recursive function using very simple base functions and predicates indeed. Let us illustrate this point by reviewing a few facts we have encountered regarding computation of partial recursive functions by programs with flowchart schemes.

FACT I Under a recursive interpretation, a program scheme computes a partial recursive function(or functions if there is more than one output variable).

FACT II Any partial recursive function $f(n)$ from nonnegative integers into nonnegative integers can be expressed as $val(P,I,n)$ where P is a three variable independent variable (all assignments of the form $y \leftarrow f(y)$) program scheme and I is an interpretation on the nonnegative integers allowing only functions $x + 1$ and $x \doteq 1$, predicate "x = 0" and constant 0 .

FACT III If Ianov schemes are restricted to the interpretation I above, only a small subclass of the recursive functions are computed in the sense that $g(n) = 1 + val(P,I,n)$ for (P,I,n) convergent and $g(n) = 0$ for (P,I,n) divergent is a total recursive function and "most" total recursive functions cannot be so expressed. However, if one selects as interpretation I the interpretation with functions px and x/p and predicates "p divides x" for every prime p and constant 1 as well as special input function 2^x and output function $\log_2 x$ then every partial recursive function $f(n)$ can be expressed as $val(P,I,n)$ for a Ianov (single register) scheme P and this particular interpretation I .

These last two facts can be obtained from Minsky's result that two counter machines are universal and FACT III justifies the original definitions of Ianov and Rutledge. Of course, the programs involved are in general complex, unnatural and highly inefficient.

The implication of these results and similar ones that could be cited is that we cannot study the relative expressive power of programming languages by merely studying the class of functions defined under simple interpretations. These considerations suggest studying abstract uninterpreted programs or schemes of one sort or another and examining when members of one class can be transformed into members of another class preserving equivalence under all interpretations. We make the following definitions, formalized later.

Two schemes P and Q are <u>translations</u> of each other if they compute the same partial function under all interpretations, that is, if they are strongly equivalent. A class C_1 of schemes is <u>translatable</u> into a class C_2 of schemes if for each P in C_1 there is a Q in C_2 such that P and Q are strongly equivalent.

In this approach, if a class C_1 is translatable into a class C_2 but not vice versa, then we consider C_2 to be more powerful and possess in some manner more expressive power than C_1. If C_1 and C_2 are incomparable - C_1 cannot be translated into C_2 and C_2 cannot be translated into C_1 - then each has advantages and special conveniences not available in the other and we wish to determine which properties lead to this incomparability.

We really need more than a mere existence theorem that a class is translatable into C_2 so that all features of C_1 can be modeled in C_2 without loss of computing power. At the very least the construction involved should be effective - there should be a total recursive function carrying any member of C_1 into a strongly equivalent member of C_2. Further we should like the translation to preserve some of the properties mentioned in Chapter IV, possibly computational equivalence, and to carry subschemes into subschemes, blocks into blocks and perhaps statements into groups of instructions so that one can build an efficient and flexible translation system.

Our general results on the comparison of flowchart schemes and recursion schemes will be:

All flowchart schemes can be translated into recursion schemes.

There are recursion schemes not translatable into flowchart schemes.

It is undecidable whether a recursion scheme is translatable into a
    flowchart scheme.

Linear recursion schemes are always translatable into flowchart schemes.

Every recursion scheme can be translated into a flowchart scheme augmented
    by one pushdown store.

Recursion schemes are equivalent to procedure augmented flowchart schemes.

In the special case of monadic recursion schemes, we shall see in Chapter VIII that:

    The classes of monadic recursion schemes and monadic flowchart schemes
        are incomparable.

    Every monadic recursion scheme can be translated into a flowchart scheme
        augmented by a simple pushdown store.

A. DEFINITIONS AND EXAMPLES

Now we are ready for some definitions. As before, one must define the base objects of the metalanguage, then the schemes written in the metalanguage, and finally the semantics, how a scheme computes a function under a given interpretation.

The basic objects are:

<u>Variables</u>	$x_1, x_2, \ldots$	as before
<u>Constants</u>	$c_1, c_2, \ldots$	as before
<u>Basis function letters</u>	$f, g, h, \ldots$	as before
<u>Predicate letters</u>	$P, Q, T, \ldots$	as before
<u>Defined function letters</u>	$F_0, F_1, F_2, \ldots$	new

"<u>terminals</u>" - basis function letters, variables, constants
"<u>nonterminals</u>" - defined function letters

To the objects needed to describe program or flowchart schemes we have added defined function letters, whose role will become clearer later. We can compose these objects into extended terms as we did before. We shall take the liberty of using "term" for "extended term" and denote what was called terms in Chapter II by "simple terms".

DEFINITION   We define <u>terms</u> inductively:

1) A variable or a constant is a term.

2) If f is an n-placed basis function letter and $t_1, \ldots, t_n$ are terms, then $f(t_1, \ldots, t_n)$ is a term.

3) If F is an n-placed defined function letter and $t_1, \ldots, t_n$ are terms, then $F(t_1, \ldots, t_n)$ is a term.

A term is <u>terminal</u> if it contains no defined function letters; otherwise it is <u>nonterminal</u>.

DEFINITION   A term t is <u>very simple</u> if t is either a variable or a constant or if $t = G(u_1, \ldots, u_n)$ or $t = f(u_1, \ldots, u_n)$ for G a defined function letter or f a basis function letter and $u_1, \ldots, u_n$ variables. A term t is <u>simple</u> if either t is very simple or $t = G(t_1, \ldots, t_n)$ or $t = f(t_1, \ldots, t_n)$ for G a defined function letter or f a basis function letter and there is a k , $1 \le k \le n$ such that t_k is a very simple term and t_i is a variable for $i \ne k$.

DEFINITION   A <u>recursion equation</u> is a statement of the form:

$$F_k(y_1,\ldots,y_m) = \text{IF} \quad T(u_1,\ldots,u_n) \quad \text{THEN} \quad t \quad \text{ELSE} \quad t'$$

where

(1) F_k is an m-placed defined function letter

(2) T is an n-placed predicate letter

(3) t and t' are terms and each variable in t or t' appears in $\{y_1,\ldots,y_m\}$

(4) $y_1,\ldots,y_m$ are m distinct variables and $\{u_1,\ldots,u_n\} \subseteq \{y_1,\ldots,y_m\}$

and this equation is said to <u>define</u> F_k .

DEFINITION   A <u>recursion scheme</u> is a finite set of recursion equations and a designated initial defined function letter F_0 such that:

(1) Each defined function letter is defined at most once.

(2) Every defined function letter appearing on the right hand side of any equation is defined exactly once.

(3) One equation defines F_0 .

We say that the scheme <u>defines</u> the function defined by F_0 .

An interpretation of a recursion scheme is defined similarly to an interpretation of a flowchart scheme. The interpretation assigns meanings to constants, predicate letters and basis function letters found in the scheme but does not, of course, assign meanings to defined function letters. A free interpretation is likewise defined as usual, to have as domain the set of all terminal terms over the set of variables, constants and basis function letters found in the scheme.

For any interpretation I we can extend the interpretation of functions and predicates to any terminal term t and any composition of predicates, and terminal terms $T(t_1,\ldots,t_n)$, in the usual way. For a variable x , $I(x)$ is the identity function. If f is an n-placed basis function letter, $t_1,\ldots,t_n$ are terminal terms interpreted as functions $I(t_1),\ldots,I(t_n)$, then $I(f(t_1,\ldots,t_n))$ is the function $I(f)(I(t_1),\ldots,I(t_n))$; if T is an n-placed predicate letter, $I(T(t_1,\ldots,t_n))$ is the Boolean function $I(T)(I(t_1),\ldots,I(t_n))$. It is sometimes convenient to extend this concept to nonterminal terms by the formula $I(F(t_1,\ldots,t_n)) = F(I(t_1),\ldots,I(t_n))$ for a defined function letter F . Further, if f is a basis function letter but at least one of $t_1,\ldots,t_n$ is nonterminal, we can let $I(f(t_1,\ldots,t_n)) = I(f(I(t_1),\ldots,I(t_n)))$ and re-evaluate when all of the arguments of f become terminal.

The definition of computation in a recursion scheme is a little more complicated than for a flowchart scheme. Computations are defined from the inside out when the equation has nested defined function letters. It has been shown by B. Rosen that evaluating recursion equations from the inside out produces a system with the

Church-Rosser property. That is, if E_1 and E_2 are expressions derived from an expression E by alternative expansion methods, then there is an expression E_3 which can be derived from both E_1 and E_2 (of course, E_3 might be either E_1 or E_2). In particular, as long as the inside-out restriction is maintained the order of expansion of functional terms cannot affect the answer. So we shall arbitrarily select whatever expansion method seems most convenient at the moment; usually we shall expand from left to right, always expanding the leftmost defined function letter whose inner terms are all terminal.

We can represent an expanded term as a tree in the obvious fashion. A variable or constant is represented by a single node labelled by itself:

$$.x \qquad or \qquad .c$$

If $t_1,\ldots,t_n$ are terms represented by trees $A_1,\ldots,A_n$, then $f(t_1,\ldots,t_n)$ is represented by a tree with root labelled f and with the roots of $A_1,\ldots,A_n$ as sons:

and similarly for $F(t_1,\ldots,t_n)$.

Computation in a recursion scheme can be represented by derivation in a type of grammar. Suppose we are computing in a recursion scheme S under an interpretation I and have so far derived a term $E = E_1 G(t_1,\ldots,t_n)E_2$ where $t_1,\ldots,t_n$ are values in the domain of I (if I is a free interpretation, $t_1,\ldots,t_n$ will be terminal terms), and G is either a basis or a defined function letter. (1) If G is a basis function letter, $G = f$, let $E_3 = I(f(t_1,\ldots,t_n))$ and write

(1) $\qquad E \implies E_1 E_3 E_2$.

(2) If G is a defined function letter, $G = F$, let the defining equation for F be

$$F(u_1,\ldots,u_n) = IF \quad T(u_{i_1},\ldots,u_{i_m}) \quad THEN \ t \ ELSE \ t'$$

and suppose first that $I(T)(t_{i_1},\ldots,t_{i_m})$ has the value TRUE. All variables in t appear in $u_1,\ldots,u_n$ so we can write t as $t(u_1,\ldots,u_n)$, a function of $u_1,\ldots,u_n$ (the dependence on some or all of these variables might be vacuous). Let $E_4 = t(t_1,\ldots,t_n)$, the result of substituting t_i for u_i everywhere in t and then write

(2) $E \Longrightarrow E_1 E_4 E_2$.

On the other hand, if $I(T)(t_{i_1},\ldots,t_{i_m})$ is FALSE we can write t' as
$t'(u_1,\ldots,u_n)$, and let $E_5 = t'(t_1,\ldots,t_n)$ and then write

(2)' $E \Longrightarrow E_1 E_5 E_2$.

We let $\overset{*}{\Longrightarrow}$ be the transitive reflexive closure of $\Longrightarrow$ - that is, $E \overset{*}{\Longrightarrow} E$
always and if $E \overset{*}{\Longrightarrow} E'$ and $E' \Longrightarrow E''$, then $E \overset{*}{\Longrightarrow} E''$.

As we have just discussed, the order in which these computations are made is
immaterial. Thus we can assume, for example, that we always perform type (1)
derivations before type (2) when possible, and within a type expand the leftmost
expression possible.

DEFINITION   Let S be a recursion scheme with initial equation $F_0(x_1,\ldots,x_n)$.
Let I be an interpretation and $\bar{a} = (a_1,\ldots,a_n)$ a selection of input values. If
there is a terminal term w (a member of the domain of I) such that
$F_0(a_1,\ldots,a_n) \overset{*}{\Longrightarrow} w$ then $(S,I,\bar{a})$ converges and $val(S,I,\bar{a}) = w$, written
$(S,I,\bar{a})\!\downarrow$ or $val(S,I,\bar{a})\!\downarrow$. Otherwise $(S,I,\bar{a})$ diverges , written $(S,I,\bar{a})\!\uparrow$ or
$val(S,I,\bar{a})\!\uparrow$.

We can prove the same relationship between computations under arbitrary
interpretations and computations under free interpretations that we did for flowchart schemes, defining $U(S)$ for a recursion scheme S in the same way as for a
program scheme. We state it without proof.

THEOREM 7.1   Let S be a recursion scheme and I an interpretation with input $\bar{a}$.
Let I^* be the free interpretation obtained from I by setting for each predicate
letter T

$$I^*(T)(t_1,\ldots,t_m) = I(T(t_1,\ldots,t_m))(\bar{a})$$

for all terminal terms $t_1,\ldots,t_m$ in $U(S)$. Then $(S,I,\bar{a})$ converges if and only
if $(S,I^*,\bar{X})$ converges and whenever $(S,I,\bar{a})$ converges,

$$val(S,I,\bar{a}) = val(S,I^*,\bar{X})(\bar{a})$$

We next illustrate these rather complicated definitions with some examples.

EXAMPLE

 We first illustrate our definitions with a computation under a free interpretation. Consider the recursion scheme with one equation:

    F(x) = IF P(x) THEN x ELSE h(F(f(x)),F(g(x)))

which we could represent in tree form:

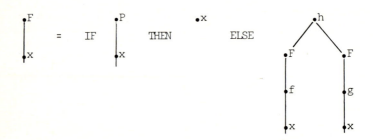

Consider the free interpretation I with I(P)(x) = I(P)(f(x)) = I(P)(g(x)) = FALSE
and I(P)(t) = TRUE elsewhere. This gives us the computation

F(x) $\Longrightarrow$ h(F(f(x)),F(g(x))) $\Longrightarrow$ h(h(F(f(f(x))),F(g(f(x)))),F(g(x)))

  $\Longrightarrow$ h(h(f(f(x)),F(g(f(x)))),F(g(x))) $\Longrightarrow$ h(h(f(f(x)),g(f(x))),F(g(x)))

  $\Longrightarrow$ h(h(f(f(x)),g(f(x))),h(F(f(g(x))),F(g(g(x)))))

  $\Longrightarrow$ h(h(f(f(x)),g(f(x))),h(f(g(x)),F(g(g(x)))))

  $\Longrightarrow$ h(h(f(f(x)),g(f(x))),h(f(g(x)),g(g(x)))) = val(S,I,x)

We can represent this computation in tree form:

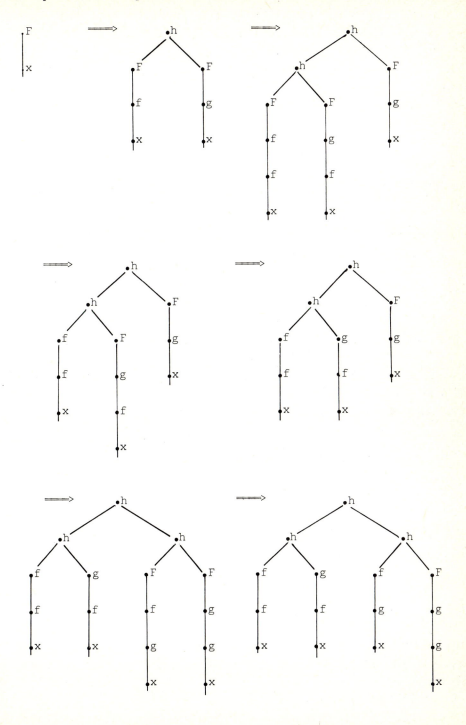

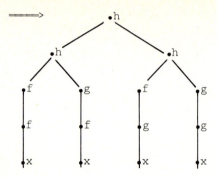

the last tree in the series being of course the tree representation of val(S,I,x) .

As a second example, consider the recursion scheme

$$F(x) = IF \ \ T(x) \ \ THEN \ \ f(x) \ \ ELSE \ \ h(x,F(g(x)))$$

under the interpretation I with domain the nonnegative integers, I(T)(x) is
"x = 0" , I(f)(x) = x + 1 , I(G)(x) = x ± 1 , and I(h)(x,y) = x·y . Under this
interpretation, the scheme becomes:

$$F(x) = IF \ \ x = 0 \ \ THEN \ \ x + 1 \ \ ELSE \ \ x·F(x ± 1)$$

The computation for input 4 is then:

$$F(4) \implies h(4,F(g(4))) \implies h(4,F(3)) \implies h(4,h(3,F(g(3))))$$

$$\implies h(4,h(3,F(2))) \implies h(4,h(3,h(2,F(g(2)))))$$

$$\implies h(4,h(3,h(2,F(1)))) \implies h(4,h(3,h(2,h(1,F(g(1))))))$$

$$\implies h(4,h(3,h(2,h(1,F(0))))) \implies h(4,h(3,h(2,h(1,f(0)))))$$

$$\implies h(4,h(3,h(2,h(1,1)))) \implies h(4,h(3,h(2,1))) \implies h(4,h(3,2))$$

$$\implies h(4,6) \implies 24$$

Not surprisingly, F defines the factorial under this interpretation. Later in this
section we shall see how to verify programs with recursion. This full expansion is
somewhat clumsy, and we would probably take the liberty of expressing the
computation in this abbreviated form:

$$F(4) \implies 4.F(3) \implies 12.F(2) \implies 24.F(1) \implies 24.F(0) \implies 24.1 \ = \ 24$$

We can define strong equivalence between recursion or program schemes as before.

DEFINITION   For schemes S and S' (recursion or program) and interpretations I and I' (with a common domain), (S,I) is <u>strongly equivalent</u> to (S',I') , written (S,I) ≡ (S',I') , if and only if for all inputs $\bar{a}$, either both (S,I,$\bar{a}$) and (S',I',$\bar{a}$) diverge or both converge and val(S,I,$\bar{a}$) = val(s',I',$\bar{a}$) . Schemes S and S' are <u>strongly equivalent</u>, S ≡ S' , if and only if for every interpretation I , (S,I) is strongly equivalent to (S',I) .

As we did for program schemes, one can establish the following result for recursion schemes:

THEOREM 7.2   Recursion schemes S and S' are strongly equivalent if and only if (S,I) is strongly equivalent (S',I) for every free (Herbrand) interpretation I .

If we try to define a "free" recursion scheme in the same way we defined a free program scheme - every path is an execution sequence - we find that although the intuitive meaning is clear, it is very hard to formalize this concept. Exactly how should one define a "path" in a recursion scheme? Or an "execution sequence"? It is possible to do so by a moderately complex tree recursion argument. Instead we will give a "syntactic" definition akin to the one we established as a theorem for program schemes.

DEFINITION   A recursion scheme S is <u>free</u> if for every free interpretation I* and every m-place test T in S , T is never applied twice to the same m-tuple $(t_1,...,t_m)$ of members of U(S) during the computation (S,I*,$\bar{X}$) .

We now give a formal definition of translatability.

DEFINITION   A class C_1 of schemes is <u>translatable</u> into a class C_2 written $C_1 \rightarrow C_2$, or $C_1 \leq C_2$, if for every P in C_1 there is a strongly equivalent Q in C_2 . Class C_1 is <u>effectively</u> translatable into C_2 if there is a total recursive function f from C_1 into C_2 such that f(P) is strongly equivalent to P for every P in C_1 .

DEFINITION   Classes C_1 and C_2 are <u>intertranslatable</u>, written $C_1 \equiv C_2$, if C_1 is translatable into C_2 and C_2 is translatable into C_1 . They are <u>effectively intertranslatable</u> if C_1 is effectively translatable into C_2 and C_2 effectively translatable into C_1 .

DEFINITION   If C_1 is translatable into C_2 but C_2 is not translatable into C_1 , write $C_1 < C_2$.

DEFINITION   Classes C_1 and C_2 are _incomparable_ if C_1 is not translatable into C_2 and C_2 is not translatable into C_1 .

There are various ways we can extend or restrict the definition of recursion scheme without affecting computing power. Some of these are very useful. We shall give two such results, leaving the proof to the reader.

First let us extend the definition of recursion equation as we did the definition of WHILE scheme. Let a _Boolean expression_ be any expression involving predicate terms $P(t_1, \ldots, t_m)$ where each t_i is a terminal term (not necessarily a variable), and the connectives AND , OR , and NOT . We define a recursion expression inductively, by saying that first any term is a recursion expression, and then that any statement of the form IF Q THEN E_1 ELSE E_2 is a recursion expression if Q is a Boolean predicate and E_1 and E_2 are recursion expressions.

LEMMA 7.3   Let R be the family of recursion schemes. Let R' be the family of schemes obtained by extending R to allow equations

$$F(u_1, \ldots, u_n) = \quad IF \quad Q \quad THEN \quad E_1 \quad ELSE \quad E_2$$

where Q is a Boolean expression and E_1 and E_2 are recursion expressions involving only $u_1, \ldots, u_n$ as variables. Then R and R' are effectively intertranslatable.

Now the alert reader will object that this is circular. For we must define the semantics of such extended equations. This can be done directly but it is probably easiest to do by saying that, for example, an equation $F(u_1, \ldots, u_n) =$ IF Q THEN E_1 ELSE E_2 where E_1 and E_2 are not terms, is an abbreviation for three equations:

$$F(u_1, \ldots, u_n) = IF \quad Q \quad THEN \quad F_1(u_1, \ldots, u_n) \quad ELSE \quad F_2(u_1, \ldots, u_n)$$
$$F_1(u_1, \ldots, u_n) = E_1$$
$$F_2(u_1, \ldots, u_n) = E_2$$

for new defined function letters F_1 and F_2 . Thus it remains only to redefine computations by substituting I(Q) for I(T) where T is a predicate letter.

We now turn to a restriction, rather than an extension, of recursion equations. First, let us permit an equation:

$$F(\overline{U}) = t$$

to abbreviate any equation

$$F(\overline{U}) = \text{IF } T(\overline{U}) \text{ THEN } t \text{ ELSE } t$$

for any term t and predicate T. That is, we permit equations without any conditional expression; the indicated action takes place in all cases. Now we define simple recursion equations and schemes.

DEFINITION   A recursion scheme S with initial function F_0 is <u>simple</u> if
1) For some integer $n \geq 1$, all defined functions are n-placed except perhaps F_0 which may be m-placed for $m \leq n$
2) The initial equation is of the form

$$F_0(x_1,\ldots,x_m) = F_1(u_1,\ldots,u_n) \text{ where } u_i = x_i \text{ for } 1 \leq i \leq m,$$
$$\text{and } u_i = x_1 \text{ for } m+1 \leq i \leq n$$

3) All other equations are of the forms:
   a) $F(u_1,\ldots,u_n) = \text{IF } T(u_{i_1},\ldots,u_{i_k}) \text{ THEN } G(u_1,\ldots,u_n) \text{ ELSE } H(u_1,\ldots,u_n)$
   b) $F(u_1,\ldots,u_n) = G(t_1,\ldots,t_n)$
   c) $F(u_1,\ldots,u_n) = f(s_1,\ldots,s_r)$
   where F, G, and H are defined function letters not equal to F_0, there is a k, $1 \leq k \leq n$, such that t_k is very simple and t_i is a variable for $i \neq k$, and there is a j, $1 \leq j \leq r$, such that s_j is either a very simple nonterminal term or a variable, and s_i is a variable for $i \neq j$, and f is a basis function.

DEFINITION   A term t is <u>linear</u> if it contains at most one nonterminal.

DEFINITION   A recursion equation of the form

$$F(\overline{U}) = \text{IF } T(\overline{V}) \text{ THEN } t \text{ ELSE } t'$$

or of the form

$$F(\overline{U}) = t$$

is <u>linear</u> if t and t' are both linear.

DEFINITION   A recursion scheme is <u>linear</u> if all its equations are linear.

DEFINITION   A recursion scheme is <u>monadic</u> if all its functions, basis, predicate and defined, are monadic.

LEMMA 7.4   The classes of recursion schemes and of simple recursion schemes are effectively intertranslatable. Furthermore, every recursion scheme S can be effectively translated into a simple recursion scheme S' such that if S is linear, monadic or linear monadic, then S' is linear, monadic or linear monadic.

The proof is left to the reader. The general idea is to convert IF-THEN expressions to type 3a) (of the definition of simple schemes) by adding new defined function letters and conditionless equations $F(\overline{U}) = t$; then the conditionless equations are converted to forms 3b) and 3c) by adding extra argument places to build up complicated terms from very simple terms. If the original defined functions have at most n argument places and the original terms contain no more than k symbols each (excluding parentheses and commas) then the new defined functions need no more than 2n+1 argument places. Special care is needed in the linear case not to violate the definition of linearity. The monadic case needs a separate approach, similar to the conversion of context-free grammars into Chomsky normal form.

B.   COMPARISON OF FLOWCHART AND RECURSION SCHEMES
   In this section we show that recursion schemes are more powerful than flowchart or program schemes. Our first result is the effective translatability of program schemes into recursion schemes. In section D we shall see a stronger form of this result, when we augment our flowchart schemes with procedures.

THEOREM 7.5   The class of program schemes with one output variable is effectively translatable into the class of recursion schemes.

PROOF

We assume that our program scheme P is written in linear sequential form with the first instruction in line 1. We use the convention that in a test statement the first transfer address is the transfer for positive (TRUE) outcome of the test. We can assume that P has input variables $x_1, \ldots, x_n$ disjoint from program variables $y_1, \ldots, y_m$ and an output variable z which is neither an input for a program variable and only appears in a halting sequence $z \leftarrow u$ STOP.

We shall, in addition to the start function F_0, have one defined function for each address in the flowchart and all the functions except F_0 shall be functions of $n+m$ variables. The values of the various variables or locations in P shall be carried along in each equation. Let us abbreviate the input variables as $\overline{X}$ and the program variables as $\overline{Y}$. Function $F_q(\overline{X}, \overline{Y})$ will compute what the final value of z would be if the computation started at instruction q with the values of the x_i and y_j specified by the arguments of F_q.

The initial equation for $F_0(\overline{X})$ will represent output given for the actual input starting at instruction 1. Each program variable is by definition assumed to be specified before it is computed on; thus any initial value assigned to it is irrelevant. So the initial equation is:

$$F_0(\overline{X}) = F_1(\overline{X}, x_1, \ldots, x_1)$$

where m copies of x_1 are added as dummy arguments, later replaced by y_i's.

If q is the address of an assignment statement

$$q. \quad y_r \leftarrow f(u_1, \ldots, u_k)$$

where by hypothesis each u_j is in $\overline{X}$ or $\overline{Y}$, then we have

$$F_q(\overline{X}, \overline{Y}) = F_{q+1}(\overline{X}, t_1, \ldots, t_m)$$

where $t_j = y_j$ for $j \neq r$ and $t_r = f(u_1, \ldots, u_k)$.

If q is the address of a store statement

$$q. \quad y_r \leftarrow u$$

with $y_r \neq z$, we have

$$F_q(\overline{X}, \overline{Y}) = F_{q+1}(\overline{X}, t_1, \ldots, t_m)$$

where $t_j = y_j$ for $j \neq r$ and $t_r = u$.

If q is the address of an assignment

$$q. \qquad y_r \leftarrow c$$

where c is a constant, we have

$$F_q(\overline{X},\overline{Y}) \;=\; F_{q+1}(\overline{X},t_1,\ldots,t_m)$$

where $t_j = y_j$ for $j \neq r$ and $t_r = c$.
If q is the address of a test statement

$$q. \qquad T(u_1,\ldots,u_k) \qquad r,s$$

where by the hypothesis each u_j is in $\overline{X}$ or $\overline{Y}$, then we have

$$F_q(\overline{X},\overline{Y}) \;=\; \text{IF } T(u_1,\ldots,u_k) \text{ THEN } F_r(\overline{X},\overline{Y}) \text{ ELSE } F_s(\overline{X},\overline{Y}) \;.$$

Since z is not a program variable the only statements involving z must be
of the form:

$$q. \qquad z \leftarrow u$$

$$q+1. \qquad \text{STOP}$$

and so we have

$$F_q(\overline{X},\overline{Y}) \;=\; u \;. \qquad \blacksquare$$

This result should be compared with the next one which exhibits a recursion
scheme which cannot be converted to flowchart form.

THEOREM 7.6   There is a recursion scheme which is not strongly equivalent to any
program scheme.

PROOF
    We give an informal argument that the particular scheme S_0 given below cannot
be translated into any program scheme.

S_0: $F(x) = \text{IF } P(x) \text{ THEN } x \text{ ELSE } h(F(f(x)),F(g(x)))$

Let us consider the behavior of S_0 under a free interpretation I_N such that $I_N(w(x)) = \text{FALSE}$ if and only if w contains fewer than N occurrences of f and g . Thus for $N = 3$, $I_3(f(g(x))) = I_3(g(f(x))) = I_3(f(f(x))) = I_3(g(g(x))) = I_3(g(x)) = I_3(f(x)) = I(x) = \text{FALSE}$ but $I_3(f(f(f(x)))) = \text{TRUE}$.

For $N = 1$, the output of (S_0,I_1,x) is $h(f(x),g(x))$. In a previous example we already computed $\text{val}(S_0,I_2,x)$ as $h(h(f(f(x)),g(f(x))),h(f(g(x)),g(g(x))))$. In general, the output under I_N can be represented as a tree:

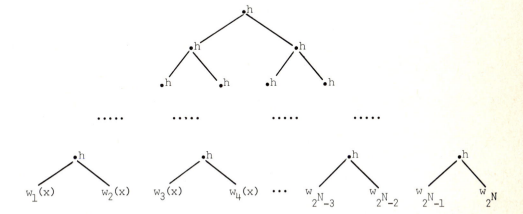

where each $w_i(x)$ is a properly parenthesized and distinct one of the 2^N strings containing parentheses and exactly N occurrences of f and g . This is a full binary tree of depth N with distinct leaves. We claim that no program scheme under I_N can compute this output.

Any term $h(t_1,t_2)$ appearing on the tree is distinct from any other subterm and t_1 and t_2 are also distinct; thus t_1 and t_2 must be computed and stored before $h(t_1,t_2)$ can be computed.

One way of thinking of this situation is to visualize a game, with a binary tree of depth N as a "board" and k markers or "pieces" (representing locations in a program scheme). Any marker can be placed on a leaf. Each node is either a leaf or has two "sons". If both sons of a node are covered with markers, then one marker can be moved up to that node and markers removed from the two sons. The object is to eventually place a marker on the root, using as few markers as possible. How many markers are needed in the worst case?

The answer is that if the tree is a full binary tree of depth N , then $N+1$ markers are necessary and sufficient. The proof is by induction on N . The case $N = 1$ is obvious, for then there are just two leaves and both must be covered before the root can be covered. Suppose this is true for depth $N-1$. The root has two sons each of which can be regarded as the root of a full binary subtree of depth $N-1$; call these nodes n_1 and n_2 . The root can be covered when and only when both n_1 and n_2 are covered. Suppose n_1 is covered first. By induction, it requires N markers to do this. Then $N-1$ of these markers are free, but one must remain on n_1 . By induction it takes N markers to cover n_2 , for a total of $N+1$. Then the root can be covered. The argument shows both that $N+1$ are required and that $N+1$ suffice.

We have really proven, using our analogy:

SUBLEMMA Let P be any program scheme and I any free interpretation. If (P,I) ever constructs a full binary tree of depth N with distinct leaves, then P must have at least $N+1$ storage locations (variables).

Thus if S_0 were strongly equivalent to a program scheme P , P would need $N+1$ locations to compute each $val(S_0, I_N, x)$ and hence need infinitely many storage locations, a contradiction. Hence S_0 is not strongly equivalent to any program scheme. ■

DEFINITION A recursion scheme S is <u>flowchartable</u> if there is a program scheme P strongly equivalent to S .

What we have really shown, but will not prove formally is:

PROPOSITION 7.7 If S is a recursion scheme such that for each n there is a free interpretation I_n for which the computation of $val(S, I_n, x)$ requires constructing a full binary tree of depth n or greater with distinct leaves, then S is not flowchartable.

We can show for always halting recursion schemes as we showed for always halting program schemes that there is a uniform bound on the length of any computation and hence on the length of the output under any free interpretation.

PROPOSITION 7.8 Any always halting recursion scheme is flowchartable.

These facts and the standard constructions we saw before allow us to show that it is not partially decidable whether a recursion scheme is flowchartable - and it also is not partially decidable whether a recursion scheme is NOT flowchartable.

THEOREM 7.9 For recursion schemes R , neither " R is flowchartable" nor " R is not flowchartable" is partially decidable.

PROOF

The proof uses the schemes in Example VII-1. For a two-tape one-way deterministic finite state acceptor $M = (K_1, K_2, \{0,1\}, \delta, q_o, q_a, q_r)$ we construct a program scheme $P(M)$ and two recursion schemes $R_1(M)$ and $R_2(M)$ such that

(1) If $L_a(M) \cap D = \phi$ then $R_1(M)$ is strongly equivalent to $P(M)$ and if $L_a(M) \cap D \neq \phi$, then $R_1(M)$ is not flowchartable.

(2) If $L_d(M) \cap D = \phi$ then $R_2(M)$ is always halting and hence flowchartable and if $L_d(M) \cap D \neq \phi$ then $R_2(M)$ is not flowchartable.

If we have proven (1) and (2) we can conclude that $R_1(M)$ is flowchartable if and only if $L_a(M) \cap D = \phi$ and that $R_2(M)$ is not flowchartable if and only if $L_d(M) \cap D \neq \phi$. Since these are not partially decidable problems for two-tape one-way deterministic finite state acceptors, we have the desired results by the standard arguments.

It remains to establish (1) and (2). We give informal justifications. If machine M never reaches state q_a on input (t,t) then $R_1(M)$ simply imitates M in the same way our previous flowchart schemes did. Thus we know in this case that $R_1(M)$ is flowchartable and can write out the strongly equivalent program scheme $P(M)$ explicitly. If M reaches q_a on input pair (t,t), then for the corresponding free interpretatinn I_t with $t_{I_t}(h(x)) = t$, $R_1(M)$ reaches the subscheme with defining letter F_{q_a} which in turn leads it into a subscheme defined by G which we know is not flowchartable. The functions and tests in G are so arranged that there is no interference from previous tests. For each n some free interpretation $I_{n,t}$ takes $R_1(M)$ to G and then leads it to construct as output a full binary tree of depth n with distinct leaves; so $R_1(M)$ is not flowchartable in this case.

We now examine $R_2(M)$. If M never diverges on (t,t) it always reaches q_a or q_r and so every occurrence of nonterminal F_q ultimately is replaced by an occurrence of F_{q_r} or F_{q_a} and hence by a terminal string. Thus $R_2(M)$ always halts and so is flowchartable. But if M diverges on (t,t) then $R_2(M)$ executes more and more of a computation that is really equivalent to S_0 which we have seen is not flowchartable. For each n there is a free interpretation $I_{t,n}$ which imitates M on (t,t) as far as concerns expansion of the F_q's but on the G_q's imitates (S_0, I_n) as previously defined and gives as output the full binary tree of depth n with distinct leaves. Hence $R_2(M)$ cannot be flowchartable if $L_d(M) \cap D \neq \phi$. ■

EXAMPLE VII-1   CONSTRUCTIONS TO PROVE THAT FLOWCHARTABILITY IS NOT DECIDABLE

Start from a deterministic two-tape one-way finite state acceptor
$M = (K_1, K_2, \{0,1\}, \delta, q_o, q_a, q_r)$.

A. PROOF THAT " R IS FLOWCHARTABLE" IS NOT PARTIALLY DECIDABLE

Recursion scheme $R_1(M)$ described below is flowchartable if and only if
$L_a(M) \cap D = \phi$

The initial equation is:

$F_0(x) = F_{q_o}(h(x), h(x), x)$

For each q in K_1 there is an equation:

$F_q(u_1, u_2, x) = IF\ T(u_1)\ THEN\ F_{\delta(q,1)}(h(u_1), u_2, x)\ ELSE\ F_{\delta(q,0)}(h(u_1), u_2, x)$

For each q in K_2 there is an equation:

$F_q(u_1, u_2, x) = IF\ T(u_2)\ THEN\ F_{\delta(q,1)}(u_1, h(u_2), x)\ ELSE\ F_{\delta(q,0)}(u_1, h(u_2), x)$

For q_r and q_a we have:

$F_{q_r}(u_1, u_2, x) = f(x)$

$F_{q_a}(u_1, u_2, x) = G(x)$

And finally $G(x)$ is defined by an equation we know is not flowchartable:

$G(x) = IF\ Q(x)\ THEN\ x\ ELSE\ h(G(f(x)), G(g(x)))$

EXAMPLE VII-1   CONTINUED

B. CONSTRUCTION OF PROGRAM SCHEME P(M)

Program scheme P(M) is constructed from two-tape one-way deterministic finite state acceptor $M = (K_1, K_2, \{0,1\}, \delta, q_o, q_a, q_r)$

Initial Subscheme

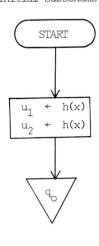

Subscheme for q in K_1

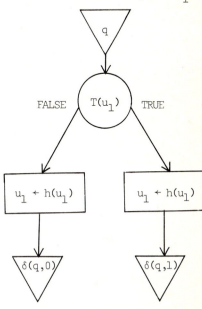

Subschemes for q_a and q_r

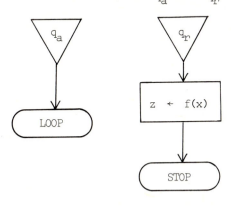

Subscheme for q in K_2

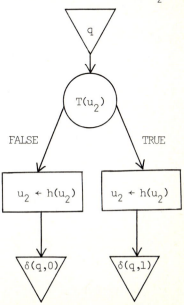

EXAMPLE VII-1   CONCLUDED

C.   PROOF THAT " R IS NOT FLOWCHARTABLE" IS NOT PARTIALLY DECIDABLE

Recursion scheme $R_2(M)$ is constructed from two-tape one-way deterministic finite state acceptor $M = (K_1, K_2, \{0,1\}, \delta, q_o, q_a, q_r)$ and is not flowchartable if and only if $L_d(M) \cap D \neq \phi$.

The initial equation is

$$F_0(x) = F_{q_o}(h(x), h(x), x)$$

For each q in K_1 there is an equation

$$F_q(u_1, u_2, v) = \text{IF } T(u_1) \text{ THEN } G_{\delta(q,1)}(h(u_1), u_2, v) \text{ ELSE } G_{\delta(q,0)}(h(u_1), u_2, v)$$

For each q in K_2 there is an equation

$$F_q(u_1, u_2, v) = \text{IF } T(u_2) \text{ THEN } G_{\delta(q,1)}(u_1, h(u_2), v) \text{ ELSE } G_{\delta(q,0)}(u_1, h(u_2), v)$$

For q_a and q_r we have:

$$F_{q_a}(u_1, u_2, v) = F_{q_r}(u_1, u_2, v) = v$$

For all q in $K_1 \cup K_2$ there is an equation

$$G_q(u_1, u_2, v) = \text{IF } Q(v) \text{ THEN } v \text{ ELSE } h(F_q(u_1, u_2, f(v)), F_q(u_1, u_2, g(v)))$$

C. LINEAR RECURSION SCHEMES ARE FLOWCHARTABLE

Many of the methods advanced for code optimization depend on presenting the program in flowchart form without any use of recursive features such as procedures. In the light of the results in the previous section it is an open and interesting problem to characterize at least some subcases of flowchartable recursion schemes and determine special cases in which it is decidable whether schemes are flow-chartable.

We now examine one special case in which we know that schemes are always flowchartable - the case of linear recursion schemes. A term was defined to be linear if it contained at most one nonterminal; a recursion scheme is linear if all terms appearing in all of its equations are linear.

We mentioned that recursion schemes could always be translated into simple recursion schemes in such a way as to preserve linearity. For our purposes, this means that in discussing linear recursion schemes we can assume that all equations are in one of the following four formats:

(1) $F(\overline{Y})$ = $G(t_1,\ldots,t_n)$ G a defined function, and each t_i terminal

(2) $F(\overline{Y})$ = $f(t_1,\ldots,t_{k-1},G(\overline{Y}),t_{k+1},\ldots,t_s)$ G a defined function and each t_i terminal and f a basis function

(3) $F(\overline{Y})$ = IF $T(y_{i_1},\ldots,y_{i_k})$ THEN $G(\overline{Y})$ ELSE $H(\overline{Y})$ G , H defined function letters

(4) $F(\overline{Y})$ = t   t terminal

Before giving a formal proof that linear recursion schemes are flowchartable we shall illustrate the concepts involved by an example which is small and yet complex enough to illustrate the general case.

EXAMPLE

$$F_0(x) = F_1(g(x),h(x))$$

$$F_1(y_1,y_2) = IF\ T(y_1,y_2)\ THEN\ f(y_1,y_2)\ ELSE\ f(F_1(g(y_2),y_1),f(y_1,y_2))$$

Consider the free interpretation I with $I(T)(g(x),h(x))$ = $I(T)(g(h(x)),g(x))$ = $I(T)(g(g(x)),g(h(x)))$ = FALSE and $I(T)(t_1,t_2)$ = TRUE elsewhere. The computation (S,I,x) proceeds as follows.

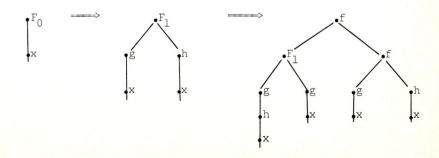

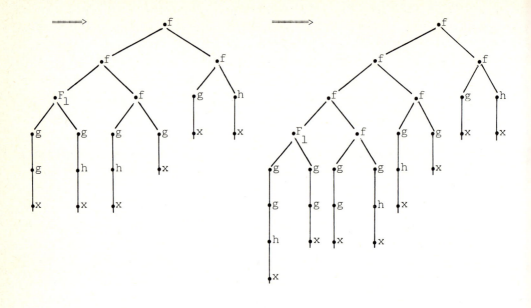

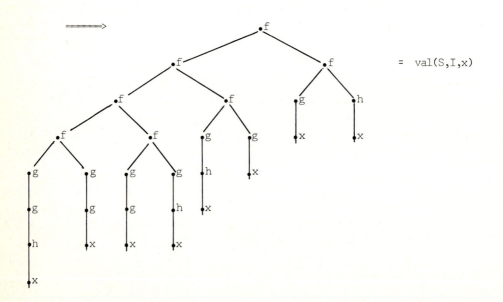

= val(S,I,x)

The output is f(f(f(f(g(g(h(x))),g(g(x))),f(g(g(x)),g(h(x)))),f(g(h(x)),g(x))),
   f(g(x),h(x)))   .

Notice that two types of action occur. The arguments of F_1 are built up in a
simple pattern - g is applied to the second argument y_2 and then $g(y_2)$
becomes the first argument while the first argument y_1 is switched into second

place unchanged. Clearly a flowchart scheme can imitate this action by alternating the FALSE branch of test $T(y_1, y_2)$ with the simultaneous compute and store instructions $(y_1, y_2) \leftarrow (g(y_2), y_1)$. Similarly the TRUE branch of test $T(y_1, y_2)$ can lead to the output statement $z \leftarrow f(y_1, y_2)$. But this is not the full output. At each step $F_1(y_1, y_2)$ is replaced by f applied to the new F_1 and to $f(y_1, y_2)$. The computation piles on as many f's as there are execution steps. To make it worse, each step also installs $f(y_1, y_2)$ as the second argument of the new occurrence of f.

Thus, in addition to building up z as indicated above, we must also, if the computation took n steps after forming F_1, build up f^n and recreate intermediate values of the arguments, proceeding backwards. Thus if $z(n)$ and $y_i(n)$ are the values after step n, we must first construct $z(n) = f(y_1(n), y_2(n))$ and then recalculate $n-1$ steps of the computation starting at the top to get $z(n+1) = f(z(n), f(y_1(n-1), y_2(n-1)))$, then $n-2$ steps of the computation yield $z(n+2) = f(z(n+1), f(y_1(n-2), y_2(n-2)))$, and so forth.

How can this be done without using a counter? The answer is that we have an implicit clock since n was exactly the number of steps required to obtain the values of $y_1(n)$ and $y_2(n)$ that first set $T(y_1, y_2)$ to TRUE. Thus we must store the initial values of the inputs and then using new variables run a separate recomputation, not to get output but just to count to n. This type of action must be repeated up to $n-1$ times and so we really need two counters. We add new variables u_i and v_i to serve as counters. In the first restart we give the u variables the values after two computation steps and the y variables the values after doing one, and store this starting value of the u variables in the v variables. Now when the u variables reach the required shut-off values the y variables are back at step $n-1$, and so we can construct that part of the tree (i.e. $z(n+1)$). Then we update the v values by one step and store this in u and v and now restart the whole computation with the y variables at their step 1 values. This time the y-computation will lag two steps behind the u-computation and end with the values for $n-2$. At the k-th restart cycle, we have the y-computation k steps behind the u-computation and end with the y variables at their time $n-k$ values and make the corresponding construction (i.e. $z(n+k)$). We always store initial (time k) values of the u variables in the v variables and have them available for the next cycle. We recognize $k = n$ because at this point the values stored in the v variables are already at the shut-off point and so we stop.

These ideas are embodied in the flowchart in Example VII-2 which is strongly equivalent to our scheme S. The construction carries over to the general case. We allow our flowchart to use multiple assignment statements $(u_1, u_2) \leftarrow (t_1, t_2)$ for t_1 and t_2 arbitrary (terminal) terms which are executed by simultaneously storing the current value of t_1 in u_1 and the current value of t_2 in u_2. As we have discussed before, these assignment statements can be simulated by standard assignment

EXAMPLE VII-2   FLOWCHART SCHEME STRONGLY EQUIVALENT TO LINEAR RECURSION SCHEME

$F_0(x) = F_1(g(x),h(x))$

$F_1(y_1,y_2) = \text{IF } T(y_1,y_2) \text{ THEN } f(y_1,y_2) \text{ ELSE } f(F_1(g(y_2),y_1),f(y_1,y_2))$

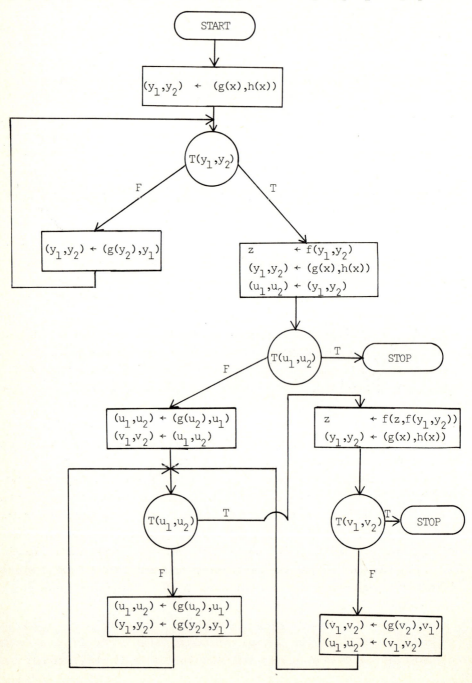

statements using new dummy variables. We have not done so because it would obscure the lines of the construction.

THEOREM 7.10   Every linear recursion scheme is flowchartable.

PROOF

We adapt the ideas of the previous construction (Example VII-2). Now we may have more than one equation. We use the fact that these equations can be assumed to be in one of four formats which we shall call Q for query, T for terminal, A for building up arguments and O for building up functions on the outside. We must not only keep track of the number of steps and store the values for the next cycle in the v variables but must also keep track of which equation is currently acting on u , which equation is acting on y and which equation will act on v when we restart. We keep track of this information mnemonically in the addresses. Thus address (R,k) will mean restart with equation k (the equation for F_k) and (i,j,k) means equation F_i is acting on y , equation F_j on u and equation F_k will act on v when we restart.

For convenience in juggling notation we assume that the recursion equations in our linear recursion scheme S define in order defined functions $F_0, F_1, \ldots$ to some F_ℓ ; the equation defining F_i is called equation i . We let the variables in $\overline{X} = (x_1, \ldots, x_n)$ and $\overline{Y} = (y_1, \ldots, y_m)$ be all distinct and assume that the start equation defines $F_0(\overline{X})$ while equation i for $i \neq 0$ defines $F_i(\overline{Y})$; this allows us to store automatically the input in separate locations. We can without loss of generality assume that all defined functions are m-placed except perhaps for F_0 . Let $\overline{U} = (u_1, \ldots, u_m)$ and $\overline{V} = (v_1, \ldots, v_m)$ contain new and distinct variables. If t is a term using the y_i as variables, we use the notation $u(t)$ for the term obtained by substituting u_i for y_i everywhere (so for example if $t = F_3(y_1, f(y_2), F_5(y_1, y_3, y_1))$, then $u(t) = F_3(u_1, f(u_2), F_5(u_1, u_3, u_1))$) .

Again, we allow our flowcharts to use multiple assignments such as $(u_1, u_2) \leftarrow (t_1, t_2)$ for arbitrary (terminal) terms t_1 and t_2 .

To an equation i we may associate various objects - an assignment statement $s(i)$ using the y variables, a corresponding assignment statement $s_u(i)$ using the u variables, an assignment statement involving z , $z(i)$, and/or query statements $q(i)$ on the y variables or $q_u(i)$ on the u variables, as well as GOTOs $d(i)$ or conditional GOTOs $d_T(i)$ and $d_F(i)$. The nature and type of these objects depend on the type of equation.

We can assume that the start equation is

$$F_0(\overline{X}) \;=\; F_1(t_1, \ldots, t_m)$$

where the t_j are terminal terms. We let $s(0)$ and $s_u(0)$ be defined by:

$$s(0): \quad (y_1,\ldots,y_m) \leftarrow (t_1,\ldots,t_m)$$

$$s_u(0): \quad (u_1,\ldots,u_m) \leftarrow (t_1,\ldots,t_m)$$

and of course $d(0) = 1$ since we transfer to equation 1.

We can assume that the other equations are in one of four forms and assign these objects as indicated below.

(1) Type A — $F_i(\overline{Y}) = F_r(t_1,\ldots,t_m)$ each t_j a terminal term.
We say that i is in A and let

$$d(i) = r$$

$$s(i): \quad (y_1,\ldots,y_m) \leftarrow (t_1,\ldots,t_m)$$

$$s_u(i): \quad (u_1,\ldots,u_m) \leftarrow (u(t_1),\ldots,u(t_m))$$

(2) Type 0 — $F_i(\overline{Y}) = f(t_1,\ldots,t_{k-1},F_r(\overline{Y}),t_{k+1},\ldots,t_s)$ each t_j terminal
We say that i is in 0 and let

$$d(i) = r$$

$$s(i) = s_u(i) = \text{the null statement}$$

$$z(i): \quad z \leftarrow f(t_1,\ldots,t_{k-1},z,t_{k+1},\ldots,t_s)$$

(3) Type Q — $F_i(\overline{Y}) = \text{IF } T(y_{i_1},\ldots,y_{i_k}) \text{ THEN } F_r(\overline{Y}) \text{ ELSE } F_s(\overline{Y})$
We say that i is in Q and let

$$d_T(i) = r$$

$$d_F(i) = s$$

$$q(i): \quad T(y_{i_1},\ldots,y_{i_k})$$

$$q_u(i): \quad T(u_{i_1},\ldots,u_{i_k})$$

(4) Type T — $F_i(\overline{Y}) = t$ t a terminal term
We say that i is in T and let

$$z(i): \quad z \leftarrow t$$

We construct a program scheme P strongly equivalent to S as follows, by subschemes. As subscheme labels we use:

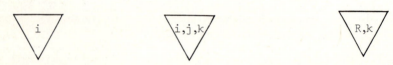

where i,j and k are equation numbers and R is a special symbol meaning restart. The scheme appears in Example VII-3. We leave it to the reader to check out its properties. ∎

EXAMPLE VII-3   CONSTRUCTION OF FLOWCHART P EQUIVALENT TO A LINEAR
                RECURSION SCHEME S .

I. Straight simulation mode

Initial subscheme:

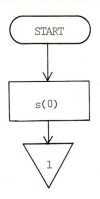

Simulation of i in A or O   Simulation of i in Q

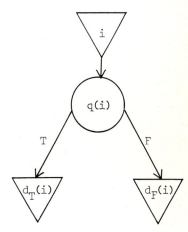

Simulation of i in T

If i = 1 or O = φ   If i ≠ 1 , O ≠ φ

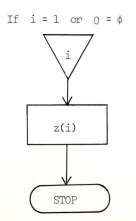

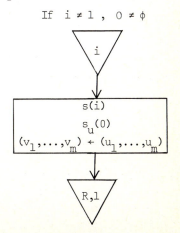

EXAMPLE VII-3 (Continued)

II. Restart subschemes

For k in A or 0

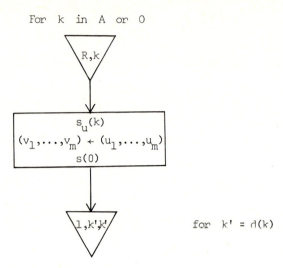

for k' = d(k)

For k in Q   For k in T

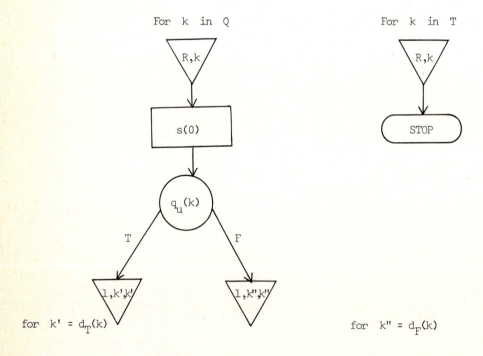

for k' = d$_T$(k)   for k" = d$_F$(k)

EXAMPLE VII-3   (Continued)

III. Clock simulation mode -   i carries the y-computation, j the
      u-computation and k is the next restart position.

Subschemes for i or j in A or 0

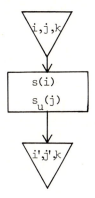

for i' = d(i) , j' = d(j)

Subscheme for j in Q , i in A or 0   Subscheme for i in Q , j in A or 0

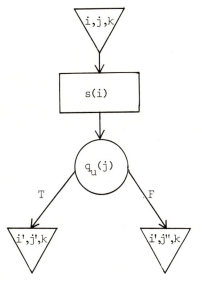

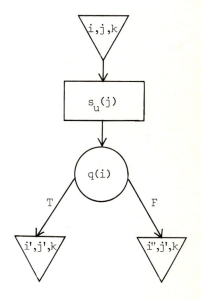

for i' = d(i) , j' = d$_T$(j) , j" = d$_F$(j)

for i' = d$_T$(i) , i" = d$_F$(i) , j' = d(j)

EXAMPLE VII-3   (Continued)

III. Clock simulation mode continued

Subschemes for i and j in Q

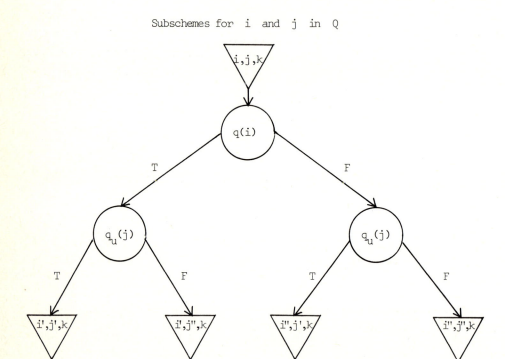

for $i' = d_T(i)$, $i'' = d_F(i)$, $j' = d_T(j)$, and $j'' = d_F(j)$

EXAMPLE VII-3   (Concluded)

IV. END OF CYCLE AND RESTART MODE - i or j in T

For i in T

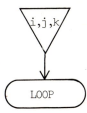

This situation cannot occur since j carries the u-computation which leads the y-computation in i and so j must reach the cutoff point - an equation in T - first.

Subscheme for j in T and i in A or Q

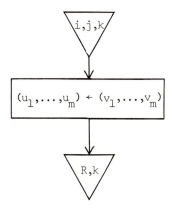

Subscheme for j in T and i in O

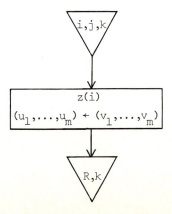

We have just shown that linear recursion schemes are flowchartable. In the last section we showed that every program scheme is translatable into a recursion scheme and our construction actually showed that every program scheme can be translated into a particular type of linear recursion scheme.

DEFINITION   A term t is <u>right linear</u> if it contains at most one nonterminal and no terminal appears to the left of any nonterminal.

Thus t is right linear if it is either terminal or else of the form $F(t_1,\ldots,t_n)$ with each t_i terminal and F a defined function letter.

DEFINITION   A recursion scheme is <u>right linear</u> if all terms appearing in all its equations are right linear.

Thus our result (Theorem 7.5) in the previous section could be phrased:

COROLLARY 7.11   The class of program schemes with one output variable is effectively translatable into the class of right linear recursion schemes.

Putting our results together yields:

THEOREM 7.12   The classes of program schemes with one output variable, of linear recursion schemes and of right linear recursion schemes are effectively inter-translatable.

This is not true for monadic recursion schemes. In the monadic case, right linear schemes are intertranslatable with Ianov schemes but the class of linear monadic recursion schemes is more powerful.

Suppose we have a recursion scheme S containing an n-placed basis function letter f and another recursion scheme S' such that all defined function letters of S' are distinct from all basis or defined function letters of S , f does not appear anywhere in S' and the initial defined function F_0' of S' is n-placed. We can define a recursion scheme S" whose defined function letters are those of S and those of S' plus f , now regarded as a defined function letter. Scheme S" contains all equations of S , all equations of S' , and in addition the equation $f(\overline{Y}) = F_0'(\overline{Y})$ defining f . Under any interpretaionn I , (S",I) computes the function (S,I') where I' is the extension of I obtained by setting $I'(f)(\overline{a}) = val(S',I,\overline{a})$ everywhere - i.e., a functional composition of S' into S . It should be clear that if S and S' are both flowchartable, so is S' .

THEOREM 7.13   The class of flowchartable recursion schemes is closed under functional composition.

Thus not only the linear recursion schemes but also their closure under functional composition is flowchartable - a fairly rich family.

D. RECURSION AUGMENTED FLOWCHART SCHEMES

In a previous section, we have shown that recursion schemes are more powerful than flowchart schemes. Now we add to the basic model of flowchart of program schemes a mechanism resembling recursive procedures and calls as defined in PL/I , for example. We find that such recursion augmented flowchart schemes are in fact equivalent in expressive power to recursion schemes. Thus we show that recursion schemes are indeed one version of the model we seek to study the power of programs when augmented by recursion, in contrast to programs without this extension but perhaps with other additions.

It is generally known that recursive procedures can be implemented using stacks. Here we provide a formal expression for this piece of "folk-lore" by showing that recursion schemes (or, as we shall actually do it, program schemes augmented by recursion) can be effectively translated into program schemes augmented by a pushdown store. We shall note without formal proof that program schemes augmented by arrays are actually more powerful than recursion schemes - a rather surprising and counterintuitive result.

As defined in Chapter Two, program schemes have basis function letters, predicate letters and constants, with "meanings" assigned by interpretations. These symbols plus the variables or storage locations are combined to form two basic kinds of instructions or statements, assignments and tests; two special instructions, STOP and START were also defined.

Recursion augmented schemes also have defined function symbols or procedure symbols; their values are assigned by the computation rather than by the interpretation. As in the definition of recursion schemes, each defined function letter or symbol F is assumed to be m-placed for some nonzero positive integer m . A recursion augmented program scheme is allowed a new type of instruction, a call.

DEFINITION   A <u>call</u> is an instruction of the form

CALL $F(y_1,\ldots,y_n)$

where F is an n-placed defined function symbol, and $y_1,\ldots,y_n$ are n distinct variables, called the <u>actual parameters</u> of the call.

Each defined function symbol appearing in a scheme must of course be defined in the scheme. This is done by appending to the scheme a special type of subroutine or subscheme called a procedure definition.

DEFINITION   A procedure <u>definition</u> is a set of instructions of the form:

> PROCEDURE $F(x_1,\ldots,x_n)$
>
> DECLARE NEW $(u_1,\ldots,u_m)$
>
> Q
>
> END   F

where

1) F is an n-placed defined function symbol, the <u>function defined by the procedure</u>;
2) $x_1,\ldots,x_n$ are n distinct variables, the <u>formal parameters</u> of the procedure;
3) $u_1,\ldots,u_m$ are m distinct variables, all different from the x_i , and the u_i are called the <u>local variables</u> of the procedure; and
4) Q , the <u>procedure body</u>, is any nonempty list of assignment instructions, test instructions and CALL instructions, involving as variables only the formal parameters and local variables of the procedure, such that START Q STOP is a program scheme with CALLs.

A recursion augmented scheme is a program scheme with definitions appended for all procedures called.

DEFINITION   A <u>recursion augmented program scheme</u> is a list $(Q,Q_1,\ldots,Q_m)$ such that Q is a program scheme with CALLs, each Q_i is a procedure definition and

1) the Q_i define all and only defined function symbols appearing in CALLs in $Q \cup Q_1 \cup \ldots \cup Q_m$ and each defined function symbol is defined only once, and
2) the variables of Q , the <u>global variables</u>, do not appear in any Q_i and the variables in Q_i are disjoint from those in Q_j for $i \neq j$.

Now we have defined the syntax of our model - how a scheme is formally put together - we must define the semantics - how a function is computed under an interpretation. Interpretations are defined as for ordinary program schemes or for recursion schemes - the defined functions are not interpreted.

We made a slight departure from our previous assumptions. Notice that we have cheated a little in the definition of a scheme. We have not explained how the division into input variables, program variables, and output variables is to be carried out. In particular, we have not explained what the requirement that on every path from START every non-input variable must be assigned to before it is computed on, means in a situation where the path contains CALLs. Such an explanation could be made but it would be complex and in some respects undesirable. For example, we wish to allow the actual parameters of a CALL to be undefined when the call is initially executed because the procedure called may return the desired values. So we abandon this requirement and instead adopt a convention that every domain of an interpretation contains a special symbol Λ meaning "undefined". Any function acting on Λ as one of its variables yields the value Λ and likewise any function acting on a value not in its domain returns Λ . This convention has some pitfalls of its own, but does allow us to sidestep some unpleasant problems. If Λ is ever the output of a program this is taken to mean that the program is ill-defined.

Let $P = (Q, Q_1, \ldots, Q_m)$ be a recursion augmented program scheme, I an interpretation of P , and $\bar{a}$ an input vector. The computation $(P, I, \bar{a})$ starts by simulating computation $(Q, I, \bar{a})$ in the usual way, until a CALL is reached. Suppose the computation $(Q, I, \bar{a})$ at step t must excecute CALL $F(y_1, \ldots, y_n)$, where F is an n-placed defined function letter defined by procedure Q_j . Let the formal parameters of Q_j be $x_1, \ldots, x_n$ and the local variables $u_1, \ldots, u_s$. By our definition all y_i and all x_i are distinct. Let u_i' be a new variable, $1 \leq i \leq s$. Let $Q_j' = Q_j \frac{\bar{x}, \bar{u}}{\bar{y}, \bar{u}'}$, the result of substituting y_i for x_i and u_i' for u_i everywhere in Q_j . Now the computation replaces CALL $F(y_1, \ldots, y_n)$ by Q_j' and proceeds to simulate subprogram (Q_j', I) . When the computation reaches the END F statement in $Q_{j'}$, it wipes out all the local variables u_i' and resumes the simulation of (Q, I) with the instruction directly following CALL $F(y_1, \ldots, y_n)$ and continues in the same way.

Thus, computation $(P, I, \bar{a})$ is at any step either simulating the main program (Q, I) or else some subprogram (Q_j', I) . It can encounter a call, CALL $G(\bar{v})$, either in the main program or in a subprogram. In either case, when it encounters this call, it takes the procedure Q_k defining G , replaces the formal parameters by the actual parameters uniformly and changes the local variables into new variables (this is necessary if, for example, G is being called by itself) and proceeds now as if CALL $G(\bar{v})$ had been replaced by this copy Q_k' of Q_k . Roughly speaking, this form of parameter passing can be considered a run-time macro-substitution.

Finally, computation $(P, I, \bar{a})$ halts if and only if it encounters the STOP instruction while in the main program (Q, I) .

EXAMPLE

We need an illustration of this somewhat complicated definition. The meanings assigned by an interpretation I have already been written down in the recursion augmented program scheme of Example VII - 4. The resulting program is a moderately poor program for computing the binomial coefficient $\binom{n}{k}$ for nonzero positive integers n and k with $1 \leq k \leq n$. One reason it is not a good program is that input is not tested for validity; another is that the algorithm - compute n! , then k! , then multiply k! by (n-k)! and divide n! by this result - is often not a safe one because of overflow. The procedure FACT(u,y) multiplies y by u! and works just if u and y are already nonzero positive integers.

The example also gives selected parts of the computation for input n = 3 and k = 2 . We enter instruction 3 with the IF test positive. Then we proceed as if a copy of the procedure body for FACT and the END statement were inserted just before instruction 4 of the main program. Notice that our definitions require a procedure definition to be, in effect, a single entry single exit subscheme so there is no ambiguity about where we enter the procedure or where we leave or where we go next, even if the main program were not a WHILE program (i.e., well-structured). The procedure definition gives us a local value TEMP . When substituting into the main program, formal parameter u becomes actual parameter x_1 , y becomes z_1 and TEMP becomes $TEMP_1$. In fact, TEMP was introduced so that we do not change the value of the global variable x_1 while executing the subroutine. Notice that in 3.4 , FACT calls itself, this time with actual parameters $TEMP_1$ and z_1 ; as this example shows, a local variable can become an actual parameter of another CALL.

EXAMPLE VII - 4   A RECURSION AUGMENTED PROGRAM FOR $\binom{n}{k}$ AND SOME COMPUTATION STEPS

Program $P = (Q, Q_1)$ input n and k output z_1

Main Program:

1. $x_1 \leftarrow n$; $x_2 \leftarrow k$

2. $z_1 \leftarrow 1$; $z_2 \leftarrow 1$

3. IF $x_1 > 1$ THEN CALL FACT(x_1, z_1) ENDIF

4. IF $x_2 > 1$ THEN CALL FACT(x_2, z_2) ENDIF

5. $x_2 \leftarrow x_1 - x_2$

6. IF $x_2 > 1$ THEN CALL FACT(x_2, z_2) ENDIF

7. $z_1 \leftarrow z_1 / z_2$

8. STOP

Procedure FACT:

PROCEDURE FACT(u, y)

DECLARE NEW (TEMP)

1. TEMP $\leftarrow u$

2. $y \leftarrow$ TEMP . y

3. TEMP $\leftarrow$ TEMP - 1

4. IF TEMP > 1 THEN CALL FACT(TEMP, y) ENDIF

END FACT

EXAMPLE VII - 4   CONTINUED

Computation steps for $n = 3$, $k = 2$

Enter instruction 3 with $val(x_1) = 3$, $val(x_2) = 2$, $val(z_1) = val(z_2) = 1$
Now proceed as if the main program were:

3. 1. $TEMP_1 \leftarrow x_1$

   2. $z_1 \leftarrow TEMP_1 \cdot z_1$

   3. $TEMP_1 \leftarrow TEMP_1 - 1$

   4.   IF $TEMP_1 > 1$ THEN CALL $FACT(TEMP_1, z_1)$ ENDIF

   END FACT

4. etc.

Enter 3.4 with $val(x_1) = 3$, $val(x_2) = 2$, $val(z_1) = 3$, $val(z_2) = 1$, and
$val(TEMP_1) = 2$

3. 4. 1. $TEMP_2 \leftarrow TEMP_1$

    2. $z_1 \leftarrow TEMP_2 \cdot z_1$

    3. $TEMP_2 \leftarrow TEMP_2 - 1$

    4.   IF $TEMP_2 > 1$ THEN CALL $FACT(TEMP_2, z_1)$ ENDIF

    END FACT
   END FACT
4. etc.

Enter 3.4.4 with $val(x_1) = 3$, $val(x_2) = 2$, $val(z_1) = 6$, $val(z_2) = 1$,
$val(TEMP_1) = 2$ and $val(TEMP_2) = 1$. Now:

3. 4.   END FACT
   END FACT
4. etc.

EXAMPLE VII - 4   CONCLUDED

Enter 4 with $\text{val}(x_1) = 3$, $\text{val}(x_2) = 2$, $\text{val}(z_1) = 6$, $\text{val}(z_2) = 1$ and
variables TEMP_1 and TEMP_2 have been destroyed.
Now proceed as if main program were:

4. 1. $\text{TEMP}_1 \leftarrow x_2$

   2. $z_2 \leftarrow \text{TEMP}_1 \cdot z_2$

   3. $\text{TEMP}_1 \leftarrow \text{TEMP}_1 - 1$

   4.   IF $\text{TEMP}_1 > 1$ THEN CALL $\text{FACT}(\text{TEMP}_1, z_2)$

   END FACT

5. etc.

Enter 4.4 with $\text{val}(x_1) = 3$, $\text{val}(x_2) = 2$, $\text{val}(z_1) = 6$, $\text{val}(z_2) = 2$, and
$\text{val}(\text{TEMP}_1) = 1$. Now:

4. END FACT

5. etc.

Enter 6 with $\text{val}(x_1) = 3$, $\text{val}(x_2) = 1$, $\text{val}(z_1) = 6$, $\text{val}(z_2) = 2$, and
TEMP_1 destroyed. Since $\text{val}(x_2)$ is not greater than 1 , proceed to 7 .

Enter 8 and halt with $\text{val}(z_1) = 6/2 = 3$. This is the output.

The next thing to observe is that we enter 3.4 with the test again positive and must insert another copy of FACT , this time just before the END FACT statement of the first copy. This time the actual parameters are, as mentioned, $TEMP_1$ and z_1 . The local variable of this CALL is not supposed to be the same as for the previous one, so we need a new variable and use $TEMP_2$; this illustrates why we must change the names of the local variables, too.

When we enter 3.4.4 the test is now false, so we go immediately to the END FACT statement. This causes variable $TEMP_2$ to be permanently destroyed, and we return to the calling subroutine. We again encounter END FACT and this time $TEMP_1$ is removed and we return to 4. of the main program.

At 4 the test is again positive, so we insert a copy of FACT with actual parameters x_2 and z_2 . Since variable $TEMP_1$ was destroyed, as far as the program is concerned it never existed. Thus, we are free to reuse $TEMP_1$; we could instead use a new variable, say $TEMP_3$. We enter 4.4 with the test negative, encounter END FACT , destroy $TEMP_1$ and return to 5 of the main program.

There are some comments on this definition we should make. It by no means reflects all possible features of procedures and calls in "real" programming languages. We have deliberately chosen only to reflect features essential to the notion of recursion and to adopt conventions and restrictions that make other concepts as simple as possible.

Some of the restrictions we have placed on our model are:

1) The values of the actual parameters are altered during the course of the procedure in accordance with the instructions of the procedure;

2) The actual parameters must be variables, not expressions (such as X + Y), and all parameters are distinct; CALL FACT(u,u) is not allowed, nor CALL FACT(x_1 - x_2,z_2) ;

3) Procedure definitions are all single entry single exit subgraphs;

4) The only global variables available to a procedure are the actual parameters;

5) All local variables and formal parameters are distinct new variables, and all local variables die at the end of the procedure subroutine.

None of these restrictions affect computing power. This can readily be shown using new temporary variables. Restriction 3) helped us in the definition of computation. All the restrictions will be useful when we adapt the verification method to handle recursion; restriction 2) is vital in this respect as without it the method in the last section of this chapter is invalid.

As we have mentioned, our definitions entail parameter passing by a kind of run-time macro-substitution. We now define a very useful equivalence preserving transformation on recursion augmented schemes, macroexpansion, which can be considered a kind of compile-time macro-substitution.

DEFINITION   Let $P = (Q,Q_1,...,Q_m)$ be a recursion augmented program scheme and let

CALL $F(y_1,\ldots,y_n)$ be an instruction in Q , with F a function symbol defined by procedure Q_k . Let Q_k be PROCEDURE $F(x_1,\ldots,x_n)$; DECLARE NEW $(u_1,\ldots,u_m)$; S_k END F , with S_k as procedure body. For $1 \le i \le m$, let u_i' be a new variable and let $S_k' = S_k\frac{\overline{x,u}}{\overline{y,u'}}$, the result of substituting y_i for x_i and u_i' for u_i everywhere in S_k and altering the addresses of instructions to avoid conflicts with addresses in Q . The scheme $P' = (Q',Q_1,\ldots,Q_m)$ obtained by replacing CALL $F(y_1,\ldots,y_n)$ by S_k' is a <u>macroexpansion</u> of P .

We note without proof that:

COROLLARY 7.14   If P' is a macroexpansion of P , then P is strongly equivalent to P' .

If an instruction CALL $F(\overline{y})$ occurs while procedure F is being executed (so this call might, for example, not appear in F itself but in another procedure called by F) this call is termed <u>recursive</u>. Otherwise it is <u>first level</u>. Any call in the main program is obviously first level, but calls inside a procedure might be first level or recursive depending on the sequence of instructions by which they are reached. A <u>complete first level macroexpansion of P</u> involves macroexpanding one by one all calls in the main program, then repeating this process as long as there are calls which are first level with respect to the original program scheme P . If P has n defined function letters (procedures) we can form P_1 by macroexpansion of all calls in P , and then form P_2 from P_1 by macroexpansion of all calls of P_1 which are first level with respect to P , then P_3 from P_2 by macroexpansion of all calls of P_2 which are first level with respect to P , and so on. By the time this has been repeated n times, all calls in P_n must be recursive with respect to P . In particular, if there is no interpretation and input under which a recursive call is executed, we can safely remove all calls from P_n (if any are there) and still have a strongly equivalent scheme which is now a program scheme without recursion.

COROLLARY 7.15   If P is a recursion augmented program scheme such that no recursive call is ever executed during any computation of P , then P is strongly equivalent to some program scheme without recursion.

Suppose in a recursion augmented scheme P , a procedure F is called and then, before this call is completed (and END F reached), F is called again. Suppose further that every test encountered during these recursive calls of F always yields the same answer (i.e., each test T either always gives answer TRUE or else always gives answer FALSE). Then the same path must be followed during the

second call of F , yielding ultimately a third call of F before the first or
second is completed, and so forth. So the program will be in an unbreakable loop.
Thus, before the first call of F is finally completed there must be some test T
and values $\bar{a}$ and $\bar{b}$ such that T is applied to both $\bar{a}$ and $\bar{b}$ before completion of the original call of F and $I(T)(\bar{a})$ = TRUE but $I(T)(\bar{b})$ = FALSE . If we
apply a complete first level macroexpansion of P , then in the resulting scheme
all calls are recursive with respect to P and so this situation must hold for
every call.

COROLLARY 7.16   Let S be obtained by a complete first level macroexpansion of
P . Whenever any procedure F is called, either it is never completed and the
computation loops, or there is some test T such that T gives different answers
for two different values during the execution of F .

Example VII - 5 gives a complete first level macroexpansion of the scheme of
Example VII - 4. All calls are now recursive with respect to the original scheme;
the process needed to be carried out only once. The resulting scheme is not
unique because we could have chosen the names of the new variables in different
ways. In particular, since the three calls expanded were independent in the sense
that at most one could be executed at a time, and local variables are destroyed
after completion of a call, we could have used the same variable, say $TEMP_1$, for
all three replacements of local variable TEMP (for that matter, we could have
used TEMP itself.)

Now we must show that our definition is "reasonable" in that the classes of
recursion schemes and of recursion augmented program schemes are effectively intertranslatable. The proof is not hard.

First suppose we have a recursion scheme S . We can, as discussed before,
assume that S is simple. In particular, we can assume that S has an initial
equation of the form

$$F_0(x_1,\ldots,x_m) = F_1(x_1,\ldots,x_m,\underbrace{x_1,\ldots,x_1}_{n-m \text{ times}})$$

and that all other equations are of the forms:

$$F(u_1,\ldots,u_n) = t \qquad t \text{ terminal}$$

$$F(u_1,\ldots,u_n) = IF \ T(u_{i_1},\ldots,u_{i_k}) \ THEN \ G(u_1,\ldots,u_n) \ ELSE \ H(u_1,\ldots,u_n)$$

EXAMPLE VII - 5   A COMPLETE FIRST LEVEL MACROEXPANSION OF EXAMPLE VII - 4

Main Program:

1. $x_1 \leftarrow n$; $x_2 \leftarrow k$

2. $z_1 \leftarrow 1$; $z_2 \leftarrow 1$

3. IF $x_1 > 1$ THEN

        3.1 $TEMP_1 \leftarrow x_1$

        3.2 $z_1 \leftarrow TEMP_1 \cdot z_1$

        3.3 $TEMP_1 \leftarrow TEMP_1 - 1$

        3.4 IF $TEMP_1 > 1$ THEN CALL $FACT(TEMP_1, z_1)$ ENDIF

   ENDIF

4. IF $x_2 > 1$ THEN

        4.1 $TEMP_2 \leftarrow x_2$

        4.2 $z_2 \leftarrow TEMP_2 \cdot z_2$

        4.3 $TEMP_2 \leftarrow TEMP_2 - 1$

        4.4 IF $TEMP_2 > 1$ THEN CALL $FACT(TEMP_2, z_2)$ ENDIF

   ENDIF

5. $x_2 \leftarrow x_1 - x_2$

6. IF $x_2 > 1$ THEN

        6.1 $TEMP_3 \leftarrow x_2$

        6.2 $z_2 \leftarrow TEMP_3 \cdot z_2$

        6.3 $TEMP_3 \leftarrow TEMP_3 - 1$

        6.4 IF $TEMP_3 > 1$ THEN CALL $FACT(TEMP_3, z_2)$ ENDIF

   ENDIF

7. $z_1 \leftarrow z_1 / z_2$

8. STOP

$$F(u_1,\ldots,u_n) = G(t_1,\ldots,t_n)$$

$$F(u_1,\ldots,u_n) = G(t_1,\ldots,t_{i-1},H(u_1,\ldots,u_n),t_{i+1},\ldots,t_n)$$

for F, G and H n-placed defined function letters and $t_1,\ldots,t_n$ terminal terms.

The main body Q of the new scheme is simply:

```
START
CALL   F₁(x₁,...,x_m,x₁,...,x₁,z)
STOP
```

with input variables $x_1,\ldots,x_m$ and output variable z .

Each defined function letter F (except F_0) becomes an n+1-placed defined function letter defined by procedure Q_F . For convenience we omit the PROCEDURE $F(u_1,\ldots,u_n,z)$ statement and the END F statement, and include the DECLARE NEW statement only when there are in fact local variables. We use the same formal parameters and local variables throughout; the names can be changed to agree with our definitions.

If the equation defining F in S is:

$$F(u_1,\ldots,u_n) = t \quad \text{for} \quad t \quad \text{terminal}$$

then the definition of the body of procedure Q_F is:

```
z ← t
```

If the equation defining F in S is:

$$F(u_1,\ldots,u_n) = \text{IF}\ \ T(u_{i_1},\ldots,u_{i_k})\ \ \text{THEN}\ \ G(u_1,\ldots,u_n)\ \ \text{ELSE}\ \ H(u_1,\ldots,u_n)$$

then the definition of the body of procedure Q_F is:

```
IF  T(u_{i₁},...,u_{i_k})  THEN CALL  G(u₁,...,u_n,z)
                           ELSE CALL  H(u₁,...,u_n,z)
ENDIF
```

If the equation defining F is

$$F(u_1,\ldots,u_n) = G(t_1,\ldots,t_n)$$

then the definition of the body of procedure Q_F is:

DECLARE NEW $(v_1,\ldots,v_n)$

$v_1 \leftarrow t_1 ; \ldots ; v_n \leftarrow t_n$

$u_1 \leftarrow v_1 ; \ldots ; u_n \leftarrow v_n$

CALL $G(u_1,\ldots,u_n,z)$

Finally, if the equation defining F is

$$F(u_1,\ldots,u_n) = G(t_1,\ldots,t_{i-1},H(u_1,\ldots,u_n),t_{i+1},\ldots,t_n) \quad \text{each } t_j \quad \text{terminal}$$

then the definition of the body of procedure Q_F is:

DECLARE NEW $(v_1,\ldots,v_n,y)$

$v_1 \leftarrow t_1 ; \ldots ; v_{i-1} \leftarrow t_{i-1}$

$v_{i+1} \leftarrow t_{i+1} ; \ldots ; v_n \leftarrow t_n$

CALL $H(u_1,\ldots,u_n,y)$

$u_1 \leftarrow v_1 ; \ldots ; u_{i-1} \leftarrow v_{i-1}$

$u_i \leftarrow y$

$u_{i+1} \leftarrow v_{i+1} ; \ldots ; u_n \leftarrow v_n$

CALL $G(u_1,\ldots,u_n,z)$

Thus we have shown

THEOREM 7.17   The class of recursion schemes is effectively translatable into the class of recursion augmented program schemes.

EXAMPLE

We can re-examine briefly two of the schemes studied in Section A of this chapter. The first scheme was:

$$F(x) = IF \ P(x) \ THEN \ x \ ELSE \ h(F(f(x)), F(g(x)))$$

This is not in the desired form. However, the scheme is so clear that we can apply the algorithm to it directly, making the necessary adjustments as we go. The main scheme is simply:

    START

    CALL F(x,z)

    STOP

and the procedure definition Q_F is just:

    PROCEDURE F(x,z)

    DECLARE NEW (u_1, u_2, y_1, y_2)

    IF P(x) THEN $z \leftarrow x$

            ELSE

                $u_1 \leftarrow f(x)$; $u_2 \leftarrow g(x)$

                CALL $F(u_1, y_1)$

                CALL $F(u_2, y_2)$

                $z \leftarrow h(y_1, y_2)$

    ENDIF

    END F

Our second example was the interpreted scheme

$$F(x) = IF \ x = 0 \ THEN \ x + 1 \ ELSE \ x.F(x \doteq 1)$$

This becomes again

    START

    CALL F(x,z)

    STOP

with procedure definition Q_F as :

```
        PROCEDURE  F(x,z)

        DECLARE NEW  (u)

        IF  x = 0  THEN  z ← x+1

                   ELSE  u ← x ∸ 1

                         CALL  F(u,z)

                         z ← x.z


        ENDIF

        END  F
```

The translation of a recursion augmented program scheme into a recursion scheme is an elaboration of the construction in the proof of Theorem 7.5.

THEOREM 7.18   The class of recursion augmented program schemes with one output variable is effectively translatable into the class of recursion schemes.

PROOF

Let $P = (Q,Q_1,\ldots,Q_p)$ be a recursion augmented program scheme with n global variables (locations in Q) $x_1,\ldots,x_n$. For each address r of an instruction in Q , we create a new defined function letter M_r which is n-placed. If F is a defined function letter in P for a procedure with m formal parameters and k local variables, we create a new m-placed defined function letter F_i for $1 \le i \le m$ and an (m+k)-placed defined function letter $F_{r,i}$ for each address r in the procedure defining F .

In the main scheme Q , an instruction

$$r. \quad x_j \leftarrow t$$

corresponds to an equation

$$M_r(x_1,\ldots,x_n) = M_{r+1}(x_1,\ldots,x_{j-1},t,x_{j+1},\ldots,x_n) \, ,$$

an instruction

$$r. \quad T(\overline{v}) \quad s,\ell$$

corresponds to equation

$$M_r(\bar{x}) = IF \ T(\bar{v}) \ THEN \ M_s(\bar{x}) \ ELSE \ M_\ell(\bar{x})$$

and if x_{j_0} is the output variable, then

    r. STOP

becomes

$$M_r(\bar{x}) = x_{j_0} \ .$$

The new feature is that if F is a procedure symbol in P defined by a procedure with m formal parameters, a call instruction in Q

    r. CALL $F(v_1,\ldots,v_m)$

now corresponds to an equation

$$M_r(x_1,\ldots,x_n) = M_{r+1}(t_1,\ldots,t_n)$$

where for $x_i = v_j$, $t_i = F_j(v_1,\ldots,v_m)$ and if $x_i \notin \{v_1,\ldots,v_m\}$, $t_i = x_i$.

Suppose F is a procedure symbol in P defined by a procedure Q_F with formal parameters $y_1,\ldots,y_m$ and local variables $y_{m+1},\ldots,y_{m+k}$. For $1 \le i \le m$, there is an equation

$$F_i(y_1,\ldots,y_m) = F_{1,i}(y_1,\ldots,y_m,\underbrace{y_1,\ldots,y_1}_{k \ times})$$

Now an instruction in Q_F

    r. $y_j \leftarrow t$

corresponds to

$$F_{r,i}(y_1,\ldots,y_{m+k}) = F_{r+1,i}(y_1,\ldots,y_{j-1},t,y_{j+1},\ldots,y_{m+k})$$

and

    r. $T(\bar{v})$ s,ℓ

to

$$F_{r,i}(\overline{y}) = IF\ T(\overline{v})\ THEN\ F_{s,i}(\overline{y})\ ELSE\ F_{\ell,i}(\overline{y})$$

while

r. END F

becomes

$$F_{r,i}(y_1,\ldots,y_{m+k}) = y_i\ .$$

Finally, a call in Q_F

r. CALL $G(v_1,\ldots,v_s)$

becomes an equation

$$F_{r,i}(y_1,\ldots,y_{m+k}) = F_{r+1,i}(t_1,\ldots,t_{m+k})$$

where $t_j = G_k(v_1,\ldots,v_s)$ if $x_j = v_k$ and $t_j = x_j$ if $x_j \notin \{v_1,\ldots,v_s\}$.

The new recursion scheme S is the set of all the equations above with initial letter M_1 . It is left to the reader to see that S is indeed strongly equivalent to P . ■

In the next section we briefly compare recursion augmented schemes with program schemes augmented by other data manipulation mechanisms - pushdown stores, labels and arrays.

E. PUSHDOWN STORES, LABELS AND ARRAYS

In this section we compare the power of recursion with other possible augmentations of program schemes: pushdown stores and arrays. The primary results are that the classes of recursion augmented program schemes and of pushdown store augmented schemes are effectively intertranslatable and that the class of array augmented program schemes is more powerful.

For this section we consider a pushdown store to be a finite but unbounded list whose entries are members of the domain of discussion. We give our definitions and constructions for the case of one pushdown store; they can easily be enlarged to cover many pushdown stores. It can be shown, although we shall not do so, that the class of program schemes augmented with two pushdown stores is effectively intertranslatable with the class of program schemes augmented with any number of pushdown stores (see the reference by Brown, Gries and Szymanski for details).

DEFINITION   A program scheme augmented by one pushdown store has a special variable π which is not an input variable and whose contents is always a list and two additional instruction forms:

   PUSH(u)

for a variable $u \neq \pi$, which makes the contents of u the new top entry in the list in π , leaving u and the rest of π unchanged, and

   $u \leftarrow$ POP

which removes the top entry in the list in π and places it in location $u \neq \pi$ and leaves the rest of π unchanged, but if π is empty (Λ) the instruction $u \leftarrow$ POP is ignored (has no effect). Variable π is always assumed to be initially empty (i.e., contain the empty list).

We make the stipulation that the pushdown store variable cannot be an input variable - so the input cannot be a list - for the same reason we will also prohibit using an array variable as an input variable (so the input cannot be an array) - namely to permit comparison of the power of schemes with these augmentations without getting anomalous results because one class has apples as input and the other has oranges.

An array variable A is really an infinite sequence $A(1),A(2),...,A(i),...$ of variables which are used as subscripted variables. We assume that we have a new "reserved" set $\underline{Z}$ of subscripts, $\underline{Z} = \{\underline{1} , \underline{2} , \underline{3} , ... \}$ which are not allowed to be members of the domain of an interpretation and are reserved for subscripting arrays. Integers used as input are assumed to be totally distinct from the members of $\underline{Z}$ and cannot be compared with them.

A program scheme augmented by an array has two sorts of variables - simple variables $u,v,x,y,z,...$ and array variables $A(v)$ where v is a simple variable. Thus any statement may contain as variable an expression $A(v)$ for v a simple variable. If v contains a subscript $\underline{i}$, then $A(v)$ is taken to refer to variable $A(\underline{i})$. Otherwise, $A(v)$ is taken to refer to $A(\underline{1})$,

the default value. Two new types of instructions are allowed. Instruction $u \leftarrow \underline{1}$
for u a simple variable, places subscript $\underline{1}$ in variable u. Instruction
$u \leftarrow v + \underline{1}$ if v contains subscript $\underline{i}$ places subscript $\underline{i+1}$ in u, u and v
must be simple variables; if v does not contain a subscript the default value
$\underline{2}$ is placed in u. If u is used as an argument of a basis function or predicate
when it contains a subscript the value Λ, undefined, is used instead.

Although this form of augmentation is called an "array" in the literature, it
behaves more like an addressible stack or list which can be everywhere accessed.

DEFINITION   A <u>program scheme augmented by an array</u> allows simple variables and
array variables $A(v)$ for v a simple variable, and subscript instructions
$u \leftarrow \underline{1}$ and $u \leftarrow v + \underline{1}$.

Again, we gave our definition for just one array variable. It is fairly easy
to see that one array gives as much power as any number of arrays. For example,
arrays A and B can be combined into array C in which $C(\underline{1})$ is $A(\underline{1})$, $C(\underline{2})$
is $B(\underline{1})$ and in general $C(\underline{2k+1})$ is $A(\underline{k+1})$ and $C(\underline{2k})$ is $B(\underline{k})$.

For convenience we shall also allow subscript instructions such as $u \leftarrow v + \underline{3}$
or $u \leftarrow \underline{3}$, which can readily be seen to be imitated by three ordinary instructions, and also permit $u \leftarrow v \underline{\bullet} 1$ which places $\underline{i}$ in u if v contains subscript $\underline{i+1}$ and otherwise places the default value $\underline{1}$ in u. It can be shown
that use of " $\underline{\bullet}$ " does not affect the power of these schemes.

Another useful mechanism is the use of labels. A scheme augmented by labels
has a special set of addresses called labels, $\{L_1,\ldots,L_n\}$ such that each label
is attached to exactly one statement; some statements can have no labels but no
statement can have more than one label and no label can refer to more than one
statement. Two new instructions are allowed: $v \leftarrow L_i$ for a label L_i and variable
v which places label L_i in location v, and a statement GOTO v which transfers control to the statement labeled L_i if v contains a label L_i; if v
does not contain a label then GOTO v is simply ignored and control passes to the
next statement in the usual way. We assume that the set of labels is disjoint from
the domain of any interpretation.

DEFINITION   A <u>program scheme augmented by labels as values</u> permits instructions
$v \leftarrow L$ and GOTO v for a label L and a variable v.

To simplify the statement of results we use the following definitions:

DEFINITION   Let R be the class of recursion schemes, P the class of program
schemes, P_R the class of program schemes augmented by recursion, P_{PDS} the class
of program schemes augmented by one pushdown store and P_A the class of program

schemes augmented by arrays. If labels are also allowed, add subscript L, so that, for example, P_{AL} is the class of program schemes augmented by arrays and labels.

Recall that if classes C_1 and C_2 are intertranslatable, we write $C_1 \equiv C_2$; if C_1 is translatable into C_2 but C_2 is not translatable into C_1 , we write $C_1 < C_2$.

So far we have seen that:

$$P < R \equiv P_R$$

We shall argue (without formal proofs) that

$$P < R \equiv P_R \equiv P_{PDS} < P_A \equiv P_{AL}$$

First we shall give a fairly detailed proof that $P_R \leq P_{PDSL}$ and then argue intuitively that the use of labels wasn't really necessary; a more complicated construction would yield a scheme in P_{PDS} .

LEMMA 7.19 $P_R \leq P_{PDSL}$

PROOF

Let $P = (Q, Q_1, \ldots, Q_p)$ be a program scheme augmented by recursion; assume all pieces are written in linear form.

The general idea is that when we call any function, we place on the pushdown store the current values of all variables which are active but not actual parameters of the call (global values if we are in the main program, formal parameters and local variables if we are in a procedure). This frees all variable names for use during the execution of the procedure and so we use formal parameters and local variables as variables. We also place on the store a label telling us where to return on completion of the call. When the call is completed, a POP instruction takes the top value of the list, which is a label, and then a GOTO statement returns control to the appropriate labeled statement; the labeled statement respecifies the actual parameter variables with the new values computed during the execution of the procedure and restores the values of the old, unchanged variables from the top of the pushdown store to their proper locations and then transfers control to the next statement to be executed.

For convenience we allow the use of a statement TRANSFER TO r where r is any address (but not a label). This is not to be confused with a GOTO v ; it simply abbreviates any unconditional transfer instruction like $T(x)$ r, r . We also assume that addresses in the main program Q are denoted by $<Q,r>$ and in the procedure defining F are denoted by $<F,r>$.

First take the main program Q. Replace any call instruction

$$<Q,r> \quad \text{CALL} \quad F(v_1,\ldots,v_n)$$

by

$$<Q,r> \quad \text{PUSH}(y_1) \; ; \; \ldots \; ; \quad \text{PUSH}(y_m)$$
$$\text{DUMMY} \leftarrow L_{Q,r}$$
$$\text{PUSH(DUMMY)}$$
$$x_1 \leftarrow v_1 \; ; \; \ldots \; ; \; x_n \leftarrow v_n$$
$$\text{TRANSFER TO} \quad <F,1>$$

where $y_1,\ldots,y_m$ are all the global values not among the actual parameters $v_1,\ldots,v_n$, $L_{Q,r}$ is a new label, DUMMY is a new variable, and $x_1,\ldots,x_n$ are the formal parameters of the procedure Q_F defining F. Also append the labeled statement:

$$L_{Q,r} \quad v_1 \leftarrow x_1 \; ; \; \ldots \; ; \; v_n \leftarrow x_n$$
$$y_m \leftarrow \text{POP} \; ; \; \ldots \; ; \; y_1 \leftarrow \text{POP}$$
$$\text{TRANSFER TO} \quad <Q,r+1>$$

Observe that the new $<Q,r>$ statement first stores all global values which are not actual parameters $(y_1,\ldots,y_m)$ on the pushdown store, then puts label $L_{Q,r}$ on top of the pushdown store, and finally lets the values of the actual parameters of the call, $v_1,\ldots,v_n$, specify the formal parameters of procedure F, $x_1,\ldots,x_n$; the x_i will be used as variables in the execution of F. Then control passes to the start of the procedure body of F. When F is completed, label $L_{Q,r}$ will be retrieved from the top of the store and a GOTO will pass control to the statement labeled by $L_{Q,r}$. Then each actual parameter of the call, v_i, will be respecified by the final value of the corresponding formal parameter, x_i, of F, the other global variables will have their proper values restored from the pushdown store and control will return to $<Q,r+1>$, the statement originally following $<Q,r>$.

This transformation is applied to every call in Q; let the result be Q'.

Now transform any procedure Q_F defining F by similar methods. Replace any call

$$\text{<F,r>} \quad \text{CALL} \quad G(u_1,\ldots,u_m)$$

by

$$\text{<F,r>} \quad \text{PUSH}(z_1) \ ; \ \ldots \ ; \quad \text{PUSH}(z_k)$$
$$\text{DUMMY} \leftarrow L_{F,r}$$
$$\text{PUSH(DUMMY)}$$
$$w_1 \leftarrow u_1 \ ; \ \ldots \ ; \quad w_m \leftarrow u_m$$
$$\text{TRANSFER TO} \quad \text{<G,1>}$$

where $z_1,\ldots,z_k$ are those formal parameters and local variables of Q_F not among the actual parameters $u_1,\ldots,u_m$ of the call, $L_{F,r}$ is a new label and DUMMY a new variable, and $w_1,\ldots,w_m$ are the formal parameters of the procedure defining G . Also append the labeled statement:

$$L_{F,r} \quad u_1 \leftarrow w_1 \ ; \ \ldots \ ; \quad u_n \leftarrow w_n$$
$$z_k \leftarrow \text{POP} \ ; \ \ldots \ ; \quad z_1 \leftarrow \text{POP}$$
$$\text{TRANSFER TO} \quad \text{<F,r+1>}$$

Finally, assume the last statement is

$$\text{<F,r>} \quad \text{END} \quad F$$

and replace it by

$$\text{<F,r>} \quad \text{DUMMY} \leftarrow \text{POP}$$
$$\text{GOTO} \quad \text{DUMMY}$$

for a new variable DUMMY . Call the result Q'_F after all these transformations. The new scheme in P_{PDSL} is simply $Q' \ ; \ Q_1' \ ; \ \ldots \ ; \ Q_p'$. ∎

Notice that the labels were used solely to tell us where to go next. Suppose there was a k-placed predicate T and values $\bar{\tau}$ and $\bar{\nu}$ such that under the current interpretation $T(\bar{\tau})$ is TRUE and $T(\bar{\nu})$ is false, and $\bar{\tau}$ is stored in variables $TRUE_1,\ldots,TRUE_k$ and $\bar{\nu}$ in $FALSE_1,\ldots,FALSE_k$ (i.e. $\bar{\tau} = (\tau_1,\ldots,\tau_k)$ and

$val(TRUE_i) = \tau_i$ for $1 \le i \le k$ and similarly for $\bar{v}$). For some n , we could assign each label to a sequence $s_1,\ldots,s_n$ of TRUEs and FALSEs. Instead of placing a label L_τ on top of the pushdown store, if L_τ were assigned to, say, the sequence of n TRUEs, we would execute $PUSH(TRUE_1)$; $\ldots$; $PUSH(TRUE_k)$ n times, thus putting n copies of $\bar{\tau}$ on top. When the time came to find L_i from the top of the store, one executes k POPs into new variables, tests by T and does this n times; a sequence of n TRUEs will then be followed by TRANSFER TO L_τ , and L_τ is now just an ordinary address. Similarly, if L_s were assigned to the sequence of 2 TRUEs and $n-2$ FALSEs we execute $PUSH(FALSE_1)$; $\ldots$; $PUSH(FALSE_k)$ $n-2$ times and then $PUSH(TRUE_1)$; $\ldots$; $PUSH(TRUE_k)$ twice. In this case, n iterations of k POPs and tests by T yields the sequence of values $T(\bar{\tau})$, $T(\bar{\tau})$, $T(\bar{v})$, $\ldots$, $T(\bar{v})$, which is now translated to TRANSFER TO L_s .

Thus if we had such a test and values, we could simulate the recursion augmented scheme by a one pushdown store scheme without labels. The trick is to locate such a test and values. This is done using a concept introduced by Constable and Gries, the <u>locator scheme</u>.

DEFINITION Let P be a program scheme possibly augmented by extra mechanisms. Let the predicates of P be $T_1,\ldots,T_n$, each T_i a k_i-placed predicate letter. A scheme P' is a <u>locator for P</u> if it has special reserved variables $TRUE_{i,j}$ and $FALSE_{i,j}$ for $1 \le i \le n$, $1 \le j \le k_i$ and special addresses $\alpha_1,\ldots,\alpha_n$ which are addresses of NULL statements with no next statement, such that for any interpretation I and input $\bar{a}$, either

(1) both $(P',I,\bar{a})$ and $(P,I,\bar{a})$ diverge, or

(2) both $(P',I,\bar{a})$ and $(P,I,\bar{a})$ enter STOP statements with the same values of the output variables, or

(3) for some i , $1 \le i \le n$, $(P',I,\bar{a})$ enters address α_i with $val(TRUE_{i,j}) = \tau_j$, and $val(FALSE_{i,j}) = v_j$, $1 \le j \le k_i$, and $I(T_i)(\tau_1,\ldots,\tau_{k_i}) = TRUE$ and $I(T_i)(v_1,\ldots,v_{k_i}) = FALSE$.

Our previous argument essentially says that if a recursion augmented scheme S has a locator S' in the class of program schemes (or indeed in P_{PDS}) then we can simulate it by a pushdown store without labels. For we start out in the locator S' . If S' either loops or halts, we are in good shape since S is guaranteed to do the same thing. If S' enters α_i , then we restart a simulation of S now using a pushdown store without labels and encoding the labels by sequences of TRUEs and FALSEs; we use $\bar{\tau} = (\tau_1,\ldots,\tau_{k_i})$ and $\bar{v} = (v_1,\ldots,v_{k_i})$ and tests $T_i(\bar{\tau})$ and $T_i(\bar{v})$ as discussed before.

LEMMA 7.20   If a recursion augmented scheme has a locator in P (or P_{PDS}),
then it is strongly equivalent to a member of P_{PDS} .

We claim that a recursion augmented scheme does indeed have a locator in P .
Recall that we observed that when a scheme executes a recursive call, then it must
use some test statement twice with opposite results before completing that call or
else it is in a loop (cf Corollary 7.16). If every call is recursive, we need not
worry about saving variable values because the call will never be completed before
locating the required test and values. This is the basis for the construction in
the next lemma.

LEMMA 7.21   Every recursion augmented scheme has a locator in P .

PROOF
    Let the recursion augmented scheme be $S = (Q,Q_1,\ldots,Q_p)$. Assume as before
that each piece is in linear form, with addresses in Q represented by $<Q,r>$
and addresses in the procedure defining F by $<F,r>$.
    Without loss of generality we can assume that all predicates are monadic; the
construction in the general case is similar but is burdened by more subscripts.
For each test T let $TRUE(T)$ and $FALSE(T)$ be new variables and α_T a new
address for the locator S' . Let $EMPTY$ be a new variable whose value is always
Λ , undefined.
    First assume that we have already applied a complete first level macroexpansion
to Q and all the calls are now recursive. This means that no call can be completed
before we go to some α_T (Corollary 7.16).
    Now put together Q and the bodies of all the procedures and apply the follow-
ing transformation to everything. Replace every test

$$<N,r> \quad T(v) \quad <N,s> \; , \quad <N,k>$$

(where N can be Q or any F and v is some variable) by

$$<N,r> \quad T(v) \quad <N,s_1> \; , \quad <N,k_1>$$
$$<N,s_1> \quad T(TRUE(T)) \quad <N,s> \; , \quad <N,s_2>$$
$$<N,s_2> \quad FALSE(T) \leftarrow TRUE(T)$$
$$TRUE(T) \leftarrow v$$
$$TRANSFER\ TO \quad \alpha_T$$

$\langle N,k_1 \rangle \quad T(FALSE(T)) \quad \langle N,k_2 \rangle \;, \quad \langle N,k \rangle$

$\langle N,k_2 \rangle \quad TRUE(T) \leftarrow FALSE(T)$

$FALSE(T) \leftarrow v$

$TRANSFER\ TO \quad \alpha_T$

where $\langle N,s_1 \rangle$, $\langle N,s_2 \rangle$, $\langle N,k_1 \rangle$, and $\langle N,k_2 \rangle$ are all assumed to be new addresses. This piece of code compares the value of $T(v)$ with either $T(TRUE(T))$ or $T(FALSE(T))$ and continues the simulation if they are the same but transfers to α_T if they are different. Notice that initially $TRUE(T)$ and $FALSE(T)$ both contain Λ (undefined). Suppose $I(T)(\Lambda) = TRUE$. If the first execution of $\langle N,r \rangle$ has $I(T)(val(v)) = TRUE$ and we do not exit at α_T , then we know that $I(T)(\Lambda) = TRUE$ and if a later execution of $\langle N,r \rangle$ has $I(T)(val(v)) = FALSE$, we shall have $I(T)(val(FALSE(T))) = I(T)(val(TRUE(T))) = I(T)(\Lambda) = TRUE$ and so have located our opposite values. If one objects to this use of the tricky convention on Λ , a more complicated construction will work, in which the first execution of $T(v)$ puts the value of v in both $TRUE(T)$ and $FALSE(T)$ regardless of outcome of the test, while the second and all subsequent executions of any test $T(u)$ compares the outcome if positive with $T(TRUE(T))$, and if negative with $T(FALSE(T))$.

Any call

$\langle N,r \rangle \quad CALL \quad F(u_1,\ldots,u_n)$

is replaced by

$\langle N,r \rangle \quad DUMMY_1 \leftarrow u_1 \;;\; \ldots \;;\; DUMMY_n \leftarrow u_n$

$x_1 \leftarrow DUMMY_1 \;;\; \ldots \;;\; x_n \leftarrow DUMMY_n$

$y_1 \leftarrow EMPTY \;;\; \ldots \;;\; y_m \leftarrow EMPTY$

$TRANSFER\ TO \quad \langle F,1 \rangle$

where the formal parameters of the procedure defining F are $x_1,\ldots,x_n$, the local variables are $y_1,\ldots,y_m$, and $DUMMY_1,\ldots,DUMMY_n$ are new variables . Since we know that the call can never be completed - either we will reach some α_T or we will loop forever - there is no need to save the values of any of the currently active variables.

When this transformation is complete, the result is the desired locator for S . ■

So putting these lemmas together we have our first result, a formal way of saying that recursion can be implemented using just one stack.

THEOREM 7.22   The class of recursion augmented program schemes is effectively translatable into the class of program schemes augmented by one pushdown store.

The translation of pushdown store schemes to recursion augmented schemes proceeds along similar lines. First we translate into a scheme with recursion and labels and then we argue that locators exist and so the labels are not really needed.

LEMMA 7.23 $P_{PDS} \leq P_{RL}$

PROOF
Let S be a program scheme augmented by one pushdown store, and let the simple variables of S be $x_1, \ldots, x_n$. Let F be an n+2-placed defined function letter. Create new variables LABEL and TOP and labels (which are also addresses) <F,r> for each address r in S plus <F,0> and <END> .
The main scheme is simply:

      1.   LABEL ← <F,1>

      2.   CALL $F(x_1, \ldots, x_n, LABEL, TOP)$

      3.   STOP

There is only one procedure, which has formal parameters $x_1, \ldots, x_n$, LABEL and TOP . The first statement in the procedure body is:

      <F,0> . GOTO LABEL

while the last statement is of course:

      <END> END F

If statement r is an assignment, then <F,r> is the same as r ; if r is $T(\bar{v})$ s,k then <F,r> is $T(\bar{v})$ <F,s> , <F,k> .
The basic idea of the construction is that the stacking of entries in the list is simulated by stacking of calls, and unstacking (popping) of entries by unstacking (completing) the calls.

So an instruction

      r. PUSH(u)

becomes

      <F,r> LABEL $\leftarrow$ <F,r+1>

             CALL $F(x_1,\ldots,x_n,LABEL,u)$

while

      r. u $\leftarrow$ POP

becomes

      <F,r> u $\leftarrow$ TOP

             LABEL $\leftarrow$ <F,r+1>

             TRANSFER TO <END>

Finally the instruction

      r. STOP

becomes

      <F,r> LABEL $\leftarrow$ <END>

             TRANSFER TO <END>

The labels stored in LABEL are used simply to point to the next statement to be executed while calls are stacked or unstacked. Since LABEL is always used as an actual parameter, its value is carried along when a new call is instituted or an old call is completed. On the other hand, TOP is never used as an actual parameter. When PUSH(u) is simulated, a new call is begun with u as the new value of the formal parameter and the old value is "left behind" in the previous procedure but is not destroyed. When v $\leftarrow$ POP is finally simulated, this new value of TOP goes into v , the call is ended and the old procedure is reentered with the previous value of TOP still there. In simulating STOP , the value of label becomes <END> permanently and the calls are unpeeled until the main scheme is reentered at 3. STOP and everything halts. ■

To complete the translation of pushdown store schemes into recursion schemes we must show how to construct a locator. The key observation is that if a pushdown store augmented scheme S with n instructions is computing under an interpretation I for which each test $I(T)$ is a constant - either always positive or always negative - then at any point at most the top n entries on the pushdown store are avaiable; the computation will never see any entries further down in the store. Hence the locator need know only the top n entries and can forget the others.

So a locator in P for S will have $n+1$ copies of S, to keep track of whether the pushdown store is empty. Execution of a PUSH instruction simulation causes transfer from copy i to copy $i+1$, for $0 \leq i \leq n-1$ but no change in copy (of S) for copy n while simulation of a POP causes transfer from i to $i-1$ for $1 \leq i \leq n$ but no such simulation occurs in copy 0. The computation starts in copy 0. Since only the top n entries need be recorded, n new variables $\pi_1, \ldots, \pi_n$ can replace pushdown store variable π. An instruction PUSH(u) can be simulated by:

$$\pi_1 \leftarrow u \; ; \quad \pi_2 \leftarrow \pi_1 \; ; \quad \cdots \; ; \quad \pi_n \leftarrow \pi_{n-1}$$

and $u \leftarrow$ POP by

$$u \leftarrow \pi_1 \; ; \quad \pi_1 \leftarrow \pi_2 \; ; \quad \cdots \; ; \quad \pi_{n-1} \leftarrow \pi_n$$

A test instruction is handled as before. Thus we can show:

LEMMA 7.24   For each scheme in P_{PDS} a locator can be found in P.

THEOREM 7.25   The class of program schemes augmented by one pushdown store is effectively translatable into the class of recursion augmented program schemes.

THEOREM 7.26 $R \equiv P_R \equiv P_{PDS}$

It should be fairly clear that a pushdown store can be regarded as a particular kind of array. Basically we only need keep track of the location of the top of the pushdown store. This is done by using a new variable, say TOP, to store the appropriate subscript. An instruction PUSH(u) is simulated by two instructions:

$$A(TOP) \leftarrow u \; ; \quad TOP \leftarrow TOP + 1$$

while an instruction $u \leftarrow$ POP is simulated by:

$$u \leftarrow A(TOP) \; ; \; TOP \leftarrow TOP \dot{-} \underline{1}$$

(we have already mentioned that the operation "$\dot{-}$" is permissible and can be eliminated by a more complicated construction in which the subscript $TOP \dot{-} \underline{1}$ is stored
in a new array as $B(TOP)$.) Initially TOP is set at $\underline{1}$. Thus:

LEMMA 7.27 $P_{PDS} \leq P_A$;   in fact the class of program schemes augmented by any
number of pushdown stores is effectively translatable into P_A .

Now we can show that arrays are more powerful than recursion, or indeed than
any number of pushdown stores. We do so by considering a functional very popular
in "schematology" called <u>leaftest</u>.

DEFINITION   Let λ and ρ be monadic basis function letters and let T be a monadic predicate letter. The functional $\underline{leaftest(\lambda,\rho,T)(x)}$ under any interpretation
I is defined by

$$leaftest(\lambda,\rho,T) = \begin{cases} x & \text{if } I(T)(\Lambda) = TRUE \text{ or } I(T)(x) = TRUE \\ x & \text{if there are } n \leq 1, \; f_1,\ldots,f_n \; \varepsilon \; \{\lambda,\rho\} \text{ such} \\ & \text{that } I(T(f_n \ldots f_1(x))) = TRUE \\ \text{undefined otherwise} \end{cases}$$

LEMMA 7.28   Leaftest can be implemented by an array augmented program scheme.

PROOF
    Leaftest is strongly equivalent to the following scheme, with array variable
A and subscript variables J and K . The idea is to test $A(J)$, the "bottom"
of the array and then, if the result is negative, put $\lambda(A(J))$ and $\rho(A(J))$ on
the "top".

1. IF NOT $T(u)$ THEN
2. $J \leftarrow \underline{1}$; $K \leftarrow \underline{1}$; $A(J) \leftarrow x$; $u \leftarrow A(J)$
3.   WHILE NOT $T(u)$ DO $K \leftarrow K + \underline{1}$; $A(K) \leftarrow \lambda(u)$; $K \leftarrow K + \underline{1}$;
                                   $A(K) \leftarrow \rho(u)$; $J \leftarrow J + \underline{1}$; $u \leftarrow A(J)$
                    ENDWHILE
    ENDIF
4. $z \leftarrow x$; STOP ■

Intuitively, the functional leaftest(λ,ρ,T) searches the following infinite tree for some node (including the root x) which tests under T to be TRUE; if it finds one it halts with answer x and otherwise searches forever.

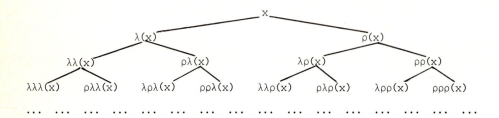

This is an infinite full binary tree. Roughly speaking, a single pushdown store cannot search such a potentially infinite tree. When we did so in Chapter VI, we added a counter whose length could be compared with the length of the store. In fact we cannot search such a tree with any number of pushdown stores unless they can find their "bottoms" - unless one can find out if the store is empty. The pushdown stores in this chapter do not have this ability. Hence leaftest cannot be done with any number of pushdown stores. However, two pushdown stores suffice if a special test "Is pushdown store i empty?" is allowed, since in that case we can use two stores to simulate the action of the array in the array augmented scheme for leaftest.

We now provide a little more detail for the claim that leaftest cannot be implemented by a program scheme with any number of pushdown stores.

LEMMA 7.29   Leaftest cannot be implemented by a program scheme augmented by any number of pushdown stores.

PROOF

The proof consists in showing that if leaftest(λ,ρ,T) could be done by just adding pushdown stores of the type described in this section, then it could be done by an ordinary program scheme without augmentations, but that is impossible.

We have argued that locators exist for schemes with one pushdown store. The same discussion applies to schemes with any number of pushdown stores. If such a scheme S has n pushdown stores and m instructions and operates under an interpretation I for which each predicate I(T) is single valued, then the scheme either halts before completing more than m instructions, and so the pushdown stores cannot have more than m entries apiece, or else after m_1 steps it enters a loop of length m_2 , $m_1 + m_2 \leq m$. For each store this loop either does not change in size or grows by at most m_2 new entries and in either case no more than the top $m_2/2$ entries are read. Thus the same result holds - in such a situation the scheme need remember at most the top m entries on the store. Hence a locator can be built which substitutes for each pushdown store π_i , m ordinary variables $\pi_{i1},\ldots,\pi_{im}$; the locator needs $(m+1)^n$ copies of S to keep track of when the stores are empty.

So if leaftest is implemented by a scheme S with n pushdown stores, there is a locator S' for S and S' is an unaugmented program scheme. Under any interpretation I , if (S',I,x) loops forever, so does (S,I,x) and leaftest has no answer. If (S',I,x) halts, it halts with the "right" answer for (S,I,x) and so for leaftest. If (S',I,x) enters the special address α then it has found values a and b for which $I(T)(a) = TRUE$ and $I(T)(b) = FALSE$. But if it ever finds a "TRUE", then it has found a solution for leaftest! So if we form S'' by placing into address α the instruction $z \leftarrow x$; STOP we have a scheme strongly equivalent to S and S'' is an unaugmented program scheme.

Thus if we can implement leaftest by a pushdown store augmented scheme, we can implement leaftest with a program scheme S'' without pushdown stores or any other augmentations. We can assume that S'' uses only basis functions λ and ρ and predicate T and that each statement of S'' is of the forms: START , STOP , $T(u)$, $u \leftarrow x$, $u \leftarrow \lambda(v)$, $u \leftarrow \rho(v)$, and $u \leftarrow v$ where x is the only input variable and is not a program or output variable, and u and v are program variables (we may have either $u = v$ or $u \neq v$). Let S'' have n program variables and m statements.

We consider two types of free interpretations. For any t let $I_t(T)(\Lambda) = I_t(T)(x) = I(T)(w(x)) = FALSE$ for $0 \leq |w| \leq t$ and let $I_t(T)$ be uniformly TRUE elsewhere; for t and $|w| = t$, let $I_{t,w}(T)(\Lambda) = I_{t,w}(T)(y(x)) = FALSE$ for $y \neq w$ and $I_{t,w}(T)(w(x)) = TRUE$.

First consider the behavior of S'' during I_t . By our hypothesis on S'' , during i steps of computation every variable must take on values of the form $w(x)$ with length w bounded by i . Thus during the first t computation steps under I_t the test $I_t(T)$ will always return the answer $FALSE$ and, since S'' certainly cannot halt until some $TRUE$ answer has been returned, the program (S'',I_t) will behave as if $I_t(T)$ were single-valued. For $t > m+1$, the program enters a cycle after at most m steps and the cycle length is $r \leq m$. What sort of values can be assumed by a variable during such a cycle? Suppose variable u has value u^0 on entering address q and on returning to q after r steps has value u^1 . Either $u^1 = y(x)$ because u has been reset during the cycle or $u^1 = y(u^0)$ or $u^1 = y(v^0)$ for $0 \leq |y| \leq r$ and a variable $v \neq u$. In the first case, as long as the cycle lasts u takes values from some finite set and is a constant, $y(x)$, at the end of the cycle. In the second case, u keeps ending the cycle with a value in $y^*(u^0)$. In the third case, the values of u depend on the behavior of v during the cycle; for $t > nm+1$ the cycle will repeat at least n times and since there are n variables fluctuations due to this third case smooth out and we have cyclic behavior. Thus for $t > nm+1$ there are a fixed finite set A of values and a fixed set B of the form $B = y_1 \overset{*}{z_1}(x) \cup \ldots \cup y_k \overset{*}{z_k}(x)$ for some k such that program (S'',I_t) enters and remains in a cycle for its first t steps during which the variables take values which are either in A or are of the form $y_i'' y_i \overset{S}{z_i}(x)$, $y_i = y_i' y_i''$ with $|y_i'' y_i \overset{S}{z_i}| \leq t$, i.e. terminal substrings of members of B bounded in length by t .

We can conclude thus that during the first t steps of (S'',I_t) the number of possible values taken on by the various variables grows at most as some polynomial in t . But the number of possible values of $w(x)$ for $|w| = t$ which must be tested grows exponentially in t . Hence for some large t there is a w in $\{\lambda,\rho\}^*$ with $|w| = t$ such that during this fixed cycle no variable ever takes on value $w(x)$ under any interpretation $I_{t'}$. Finally, if we consider the behavior of S'' under $I_{t,w}$ for this w , we see that the resulting program never gets a chance to test $w(x)$ and since it can leave the cycle only by testing $w(x)$ it is stuck in this cycle and so diverges, although leaftest is defined for this interpretation $I_{t,w}$ and input x . Hence no program scheme and thus no pushdown store scheme can implement leaftest. ∎

THEOREM 7.30 $R \equiv P_R \equiv P_{PDS} < P_A$; the class of program schemes augmented by arrays is not translatable into the class of program schemes augmented by any number of pushdown stores.

There are a few other things one can mention. First, our argument applies only to pushdown stores defined so as not to know their "bottoms". We leave it as an exercise to the reader to construct a program scheme for leaftest using two pushdown stores plus instructions "IF EMPTY(π_i) THEN ... ELSE ...". Next, it can be shown that n pushdown stores can be simulated by two. The general idea is to construct a locator for the n pushdown store machine; the locator uses no pushdown stores. Then the TRUE and FALSE values can be used to mark the bottom of a store, and separate the n pushdown stores all stacked up on one store (alternating the "real" entries with the marked TRUE and FALSE values with, say, TRUE marking the bottom of a store and FALSE for intermediate entries). Each store is then accessed by transferring all the entries above it to the second store, suitably interleaved with the marked values, and then transferring back. However, one pushdown store does not suffice; two are more powerful than one. The functional used to show this is a variant of leaftest.

DEFINITION   The functional Eleaftest($\lambda,\rho,$T) is defined by:

$$\text{Eleaftest}(\lambda,\rho,T)(x,y,z) = \begin{cases} \text{leaftest}(\lambda,\rho,T)(x) & \text{if } I(T)(y) = \text{TRUE} \\ & \text{and } I(T)(z) = \text{FALSE} \\ x & \text{otherwise} \end{cases}$$

We leave it to the reader as an exercise to implement Eleaftest using two pushdown stores (with no test for emptiness this time). The point is that now y and z can be used to mark the bottom of the two pushdown stores and the "real" entries corresponding to A(J) or A(K) in the proof of Lemma 7.28 are interleaved with the "markers" y and z .

It can be shown that if Eleaftest were implementable in P_{PDS} , then so would leaftest be also. Hence Eleaftest is not implementable in P_{PDS} .

COROLLARY 7.31   The class of program schemes augmented by two pushdown stores is not translatable into the class of program schemes augmented by one pushdown store.

Using simple simulation techniques it can be shown that the class of program schemes augmented by pushdown stores and labels is effectively intertranslatable with the class P_{AL} of program schemes augmented by arrays and labels. It is also true that P_A and P_{AL} are intertranslatable, but the translation from P_{AL} to P_A is not effective!

Consider schemes without any tests. A scheme in P_A without any tests is either always halting or never halting and a simple examination of the graph will show which one. However, it is undecidable whether a scheme in P_{AL} without any tests is always halting! The proof consists in simulating with such a scheme the behavior of a Turing machine on an initial tape consisting of all 0's . So if there were an effective translation from P_{AL} to P_A , then this question would be decidable. The translation from P_{AL} to P_A is nonconstructive and depends on having an oracle tell you about the behavior of certain test-free schemes. Details can be found in the reference by Constable and Gries.

F.   VERIFICATION OF PROGRAMS WITH RECURSION

We conclude this chapter by discussing briefly the verification of programs with procedures and calls. We use the model of a recursion augmented program scheme in order to do so conveniently.

At first glance it might seem as if our verification conditions would have to · keep track of the contents of a pushdown store implementation of recursion. For the final output will depend of course not just on the final output of the call being executed, but where it came from and what is the stack of calls and "saved" variables waiting to be completed. However, this is not really necessary.

First we discuss a version of the verification procedure which provides a sufficient condition for partial correctness - if the procedure gives a positive answer, then the program is indeed partially correct for the given input and output criteria. However, the condition is not necessary - the program can be partially correct yet no choice of inductive assertions will make the procedure "work". This leads us to the complete procedure, which is rather more complex and lengthy.

Suppose our program (P,I) comes from an underlying scheme P with procedures and calls as defined in Section A of this chapter, and let the input criterion be A and the output criterion B. We first define critical points and inductive assertions as before. Then we add to the list of critical points every point directly before and directly after a call. Some care needs to be exercised in assigning inductive assertions to these calling points.

To each procedure F we assign two inductive assertions $_FA$ and $_FB$ which are written solely in terms of the formal parameters of procedure F; that is, the only free variables in $_FA$ and $_FB$ are the formal parameters of F.

Now consider a call in (P,I):

$\quad$ k. $\quad$ CALL $F(u_1,\ldots,u_n)$

We have carefully required that symbols $u_1,\ldots,u_n$ be variables and that they be all distinct and further be all distinct from the formal parameters of procedure F, say $x_1,\ldots,x_n$. At this point, these requirements become crucial. The two critical points of interest can be called k_A and k_B, the points just before and just after the call of F. To critical point k_A assign the inductive assertion $_FA\frac{\bar{x}}{\bar{u}}$ which is the result of substituting u_i for x_i everywhere in $_FA$ and to critical point k_B assign $_FB\frac{\bar{x}}{\bar{u}}$, the result of substituting u_i for x_i in $_FB$.

We must consider the procedures to be subroutines or subprograms in the program. So we take each procedure body Q_F and play the same game. To the entry point of Q_F we attach inductive assertion $_FA$ and to the exit point we attach inductive assertion $_FB$. We choose the other critical points to cut all cycles and to include all points directly before or directly after calls. We assign inductive assertions to critical points freely, except that for a call

$\quad$ k. $\quad$ CALL $G(\bar{v})$

if the formal parameters of G are $\bar{y}$, we assign to k_A, the point just before this call of G , the inductive assertion $_G A \frac{\overline{y}}{v}$ and to k_B , the point just after this call has been completed, the assertion $_G B \frac{y}{v}$.

After all this has been done, we apply the usual verification procedure to the main program and to each procedure body - constructing verification conditions and sending them to a THEOREM PROVER just as before. We claim that if all the verification conditions hold for the main program and all procedures, then the whole program is partially correct for A and B .

Why can we make this claim? The idea is simple but subtle. If the program does not terminate for a particular input, say $\overline{a}$, we are uninterested in the outcome. If it does terminate for input $\overline{a}$, there must be some k such that no more than k calls are executed during the entire computation $(P,I,\overline{a})$. Now make k complete first level macroexpansions of (P,I) and call the result (P',I) . Each time a call of F is macroexpanded, put into the diagram all the critical points and inductive assertions with the appropriate substitutions of actual parameters for formal parameters. Because of the way in which we have chosen inductive assertions before and after calls, the points before and after the macroexpansion of F will have attached the same inductive assertions as before. Finally, when we are all done, replace any remaining calls by a LOOP instruction.

As far as input $\overline{a}$ is concerned, the old program (P,I) and the new program (P',I) are identical - they must both converge with the same answer. The only difference between (P,I) and (P',I) in execution is the inserted LOOP statements. If they are never reached, the programs are strongly equivalent. We know that for input $\overline{a}$ they can never be reached because for this input, the program does not nest calls more than k deep. All the verification conditions of (P',I) appear among the verification conditions of (P,I) , since all the paths appeared either in the main program or the procedure bodies, and we do not construct verification conditions over a LOOP statement (or if we do, we construct the condition that is uniformly TRUE). Hence, since the verification conditions hold for (P,I) , they certainly hold for (P',I) . But (P',I) has no procedures or calls and hence by our previous arguments, we can conclude that (P',I) is partially correct with respect to A and B . Thus (P,I) is partially correct with respect to A and B for the particular input $\overline{a}$. But this holds for all inputs. So (P,I) is partially correct for the given criteria as claimed.

Unfortunately this procedure will not work even in some very simple cases where partial correctness is transparent. Consider the very trivial program:

```
IF  x₁ = x₂  THEN CALL  F(x₂,z)

              ELSE  IF  x₁ > x₂  THEN  u ← x₂+1

                                       CALL  F(u,z)

                          ELSE  u ← x₁

                                CALL  F(u,z)

                  ENDIF

ENDIF

STOP

PROCEDURE  F(u,v)

v ← u²

END  Γ
```

This program is obviously partially correct with respect to $A(x_1,x_2)$:

x_1 and x_2 are integers

and $B(x_1,x_2,z)$:

If $x_1 = x_2$, then $z = x_2^2$; if $x_1 > x_2$, then $z = (x_2+1)^2$;
if $x_1 < x_2$, then $z = x_1^2$

It should be clear that the procedure as just described cannot handle this program. For the inductive assertion $_F B$ attached to the critical point after each CALL $F(x_2,z)$ or $F(u,z)$ will have as free variables only z and x_2 or u , the actual parameters, but the output criterion B involves x_1 and x_2 and its value depends on the relationship of x_1 and x_2 as well as the relationship between z and x_2 . We have so far provided no way to carry over a CALL assertions regarding variables not involved in the CALL.

An obvious first stab at a solution presents itself. Let the critical points around CALLS have extra assertions for the variables not involved in the CALL. If the CALL at address k in the main program is a call of procedure F , attach to the point k_A just before the CALL any inductive assertion of the form $C \wedge {}_F A'$ where $_F A'$ is the appropriate version of $_F A$ and C is any assertion involving as free variables only the global variables which do not appear in the actual parameters of the CALL. Then attach to k_B directly following the CALL, $C \wedge {}_F B'$ where $_F B'$ is the corresponding version of $_F B$. Similarly, if the CALL of F at address k occurs within the procedure body of procedure G , the extra assertion C will have as free variables those formal parameters and local variables of procedure G which are not involved in the call of F . However, the input assertion F remains just $_FA$, while the output assertion is $_FB$. Since variables that are not actual parameters do not change during the execution of the CALL, there is no problem in attaching C to k_A and k_B and no need to use inductive assertion C in verifying procedure F ; if C is true at k_A it must also be true at k_B . So we can confidently state that if this amended procedure comes up with a positive result, this program is partially correct for the given input and output criteria.

Even this patch is not quite enough. Our simple example shows that a condition C on x_1 or on x_1 and x_2 but not on u , is not enough. All the active variables must be tied together for the verification procedure to return a positive answer. But the actual parameters may change in value during a CALL, so we would have to put the added assertions into the verification process for the procedure called. This can multiply itself indefinitely and so is obviously unsatisfactory.

There are several ways of cleaning this up. We now present just one. We notice that part of the problem is that procedures are really kinds of programs which we verify separately. In our main verification procedure, we demanded that the input variables be unchanged during the whole program, in order to be able to make clean statements about the relationship between the final values of output variables with the initial values of input variables. One of our difficulties is that we have not done this for procedures. Let us see how we can do it!

Let variable u appearing in the body Q of the main program or in the body Q_F of a procedure be deemed to be "changed" during Q or Q_F if it appears either in the left hand side of an assignment statement or in a CALL of G such that the corresponding formal parameter v of G is changed during Q_G . Otherwise it is "unchanged". It should be evident that it is decidable whether or not u is "unchanged" - flag all variables appearing on the left hand side of an assignment statement; if a formal parameter v is flagged in Q_F , flag any variable appearing in the corresponding place of any call of F ; continue until all variables are flagged or no new ones can be flagged; the flagged ones are "changed". The point of this definition is that a changed variable may or may not be changed during a particular execution sequence, but an unchanged variable cannot possibly be changed in any computation.

We give a technical meaning to the formal term "dummy". If u is a variable appearing in a call

      k. CALL $F(...,u,...)$

in the main program, then u is a dummy at k if u is not an input or an output
variable and the only statements involving u other than k appear after k in
the main program and are of the form v ← u for v ≠ u ; in particular, u cannot
appear on the left hand side of an assignment statement, in a test, or in any other
call. If u is a variable appearing in a call

Gk. CALL F(...,u,...)

in the body Q_G of a procedure G (which may or may not be equal to F), then
u is a dummy at Gk if u is a local variable in G and the only statements
involving u other than Gk appear after Gk in Q_G and are of the form v ← u
for v ≠ u ; in particular, u cannot appear on the left hand side of an assignment statement, in a test, or in any other call.

   Now we place on our programs two additional restrictions on the use of variables
in CALLs. They are:
1) No input variable is changed.
2) The formal parameters of any procedure F can be described as $x_1,...,x_n,y_1,...,y_m$
    where the x_i are unchanged in F and any call of F can be described as

k. $F(u_1,...,u_n,v_1,...,v_m)$

where the v_j are dummies at k .
   We have already observed that condition 1) can easily be met by transferring
the contents of any input variable into a copy variable. If we have a procedure F
with formal parameters $x_1,...,x_n$, we add new formal parameters $y_1,...,y_n$ and
start Q_F with the assignments $y_1 ← x_1$; ... ; $y_n ← x_n$ and then let the rest of
the procedure have y_i substituted for x_i everywhere. For a call of F

k. CALL $F(u_1,...,u_n)$

we let $u_1',...,u_n'$ be n new variables not appearing anywhere else and substitute:

k. CALL $F(u_1,...,u_n,u_1',...,u_n')$
k'. $u_1 ← u_1'$; ... ; $u_n ← u_n'$

This is all right since the x_i are now unchanged in F and the u_i' are all new
and are never again used.
   Once we are assured that the CALLs obey 2) we are in business. Now for procedure F with unchanged formal parameters $\bar{x} = (x_1,...,x_n)$ and other formal
parameters $\bar{y} = (y_1,...,y_m)$ we let input criterion $_FA$ involve all the unchanged

formal parameters, $\overline{x}$, but output criterion $_F B$ may involve all the formal parameters of F , $\overline{x}$ and $\overline{y}$. To verify the procedure body for F we use input criterion $_F A$ and output criterion $_F B$. Suppose we have a call of F (whether in the main program, in the procedure body Q_F of F or in the procedure body Q_G of any other call of F) , say

k. CALL $F(u_1, \ldots u_n, v_1, \ldots, v_m)$

with the u_i corresponding to the unchanged formal parameters (x_i) and the dummies v_i corresponding to the y_i's . We attach to critical point k_A an inductive assertion of the form

$$C_k \wedge {}_F A \frac{\overline{x}}{\overline{u}}$$

and to k_B the corresponding assertion

$$C_k \wedge {}_F B \frac{\overline{x}, \overline{y}}{\overline{u}, \overline{v}}$$

where C_k may involve as free variables the u_i as well as any other active variables which are not dummies (any global variables if this is the main program or formal parameters and local variables if this is a procedure body). Since the additional assertions C_k involve only variables unchanged in the procedure, we are free to carry such assertions over a procedure without further checking.

Now we have a method that is both necessary and sufficient to demonstrate partial correctness. We have already seen that if these verification conditions all hold, then the program is indeed partially correct for the given criteria. The arguments used in Chapter V can be adapted to show that if partial correctness holds, then some choice of inductive assertions will make the verification conditions true.

EXAMPLE

First examine Example VII - 6. This is one possible version of Example VII - 4 altered to meet the conditions of our verification procedure. Of course, one need not in general transform the program itself; one can in practice apply the verification technique "as if" the transformation had already been made, provided extreme care is taken with the identity of the various variables and parameters.

The critical points in Example VII - 6 are the initial and final points, 1 and 8 , in the main program and the initial and final points F1 and F4 in procedure FACT , as well as the points just before CALLS in the main program, 3.1- , 4.1-, and 6.1- , F3.1- in the procedure, and the points after calls, 5.1+ , 4.1+ ,

6.1+ and F3.1+ . The example shows the input and output criteria for the main program and for the procedure. Additional inductive assertions are attached to each of the calling points, as indicated by assertions C_3 , C_4 , C_6 and C_F . There are 10 paths to check in the main program (2 are inconsistent and so cause no problems) and 3 in the procedure.

EXAMPLE VII - 6   EXAMPLE VII - 4 EDITED FOR VERIFICATION PROCEDURE

Main Program   † indicates critical points
Input variables n,k

† 1. $x_1 \leftarrow n$; $x_2 \leftarrow k$

2. $z_1 \leftarrow 1$; $z_2 \leftarrow 1$

3. IF $x_1 > 1$ THEN

†

3.1   CALL FACT(x_1,z_1,v_1,w_1)

†

3.2 $z_1 \leftarrow w_1$

ENDIF

4. IF $x_2 > 1$ THEN

†

4.1   CALL FACT(x_2,z_2,v_2,w_2)

†

4.2 $z_2 \leftarrow w_2$

ENDIF

5. NEW $\leftarrow x_1 - x_2$

6. IF NEW > 1 THEN

†

6.1   CALL FACT(NEW,z_2,v_3,w_3)

†

6.2 $z_2 \leftarrow w_3$

ENDIF

7. $z_1 \leftarrow z_1/z_2$

† 8. STOP

EXAMPLE VII - 6 -- CONTINUED

Procedure Program

PROCEDURE   FACT(u,y,u_1,y_1)

DECLARE NEW (TEMP$_1$,TEMP$_2$)

† F1. $y_1 \leftarrow u.y$

F2. $u_1 \leftarrow u - 1$

F3. IF $u_1 > 1$ THEN

†

F3.1   CALL   FACT(u_1,y_1,TEMP$_1$,TEMP$_2$)

†

F3.2 $y_1 \leftarrow$ TEMP$_2$

ENDIF

† F4. END FACT

EXAMPLE VII - 6   CONTINUED   -   VERIFICATION OF EXAMPLE VII - 4

Input criterion $A(n,k)$: n,k integers, $1 \leq k \leq n$

Output criterion $B(n,k,z_1)$: $A(n,k)$, $z_1 = \binom{n}{k}$

Extra inductive assertions

For 3.1 $C_3(n,k,x_1,x_2,z_1,z_2)$: $A(n,k)$, $x_1 = n$, $x_2 = k$, $z_1 = z_2 = 1$

For 4.1 $C_4(n,k,x_1,x_2,z_1,z_2)$: $A(n,k)$, $x_1 = n$, $x_2 = k$, $z_1 = n!$, $z_2 = 1$

For 6.1 $C_6(n,k,x_1,x_2,z_1,z_2,NEW)$: $A(n,k)$, $x_1 = n$, $x_2 = k$, $NEW = n-k$,

        $z_1 = n!$, $z_2 = k!$

For procedure FACT:

Input criterion $_FA(u,y)$: u,y integers, $y \geq 1$, $u > 1$

Output criterion $_FB(u,y,u_1,y_1)$: $_FA(u,y)$, $u_1 = u - 1$, $y_1 = u! \cdot y$

For F3.1 $C_F(u,y,u_1,y_1)$: $_FA(u,y)$, $u_1 = u - 1$, $y_1 - u.y$

Verification conditions:

1) For path 1 , 2 , 3 , 3.1-

   $A(n,k) \wedge (n > 1) \supset {}_FA(n,1) \wedge (n = n) \wedge (k = k) \wedge (1 = 1 = 1)$

2) For path 1 , 2 , 3 , 4 , 4.1-

   TRUE since this path is impossible

3) For path 1 , 2 , 3 , 4 , 5 , 6 , 6.1-

   TRUE since this path is impossible

4) For path 1 , 2 , 3 , 4 , 5 , 6 , 7 , 8

   $A(n,k) \wedge (n \leq 1) \wedge (k \leq 1) \wedge (n-k \leq 1) \supset [A(n,k) \wedge [1 = \binom{n}{k}]]$

5) For path 3.1+ , 3.2 , 4 , 4.1-

   $[_FA(x_1,z_1) \wedge (v_1 = x_1-1) \wedge (w_1 = x_1! \cdot z_1) \wedge A(n,k) \wedge (x_1 = n) \wedge (x_2 = k) \wedge$

   $(z_1 = z_2 = 1) \wedge (x_2 > 1)] \supset [_FA(x_2,z_2) \wedge A(n,k) \wedge (x_1 = n) \wedge (x_2 = k) \wedge (z_1 = n!)$

   $\wedge (z_2 = 1)]$

6) For path 3.1+ , 3.2 , 4 , 5 , 6 , 6.1-

   $[_FA(x_1,z_1) \wedge (v_1 = x_1-1) \wedge (w_1 = x_1! \cdot z_1) \wedge A(n,k) \wedge (x_1 = n) \wedge (x_2 = k) \wedge$

   $(z_1 = z_2 = 1) \wedge (x_2 \leq 1) \wedge (x_1 - x_2 > 1)] \supset [_FA(x_1-x_2,z_2) \wedge A(n,k) \wedge (x_1 = n) \wedge$

   $(x_2 = k) \wedge (x_1-x_2 = n-k) \wedge (w_1 = n!) \wedge (z_2 = k!)]$

EXAMPLE VII - 6   CONTINUED

7) For path 3.1+ , 3.2 , 4 , 5 , 6 , 7 , 8

$[_FA(x_1,z_1) \wedge (v_1 = x_1-1) \wedge (w_1 = x_1! \cdot z_1) \wedge A(n,k) \wedge (x_1 = n) \wedge (x_2 = k) \wedge$
$(z_1 = z_2 = 1) \wedge (x_2 \leq 1) \wedge (x_1 - x_2 \leq 1)] \supset [A(n,k) \wedge [w_1/z_2 = \binom{n}{k}]]$

8) For path 4.1+ , 4.2 , 5 , 6 , 6.1-

$[_FA(x_2,z_2) \wedge (v_2 = v_2-1) \wedge (w_2 = x_2! \cdot z_2) \wedge A(n,k) \wedge (x_1 = n) \wedge (x_2 = k) \wedge$
$(z_1 = n!) \wedge (z_2 = 1) \wedge (x_1-x_2 > 1)] \supset [_FA(x_1-x_2,w_2) \wedge A(n,k) \wedge (x_1 = n) \wedge$
$(x_2 = k) \wedge (x_1-x_2 = n-k) \wedge (z_1 = n!) \wedge (w_2 = k!)$

9) For path 4.1+ , 4.2 , 5 , 6 , 7 , 8

$[_FA(x_2,z_2) \wedge (v_2 = x_2-1) \wedge (w_2 = x_2! \cdot z_2) \wedge A(n,k) \wedge (x_1 = n) \wedge (x_2 = k) \wedge$
$(z_1 = n!) \wedge (z_2 = 1) \wedge (x_1-x_2 \leq 1)] \supset [A(n,k) \wedge [z_1/w_2 = \binom{n}{k}]]$

10) For path 6.1+ , 6.2 , 7 , 8

$[_FA(NEW,z_2) \wedge (v_3 = NEW-1) \wedge (w_3 = NEW! \cdot z_2) \wedge A(n,k) \wedge (x_1 = n) \wedge (x_2 = k) \wedge$
$(NEW = n-k) \wedge (z_1 = n!) \wedge (z_2 = k!)] \supset [A(n,k) \wedge [z_1/w_3 = \binom{n}{k}]]$

EXAMPLE VII - 6   CONCLUDED

Verification conditions for the Procedure FACT.

1) For path F1 , F2 , F3 , F3.1-

   $[_FA(u,y) \wedge (u-1 > 1)] \supset [_FA(u,y) \wedge (u-1 = u-1) \wedge (u.y = u.y) \wedge _FA(u-1,u.y)]$

2) For path F1 , F2 , F3 , F4

   $[_FA(u,y) \wedge (u-1 \leq 1)] \supset [_FA(u,y) \wedge (u-1 = u-1) \wedge (u.y = u! \cdot y)]$

3) For path F3.1+ , F3.2 , F4

   $[_FA(u_1,y_1) \wedge (TEMP_1 = u_1-1) \wedge (TEMP_2 = u_1! \cdot y_1) \wedge _FA(u,y) \wedge (u_1 - u-1) \wedge$
   $(y_1 = u.y)] \supset [_FA(u,y) \wedge (u_1 = u-1) \wedge (TEMP_2 = u!.y)]$

VIII. MONADIC RECURSION SCHEMES

We now focus attention on the special case of monadic recursion schemes.

DEFINITION   A recursion scheme is <u>monadic</u> if all of its defined and basis function letters and all of its predicate letters are monadic.

Our first result is that the classes of monadic recursion schemes and monadic program schemes are incomparable. We use a somewhat different argument than before to establish the existence of a monadic recursion scheme not translatable into any monadic program scheme. In the case of monadic schemes we save ourselves much notational complication by omitting parentheses and writing $F(x)$ as Fx and $f(g(x))$ as fgx ; we often take the additional liberty of omitting the x since its position is obvious.

A. A MONADIC RECURSION SCHEME WHICH IS NOT FLOWCHARTABLE

THEOREM 8.1   The monadic recursion scheme

$$S: \quad Fx = IF \ \ Tx \ \ THEN \ \ x \ \ ELSE \ \ gFFfx$$

is not translatable into any strongly equivalent monadic program scheme.

PROOF

In this example we see that, freely speaking, a simulating program scheme would run out of time rather than space.

For each integer $n \geq 1$, consider a "counting" free interpretation I_n defined as follows. For an expression E in $\{f,g\}^* x$, let $r(E)$ be the number of occurrences of f in E minus the number of occurrences of g in E . Let

$$I_n(T)(E) = FALSE \quad if \ \ E = x \ \ or \ \ r(E) \ \ is \ not \ divisible \ by \ \ n$$
$$I_n(T)(E) = TRUE \quad if \ \ E \neq x \ \ and \ \ r(E) \ \ is \ divisible \ by \ \ n$$

For $n \geq 1$ we define an expression h_n as follows by induction on n :

$$h_1 = e \quad the \ empty \ tape$$

$$h_n = h_{n-1}f^{n-1}g^{n-1}h_{n-1} \quad for \ \ n \geq 2$$

We show by induction on n that $\text{val}(S,I_n,x) = g^n h_n f^n x$ for $n \geq 1$. It is evident for $n = 1$. Assume $n \geq 2$. Define a function F_n by $F_n(E) = \text{val}(S,I_n,E)$ for any terminal term E. Since $I_n(T)(E) = \text{FALSE}$ for $E = x$, we see that $F_n(x) = g(F_n(F_n(fx)))$.

Suppose we are computing under an interpretation I_n. It can be shown by induction on $r+(n-s)$ that for $1 \leq r \leq s \leq n$, if t_s is in $\{f,g\}^+$ with $r(t_s) = s$, then there are t_{s-1} and t_{s-r} in $\{f,g\}^+$ with $r(t_{s-1}) = s-1$ and $r(t_{s-r}) = s-r$ such that

$$(gF)^r t_s x \xrightarrow{\ *\ } (gF)^{r-1} t_{s-1} x \xrightarrow{\ *\ } t_{s-r} x .$$

For $n \geq 2$ the computation can be divided into phases:

$$Fx \Longrightarrow gF^2 fx \xrightarrow{\ *\ } (gF)^{n-1} E_{n-1} x \xrightarrow{\ *\ } (gF)^{n-2} E_{n-2} x \xrightarrow{\ *\ } \ldots$$

$$\xrightarrow{\ *\ } gFE_1 x \xrightarrow{\ *\ } E_0 x = \text{val}(S,I_n,x)$$

where each E_i is an appropriate word in $\{f,g\}^*$ with $r(b_i) = i$; in particular $E_{n-1} = gf^n$. Similarly, if we now compute under I_{n+1} instead of I_n, and follow (S,I_{n+1},fx) with input fx instead of x we have:

$$Ffx \Longrightarrow gF^2 f^2 x \xrightarrow{\ *\ } (gF)^{n-1} gF^2 f^{n+1} x \Longrightarrow (gF)^{n-1} gf^{n+1} x =$$

$$(gF)^{n-1} E_{n-1} fx \xrightarrow{\ *\ } (gF)^{n-2} E_{n-2} fx \xrightarrow{\ *\ } \ldots$$

$$\xrightarrow{\ *\ } gFE_1 fx \xrightarrow{\ *\ } E_0 fx = \text{val}(S,I_{n+1},x)$$

where the expressions E_i are the same as for (S,I_n,x) ! Thus we have $\text{val}(S,I_{n+1},fx) = \text{val}(S,I_n,x)(fx)$. Indeed for any E in $\{f,g\}^+$ with $r(E) = 1$, we can write (recalling that $F_n(x)$ is itself a formal function since I_n is a free interpretation) $F_{n+1}(Ex) = F_n(x)(Ex)$.

Thus if we have shown that $F_n(x) = g^n h_n f^n x$ for $n \geq 1$, we have
$$F_{n+1}(x) = gF_{n+1}(F_{n+1}(fx)) = gF_{n+1}(F_n(x)(fx)) = gF_{n+1}(g^n h_n f^n x(fx))$$
$$= gF_{n+1}(g^n h_n f^{n+1} x) = gF_n(x)(g^n h_n f^{n+1} x) = g(g^n h_n f^n x(g^n h_n f^{n+1} x))$$
$$= g^{n+1} h_n f^n g^n h_n f^{n+1} x = g^{n+1} h_{n+1} f^{n+1} x .$$ This shows that $F_n(x) = g^n h_n f^n x$ for all $n \geq 1$.

If we set $m_n = |h_n|$, we see that $m_1 = 0$, $m_2 = 2$ and for $n \geq 1$, $m_{n+1} = 2n + 2m_n$. Expanding this recurrence relation, we get the series expression:

$$m_{n+1} = \sum_{k=0}^{n-1} 2^{k+1}(n-k)$$

and hence $m_{n+1} = 2^{n+2} - 2(n+1) - 2$.

So we have $|val(S,I_n,x)| = 2^{n+1} - 1$. We claim that no flowchart scheme can exhibit this growth pattern under I_n . Suppose P is any flowchart scheme such that (P,I_n,x) converges. Suppose P has m registers of all kinds - input variable, program variables, output variables - and k instructions. Since the outcome of the only test $I_n(T)(t)$ depends solely on whether or not n divides $r(t)$ or $t = x$, as far as program (P,I_n) is concerned the values of the registers fall in $n + 1$ equivalence classes, determined by whether $t = x$ or whether $t \neq x$ and $r(t)$ is congruent to $j \bmod n$ for $0 \leq j \leq n-1$. If the computation contains more than $k(n+1)^m$ steps, then it must twice enter the same instruction with the values in the m registers in the same equivalence classes as before; hence it is in an unbreakable loop. Thus if (P,I_n,x) converges, it does so within $k(n+1)^m$ steps. There is some constant c such that each instruction can increase the length of the value of a variable under I_n by at most c . Hence $|val(P,I_n,x)| \leq ck(n+1)^m$. For n large this is strictly less than $|val(S,I_n,x)|$ and so $val(P,I_n,x) \neq val(S,I_n,x)$. Hence P cannot be strongly equivalent to S . ∎

We have shown that the class of monadic recursion schemes is not translatable into the class of monadic program schemes. Before showing that the two classes are in fact incomparable let us consider briefly how we can compute the value of a monadic recursion scheme using a simple pushdown store.

We use a pushdown store with the top at the right and start with the defined letter of the start equation alone on the top of the store. The output is generated in an output register. We start with the input (the initial value of x) in this output register. At any step:

(1) If the top of the store is a basis function letter, say f , apply it to the output register and if a is in the output register replace a by $I(f)(a)$ and erase f from the top of the pushdown store.

(2) If the top of the pushdown store is a defined function letter, say F , and the recursion expression defining F is IF Tx THEN Ex ELSE E'x apply $I(T)$ to the value of the output register, a , and if $I(T)(a)$ is TRUE replace F by E on the top of the pushdown store and otherwise replace F by E' .

(3) If the pushdown store is empty, STOP and print the value of the output register.

The pushdown stores considered in the previous chapter contain as individual items members of any domain. In the case of monadic schemes we can get away with a simpler and stricter definition of a store. We can regard a store as a special variable u whose value under any interpretation must be a member of Γ^* for a fixed vocabulary Γ and to which we can apply as functions only POP(u) (which erases the rightmost symbol, if any, of u regarded as the top of the stack) and PUSH(u,A) (which adds A to the top (right) of u for any A in Γ). The only predicates applicable to u are EMPTY(u) which is TRUE if and only if u is empty, $u = e$, and for each A in Γ, TOP(u,A) which is true if and only if A is the top (rightmost) symbol of u. The store is always empty at the start of any computation. Further all assignments and tests involving u cannot involve any other variable.

Thus we have really established the following result:

THEOREM 8.2   The class of monadic recursion schemes is translatable into the class of Ianov schemes augmented by a simple pushdown store.

PROOF

We extend the definition of a pushdown store variable to allow functions PUSH(u,w) for any string w over the pushdown store vocabulary Γ^* ; obviously that can be simulated by $|w|$ instructions of the form PUSH(u,A) .

We can assume that our monadic recursion scheme S has basis functions $f_1,\ldots,f_m$ and defined functions $F_0,F_1,\ldots,F_n$ with Γ_0 initial and that each function F_i is defined by an equation

$$F_i x = \text{IF } T_i x \text{ THEN } E_i x \text{ ELSE } E_i' x$$

The strongly equivalent program scheme with one pushdown store can be described by the WHILE scheme in Example VIII-1. It is obviously a single register Ianov scheme augmented by one simple pushdown store.   ∎

We have shown that in the monadic case one simple pushdown store suffices. Similar to this definition of the augmentation of a flowchart scheme by a simple pushdown store one can define a counter as a reserved variable u whose values can only be non-negative integers and to which can only be applied the functions $u + 1$ and $u \doteq 1$ and the predicate $u = 0$. As in the case of an added pushdown store, all assignments to or by u must be independent variable - that is $u \leftarrow f(v)$ and $v \leftarrow f(u)$ are forbidden for $v \neq u$ and any f .

The proof of Theorem 8.1 can be modified to show that:

THEOREM 8.1'   The monadic recursion scheme S: $Fx = \text{IF } Tx \text{ THEN } x \text{ ELSE } gFFfx$ is not translatable into any strongly equivalent monadic program scheme augmented by one counter.

EXAMPLE VIII-1   WHILE SCHEME TO IMPLEMENT A MONADIC RECURSION SCHEME

```
START
y ← x
u ← PUSH(u,F₀)
WHILE  NOT EMPTY(u)  DO
```

$$y \gets x$$

IF TOP(u,f_1) THEN $y \gets f_1(y)$; u ← POP(u) ENDIF

IF TOP(u,f_2) THEN $y \gets f_2(y)$; u ← POP(u) ENDIF

....

IF TOP(u,f_m) THEN $y \gets f_m(y)$; u ← POP(u) ENDIF

IF TOP(u,F_0) THEN u ← POP(u)

     IF $T_0 x$ THEN u ← PUSH(u,E_0)

        ELSE u ← PUSH(u,E_0')

     ENDIF

ENDIF

IF TOP(u,F_1) THEN u ← POP(u) ;

     IF $T_1 x$ THEN u ← PUSH(u,E_1)

        ELSE u ← PUSH(u,E_1')

     ENDIF

ENDIF

....

IF TOP(u,F_n) THEN u ← POP(u) ;

     IF $T_n x$ THEN u ← PUSH(u,E_n)

        ELSE u ← PUSH(u,E_n')

     ENDIF

ENDIF

```
ENDWHILE
z ← y
STOP
```

However, it is known that two counters can imitate a simple pushdown store over a fixed vocabulary (or, for that matter, any number of such pushdown stores); the simulation does not require additional variables beyond the reserved counter variables. Hence one can show that:

THEOREM 8.2'   The class of monadic recursion schemes is effectively translatable into the class of Ianov program schemes augmented by two counters.

When one turns to general recursion schemes one runs into a problem. The pushdown store must record not only the basis and defined function letters but also the actual values of the functions. The proof we used to establish that a particular recursion scheme was not flowchartable also shows that it does not suffice to record the basis function letters and names of registers in which the values of arguments are stored - the actual values cannot then be computed with a finite number of registers. Hence the domain must be encoded into some finite alphabet. This either requires placing some restriction on domains or else admitting that the encoding of the domains need not be uniform and that the specification of the pushdown store(s) can vary. So, in the previous chapter we considered what might be called a "complex" pushdown store - the individual entries were not members of a fixed vocabulary but rather members of the domain of the interpretation - contents of the variables - such a store is really a list of lists. It cannot necessarily be translated uniformly into counters.

B. VALUE LANGUAGES
     A very powerful technique for comparing monadic recursion schemes with monadic program schemes was introduced by Luckham and Garland. It uses results from formal language theory in an interesting way. The basic concepts are those of a value language and an interpreted value language, formal languages which describe some of the properties of a given scheme.
     In describing the output $val(S,I,\overline{X})$ of a monadic scheme under a free interpretation I we omit parentheses, as discussed before.

DEFINITION   For a recursion scheme S the value language of S , L(S) , is the language:

$$\{ \ val(S,I,\overline{X}) \ \ | \ \ I \ \ free \ interpretation, \ \ val(S,I,\overline{X})\!\downarrow \ \}$$

DEFINITION   For a program scheme P the <u>value language</u> of P , L(P) , is the language:

$$\{ \text{val}(P,I,\overline{X}) \mid I \text{ free interpretation, } \text{val}(P,I,\overline{X}){\downarrow} \}$$

Our observations on Ianov schemes can be expressed as follows.

THEOREM 8.3   The value language of a Ianov scheme is a regular set.

For monadic recursion schemes and certain subcases of monadic program schemes such as Ianov schemes we can also define the <u>interpreted value language</u>.

To give a uniform definition, let us represent TRUE by 1 and FALSE by 0 and define the <u>interpreted value language $L\#(S)$ of a monadic recursion scheme S</u> with r tests $T_1,\dots,T_r$ as the set of all words of the form:

$$P_n f_n \cdots P_1 f_1 P_0 x$$

such that there is a free interpretation I for which:

(1) either $n = 0$ and $\text{val}(S,I,x) = x$ or $n \geq 1$ and
  $\text{val}(S,I,x) = f_n f_{n-1} \cdots f_1 x$,

(2) $P_0 = I(T_r)(x)\, I(T_{r-1})(x)\, \dots\, I(T_1)(x)$, and

(3) for $1 \leq i \leq n$, $P_i = b_{ir} \cdots b_{i1}$, where $b_{ij} = I(T_j)(f_i f_{i-1} \dots f_1 x)$.

EXAMPLE

Consider the monadic recursion scheme

$$S_1: \quad F_0 x = \text{IF } T_1 x \text{ THEN } F_1 x \text{ ELSE } F_2 x$$
$$F_1 x = \text{IF } T_2 x \text{ THEN } f F_0 f x \text{ ELSE } f h f x$$
$$F_2 x = \text{IF } T_2 x \text{ THEN } g F_0 g x \text{ ELSE } g h g x$$

The value language of S_1 is easily seen to be:

$$L(S_1) = \{ w h w^R x \mid w \in \{f,g\}^+ \}$$

(where w^R is w written backwards). The interpreted value language of S_1 is:

$$L\#(S_1) = \{ P_{n+1} \alpha_1 P_n \cdots \alpha_n P_1 h P_0 \alpha_n 0 i_n \alpha_{n-1} 1 i_{n-1} \cdots \alpha_1 1 i_0 x \mid n \geq 0 ,$$
$$i_0,\dots,i_n \in \{0,1\}, P_0, P_1,\dots,P_{n+1} \in \{00,01,10,11\} ,$$
$$\text{for } 0 \leq k \leq n , \text{ if } i_k = 0 \text{ then } \alpha_k = g \text{ and if}$$
$$i_k = 1 \text{ then } \alpha_k = f \}$$

Now examine the monadic recursion scheme:

$$S_2: \quad G_0 x = \text{IF } T_1 x \text{ THEN } fG_1 fx \text{ ELSE } gG_1 gx$$

$$G_1 x = \text{IF } T_2 x \text{ THEN } G_0 x \text{ ELSE } hx$$

It is clear that $L(S_2) = L(S_1)$. However, S_1 is not strongly equivalent to S_2 . For example, consider the free interpretation I defined by

$$I(T_1)(x) = 1 \quad, \quad I(T_2)(x) = 0$$

$$I(T_1)(fx) = I(T_2)(fx) = 1$$

$$I(T_1)(ffx) = I(T_2)(ffx) = 0$$

and $I(T_1)(E) = I(T_2)(E) = 0$ elsewhere. In S_1 we have:

$$F_0 x \implies F_1 x \implies fhfx = \text{val}(S_1,I,x)$$

But in S_2 :

$$G_0 x \implies fG_1 fx \implies fG_0 fx \implies ffG_1 ffx$$

$$\implies ffhffx = \text{val}(S_2,I,x) \neq \text{val}(S_1,I,x) \quad .$$

Now $00f00h11f01x$ is in $L\#(S_1)$ but not in $L\#(S_2)$ while $00f00f00h00f11f01x$ is in $L\#(S_2)-L\#(S_1)$. The reader can verify that $fhfx = \text{val}(S_2,I_1,x)$ and $ffhffx = \text{val}(S_1,I_2,x)$ for free interpretations I_1 and I_2 with $I_1(T_1)(x) = 1$ and $I_1(T_2)(fx) = 0$, and $I_2(T_1)(x) = I_2(T_2)(x) = I_2(T_1)(fx) = 1$ and $I_2(T_2)(fx) = 0$; $I_1(T_1),I_1(T_2),I_2(T_1)$ and $I_2(T_2)$ can be arbitrary elsewhere.

If two schemes are strongly equivalent they must give the same output under all interpretations and all inputs and hence under all free interpretations; thus the value languages must certainly be the same. If S is an extension of S' - that is, whenever $(S',I,\bar{a})$ converges, $(S,I,\bar{a})$ converges and $\text{val}(S,I,\bar{a}) = \text{val}(S',I,\bar{a})$ - certainly the set of outputs of S' must be a subset of the set of outputs of S . So we can establish the following simple facts about value and interpreted value languages.

FACTS

(1) For any schemes S and S' , if S and S' are strongly equivalent then $L(S) = L(S')$; if S is an extension of S' , then $L(S') \subseteq L(S)$.

(2) For any two classes C_1 and C_2 of schemes, if C_1 is translatable into C_2, then:

$$\mathscr{L}(C_1) = \{L(S) \mid S \in C_1\} \subseteq \mathscr{L}(C_2) = \{L(S) \mid S \in C_2\} .$$

Hence, if there is a scheme S in C_1 such that $L(S) \notin \mathscr{L}(C_2)$ then S is not translatable into C_2 and C_1 is not translatable into C_2.

(3) For monadic recursion schemes S and S', S is strongly equivalent to S' if and only if $L\#(S) = L\#(S')$.

(4) If C_1 and C_2 are two classes of monadic recursion schemes then C_1 is translatable into C_2 if and only if

$$\mathscr{L}\#(C_1) = \{L\#(S) \mid S \in C_1\} \subseteq \mathscr{L}\#(C_2) = \{L\#(S) \mid S \in C_2\} .$$

Fact (3) is also true for Ianov schemes. For arbitrary monadic one input one output program schemes it is possible to have $L\#(S) = L\#(S')$ with S not strongly equivalent to S' even if S is Ianov and S' always halting. For an example consider the schemes below:

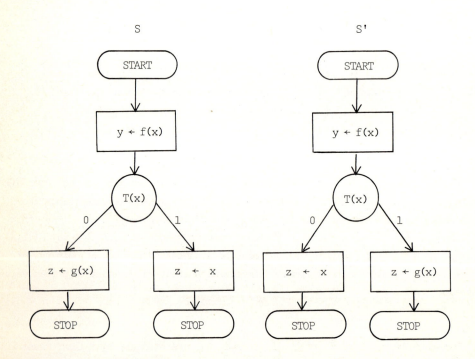

We have $L\#(S) = L\#(S') = \{p_1x, p_2gp_1x \mid p_1, p_2 \in \{0,1\}\}$ but $S \not\equiv S'$; S and S' are not even weakly equivalent. The point is that due to resets $(z \leftarrow g(x)$ and $z \leftarrow x$) the string tested ($f(x)$) doesn't appear in the output and so the definition of $L\#(S)$ is in this case artificial and irrelevant.

For monadic recursion schemes S and S' it is possible to have $L(S) = L(S')$ even if S is not strongly equivalent to S' - the same output might be given but for different interpretations; we saw this in the previous example.

First we show that the reversal of the interpreted value language of a monadic recursion scheme is a deterministic context-free language. This construction is effective. Hence the strong equivalence problem for monadic recursion schemes is decidable if the equivalence problem for deterministic context-free languages is decidable. (E. Friedman has recently shown that the converse is also true - if the strong equivalence problem for monadic recursion schemes were decidable then the equivalence problem for deterministic context-free languages would be decidable. Hence the strong equivalence problem for monadic recursion schemes is precisely the same as a well-known open problem - the equivalence problem for deterministic context-free languages.)

THEOREM 8.4   The reversal of the interpreted value language of a monadic recursion scheme is a deterministic context-free language.

PROOF
    We take the reversal of the interpreted value language simply because the input tape on a pushdown store acceptor is read from left to right while we write the composition of functions from right to left.

Let be S be a monadic recursion scheme with r tests $T_1, \ldots, T_r$, $r \geq 1$, and equations:

$$F_i x = \text{IF } T_{k_i} x \text{ THEN } E_{i,1}x \text{ ELSE } E_{i,0}x$$

for $0 \leq i \leq n$ and initial equation F_0 .
    Our deterministic pushdown acceptor will have as states [START], [STOP], [DEAD], and a state [w] for each w in $\{0,1\}^*$ with $0 \leq |w| \leq r$; we let e stand for the empty string, with $|e| = 0$.
    The transition function δ of our pushdown store machine starts off, with the pushdown store initially empty:

$$\delta([\text{START}], x, e) = ([e], F_0)$$

This transition causes x to be read on the input tape, places F_0 on the top (right) of the pushdown store and transfers to state [e] .

For w in $\{0,1\}^*$ and $0 \le |w| \le r-1$, the transition:

$$\delta([w],p,Z) = ([wp],Z)$$

for any p in $\{0,1\}$ and any condition Z of the pushdown store (i.e. $Z = e$, $Z = F_i$ or $Z = f$ for a basis function f), causes the machine to collect in its finite state control the outcomes of the r tests under the interpretation described by the input word.

If the machine has collected the required outcomes of the r tests, it is in a state $[w]$ with $w = b_1 \ldots b_r$, each b_j in $\{0,1\}$. If the top symbol of the pushdown store is now F_i , there is a transition

$$\delta([w],e,F_i) = ([w],E_{i,b_{k_i}})$$

which replaces F_i by $E_{i,1}$ or $E_{i,0}$ depending on whether the outcome of test T_{k_i} is supposed to be 1 or 0 as indicated by the input tape; thus the machine simulates the computation of S . If the top symbol of the pushdown store is now f for a basis function letter f , the transition is, for w in $\{0,1\}^+$ with $|w| = r$,

$$\delta([w],f,f) = ([e],e)$$

which means the machine must now consult its input tape for the outcome of the tests on the new value.

When the pushdown store is empty and we have collected the test outcomes, we can accept:

$$\delta([w],e,e) = ([STOP],e)$$

for $w \in \{0,1\}^+$ and $|w| = r$.

The machine accepts all and only input words which lead it from initial state [START] with empty pushdown store to accepting state [STOP] with empty pushdown store.

Any transition not described above leads into the dead state [DEAD] (e.g. $\delta([w],f,g) = ([DEAD],g)$ for f and g basis functions and $f \ne g$ or $|w| \ne r$, and $\delta([STOP],a,Z) = ([DEAD],Z)$ for any input a and pushdown store condition Z) and the dead state can never be left – $\delta([DEAD],a,Z) = ([DEAD],Z)$ everywhere.

Clearly the language accepted by this deterministic pushdown store acceptor is $(L\#(S))^R$, the reversal of $L\#(S)$ and hence $(L\#(S))^R$ is deterministic context-free. ∎

A term in a monadic recursion scheme is <u>right linear</u> if either it contains no defined function letters or else is of the form Fyx for F a defined function letter and y a (possibly empty) string of basis function letters; such a term is <u>left linear</u> if it either contains no defined function letters or else is of the form yFx for F a defined function letter and y a (possibly empty) string of basis function letters. A monadic recursion scheme S is <u>right linear</u> if in each equation

$$Fx \ = \ IF \ Tx \ THEN \ Ex \ ELSE \ E'x$$

both E and E' are right linear. We define left linear monadic recursion schemes in similar ways.

Our previous construction can be adapted to show:

COROLLARY 8.5   The reversal of the interpreted value language of a linear monadic recursion scheme is a deterministic linear context-free language (the language accepted by a deterministic single-turn pda).

COROLLARY 8.6   The reversal of the interpreted value language of a right linear or left linear monadic recursion scheme is a regular set.

Now Valiant has shown that the equivalence problem for deterministic finite-turn pdas is decidable, hence:

COROLLARY 8.7   The strong equivalence problem is decidable for monadic linear recursion schemes.

To get the value language $L(S)$ from $(L\#(S))^R$ one reverses the words and erases the sequence of 0's and 1's indicating the outcome of tests for a given interpretation. The families of context-free, of linear, and of regular languages are all closed under reversal and erasing so we have at once:

THEOREM 8.8   The value language of a
(1) monadic recursion scheme is context-free,
(2) linear monadic recursion scheme is linear context-free, and
(3) right linear monadic recursion scheme is regular.

We note in passing that it is easy to show that a few converses hold (provided of course we remove the end x):

(1) Every context-free language is the value language of some monadic recursion scheme.

(2) Every linear context-free language is the value language of some linear monadic recursion scheme.

(3) Every regular set is the value language of some right linear monadic recursion scheme.

However not every deterministic context-free language - even if it is in the right format - is the reversal of the interpreted value language of some monadic recursion scheme: the regular set $x0(f0)^*$ is an obvious example. We can show:

THEOREM 8.9   Every context-free language is the value language of some free monadic recursion scheme.

PROOF

If L is a context-free language, there is a reverse standard form context-free grammar $G = (V,\Sigma,P,S)$ such that $L = L(G)$ and all rules of P are of the forms

$$S \to e$$
$$Z \to ya \qquad\qquad a \in \Sigma \ , \ y \in (V - \{S\})^* \ .$$

For Z in $V - \Sigma$, let $r(Z)$ be the number of rules with left hand side Z and let $r = \text{Max } \{r(X) \mid Z \in V - \Sigma\}$. For $1 \le i \le r$ let T_i be a binary test. For each Z in $V - \Sigma$ assume that the rules with left hand side Z are ordered in some way: $Z \to y_{Z1}a_{Z1}$, $Z \to y_{Z2}a_{Z2}$, $\cdots$, $Z \to y_{Zr(Z)}a_{Zr(Z)}$. Create a new and distinct defined function letter F_{Zi} for each i , $1 \le i \le r(Z)$. The terminals in Σ are now considered to be basis function letters.

If $S \to e$ is in P and $r(S) = 1$, then the only equation is

$$F_{S1}x = x \quad .$$

If $S \to e$ is in P and $r(S) \ge 2$, then the start equation is

$$F_{S1}x = \text{IF } T_1x \text{ THEN } x \text{ ELSE } F_{S2}x \quad .$$

If $S \to e$ is not in P and $r(S) = 1$, and the only rule is $S \to ya$ then the only equation is

$$F_{S1} = yax \ .$$

Otherwise, $r(S) \geq 2$, and if the first rule for S is $S \rightarrow ya$, the start equation is

$$F_{S1} = IF \ T_1 x \ THEN \ yax \ ELSE \ F_{S2} x \ .$$

For $(Z,i) \neq (S,1)$ and $1 \leq i \leq r(Z) = 1$, there is an equation

$$F_{Zi} x = IF \ T_i x \ THEN \ y_{Zi} a_{Zi} x \ ELSE \ F_{Z \ i+1} x \ .$$

For $(Z, r(Z)) \neq (S,1)$ there is an equation

$$F_{Zr(Z)} x = IF \ T_{r(Z)} x \ THEN \ y_{Zr(Z)} a_{Zr(Z)} x \ ELSE \ y_{Zr(Z)} a_{Zr(Z)} x \ .$$

These equations form a monadic recursion scheme $S(G)$ and it can be verified that
(1) $S(G)$ is a _free_ monadic recursion scheme
(2) $L(S(G)) = Lx$. ∎

We can examine a few schemes. Flowchart scheme P_1 in Example VIII-2 uses the u variable as a counter. First it finds the first n such that $f^n x$ tests out to 1, simultaneously constructing v as $a^n x$. Then u is reset to fx and the scheme again searches for the first m such that $f^m x$ tests to 1; since $m = n$, v is recomputed as $b^n a^n x$. Finally u is reset to fx and the search is repeated, with v ending as $a^n b^n a^n x$ and then the contents of v are transferred to output register z and the computation halts. So the value language of P_1 is $val(P_1) = \{a^n b^n a^n x \mid n \geq 1\}$ which is not context-free. Hence P_1 is not strongly equivalent to any monadic recursion scheme.

THEOREM 8.10   There is a monadic program scheme which is not strongly equivalent to any monadic recursion scheme.

THEOREM 8.11   The classes of monadic recursion schemes and monadic program schemes are incomparable.

EXAMPLE VIII-2 - Monadic flowchart scheme P_1 is not translatable into
any strongly equivalent monadic recursion scheme.

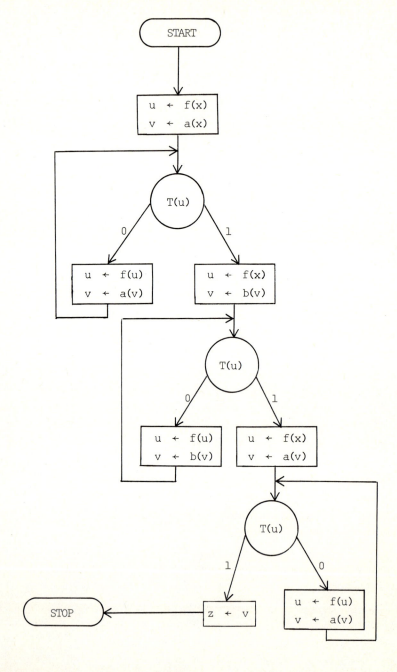

The value language of P_1, $L(P_1) = \{a^n b^n a^n x \mid n \geq 1\}$ is not Context-Free

Scheme P_2 in Example VIII-3 shows that a flowchart scheme may not be translatable into a monadic recursion scheme even if the value language is context-free. The reason is that P_2 really combines two schemes. If $T(x) = 1$, P_2 enters P_1 and if R is the regular set of all words ending in $1x$ then $L\#(P_2) \cap R = L\#(P_1) \cap R$ and if h is the homomorphism which erases the 0's and 1's, $h(L\#(P_2) \cap R) = h(L\#(P_1) \cap R) = L(P_1)$ which is not context-free; since the family of context-free languages is closed under intersection with regular sets and homomorphism, $L\#(P_2)$ is not context-free and so P_2 cannot be translated into any monadic recursion scheme. On the other hand, if $T(x) = 0$, P_2 enters a scheme which is essentially a Ianov scheme and whose value language is the regular set $aa^*bb^*aa^*x$. Since $L(P_1) \subset aa^*bb^*aa^*x$, $L(P_2) = L(P_1) \cup aa^*bb^*aa^*x = aa^*bb^*aa^*x$ and hence $L(P_2)$ is context-free and even regular.

In Example VIII-4, P_3 is a flowchart scheme the reversal of whose interpreted value language is deterministic context-free. Indeed,

$$(L\#(P_3))^R = \{x0(a0)^{2n}a1bp_1\ldots bp_m \mid n \geq 0 , m = 2(2n+1) , p_1,\ldots,p_m \in \{0,1\} \}$$

$$\cup \{x0(a))^{2n+1}a1bp_1\ldots bp_m \mid n \geq 0 , m = 2n+2 , p_1,\ldots,p_m \in \{0,1\} \}$$

$$\cup \{x1\}$$

which is deterministic context-free and even realtime. However, the final outcome depends on whether the number of a's read until the test of $a^n x$ yields 1 is an even or an odd number. This requires two states which record whether the whole sequence of a's is even or odd. But the deterministic pda for the reversal of an interpreted value language has a property which might be called "r+1-definite".

DEFINITION A deterministic pda $M = (K,\Sigma,\delta,q_o,F)$ is k-definite for an integer $k \geq 0$, if and only if for all inputs w,w' and x , if $|x| \geq k$, then

$$(q_o,wx,e) \vdash^* (q,e,y) \quad \text{and} \quad (q_o,w'x,e) \vdash^* (q',e,y')$$

imply $q = q'$. We call $L(M)$, the language accepted by M by final state and empty pushdown store, a k-definite deterministic context-free language.

In this definition, we allow our deterministic pdas to block (rather than enter a DEAD state). We can adapt our previous construction to show that under these definitions:

THEOREM 8.4' The reversal of the interpreted value language of a monadic recursion scheme with r tests is an (r+1)-definite deterministic context-free language.

EXAMPLE VIII-3 - Flowchart scheme P_2 is not translatable into
any monadic recursion scheme

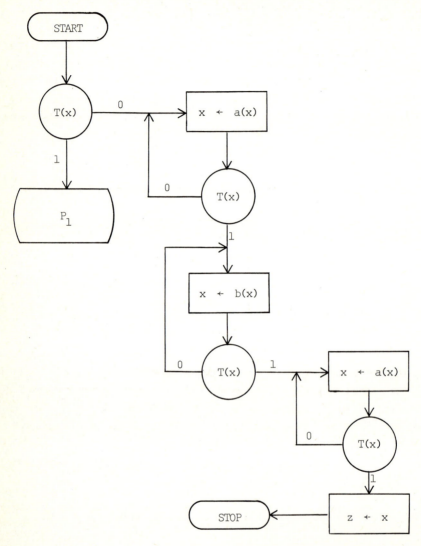

The value language of P_2 is $L(P_2)$ = aa*bb*aa*x which is regular; however,
the interpreted value language $L\#(P_2)$ is not context-free, since if h is
the homomorphism that erases the test outcomes and R the regular set of
words ending in 1x , $h(L\#(P_2) \cap R) = L(P_1)$ which is not context-free.

EXAMPLE VIII-4 - Flowchart scheme P_3 is not strongly equivalent
to any monadic recursion scheme even though
$(L\#(P_3))^R$ is deterministic context-free

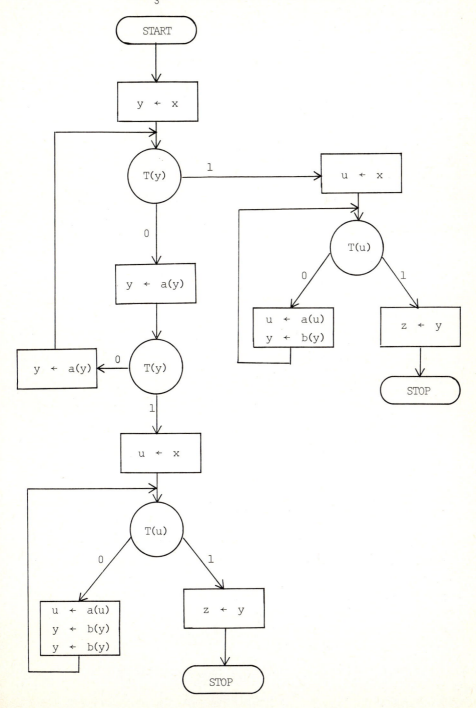

Now $(L\#(P_3))^R$ is not 2-definite (or even k-definite for any k) and so P_3 cannot be translated into any strongly equivalent monadic recursion scheme.

We can extend these constructions a little further to show that every recursively enumerable set can be obtained as the value language of a monadic program scheme (subject to addition of the final x, of course).

THEOREM 8.12   Every recursively enumerable set is the value language of some monadic program scheme.

PROOF

Just as we showed that for every Turing machine T there is a two-tape one-way deterministic finite state acceptor M_T such that T halts on the initially blank tape if and only if $L_a(M_T) \cap D = \phi$, so it can be shown that for any recursively enumerable language $L \subseteq \Sigma^*$ and a marker $\$$ not in Σ , there is a deterministic two-tape one-way finite state acceptor M with input vocabulary $\Sigma \cup \{\$,0,1\}$ such that:

(1) If (z,z) is in $L_a(M) \cap D$, then $z = w\$t$ for some w in L .

(2) For each w in L there is a finite tape t containing only 0's and 1's such that $(w\$t,w\$t)$ is in $L_a(M) \cap D$ and M does not accept $(w\$t,w\$t)$ until after it has read past the $\$$ on both tapes.

If T is a Turing machine which accepts L , machine M searches for pairs $(w\$t,w\$t)$ where w is in Σ^* and t is an encoding in binary of a computation of T accepting w as input. Thus in effect

$$t = h(q_0 w\text{¢}ID_1 \text{¢}ID_2 \ldots \text{¢}ID_n\text{¢})$$

where $q_0 w \vdash ID_1 \vdash ID_2 \vdash \ldots \vdash ID_n$, ID_n is an accepting instantaneous description of T , and h is a homomorphism mapping the symbols of the instantaneous descriptions into 0's and 1's in a one-to-one uniquely decodable fashion.

Let $M = (K_1, K_2, \Sigma \cup \{\$,0,1\}, \delta, q_0, q_a, q_r)$. We assume that $\$, 0$, and 1 are not in Σ . For convenience, order $\Sigma = \{a_1, \ldots, a_m\}$ and let $a_{m+1} = \$$, $a_{m+2} = 0$ and $a_{m+3} = 1$.

In Example VIII-5 we construct by subschemes a program scheme $P(M)$ with output variable z such that

$$L(P(M)) = \{w^R x \mid \exists(w\$t,w\$t) \in L_a(M) \cap D, \ w \in \Sigma^*\} = L^R x .$$

This suffices, since the family of recursively enumerable languages is closed under reversal.

EXAMPLE VIII-5

CONSTRUCTION of flowchart scheme $P(M)$ from two-tape one-way deterministic finite state acceptor $M = (K_1, K_2, \Sigma \cup \{\$, 0, 1\}, \delta, q_o, q_a, q_r)$. For any free interpretation I , $(P(M), I, x)\downarrow$ if and only if $(t_I, t_I) \in L_a(M) \cap D$ and in that case $t_I = w\$t'$, $w \in L$, and $val(P(M), I, x) = w^R x$.

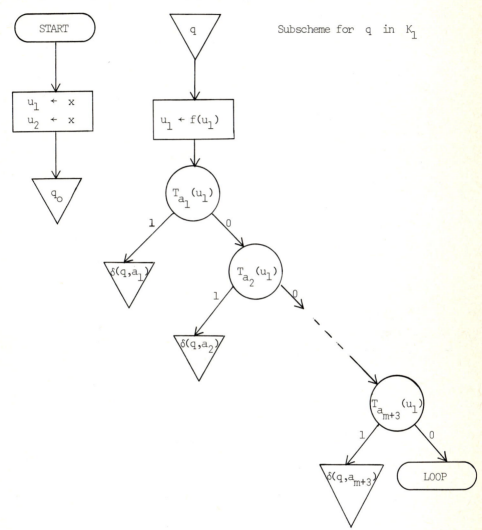

Subscheme for q in K_1

EXAMPLE VIII-5 (Continued)

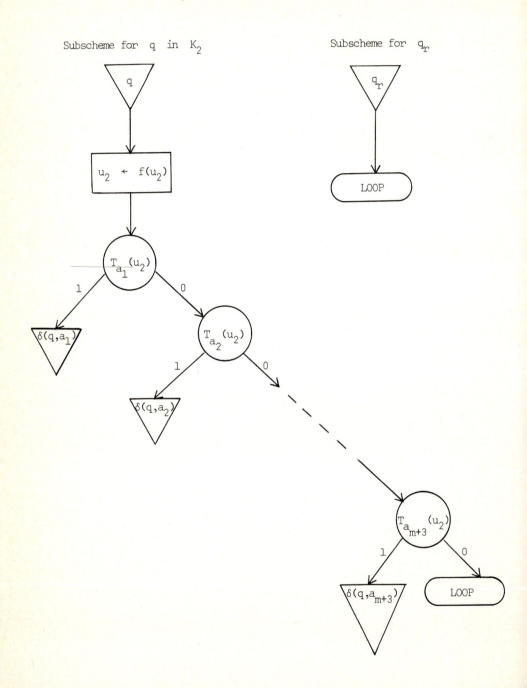

EXAMPLE VIII-5 (Concluded)

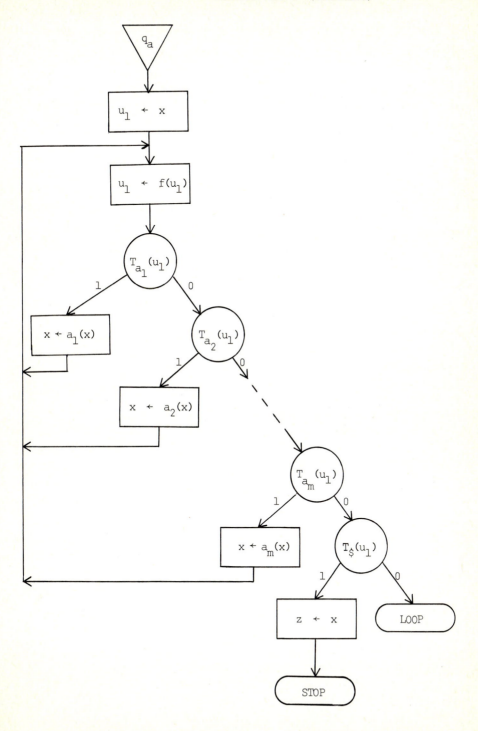

Our construction deviates slightly from the previous ones of this type in that we have one test T_{a_i} for each a_i in $\Sigma \cup \{\$,0,1\}$. We always apply these tests in sequence from a_1 to a_{m+3}. Call a free interpretation I "useful" if for every $j \geq 1$ there is an i, $1 \leq i \leq m+3$ such that $I(T_{a_i})(f^j x) = 1$ and otherwise let I be "useless". If I is useful, let $b_j = a_k$ where $k = \text{Min}\{i \mid I(T_{a_i})(f^j x) = 1\}$. Scheme $P(M)$ is set to loop for a useless interpretation once it is known to be useless – i.e., $f^j x$ is encountered with $I(T_{a_i})(f^j x) = 0$ for $1 \leq i \leq m+3$ – and so we need not worry about useless interpretations. If I is useful, let $t_I = b_1 \ldots b_j \ldots$.

This time $P(M)$ is built so that for a useful free interpretation I, computation $(P(M),I,x)$ simulates M on input (t_I,t_I). In particular, computation $(P(M),I,x)$ reaches subscheme q_a if and only if M accepts (t_I,t_I), i.e. (t_I,t_I) is in $L_a(M) \cap D$. If $P(M)$ reaches q_a, then we must have $t_I = w\$t'$ for some w in L. Thereupon $P(M)$ resets u_1 to x and rechecks the values of the tests on the $f^{j+1} x$. This time $P(M)$ records the fact that $b_j = a_k$ by reassigning $x \leftarrow a_k x$. When $P(M)$ reaches $b_j = \$$ it transfers the contents of x, $w^R x$, to z and halts with $\text{val}(P(M),I,x) = w^R x$. Thus $\text{val}(P(M),I,x) = w^R x$ for w in L. This is the only way in which $P(M)$ can give output on a free interpretation, so $L(P(M))$ has the desired properties. ∎

C. FREE MONADIC RECURSION SCHEMES

It is undecidable whether a monadic program scheme is free. But it is fairly easy to see that it is decidable whether a monadic recursion scheme is free. Recall that a monadic recursion scheme S is free if and only if during every computation of S under every free interpretation of S no test T of S is twice applied to the same expression Ex.

If we construct the pushdown store automaton which accepts the reversal of the interpreted value language of a monadic recursion scheme S we see that there are only two cases in which S can fail to be free:

(1) If some defined function letter F appears on the top of the pushdown store and then without erasing the store or advancing the input, a defined function letter G appears on top, and the equations for F and G have the same test.

(2) If some defined function F appears on the top of the pushdown store, an occurrence of a defined function letter G appears below, and G is reached without advancing the input tape, and the equations for F and G have the same test.

Case (1) means that in the derivation under some free interpretation we have $F_0 x \overset{*}{\Longrightarrow} uFtx \overset{*}{\Longrightarrow} uvGtx$ where t is a string of basis functions and the second derivation takes at least one step, and the same test T is associated with the equations for F and G. Then test T must test tx twice and so S is not free. If we form a context-free grammar from S in the straightforward way - i.e. an equation $Gx = IF\ Tx\ THEN\ Ex\ ELSE\ E'x$ becomes two productions $G \rightarrow E$ and $G \rightarrow E'$ - we observe that it suffices to test whether $F_0 \overset{*}{\Longrightarrow} uFt$ and $F \overset{k}{\Longrightarrow} vG$ for $k \neq 0$ in the resulting grammar. If this condition does not occur, condition (1) cannot occur in the original scheme. If it does and $F_0 x \overset{*}{\Longrightarrow} uFtx$ does not occur for any free interpretation in S, then S cannot be free; similarly if $F_0 x \overset{*}{\Longrightarrow} uFtx$ but then $Ftx \overset{*}{\Longrightarrow} vGtx$ is impossible. But if both occur, then S cannot be free. However, standard methods show that it is decidable for context-free grammars whether there are u, F, t, v such that $F_0 \overset{*}{\Longrightarrow} uFt$ and $F \overset{k}{\Longrightarrow} vG$ for $k \neq 0$.

The other case, (2), is handled similarly, This really applies to the situation $F_0 x \overset{*}{\Longrightarrow} uGvFtx$ and $Ftx \overset{*}{\Longrightarrow} tx$ and $vtx \overset{*}{\Longrightarrow} tx$ for t a string of basis functions and v a string of defined functions. Again, it is decidable for context-free grammars whether this situation holds; if it does, either S is already not free because the corresponding derivations in the scheme cannot hold for any free interpretation, or the existence of this situation under any free interpretation violates the definition of "freeness". So we have proven the following result of Ashcroft, Manna and Pneuli:

THEOREM 8.13   It is decidable whether a monadic recursion scheme is free.

If a monadic recursion scheme S is free, then neither (1) nor (2) can hold. If S has n defined functions, then every n steps of a comuutation must add at least one new basis function letter in the argument of the defined function letter being computed upon. Similarly, no more than n defined function letters in a row can be "erased". If we pursue these conditions into the formation of the deterministic pushdown store automaton for the reversal of the interpreted value language of such a scheme, one can show that (Ashcroft, Manna, Pneuli):

THEOREM 8.14   The strong equivalence problem for free monadic recursion schemes is decidable.

By contrast, E. Friedman has shown:

THEOREM 8.15   The weak equivalence problem for free monadic recursion schemes is undecidable.

D. WEAK TRANSLATABILITY

We can carry the ideas in the proof that every recursively enumerable set is
the value language of some monadic program scheme one step forward and show that in
a certain sense we can translate monadic recursion schemes into monadic program
schemes, this notion of translatability being weak translatability.

There are alternative definitions of "weak translatability". The following
definition is rather "strong". "Weaker" versions omit condition (3).

DEFINITION   A scheme S is <u>weakly translatable</u> into a scheme S' if
(1) L(S) = L(S')
(2) For any interpretation I and input $\bar{a}$, if computation $(S',I,\bar{a})$ converges,
     then computation $(S,I,\bar{a})$ converges and $val(S,I,\bar{a}) = val(S',I,\bar{a})$
(3) For any interpretation I of S restricted to the function and predicate
     letters of S , there is an interpretation I' of S' compatible with S
     such that (S,I) is strongly equivalent to (S',I') .

THEOREM 8.16   Every monadic recursion scheme is weakly translatable into a monadic
program scheme.

PROOF
Let S be a monadic recursion scheme. By methods similar to the proof of
Chomsky normal form for context-free grammars we can convert the equations of S
to the forms:

    Fx = IF Qx THEN Gx ELSE Hx
    Fx = Gx
    Fx = GHx
    Fx = tx

for t a terminal term and F,G,H defined function letters.
Assume that S is in this form and that S has defined function letters
$F_0,F_1,\ldots,F_n$ with F_0 the initial function letter.
The program scheme P(S) we shall construct in Example VIII-6 has an extra
test T which does not appear in S and which we assume to be an n+2-way test
with possible outcomes $0,1,\ldots,n,\$$ for some new symbol $; such a test could be
simulated by binary tests in the standard way. Scheme P(S) has variables
x , u , v , and z . Register z holds the eventual output and register x is
input and program variable. The registers u and v are special program variables
which simulate the pushdown store of a pushdown store machine implementing the
computations of S .

EXAMPLE VIII-6

WEAK TRANSLATION OF A RECURSION SCHEME S INTO FLOWCHART SCHEME

Let the subscheme: Abbreviate subscheme:

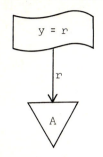

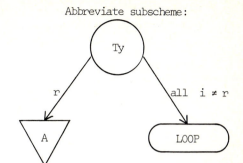

Initial subscheme:

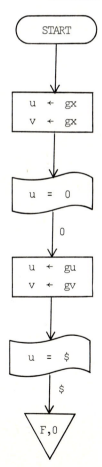

EXAMPLE VIII-6 (Continued)

II. Subschemes for updating the Pushdown store Simulation

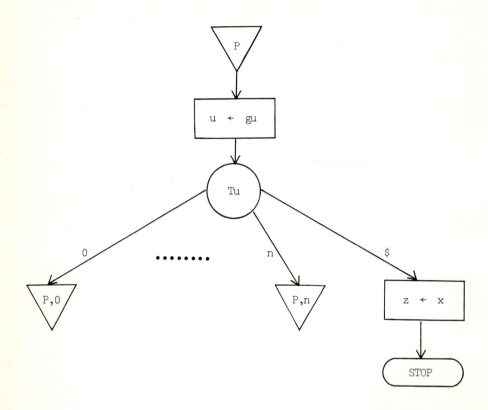

EXAMPLE VIII-6 (Continued)

II. Subschemes for updating the Pushdown store Simulation (Continued)

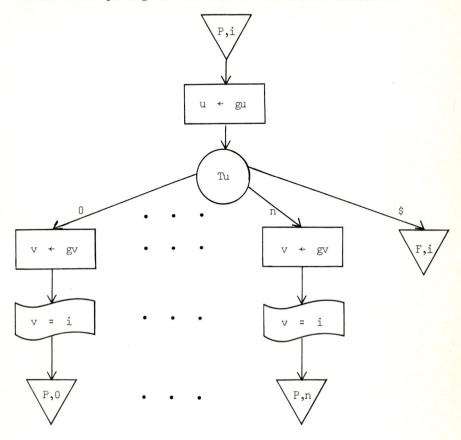

EXAMPLE VIII-6 (Continued)

III. Subschemes for Simulating the Recursion Scheme

IF EQUATION i IS: $F_i x = F_r x$ IF EQUATION i IS: $F_i x = F_r F_s x$

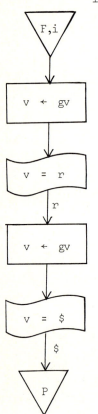

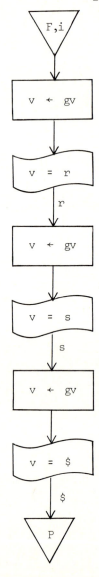

EXAMPLE VIII-6 (Concluded)

III. Subschemes for Simulating the Recursion Scheme - (Continued)

IF EQUATION i IS:

$F_i x = tx$ t terminal

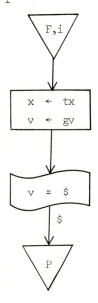

IF EQUATION i IS:

$F_i x = $ IF Qx THEN $F_r x$ ELSE $F_s x$

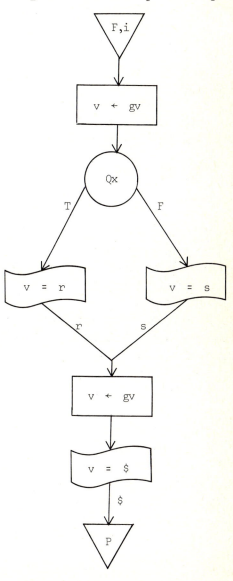

We relate a free interpretation I and a tape t_I by setting $a_j = F_i$ if $I(T)(g^jx) = i$ with $0 \le i \le n$ and $a_j = \$$ if $I(T)(g^jx) = \$$ and defining:

$$t_I = a_1 \ldots a_j \ldots$$

Given a free interpretation I of S there is a tape

$$p_I = F_0\$w_1\$w_2\$\ldots$$

where under interpretation I in S :

$$F_0x \implies w_1x \implies w_2x \implies \ldots$$

and if (S,I,x) converges in n steps:

$$p_I = F_0\$w_1\$w_2\$\ldots\$w_n\$\$$$

and otherwise p_I is infinite. Thus p_I contains the successive pushdown store contents of the pushdown store machine executing (S,I) separated by $\$$'s and ending in $\$\$$ to represent the fact that the pushdown store is empty when (S,I,x) converges; if (S,I,x) does not converge, the tape p_I is infinite.

An extension I' of I to $P(S)$ is called "useful" if either p_I is infinite and $t_{I'} = p_I$ or p_I is finite and $t_{I'} = p_It'$ for some tape t' ; thus t_I is a record of the pushdown store contents of the machine executing (S,I) . Otherwise I' is "useless". The scheme $P(S)$ is built to loop whenever I' is "useless" so that we need only consider the effect of useful free interpretations of $P(S)$.

The variables u and v are used to ensure that an interpretation is "useful" and to keep track of the proper equation to simulate. Initially they are both set to gx . Next the test T on gx and then ggx makes sure we start with $t_I = F_0\$$. Variables u and v behave like the heads of a finite state acceptor with two heads which reads t_I and tries to verify that it is useful.

Initially we enter - on free interpretation I - subscheme $<F,0>$ after determining that t_I starts with $F_0\$$ and having, figuratively speaking, both u and v heads at $\$$ - that is, u and v are both specified at g^2x , $I(T)(gx) = 0$ and $I(T)(g^2x) = \$$. This is shown at the top of the diagram on the next page.

Initially, from START to <F,0> :

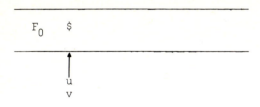

For $F_i x = F_r x$

From <F,i> :

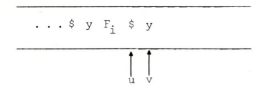

To <P> :

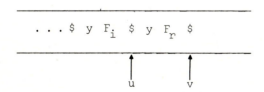

To <F,r> :

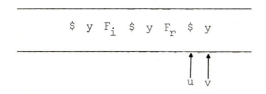

Now suppose that at some step in the computation of $(P(S),I,x)$, we are at subscheme $<F,i>$ and have verified that the tape t_I starts with $F_0\$w_1\$...\$yF_i\$y$ where t_I represents the proper pushdown store contents through yF_i , yF_i is the current pushdown store contents, variable x contains the proper value of the argument of F_i , and "head" u is sitting on "$\$$" and head v at the rightmost symbol of y (or on $\$$ if $y = e$) . This situation is diagrammed on page 8-32 , second picture from the top. There are four possibilities.

If $F_ix = F_rx$ then $P(S)$ first reassigns v as gv , ensures that gv tests to r , reassigns v to gv and tests that this yields $\$$ under T . Thus it enters subscheme $<P>$ having checked that t_I starts with $F_0\$w_1\$...\$yF_i\$yF_r\$$ and head u is on the next to last "$\$$" and v on the last "$\$$" . This is the third picture on page 8-32. Finally in subscheme P the computation verifies that t_I starts with $F_0\$w_1\$...\$yF_r\$yF_r\$y$ by moving head v to the rightmost symbol of y and u to the last "$\$$" encountered to date. In the process it observes that F_r is the top of the last complete pushdown store and so proceeds to subscheme $<F,r>$ as shown in the last picture on page 8-32. If the simulation was "correct" at $<F,i>$, it is still correct.

Second, suppose $F_ix = F_rF_sx$. This case appears on page 8-34. First in subscheme $<F,i>$ we verify that $I(T)(gv) = r$, then $I(T)(ggv) = s$ and finally $I(T)(gggv) = \$$. This checks that t_I starts $F_0\$w_1\$...\$yF_i\$yF_rF_s\$$ and moves head v to the last "$\$$" with u still on the next to last "$\$$" as shown in the second picture on the next page; this situation holds as we enter subscheme P . Then we verify that t_I starts with $F_0\$...\$yF_i\$yF_rF_s\$yF_r$ as head u moves to the last "$\$$" and v to the last "F_r" and we enter subscheme $<F,s>$, having noticed that F_s is the top of the last complete pushdown store contents found on t_I to date. Again, if the simulation was correct at $<F,i>$ it is still correct.

Next, suppose that $F_ix = IF\ Qx\ THEN\ F_rx\ ELSE\ F_sx$. In this case subscheme $<F,i>$ first tests $I(Q)(x)$ and on TRUE behaves as if the equation were $F_ix = F_rx$ and on FALSE as if it were $F_ix = F_sx$. We have already illustrated this form of behavior.

Finally consider the case $F_ix = tx$ for t a terminal string. This is illustrated on page 8-35. There are two cases. The case $y = y'F_j$ appears on the top of the illustration. Now we have verified that t_I starts with $F_0\$w_1\$...\$y'F_jF_i\$y'F_j$ and u sits on the last "$\$$" and v on the last "F_j" . In moving from $<F,i>$ to $<P>$ this time we reassign $x \leftarrow tx$, verify that "$\$$" is the next symbol on t_I and move v to this position. Then we pass from $<P>$ to $<F,j>$ verifying that t_I starts with $F_0\$w_1\$...\$y'F_jF_i\$y'F_j\$y'$ and moving u to the last "$\$$" and v to the rightmost symbol of y' . This is shown in the top three pictures of the illustration on page 8-35. Again, everything checks out.

For $F_i x = F_r F_s x$

From <F,i> :

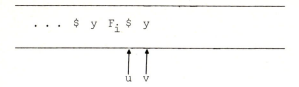

To <P> :

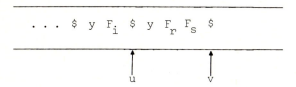

To <F,s> :

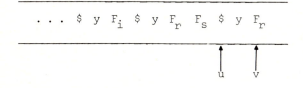

For $F_i x = tx$ t   terminal

<u>Either</u>

     From   <F,i> :

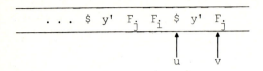

     To   <P> :

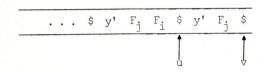

     To   <F,j> :

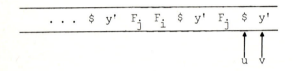

<u>Or</u>

     From   <F,i> :

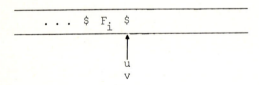

     To   <P> :

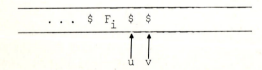

     To   <STOP> :

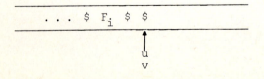

In the last case, $F_i x = tx$, t a terminal string and $y = e$ so that we have verified that t_I starts with $F_0 \$ w_1 \$ \ldots \$ F_i \$$ and both u and v sit on the last "\$" . This is shown in the last three parts of the illustration on page 8-35. We reassign $x \leftarrow tx$, then check that the next symbol of "\$" , and move v to this position. Now we move u right and meet this "\$" . So we know that t_I starts with $F_0 \$ w_1 \$ \ldots \$ F_i \$ \$$ and this is p_I since the pushdown store contents are empty. The computation ends and we go to the STOP statement placing the current contents of x in the output register z .

Thus if I is a useful free interpretation of $P(S)$, $P(S)$ simulates S on the restriction of I to the functions and predicates of S ; if computation $(P(S),I,x)$ converges, then $\mathrm{val}(P(S),I,x) = \mathrm{val}(S,I,x)$. So for any useful interpretation I , $(P(S),I)$ is strongly equivalent to (S,I) . If I is useless, then eventually $(P(S),I,x)$ encounters a "wrong" symbol on t_I and loops. On the other hand, any free interpretation I of S alone has an extension to some useful free interpretation I' of $P(S)$ according to the formula $t_{I'} = p_I$ for (S,I,x) divergent and $t_{I'} = p_I t'$ for (S,I,x) convergent and any choice of t' . Hence S is weakly translatable to $P(S)$ as desired. ■

APPENDIX A   -   PROGRAM SCHEMES AND THE FIRST ORDER PREDICATE CALCULUS

We wish to present a few of the basic ideas of the first order predicate calculus, using as a starting point the ideas of interpretations of schemes which we have already encountered.

We are dealing with a particular formal metalanguage which extends the meta-language used to define and describe program schemes. The alphabet used contains the symbols used in defining program schemes:

variables
constants
function letters
predicate letters
parentheses and commas

but adds to them

equality symbol: =
logical symbols: $\land$, $\lor$, $\rceil$, $\supset$, $\equiv$
quantifiers: $\exists$, $\forall$

We extend the definition of terms to give us (extended) functional terms, atomic formulae, and well-formed formulae. All these are defined inductively.

DEFINITION   The following expressions are <u>functional terms</u>.

1) If x is a variable, x is a functional term.

2) If c is a constant, c is a functional term.

3) If f is an n-placed function letter and $t_1,\ldots,t_n$ are functional terms, then $f(t_1,\ldots,t_n)$ is a functional term.

DEFINITION   An <u>atomic formula</u> is defined as follows.

1) If P is an n-placed predicate letter and $t_1,\ldots,t_n$ are functional terms, then $P(t_1,\ldots,t_n)$ is an atomic formula.

2) If t_1 and t_2 are functional terms, then $(t_1 = t_2)$ is an atomic formula.

DEFINITION   A <u>well-formed formula</u> (<u>wff</u>) is defined as follows.

1) Every atomic formula is a wff.

2) If x is a variable and α is a wff, then $\exists x \alpha$ and $\forall x \alpha$ are wffs.

3) If α and β are wffs, then the following are wffs:

$$(\rceil\alpha) , (\alpha \lor \beta) , (\alpha \land \beta) , (\alpha \supset \beta) , (\alpha \equiv \beta)$$

A wff formed without any application of 2) is <u>quantifier-free</u>. A quantifier-free wff containing no usage of " = " is a <u>Boolean expression</u>.

The quantifier " ∃x " is usually translated "there exists an x " while " ∀x " is translated as "for all x " . We shall give more precise semantics for these symbols by extending the concept of an interpretation to a wff. First we must distinguish between those variables appearing "free" in a wff and those which are "bound" by the quantifiers. These definitions are also inductive.

DEFINITION   Any appearance of a variable in a wff is either <u>free</u> or <u>bound</u> by these rules:

1) Any appearance of a variable in a quantifier-free wff is free.

2) A variable appearing free in a wff α appears free in $(\daleth\alpha)$; a free appearance of a variable in α or β is free in $(\alpha \vee \beta)$, $(\alpha \wedge \beta)$, $(\alpha \supset \beta)$, and $(\alpha \equiv \beta)$.

3) If x and y are distinct variables and α is a wff, then any appearance of x is free in $\exists y\alpha$ or $\forall y\alpha$ if it is free in α .

4) Any appearance of a variable x that is not free by (1) - (3) is bound; in particular, any occurrence of x is bound in $\exists x\alpha$ and $\forall x\alpha$ for any wff α .

For example, all variables appear free in $(\daleth((x = c) \equiv (y = z)))$ or $(P(x,f(x),g(x,z)) \equiv Q(x))$. Variable x is free and variable y is bound in wff $(\forall y P(x,x,y) \equiv Q(x))$; this wff, as we shall shortly see, can be regarded as a formula of one variable, x ; it is not a function of y . The situation can be more complicated; e.g. in the wff $(\forall x\forall y P(x,x,y) \supset (\daleth\forall y P(y,x,x)))$, the first two appearances of x - in $P(x,x,y)$ - are bound by the quantifier x but the second two appearances of x - in $P(y,x,x)$ - are free. When we wish to avoid this sort of confusion, we can restrict attention to "pretty wffs" in which either every appearance of a variable x is free or else every appearance of x is bound.

DEFINITION   The following wffs are <u>pretty wffs</u>.

1) Every atomic formula is a pretty wff.

2) Let x be a variable. If α is a pretty wff such that x appears free in α and all appearances of x in α are free, then $\exists x\alpha$ and $\forall x\alpha$ are pretty wffs.

3) Let α and β be pretty wffs. Then $(\daleth\alpha)$ is a pretty wff. The wffs $(\alpha \vee \beta)$, $(\alpha \wedge \beta)$, $(\alpha \supset \beta)$, and $(\alpha \equiv \beta)$ are pretty wffs unless there is a variable x such that x appears free in α but bound in β or free in β but bound in α .

DEFINITION   A <u>sentence</u> is a wff with no free variables. A <u>pretty sentence</u> is a pretty wff with no free variables.

Now we must define interpretations for functional terms, atomic formulae, wffs and sentences. Basically we have as before:

DEFINITION   An _interpretation_ I consists of a nonempty domain D and an assignment of each constant c to a member $I(c)$ of domain D and

1) for each n-placed function letter f a total function $I(f)$: $D^n \to D$, and

2) for each n-placed predicate letter P a total Boolean function

$$I(P): D^n \to \{\text{TRUE},\text{FALSE}\}$$

First we must extend the definition of I to arbitrary functional terms. For this purpose we consider any member a of the domain D of I to be a functional term.

DEFINITION   We define $I(t)$ for a functional term t not containing a variable by:

1) For a constant c , $I(c)$ is the member of D assigned to c .

2) For a member a of D , $I(a) = a$.

3) If $t_1,\dots,t_n$ are functional terms not containing variables, and f is an n-placed functional letter, then

$$I(f(t_1,\dots,t_n)) = I(f)(I(t_1),\dots,I(t_n)) .$$

DEFINITION   If t is any functional term containing precisely the n distinct variables $x_1,\dots,x_n$ and no others, then by $I(t)$ we mean that function, $I(t)$: $D^n \to D$ defined by $I(t)(a_1,\dots,a_n) = I(t(a_1,\dots,a_n))$ for all $a_1,\dots,a_n \in D$, where $t(a_1,\dots,a_n)$ is formed from t by substituting a_i for x_i everywhere.

We can make similar definitions for atomic formulae.

DEFINITION   We define $I(\alpha)$ for an atomic formula α not containing a variable by:

1) If P is an n-placed predicate letter and $t_1,\dots,t_n$ are functional terms not containing variables, then

$$I(P(t_1,\dots,t_n)) = I(P)(I(t_1),\dots,I(t_n)) .$$

2) If t_1 and t_2 are functional terms not containing variables, then

$$I((t_1 = t_2)) = \begin{cases} \text{TRUE} & \text{if } I(t_1) = I(t_2) \\ \text{FALSE} & \text{otherwise} \end{cases}$$

DEFINITION   If α is any atomic formula containing precisely the n distinct variables $x_1,\dots,x_n$ and no others, then by $I(\alpha)$ we mean that Boolean function, $I(\alpha)$: $D^n \to \{\text{TRUE},\text{FALSE}\}$ defined by $I(\alpha)(a_1,\dots,a_n) = I(\alpha(a_1,\dots,a_n))$ for all $a_1,\dots,a_n$ in D , where $\alpha(a_1,\dots,a_n)$ is formed from α by substituting a_i for x_i everywhere.

Thus " = " is interpreted as equality, relative to I , as we intend it to be. So $I((f(x) = f(x))(a)$ will be TRUE for any interpretation I and any member a of the domain of I , but $I((f(a) = g(a)))$ may be TRUE or FALSE, depending on I and a ; for example, if $I(f)$ and $I(g)$ are the same function for a particular I then it will always be TRUE while if $I(f)(a) \neq I(g)(a)$, it is FALSE. As another example, if D is the integers, $I(f)(a,b) = a+b$, $I(g)(a) = a^2$ and $I(P)(a) = $ TRUE if and only if $a = 0$, then we can compute:

$$I(f(a,g(b))) = a+b^2 \; ; \quad I(g(f(b,a))) = (b+a)^2 \; ; \quad I(P)(g(a)) = \text{TRUE} \text{ if}$$
$$\text{and only if} \quad I(P)(a) = \text{TRUE} \text{ if and only if} \quad a = 0 \; .$$

For this interpretation, e.g., $f(g(f(x,y)),f(y,z))$ is that function of variables x,y and z denoted by $((x+y)^2 + (y+z))$.

Now we must explain the semantics of the logical connectives. Informally, they have meanings you are probably acquainted with. Connective " $\wedge$ " is "AND" , connective " $\vee$ " is "OR" , " $\daleth$ " is "NOT" , " $\supset$ " is "IMPLIES" , while " $\equiv$ " is "IF AND ONLY IF" . Occasionally we use the English words rather than the formal symbols as a matter of convenience. We now give the formal definitions of these concepts. In this definition, recall that we allow members of the domain of I to play the same role as constants or free (but not bound) variable in wffs.

DEFINITION   Let α and β be wffs which contain no free variables but might contain free occurrences of members of the domain of interpretation I . Then

1) $I((\daleth\alpha))$ = $\begin{cases} \text{TRUE} & \text{if } I(\alpha) = \text{FALSE} \\ \text{FALSE} & \text{if } I(\alpha) = \text{TRUE} \end{cases}$

2) $I((\alpha \vee \beta))$ = $\begin{cases} \text{TRUE} & \text{if either } I(\alpha) = \text{TRUE or } I(\beta) = \text{TRUE} \\ \text{FALSE} & \text{if both } I(\alpha) = \text{FALSE and } I(\beta) = \text{FALSE} \end{cases}$

3) $I((\alpha \wedge \beta))$ = $\begin{cases} \text{TRUE} & \text{if } I(\alpha) = I(\beta) = \text{TRUE} \\ \text{FALSE} & \text{if either } I(\alpha) = \text{FALSE or } I(\beta) = \text{FALSE} \end{cases}$

4) $I((\alpha \supset \beta))$ = $\begin{cases} \text{TRUE} & \text{if } I(\alpha) = \text{FALSE or } I(\beta) = \text{TRUE} \\ \text{FALSE} & \text{if } I(\alpha) = \text{TRUE and } I(\beta) = \text{FALSE} \end{cases}$

5) $I((\alpha \equiv \beta))$ = $\begin{cases} \text{TRUE} & \text{if } I(\alpha) = I(\beta) \\ \text{FALSE} & \text{if } I(\alpha) \neq I(\beta) \end{cases}$

There are one or two points to notice in this last definition. One is the significance of the implication symbol " ⊃ " in 4). In a sentence " α ⊃ β " , " α IMPLIES β " , wff α is the "hypothesis" and β is the "conclusion". The sentence has value TRUE under I if either α and β are TRUE, or α is FALSE and β is TRUE or α is FALSE and β is FALSE and is only FALSE when the hypothesis is TRUE but the conclusion FALSE. Thus if " α ⊃ β " is TRUE and the hypothesis is TRUE, we can conclude that the conclusion is TRUE; but if the hypothesis is FALSE we can make no comment about the conclusion. We sometimes say that such an implication is "vacuously TRUE" if the hypothesis is FALSE.

We can readily show that the connectives AND and OR are associative in the sense that $I((\alpha \wedge (\beta \wedge \gamma))) = I(((\alpha \wedge \beta) \wedge \gamma))$ for any interpretation I and similarly $I((\alpha \vee (\beta \vee \gamma))) = I(((\alpha \vee \beta) \vee \gamma))$. For these reasons it is customary to omit parentheses and write $(\alpha_1 \wedge ... \wedge \alpha_n)$ or $(\alpha_1 \vee ... \vee \alpha_n)$ when, hopefully, no ambiguity can occur; the first expression is often called a conjunction of the conjuncts $\alpha_1,...,\alpha_n$ and the second a disjunction of the disjuncts $\alpha_1,...,\alpha_n$.

Now we must define the semantics of our sentences with quantifiers. Notice that in our definitions, logical connectives have precedence over quantifiers. Thus in evaluating $I((\daleth(\forall x P(x) \wedge (\daleth \forall x \forall y Q(x,y)))))$, we first peel off the NOT and evaluate $I((\forall x P(x) \wedge (\daleth \forall x \forall y Q(x,y))))$; to do this, we evaluate the two conjuncts, $\forall x P(x)$ and $(\daleth \forall x \forall y Q(x,y))$ etc. Finally we are driven inside and must start by evaluating $I(\forall x P(x))$ and $I(\forall x \forall y Q(x,y))$. In the latter case we also go inwards, and for each a , examine $I(\forall y Q(a,y))$, etc. This is implied by our next definitions.

DEFINITION   Let $\alpha(x)$ be a pretty wff containing x as a free variable and no other free variables. Then we can extend the definition of I :

1) $I(\exists x \alpha(x))$ = $\begin{cases} \text{TRUE} & \text{if there is an a in D with } I(\alpha(a)) = \text{TRUE} \\ \text{FALSE} & \text{if } I(\alpha(a)) = \text{FALSE for all a in D .} \end{cases}$

2) $I(\forall x \alpha(x))$ = $\begin{cases} \text{TRUE} & \text{if } I(\alpha(a)) = \text{TRUE for all a in D} \\ \text{FALSE} & \text{if there is an a in D such that } I(\alpha(a)) = \text{FALSE} \end{cases}$

where $\alpha(a)$ is the sentence obtained by substituting a for x everywhere in α .

DEFINITION   Let $\psi(x_1,...,x_n)$ be a pretty wff containing as free variables all and only the distinct variables $x_1,...,x_n$. By $I(\psi(x_1,...,x_n))$ we denote the Boolean function $I(\psi(x_1,...,x_n)): D^n \to \{TRUE,FALSE\}$ defined by setting $I(\psi(x_1,...,x_n))(a_1,...,a_n) = I(\psi(a_1,...,a_n))$ for all $a_1,...,a_n$ in D , where $\psi(a_1,...,a_n)$ is the result of substituting a_i for x_i everywhere in ψ .

One consequence of this definition which will be important in applications to program verification is that $\forall x(\alpha_1 \wedge \ldots \wedge \alpha_n)$ is logically equivalent to $(\forall x\ \alpha_1 \wedge \ldots \wedge \forall x\ \alpha_n)$ in the sense that for any interpretation I, $I(\forall x(\alpha_1 \wedge \ldots \wedge \alpha_n)) = I((\forall x\ \alpha_1 \wedge \ldots \wedge \forall x\ \alpha_n))$; in other words, universal quantification ($\forall$) distributes over conjunction. This is not true of existential quantification ($\exists$) but existential quantification distributes over disjunction - $\exists x\ (\alpha_1 \vee \ldots \vee \alpha_n)$ is logically equivalent to $(\exists x\ \alpha_1 \vee \ldots \vee \exists x\ \alpha_n)$ - while universal quantification does not distribute over disjunction.

DEFINITION A pretty sentence ψ is <u>satisfiable</u> (consistent) if there is an interpretation I such that $I(\psi) = $ TRUE . If $I(\psi) = $ TRUE , we call I a <u>model</u> for ψ . If $I(\psi) = $ FALSE for every interpretation I , then ψ is <u>inconsistent</u>. Pretty sentence ψ is <u>valid</u> (is a <u>theorem</u>) if $I(\psi) = $ TRUE for every interpretation I or, equivalently, $\lnot\psi$ is inconsistent; we sometimes write $\vdash \psi$ in this case. If $\vdash (\psi \equiv \xi)$, then ψ and ξ are said to be <u>logically equivalent</u>; if $\vdash (\psi \supset \xi)$, then we say that ψ <u>logically implies</u> ξ .

REMARK

It is possible to define $I(\psi)$ for any arbitrary sentence ψ . We let $\psi(x_1,\ldots,x_n)$ denote a wff such that each x_i is a variable appearing free in that wff, all x_i are distinct and no other variable appears free although all occurrences of x_i may not be free. Then $\psi(a_1,\ldots,a_n)$ denotes substituting a_i for all and only <u>free</u> occurrences of x_i . Then the definition of $I(\psi)$ is the same as for pretty sentences. Note that for any wff $\psi(x_1,\ldots,x_n)$, there is pretty wff $\xi(x_1,\ldots,x_n)$ such that

$$\vdash \forall x_1 \ldots \forall x_n\ (\psi(x_1,\ldots,x_n) \equiv \xi(x_1,\ldots,x_n))$$

The advantage of using a pretty wff or pretty sentence is that if any occurrence of x is free, all occurrences are free. The disadvantage is that many more names of variables may be needed for the bound variables.

APPLICATIONS TO PROGRAM SCHEMES

Suppose P is a program scheme with n input and m output variables and $\rho(\overline{X},\overline{Z})$ is a pretty wff using the same alphabet of function, predicate and variables symbols (possibly including constant symbols) where $\overline{X} = (x_1,\ldots,x_n)$ and $\overline{Z} = (z_1,\ldots,z_m)$, each x_i and z_j a variable. That is, the x_i and z_j appear free in ρ , are all distinct, all occurrences are free and no other variables appear free in ρ . An interpretation I of P with domain D can be considered to be an interpretation of $\rho(\overline{X},\overline{Z})$ and to define a function

$$(\rho,I)(\overline{a},\overline{b}) = I(\rho(\overline{a},\overline{b}))\ \text{for}\ \overline{a}\ \text{in}\ D^n ,\ \overline{b}\ \text{in}\ D^m$$

as shown above. Thus it makes sense to say, e.g., that (P,I) is totally correct with respect to (ρ,I) .

DEFINITION   Scheme P is <u>partially correct</u> with respect to input criterion $\psi(\overline{X},\overline{Z})$ and output criterion $\rho(\overline{X},\overline{Z})$ if for all interpretations I , (P,I) is partially correct with respect to (ψ,I) and (ρ,I) .

DEFINITION   Scheme P is <u>totally correct</u> with respect to input criterion $\psi(\overline{X},\overline{Z})$ and output criterion $\rho(\overline{X},\overline{Z})$ if for all interpretations I , (P,I) is totally correct with respect to (ψ,I) and (ρ,I) .

When we omit the input criterion we assume that it is the "courtesy wff" TRUE, standing for any always true wff (e.g. $(x = x)$) .

Such a formula $\rho(\overline{X},\overline{Z})$ can be considered to be <u>functional</u> if for every interpretation I and every $\overline{a}$ in the domain of I , there is at most one $\overline{b}$ for which $I(\rho(\overline{a},\overline{b})) = \text{TRUE}$. The methods of Chapter III can be used to show that:

THEOREM A-1   Given an always halting program scheme P , we can construct a quantifier-free wff ρ such that P is totally correct with respect to TRUE and ρ .

This is not necessarily true for schemes with loops. The always halting scheme in Example A-1 is totally correct with respect to TRUE and:

$$(((P(f(x)) \wedge P(g(x))) \supset (z = h(x,x))) \wedge ((P(f(x))$$
$$\wedge (\daleth P(g(x)))) \supset (z = h(x,g(x)))) \wedge ((\daleth P(f(x))) \supset (z = h(x,f(x)))))$$

We take a somewhat different approach in Chapter V in discussing partial correctness for arbitrary programs. From a program scheme P one constructs a quantifier-free wff $W(P,A,B)$ which contains besides the predicate and function letters of P , special predicate letters A and B plus others $A_1,\ldots,A_n$. A program (P,I) is thought to apply interpretation I not just to P to get (P,I) but also to A and B to get input criterion $I(A)$ and output criterion $I(B)$. An interpretation I' extends I by using the same domain but attaching meanings to $A_1,\ldots,A_n$ which are uninterpreted by I . The wff $W(P,A,B)$ can be considered to be $W(P,A,B)(\overline{X},\overline{Z})$, i.e., a function of the input variables $\overline{X}$ and output variables $\overline{Z}$. The main point of that chapter is that:

THEOREM A-2   There is an extension   I'   of   I   which is a model for

$$\forall \overline{X} \, \forall \overline{Y} \ \ W(P,A,B)$$

if and only if   (P,I)   is partially correct with respect to   I(A)   and   I(B) .

This enables one to detail an interactive verification procedure for flowchart based programs such that if the procedure returns a yes answer, then the program is indeed partially correct with respect to the given input and output criteria. The catch, discussed in Chapter V and justified in Chapter VI, is that it may not be possible to find   I' .   In fact, there can be no mechanical procedure which, when   I'   exists, will eventually locate it and establish the validity of the interpreted formula.

EXAMPLE A-1   TOTAL CORRECTNESS FOR AN ALWAYS HALTING SCHEME

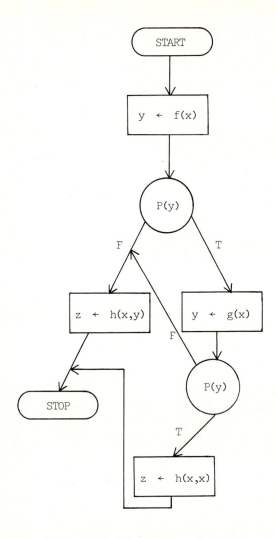

This scheme is totally correct with respect to TRUE and the wff:

$$(((P(f(x)) \land P(g(x))) \supset (z = h(x,x))) \land ((P(f(x)) \land (\daleth P(g(x)))) \supset (z = h(x,g(x))))$$
$$((\daleth P(f(x))) \supset (z = h(x,f(x))))))$$

EXERCISES

CHAPTER II

2.1.   For this problem use <u>only</u> schemes <u>without</u> identity or reset statements
        (i.e. y ← x , for x and y variables) or equality tests (i.e. x = y
        for x and y variables) or constants.

        (a) Given two schemes P and P' , each with n input and m output
             variables, show how to construct a scheme P" such that P is totally
             equivalent to P' if and only if P" always halts.

        (b) Given a scheme P with n input and m output variables, show how to
             construct schemes P' and P" with n+1 input and 1 output vari-
             ables such that P always halts if and only if P' is strongly equiva-
             lent to P" .

        (c) Prove that the termination problem (does P halt for all interpretations
             and all inputs?) is decidable if and only if the total equivalence prob-
             lem (do P' and P" always halt and give the same answer for all inter-
             pretations and all inputs?) is decidable.

        (d) Prove that if the strong equivalence problem (for all interpretations
             and all inputs do P and P' either both diverge or both halt with
             the same answer) is decidable, then the termination problem is decidable.

2.2   Call P the set of program schemes under the linear form definition given
        in Section C .

        (a) Consider the class P_1 of program schemes which enlarges P to allow
             multiple assignment statements:

             k. $(x_1,\ldots,x_n) \leftarrow (f_1(y_{11},\ldots,y_{1m_1}),\ldots,f_n(y_{n1},\ldots,y_{nm_m}))$

             Execution of such an instruction involves simultaneous assignments.
             For example, if at some stage in a computation under interpretation I ,
             a is assigned to x and b to y , execution of

             7. $(x,y) \leftarrow (f(x), g(x,y))$

             places I(f)(a) in x and I(g)(a,b) in y and transfers control to
             8 . Show that given P_1 in P_1 one can construct a strongly equivalent
             scheme P in P .

(b)   Now enlarge P_1 to allow multiple-valued tests, i.e., instructions:

   k. $T(y_1, \ldots, y_r)$ $m_1, \ldots, m_t$

   which transfer control to m_i if the output of the test predicate is
   i . Call this family of schemes P_2 . Give formal definitions of
   schemes, interpretations and computations in P_2 . Devise a decent
   (intuitively satisfying and not too long winded) definition of "equivalence" under which each member of P_2 is equivalent to some member of
   P .

2.3.   For an interpretation I with domain D and for integers n,m let an
   (I,n,m)-predicate be any total function from $D^n \times D^m$ into $\{TRUE, FALSE\}$.

   (a)   Let P and P' be two schemes with n input and m output variables.
   Prove that P is strongly equivalent to P' if and only if the following condition holds for every interpretation I and (I,n,m)-
   predicate ψ : (P,I) is partially correct with respect to ψ if and
   only if (P',I) is partially correct with respect to ψ .

   (b)   Following the model of (a) , devise means of expressing in terms of
   partial correctness the properties: P always halts; P totally
   equivalent to P' ; (P,I) totally correct with respect to ψ .

   HINTS:
   (a)   In proving that the condition cited implies that $P \equiv P'$, consider
   predicates like " $\psi(\bar{a},\bar{b}) = TRUE$ if and only if $(P,I,\bar{a})\downarrow$ " to show
   that (P,I) and (P',I) diverge for the same inputs. Then establish
   strong equivalence.

   (b)   Consider predicates such as " $\psi_{\bar{a}}(\bar{c},\bar{b}) = FALSE$ if and only if $\bar{a} = \bar{c}$ "
   and conditions such as " (P,I) is not partially correct with respect
   to any $\bar{a}$."

2.4.   Show informally that the transformations in Example II - 4 take a scheme into
   a strongly equivalent scheme (preserve strong equivalence).

2.5.   For the schemes in Example E - 1, all with input variable x and output
   variable y , prove that $A \equiv B \equiv C$. It may be easier to show first $A \equiv B$
   and then $B \equiv C$, using a sequence of "easy" transformations (i.e. substitutions of one subprogram for another which clearly preserve strong equivalence)

to go from A to B and C to B . Display and explain carefully all
steps. If your explanations are clear enough and your steps are small and
comprehensible enough, no formal justifications need be given.

CHAPTER III

3.1.   Examine Scheme A in Example E - 2. Prove that it always halts and find
        the longest computation. Then construct the simplest strongly equivalent
        tree scheme you can find (its computation may or may not be shorter than
        those in the original scheme; there is not necessarily a unique answer).
        There are at least two approaches to proving that the scheme always halts.
        You may list the addresses of assignment statements executed, the respeci-
        fications of the y_i and what must be the value of $T(y_i)$ if the computa-
        tion is to continue, making allowances for choices (compare our treatment
        of Example II - 3). Or you may draw a version of the execution sequence
        tree (as in Example III - 1), recording at each node only important informa-
        tion such as the address of the executed statement and the new values of the
        y_i for an assignment or the values tested for a test statement; since we
        always have $\text{val}(y_i,j) = f^n(x)$ for some n , you can save space by record-
        ing only n .

3.2.   Repeat #3.1 for Scheme C in Example E - 2.
        HINT: This problem is very lengthy if done just by trial and error - for
        example, the value of z on halting can be $f^n(x)$ for $n > 30$. It may
        help first to notice that it suffices to consider interpretations I with
        domain the integers, $I(f)(n) = n+1$, and initial input $x = 0$ and then
        to prove small lemmas such as:
            If the computation enters point β with $\text{val}(y_1) = i$, $\text{val}(y_2) = j$
            and $\text{val}(y_3) = k$, $i < k < j$, $I(T)(i) = I(T)(j) = 0$ and $I(T)(\ell) = 1$
            for $i < \ell < j$, either the computation halts or it eventually passes
            points δ and α once and enters point β with $\text{val}(y_1) = j$,
            $\text{val}(y_2) = 2j+1-i$, $\text{val}(y_3) = k+2$, $I(T)(2j+1-i) = 0$ and $I(T)(\ell) = 1$
            for $j < \ell \le 2j-i$.

3.3.   Improve the proof in Section C that freeness is undecidable by using the
        correspondence problem to show that freeness is undecidable for schemes with
        one monadic predicate letter and two monadic function letters (i.e. show how
        to construct for A and B a scheme $P(A,B)$ with one monadic predicate and
        two monadic functions such that $P(A,B)$ is not free if and only if the cor-
        respondence problem has a solution).

3.4.   (open problem)   Is freeness decidable for schemes with one monadic function
       letter and any number of monadic predicate letters?

3.5.   Prove that it is decidable:
       (a) Whether a liberal scheme is already free.

       (b) Whether a liberal scheme is always halting.

       (c) Whether two liberal schemes are totally equivalent.

3.6.   A scheme P is _progressive_ if in every path through P , whenever only
       test statements intervene between an assignment statement $u \leftarrow f(v_1, \ldots v_r)$
       and a subsequent assignment statement $v \leftarrow g(y_1, \ldots, y_s)$, then u is one
       of the y_i - i.e., the assignment location of each assignment statement
       must be one of the retrieval locations of the next assignment statement if
       any.
       (a) Show that every progressive scheme is liberal and hence strongly equiva-
            lent to some free scheme.

       (b) Show that it is decidable whether a scheme is progressive.

       (c) Exhibit a liberal scheme which is not strongly equivalent to any progres-
            sive scheme.

3.7.   An _independent variable (IV) scheme_ P contains only monadic tests and
       assignments of the form $y \leftarrow f(y)$ where f is a monadic function letter.
       Prove that given an IV scheme P we can effectively construct a strongly
       equivalent free IV scheme P' .

3.8.   Prove that for a program scheme P , the domain $U(P)$ of a free interpreta-
       tion is always a context-free language.

CHAPTER IV

4.1.   Examine the lattice of implications among the various types of structural
       similarity defined in Section A . Justify the absence of other lines in the
       upper quadrangle by finding:
       (a) two schemes that are strongly structurally similar but neither is a homo-
            morphic image of the other, and

(b) two schemes that are not strongly structurally similar but one is a homomorphic image of the other.

4.2. Repeat #4.1 for the next quadrangle by finding:
(a) two schemes that are structurally similar but not strongly computationally isomorphic, and

(b) two schemes that are strongly computationally isomorphic but not structurally similar.

4.3. Complete #4.1 and #4.2 by finding:
(a) two schemes that are computationally isomorphic but not strongly computationally equivalent,

(b) two schemes that are strongly computationally equivalent but not computationally equivalent, and

(c) two schemes that are strongly equivalent but not computationally equivalent.

4.4. Prove the Block Replacement Lemma. (Notice that the difficulty is that B_1 can be a subblock of B - i.e. a subgraph which is a block - without having been added as a block.)

4.5. Examine scheme A in Example E - 3. Show why scheme A is not tree-like. Find a tree-like scheme A' strongly equivalent to A and then exhibit the division of A' into major blocks, as in Example IV - 4.

4.6. Prove that if B is a well-structured scheme, then:

$$DO \ B \ UNTIL \ Q(\overline{u}) \ ENDUNTIL$$

and

$$DO \ B \ UNTIL \ NOT \ Q(\overline{u}) \ ENDUNTIL$$

are well-structured schemes. Their semantics appear in Example E - 3, Diagram 2.

4.7. Prove that the extended test statements in (2) in Section E are well-structured schemes.

4.8.   Complete #4.5 by finding an extended WHILE scheme strongly equivalent to Scheme A of Example E - 3.

CHAPTER V

5.1.   (a) For scheme P_1 and the tagged points indicated on Diagram 1 of Example E - 4 write out in terms of f,g,c,A,B,A_α , and A_β the path verification conditions necessary to prove P_1 partially correct for A and B .

   (b) Now let I be the interpretation with domain the natural numbers setting constant c at 0 , $I(f)(n) = n + 1$, $I(g)(n) = n \doteq 1$, and $I(T)(n)$ is TRUE if and only if $n = 0$. Express the program (P_1,I) as a structured program using IF ... THEN ... ELSE ... ENDIF and WHILE ... DO ... ENDWHILE etc.

   (c) Now assign $A(x)$: $x \geq 0$

$$A_\alpha(x,y_1,z) \quad : \quad (0 \leq y_1 \leq x) \wedge (z = 2^{x-y_1})$$
$$A_\beta(x,y_1,y_2,z) : \quad (0 < y_1 \leq x) \wedge (0 \leq y_2 \leq z) \wedge (z = (2(2^{x-y_1}) \doteq y_2))$$
$$B(x,z) \qquad : \quad z = 2^x$$

   Show that (P_1,I) is partially correct with respect to A and B by first generating the verification conditions for (P_1,I) and this choice of inductive assertions A_α and A_β and of input predicate B , and then checking the verification conditions. You may be reasonably informal in establishing that the verification conditions hold for all x,y_1,y_2 and z in the domain of I .

5.2.   Consider structured program (P_2,I) in Diagram 2 of Example E - 4 which is an already interpreted WHILE program. Let the input predicate $A(x)$ be true if and only if x is a nonzero positive integer and let the output predicate $B(x,z)$ be true if and only if $z = x^2$. Show that (P_2,I) is partially correct with respect to A and B by finding suitable inductive assertions $A_\alpha(x,y_1,y_2,z)$ and $A_\beta(x,y_1,y_2,z)$ for the tagged points, generating the appropriate verification conditions, and showing that these conditions hold over the domain of the natural numbers. You may be reasonably informal in establishing that the verification conditions hold.

5.3. Construct a structured program (P_3, I) which is totally correct for A and B where $A(x)$ is true if and only if x is a nonzero positive integer and $B(x,z)$ is true if and only if z is the xth prime; take 2 as the first prime. Start the process of verifying that your program is partially correct by selecting appropriate tagged points t , generating verification conditions in terms of the symbols A_t and then assigning suitable inductive assertions to the A_t . Then write out the conditions in full and informally check them out. Your program may use as constants only 0,1,2 , as functions only $n + 1$, $n \pm 1$, and n.m (multiplication) and as predicates only n = 0? (check for zero) and n = m? (check for equality).

CHAPTER VI

6.1. Complete the proof of Lemma 6.5.

6.2. A scheme P is a <u>2-variable independent variable (IV) scheme</u> if it has exactly 2 variables y_1 and y_2 , both of which are input, program, and output variables, if it has only monadic tests, and if the only assignments are of the forms $y_1 \leftarrow f(y_1)$ and $y_2 \leftarrow f(y_2)$.

(a) Given two two-tape one-way deterministic finite state acceptors M_1 and M_2 , show how to construct two 2-variable IV schemes P_1 and P_2 such that M_1 is equivalent to M_2 (i.e., $L_a(M_1) = L_a(M_2)$ and $L_r(M_1) = L_r(M_2)$) if and only if P_1 is strongly equivalent to P_2 .

(b) Given two 2-variable IV schemes P_1 and P_2 , show how to construct two two-tape one-way deterministic finite state acceptors M_1 and M_2 such that M_1 is equivalent to M_2 if and only if P_1 is strongly equivalent to P_2 .

(c) Show that the strong equivalent problem for 2-variable IV schemes is decidable if and only if the equivalence problem for two-tape one-way deterministic finite state acceptors is decidable.

(d) Show that strong equivalence is undecidable for 2-variable IV schemes with resets (statements $y_i \leftarrow x$ or $y_i \leftarrow y_j$ for $i \neq j$).

HINTS: In (a) and (d) you want constructions like Examples VI - 1 to VI - 5; in (a) notice that now you are considering $L_a(M_i)$ everywhere, not just on the diagonal and cannot start with $y_1 \leftarrow f(x)$ and $y_2 \leftarrow f(x)$; but in (d) you want to consider behavior on the diagonal, since you are now allowed to use $y_1 \leftarrow x$ or $y_2 \leftarrow x$. In (b) , it is perhaps useful to first employ transformation t from Section D of Chapter III. If P_1 has tests $T_1, \ldots T_k$, a free interpretation I will correspond to an input to Tape i of the form $t_{Ii} = P_{01} \cdots P_{0k} f_1 \cdots P_{m1} \cdots P_{mk} f_{k+1} \cdots$ where $P_{0j} = I(T_j)(y_i)$, $P_{mj} = I(T_j)(f^m(y_i))$ and (P_1, I, x) computes at some point $f_{k+1} \cdots f_1(y_1)$; the behavior of computation (P_1, I, x) is then correlated with the behavior of M_1 on (t_{I1}, t_{I2}) , etc.

REMARK: It is known that the strong equivalence problem for 2-variable IV schemes is decidable (see Bird, M., "The Equivalence Problem for Deterministic Two-Tape Automata," J. Computer System Sciences, 7 (1973) 218-236.)

6.3. Prove that the following are undecidable for 2-variable independent variable schemes P_1 and P_2 :
   (a) whether there is any free interpretation I such that (P_1, I, x) and (P_2, I, x) both halt.

   (b) whether P_1 is weakly equivalent to P_2.

   HINTS: In (a) , use the Correspondence Problem; construct for (A, B) two 2-variable IV schemes $P(A)$ and $P(B)$ such that there is an I for which both $(P(A), I, x)$ and $(P(B), I, x)$ halt if and only if the correspondence problem has a solution. Use the outcome of tests on $f^m(y_1)$ to indicate the number of one of the n members of A (or B) and the outcome of tests on $f^m(y_2)$ to write out that member; combine the ideas of Examples III - 3 and VI - 1. In (b) , modify the construction of (a) .

6.4. Recall that P_1 is an extension of P_2 if $val(P_1, I, \bar{a}) = val(P_2, I, \bar{a})$ whenever $val(P_2, I, \bar{a})$ is defined. Prove that for 2-variable IV schemes P_1 and P_2 it is undecidable whether P_1 is an extension of P_2 .

   HINT: Use a construction similar to the one in 6.3. This time, set the output values so $P(A)$ is an extension of $P(B)$ if and only if the correspondence problem for (A, B) has no solution.

6.5. Prove that the two problems in 6.3a and 6.4 are decidable for Ianov schemes.

6.6. Show that it is partially decidable whether a scheme is <u>not</u> free.

6.7. A <u>free finite partial interpretation</u> I of a scheme P has domain $U(P)$, assigns $I(f)(t_1,\ldots,t_n) = f(t_1,\ldots,t_n)$ for each n-placed function letter f and $t_1,\ldots,t_n$ in $U(P)$, but there is a finite subset D of $U(P)$ such that for each n-placed test T, T is only defined on D^n. A free interpretation I' <u>completes</u> I if it is a complete free interpretation (i.e. $I'(T)$ is everywhere defined for each predicate T) and agrees with I wherever I is defined.

(a) Show that a scheme P_1 fails to be an extension of P_2 if and only if there is a free finite partial interpretation I such that $(P_2,I,\overline{X})$ converges but either $(P_1,I,\overline{X})$ converges with $val(P_1,I,\overline{X}) \neq val(P_2,I,\overline{X})$ or there is a completion of I under which P_1 diverges.

(b) Show that for independent variable schemes it is partially decidable whether P_1 is not an extension of P_2.

(c) Show that for independent variable schemes it is partially decidable whether P_1 is not strongly equivalent to P_2.

(d) Is (b) true for arbitrary schemes – is it partially decidable whether P_1 fails to be an extension of P_2?

HINT: In (b), assume P_1 and P_2 to be free and use (a); in (c), use (b).

6.8. Use the definition of progressive in Exercise 3.6. Modify the proof that strong equivalence is decidable for Ianov schemes to show that strong equivalence is decidable for progressive **schemes**.

CHAPTER VII

7.1. Let R be the family of recursion schemes. Let R' be the family of schemes obtained by extending R to allow equations

$$F(u_1,\ldots,u_n) = IF\ Q\ THEN\ E_1\ ELSE\ E_2$$

where Q is a Boolean expression and E_1 and E_2 are recursion expressions involving only $u_1,\ldots,u_n$ as variables.

(a) Complete the definition of R' by providing semantics – how a scheme in R' computes a function under an interpretation.

(b) Show that R and R' are effectively intertranslatable.

7.2. Prove that the families of recursion schemes and of simple recursion schemes are effectively intertranslatable (Lemma 7.4).

7.3. Prove that the families of linear recursion schemes and of simple linear recursion schemes are effectively intertranslatable (Lemma 7.4).

7.4. Prove that any always halting recursion schemes is flowchartable (Proposition 7.8).

7.5. Let P be a recursion augmented flowchart scheme. Show that if P' is a macroexpansion of P, then P is strongly equivalent to P' (Corollary 7.14). Give an algorithm for performing a complete first level macroexpansion of P.

7.6. Let P_R be the class of recursion augmented schemes defined in Section D of Chapter VII. Constable and Gries define a slightly different class P'_R using an alternative method of parameter passing. A scheme in P'_R contains a main scheme and procedure definitions. In this case, a procedure definition Q_F contains at the start, in addition to a statement of formal parameters and local variables, a statement RETURN(z) where z is a new variable, the <u>output variable</u>, which can also appear in the instructions and calls of Q_F. A <u>call</u> has the form $v \leftarrow F(u_1,\ldots,u_n)$. If procedure Q_F has formal parameters $x_1,\ldots,x_n$, and output variable z, then the scheme executes as if call $v \leftarrow F(u_1,\ldots,u_n)$ were replaced by

$$x_1' \leftarrow u_1 ; \ldots ; x_n' \leftarrow u_n$$
$$Q'_F$$
$$v \leftarrow z'$$

where $x_1',\ldots,x_n',z'$ are new variables, and Q'_F is a copy of the body of Q_F with x_i' replacing x_i and z' replacing z everywhere. The important point is that execution of the call of F does not change the value of $u_1,\ldots,u_n$ (as it does for schemes in P_R) but after completion of the call v is respecified. Prove that P_R and P'_R are effectively intertranslatable. Thus the method of parameter passing selected does not affect expressive power.

7.7. Construct a flowchart scheme augmented by one pushdown store strongly equivalent to the recursion scheme:

$$F(x) = IF \ P(x) \ THEN \ x \ ELSE \ h(F(f(x)),F(g(x))).$$

7.8. Show that for any recursion augmented program scheme P there is a strongly equivalent recursion augmented program scheme P' using only <u>one</u> procedure F .

HINT: Consider the translations between recursion and pushdown store augmented schemes.

7.9. Construct an implementation of $leaftest(\lambda,\rho,T)(x)$ using only two push-down stores but allowing instructions of the form:

$$IF \ \pi_i \ IS \ EMPTY, \ TRANSFER \ TO \ r \ , \ ELSE \ TRANSFER \ TO \ s$$

where π_i can be pushdown store π_1 or pushdown store π_2 , and r and s are addresses. Then construct an implementation for $Eleaftest(\lambda,\rho,T)(x,y,z)$ using only two pushdown stores and not permitting such instructions (cf. Lemmas 7.28 and 7.29 and Corollary 7.31).

7.10. Construct a recursion augmented scheme P without iteration (the main scheme and all procedure bodies are trees - no loops) and an interpretation I with domain the nonnegative integers and using only dyadic function, $\alpha(n,m) = n+m$, constant 0 and predicate $E(n,m)$ which is true if and only if $n = m$, such that program (P,I) is totally correct for input criterion " x is a nonnegative integer" and output criterion " $x^2 = z$ ". Then prove that your program is partially correct for the given input and output criteria.

HINT: Use the fact that for $n \geq 1$, n^2 is the sum of the first n odd numbers.

CHAPTER VIII

8.1. Prove that the class of monadic recursion schemes is effectively intertrans-latable with the class of simple monadic recursion schemes.

8.2. Prove that the class of linear monadic recursion schemes is effectively inter-translatable with the class of **simple linear** monadic recursion schemes.

8.3. Prove that for monadic recursion schemes S and S' , S is strongly equiva-
      lent to S' if and only if L#(S) = L#(S') , where L#(S) is the inter-
      preted value language of S .

8.4. Prove that the reversal of the interpreted value language of a right linear
      monadic recursion scheme is a regular set (Corollary 8.6). Give an example
      of a linear monadic recursion scheme which is not strongly equivalent to any
      right linear monadic recursion scheme.

EXAMPLE E-1 - DIAGRAM 1

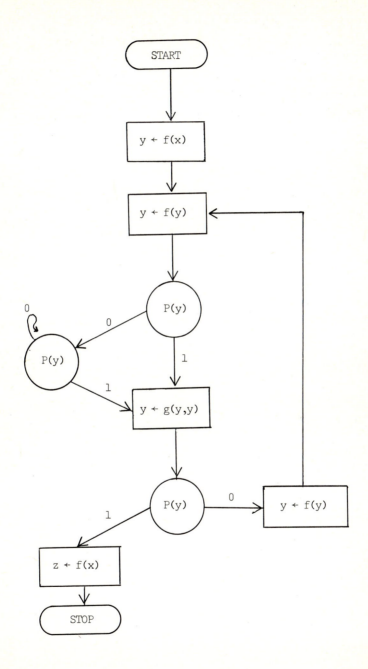

S c h e m e   A

EXAMPLE E-1 - DIAGRAM 2

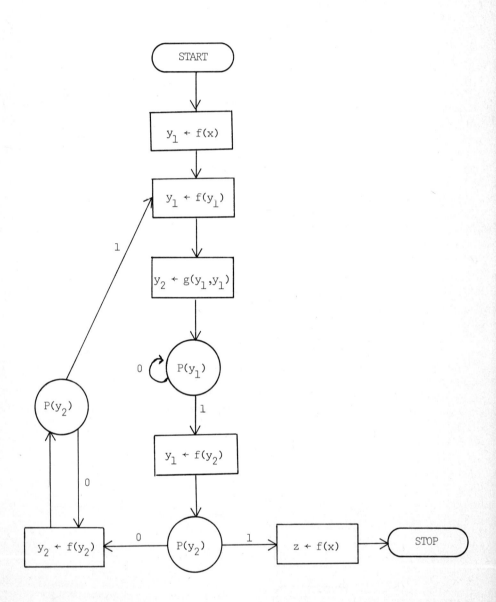

S c h e m e   B

EXAMPLE E-1 - DIAGRAM 3

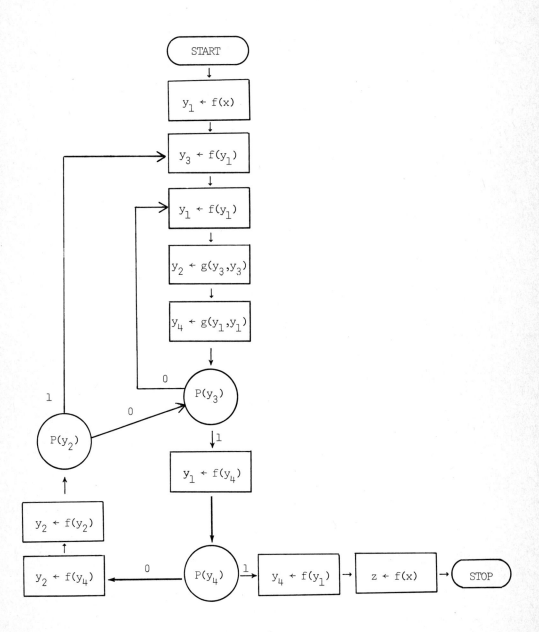

S c h e m e   C

EXAMPLE E-2 - DIAGRAM 1

SCHEME A

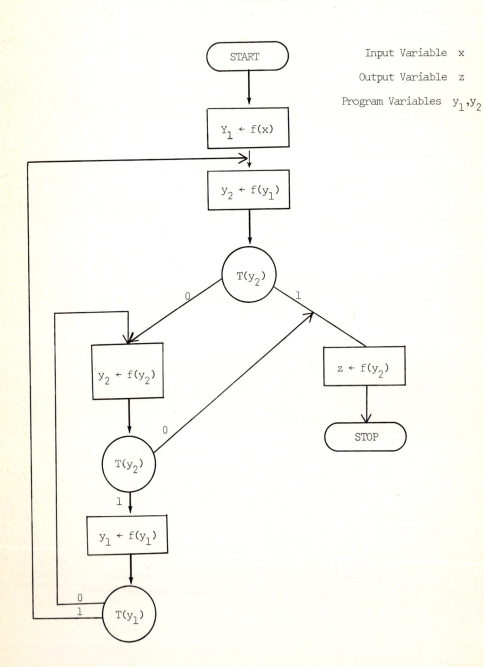

Input Variable x

Output Variable z

Program Variables y_1, y_2

EXAMPLE E-2 - DIAGRAM 2

SCHEME B

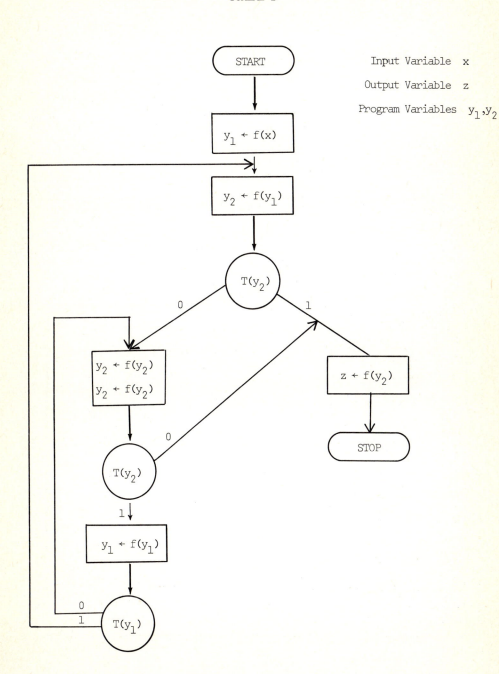

EXAMPLE E-2 - DIAGRAM 3

SCHEME C

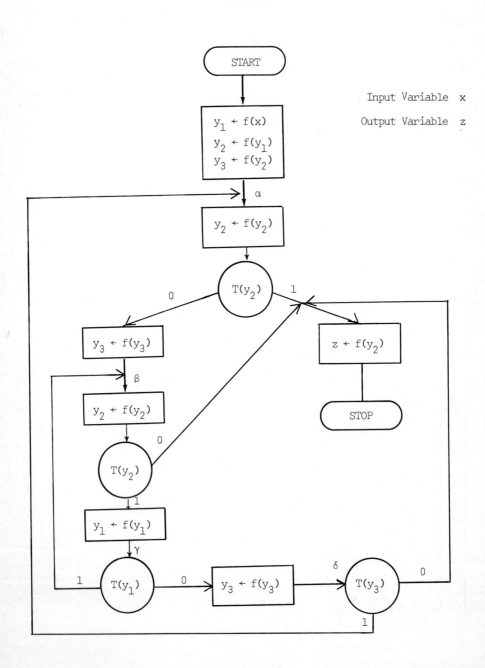

Input Variable x

Output Variable z

EXAMPLE E-3 - DIAGRAM 1

SCHEME A

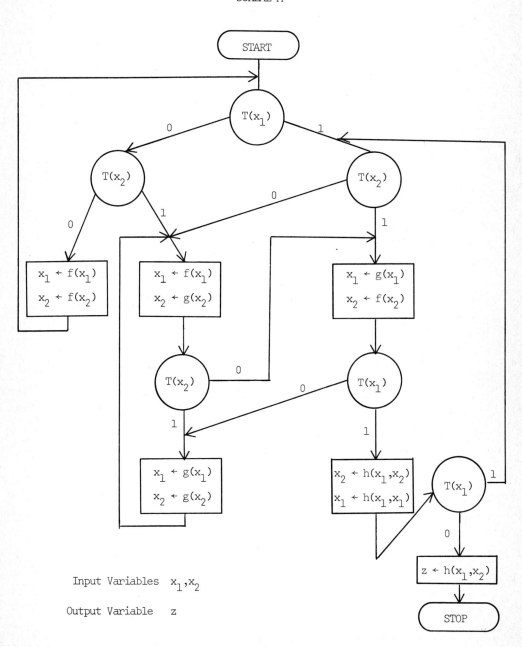

Input Variables x_1, x_2

Output Variable z

EXAMPLE E-3 - DIAGRAM 2

DO UNTIL

   Let B be a single entry single exit well-structured schemes, which are not
zero entry or zero exit, Q be an m-placed predicate letter, and $\bar{u}$ a vector of
m variables, then B_1 and B_2 are defined below.

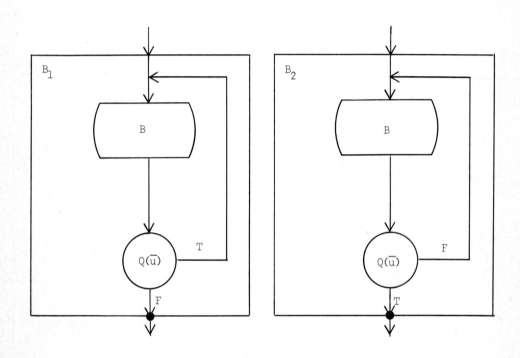

B_1: DO B UNTIL NOT Q($\bar{u}$) ENDUNTIL B_2: DO B UNTIL Q($\bar{u}$) ENDUNTIL

EXAMPLE E-4 - DIAGRAM 1

SCHEME P_1

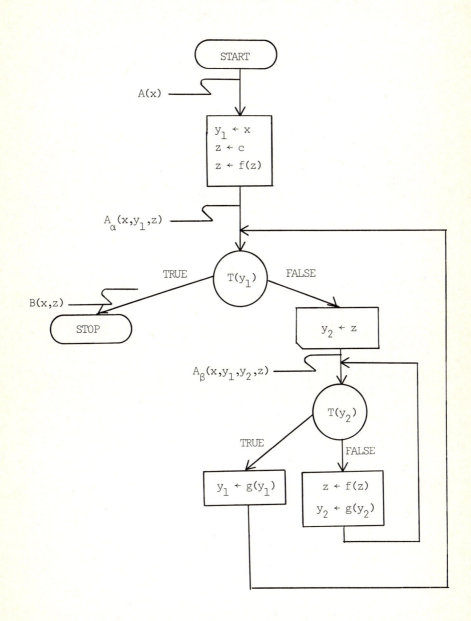

EXAMPLE E-4 - DIAGRAM 2

A(x) _____⌐ ——— START

$y_1 \leftarrow x$

$y_2 \leftarrow 0$

$z \leftarrow 0$

$y_2 \leftarrow y_2 + 1$

$A_\alpha(x,y_1,y_2,z)$ _____⌐ ——WHILE $y_1 \neq 0$ DO

$y_3 \leftarrow y_2$

$A_\beta(x,y_1,y_2,z)$ _____⌐ ——WHILE $y_3 \neq 0$ DO

$z \leftarrow z + 1$

$y_3 \leftarrow y_3 \doteq 1$

ENDWHILE

$y_1 \leftarrow y_1 \doteq 1$

$y_2 \leftarrow y_2 + 1$

$y_2 \leftarrow y_2 + 1$

ENDWHILE

STOP

B(x,z) _____⌐

STRUCTURED PROGRAM (P_2,I)

BIBLIOGRAPHY

Since this is a set of lecture notes rather than a research monograph I have provided neither an exhaustive list of papers and books on the subject nor a chronological account of who-did-what-when. The bibliography simply contains a chapter by chapter record of those articles which influenced   selection and presentation of material; the books listed for Chapter VI and Appendix A (on logic and recursive function theory) are meant to supply background material for the interested reader. My choice of references has no implications whatsoever as to priority, superiority or significance, but simply reflects my own eclectic approach and personal idiosyncracies. I apologize in advance to all those whose work would have appeared in any complete or chronological listing.

CHAPTERS II AND III

Garland, S. J. and D. C. Luckham, "Program schemes, recursion schemes, and formal language," J. Computer System Sciences, 7 (1973) 119-160.

Luckham, D. C., Park, D. M., and M. S. Paterson, "On Formalized Computer Programs," J. Computer System Sciences, 4 (1970) 220-249.

Manna, Zohar, "The Correctness of Programs," J. Computer System Sciences, 3 (1969) 119-127.

Manna, Zohar, "Program Schemas," in Currents in the Theory of Computing, Alfred V. Aho (editor), Prentice-Hall (1973) Englewood Cliffs, New Jersey, pp. 90-142.

Paterson, M. S., "Equivalence problems in a model of computation," Ph.D. Thesis, University of Cambridge, Cambridge, England, 1967.

CHAPTER IV

Ashcroft, E. and Z. Manna, "The translation of 'Go To' Programs to 'WHILE' Programs," Booklet TA-2, Preprints of the IFIP Congress 1971, Ljubljana, Yugoslavia, August, 1971.

Dijkstra, E., "GoTo Statement Considered Harmful," Communications Association Computing Machinery, 11 (1968) 147-148.

Dijkstra, E., "Notes on Structured Programming," in Structured Programming, O. J. Dahl, E. W. Dijkstra, and C. A. R. Hoare (editors), Academic Press (1972) London, pp. 1-82.

CHAPTER IV (Continued)

Manna, Zohar, "Program Schemas," in Currents in the Theory of Computing, Alfred V. Aho (editor), Prentice-Hall (1973) Englewood Cliffs, New Jersey, pp. 90-142.

Meyer, A. R. and D. M. Ritchie, "The Complexity of Loop Programs," Proceedings ACM 22nd National Conference, 1967, Psychonetics, Narbeth, Pennsylvania, pp. 465-469.

Mills, H. D., "Mathematical Foundations for Structured Programming," Report FSC 72-6012, Federal Systems Division, IBM, Gaithersburg, Maryland (1972).

Wulf, W. A., "Programming without the Go To," Booklet TA-3, Preprints of the IFIP Congress 1971, Ljubljana, Yugoslavia, August, 1971.

CHAPTER V

Hoare, C. A. R., "An Axiomatic Basis for Computer Programming," Communications Association for Computing Machinery, 12 (1969) 576-580.

Kernighan and Plauger, The Elements of Programming Style, McGraw-Hill, New York, 1974.

King, J. C., "A Program Verifier," Ph.D. Thesis, Carnegie-Mellon University, Pittsburg, Pennsylvania, September 1969.

Manna, Zohar, "The Correctness of Programs," J. Computer System Sciences, 3 (1969) 119-127.

Manna, Zohar, "Mathematical Theory of Partial Correctness," J. Computer System Sciences, 5 (1971) 239-253.

Manna, Zohar, "Properties of Programs and the First-Order Predicate Calculus," J. Association Computing Machinery, 16 (1969) 244-255.

CHAPTER VI

Davis, M., Computability and Unsolvability, McGraw-Hill, New York (1958).

Garland, S. J. and D. C. Luckham, "Program Schemes, recursion schemes, and formal languages," J. Computer System Sciences, 7 (1973) 119-160.

Hermes, H., Enumerability, Decidability, Computability, Academic Press, New York for Springer-Verlag, Berlin (1965).

CHAPTER VI (Continued)

Luckham, D. C., Park, D. M. and M. S. Paterson, "On Formalized Computer Programs," J. Computer System Sciences, 4 (1970) 220-249.

Paterson, M. S., "Equivalence problems in a model of computation," Ph.D. Thesis, University of Cambridge, Cambridge, England, 1967.

Péter, R., Recursive Functions, Academic Press, New York, 1967.

Rutledge, J., "On Ianov's Program Schemata," J. Association Computing Machinery, 11 (1964) 1-9.

Yasuhara, A., Recursive Function Theory and Logic, Academic Press, New York, 1971.

CHAPTER VII

Brown, S., Gries, D. and T. Szymanski, "Program Schemes with Pushdown Stores," SIAM Journal Computing, 1 (1972) 242-268.

Constable, R. L. and D. Gries, "On Classes of Program Schemata," SIAM Journal Computing, 1 (1972) 66-118.

Hoare, C. A. R., "Procedures and Parameters: An Axiomatic Approach," in Symposium on Semantics of Algorithmic Languages, E. Engeler (editor), Springer-Verlag, New York, 1971, 102-116.

Paterson, M. S. and C. E. Hewitt, "Comparative Schematology," Record Project MAC Conference on Concurrent Systems and Parallel Computation, Woods Hole Massachusetts, June 1970, ACM, 119-128.

Strong, H. R., "Translating Recursion Equations into Flow Charts," J. Computer System Sciences, 5 (1971) 254-285.

CHAPTER VIII

Ashcroft, E., Manna, Z. and A. Pneuli, "Decidable Properties of Monadic Functional Schemas," in Theory of Machines and Computations, Z. Kohavi and A. Paz (editors), Academic Press, 1971, pp. 3-18.

Chandra, A., "On the Properties and Applications of Program Schemes," Ph.D. Thesis, Stanford University, Stanford, California, March 1973.

Friedman, E. P., "Equivalence Problems in Monadic Recursion Schemes," Proceedings 14th Annual Symposium on Switching and Automata Theory, Iowa City, Iowa, 1973, 26-33.

Garland, S. J. and D. C. Luckham, "Program schemes, recursion schemes, and formal languages," J. Computer System Sciences, 7 (1973) 119-160.

Valiant, L. G., "The Decidability of Equivalence for Deterministic Finite-Turn Pushdown Automata," Proceedings 6th Annual ACM Symposium on Theory of Computing, Seattle, Washington, (1974) 27-32.

APPENDIX A

Enderton, H. B., A Mathematical Introduction to Logic, Academic Press, New York, 1972.

INDICES

In the Index of Notation and the Index of Terms, the page reference is usually to either the location of the appropriate definition or to the place where the notation or term is first introduced.

INDEX OF NOTATION

INDEX OF TERMS